JAMES WINTER is a member of the History Department at the University of British Columbia.

Robert Lowe was one of those rare specimens, an English intellectual in politics, a man who had a thorough theoretical grasp of the ideas of Locke, Adam Smith, Bentham, and the political economists. A member of the House of Commons from 1852 to 1880, and chancellor of the exchequer and later home secretary in Gladstone's first ministry, he was one of the most interesting and influential figures in the British Parliament of his day.

He was fully conscious of the radical implications of applying free trade to every aspect of the world he lived in, while at the same time aware of the important criticisms of his free-trade, utilitarian position. He was also extraordinarily ambitious and eager for recognition. Nevertheless, he was willing to accept the suspicions and unpopularity entailed by his stand, and set out to apply his theories during a long career in public service and journalism.

He worked steadily, and with considerable effect, in New South Wales as well as in Britain to rationalize business law, the civil service, education, and national health, with the goal of establishing a 'meritocracy' – a society structured according to standards of intelligence and talent.

He consistently showed courage and rigour in pressing his liberal premises to their logical extensions. Anyone who has read the remarkable debate on the Reform bill of 1866 has been struck by the force of his case against the extension of the franchise to urban working men. Just as in the sixties he defended 'old' liberalism and free trade against the attacks of the democrats, so in the seventies and eighties he defended them against the 'new' liberals.

This careful consideration of the events and legislative acts and proposals with which Lowe was involved will be of great interest to students of the nineteenth century. It offers new materials and interpretations to historians not only in Britain and Australia, but also in Canada and the United States. The intrinsic interest of Lowe's life and Dr Winter's balanced and lively account make this a most enjoyable book.

James Winter

ROBERT LOWE

University of
Toronto Press

TORONTO AND BUFFALO

© University of Toronto Press 1976
Toronto and Buffalo
Printed in Canada

Library of Congress Cataloging in Publication Data

Winter, James, 1925–
Robert Lowe.

Bibliography: p.
Includes index.
1. Sherbrooke, Robert Lowe, Viscount, 1811–1892.
2. Great Britain – Politics and government – 1837–1901.
DA565.S5W56   941.081'092'4 [B]   75-43814
ISBN 0-8020-5323-8

To Lucile Winter

Contents

ILLUSTRATIONS

frontispiece Robert Lowe, photo by Lock and Whitfield
(National Portrait Gallery)

The Rev. Robert Lowe (A.P. Martin, *Robert Lowe*, I, 44)

Mr Lowe, MP (*Penny Illustrated Paper*, 29 March 1866, NPG)

Georgiana Lowe (Martin, *Robert Lowe*, I, 106)

'The Rival Conjurors' (*Punch*, 24 April 1869)

Robert Lowe (sketch for *Punch*, NPG)

Acton Smee Ayrton (*Vanity Fair*, 23 Oct. 1869)

Robert Lowe (*Vanity Fair*, 27 Feb. 1869)

Viscount Sherbrooke, portrait by George Frederic Watts (NPG)

Acknowledgments

Among the many librarians, colleagues, and scholarly associates who have assisted me with their advice and criticism, I owe a special debt of gratitude to David Roberts, John Norris, Marjorie Sinel, George Taylor, Catherine Sosnowsky, and Eric Sager. Corpus Christi College, Cambridge, sheltered me while the manuscript was prepared for publication. The Canada Council, the J.S. Ewart Foundation, and research grants from the University of British Columbia made it possible for me to consult archives in Canada, the United States, the United Kingdom, and Australia. The Broadlands Papers were used by permission of the Trustees of the Broadlands Archives and the Royal Archives by the gracious permission of Her Majesty the Queen. I wish also to thank Mrs R.T. Sneyd for allowing me to use the Robert Lowe Papers in the National Register of Archives in London and the editor and archivist of *The Times* for giving me access to the Delane Papers. Publication was made possible by a grant from the Humanities Research Council, using funds provided by the Canada Council, and by a grant to the University of Toronto Press from the Andrew W. Mellon Foundation.

Introduction

Robert Lowe was born in 1811 and died at the age of eighty-one. An albino, whose eyes were painfully sensitive to light, he lived most of his life in anticipation of the blindness which finally overcame him in advanced old age, yet the goals he set for himself and pursued with extraordinary determination and consistency lay, as he put it, 'in the open arena of life.' That arena was a wide one, and his achievements there were many and diverse. As a politician, barrister, and journalist he helped to shape the institutions and traditions of New South Wales; back home in England he caught the attention of political leaders by his speeches on colonial reform and by his reputation as a writer for *The Times*. The Whigs lost no time in finding him a seat in the House of Commons and promoting him to government offices. During the 1850s and 1860s, when *The Times* was at the peak of its influence over opinion and politicians, he wrote many of the newspaper's leading articles and helped to direct its policies, particularly on affairs in British North America and the United States. In that same period, as a junior minister in the Aberdeen coalition, he helped to reform the Indian Civil Service and to codify the Indian civil and criminal law. In Palmerston's first ministry he was instrumental in passing legislation giving businessmen and investors easy access to the protection of limited liability. In Palmerston's second ministry he assisted Sir John Simon in his battle to create a national health service; also he put through a Revised Code of Education which set the pattern of elementary education for nearly two generations. When his own party brought in a Reform bill in 1866, he deeply stirred Parliament with his protest against this attempt to extend the franchise to the urban working man. In spite of his rebellious act and to a certain extent because of it, Gladstone chose Lowe to be chancellor of the exchequer in the great reform ministry formed in

1868. At that office he carried through a major reform of the civil service, a significant step towards his lifetime goal: the establishment of rule by educated intellect rather than rule by birth and privilege.

It would seem that a life so full as this deserved to be remembered, yet, as James Bryce noted after his death, the Victorian period contains few examples of such a 'rapid obscuration of a reputation.' Lord Bryce thought he knew the reasons: Lowe's transitory fame as a political philosopher came about because he was able to make a rather crude abstract from the ideas of Bentham, Plato, and de Tocqueville, piece it together, and decorate it with literary allusions flattering to an educated class which 'plumed itself upon its culture.' Then he served this compilation up 'in so terse, bright, and painted a form that it made the ordinary country gentleman fancy himself a philosopher while he listened to it in the House or repeated it to his friends at the club.' Thus when the passage of time demonstrated the falseness of all his gloomy predictions about the consequences of democracy, people ceased to listen and remember. In addition, Bryce wrote, Lowe was 'deemed a hard-natured man,' lacking in compassion, and as merciless in attack as he was feeble in defence. Thus he found it difficult to attract or hold a following either among the ruling classes or the general populace.[1]

The growing appreciation for things Victorian in the mid-twentieth century and our disillusionment with the kind of liberal optimism that Bryce expressed have brought a number of scholars to reconsider this judgment. Asa Briggs, in a perceptive essay in *Victorian People*, treats Lowe's opinions and predictions critically but with respect. In 1966 Ruth Knight published a careful study of his career in Australia and concluded that personality defects rather than inconsistency or superficiality prevented him receiving full recognition for his 'genius.' Even his part in shaping the course of elementary education in Britain, frequently denounced by historians of the subject, has begun to receive more sympathetic attention. Thus a new look at Lowe's contribution to the history of Victorian Britain seems in order, particularly since the official life which Lowe and his wife commissioned A.P. Martin to write in the late 1880s is an appreciation rather than a balanced examination.[2]

Lowe is worth remembering not merely for what he accomplished but also for what he represented. He was, perhaps more than any other mid-Victorian minister, the embodiment of classical liberalism. An intellectual in politics, he had a firm grasp of the theoretical premises which he held so rigidly; he had read and absorbed the works of Locke, Ricardo, Malthus, McCullock, and Bentham, and he had carefully considered the counter-arguments put by Hegel, Carlyle, Coleridge, Matthew Arnold, and Alfred Marshall. The position he worked out during the agitations for parliamentary reform and the abolition of the corn laws in the thirties he held on to with undiminished assurance forty years later. He was proud of his steadfastness in the old-liberal faith when it seemed that all those about him were losing theirs. To an audience of constituents in the late 1850s he said: 'I have suffered in different ways for my opinions when they were not quite so popular as they are now; but it was my fortune early in life to take up a set of opinions on politics which I never have been obliged to change. The times have come to me instead of my being compelled to go to the times.' Twenty years later he was still making this assertion of consistency although he was no longer claiming that he and the times were in accord.[3]

He was sometimes unbearably self-righteous about his willingness to pursue the logic of his presuppositions to its conclusions, regardless of the consequences to his reputation and career. As we shall see, some of this boldness was rhetorical; when in a position to implement his views he could, on occasion, show great ingenuity in finding excuses for making compromises. Nevertheless there is substance to his claim that he was more willing than most of his political colleagues to martyr himself in the liberal cause. And because he was clear in his mind about the policies he should consistently adopt and because he was, as Walter Bagehot once noted, 'not only bold enough to propose anything, but bold enough to undertake to explain anything,' he does provide us with a model of mid-century, classical liberalism. Had he been an innovative thinker, had he possessed the subtlety of a Bagehot or the philosophical power of a Mill, he would have been atypical and therefore less valuable as a specimen of a type.[4]

The chapters which follow will treat Lowe as a human being and not as an abstraction. Therefore it might be useful here to speculate what a man would need to believe were he convinced, as Lowe frequently proclaimed himself to be, that liberalism implied the creation of what we have come to call a 'meritocracy' – a society structured according to the standards of intelligence and talent. His tenets, were he rigorous with himself, would be:

1 That the values of efficiency, rationality, and technological, scientific, and industrial progress are the values needed to construct the good society and that merit should be defined as the quality necessary to achieve those values.

2 That the moral code and the cultural life of the community should give support to the values described above. (Therefore he will be antagonistic towards mysticism, sentimentalism, and humanitarianism.)

3 That social and economic inequality is a fact of life; it is also a social utility, providing that the higher rewards go to people equipped with and prepared to use above-average intelligence.

4 That those aspects of democracy are disadvantageous which give the intellectually or morally 'inferior' a sense that they are of equal value to the community or which make it possible for the less able to make

policy decisions and impose them on the more able. (He might, however, approve of policies and institutions which serve to check the tendency of an élite, even an intellectual élite, to behave self-interestedly or arrogantly.)

5 That traditional privileges and the inheritance principle are socially counter-productive and must be abolished.

6 That the most effective machinery for detecting merit and directing people into appropriate niches is a school system, divided into grades which correspond to the various gradations within the social structure; that progress through school should be regulated, at the lower levels at any rate, by standardized, 'objective' testing; and that the curriculum should provide training in skills relevant to the role a youth is expected eventually to fill.[5]

Most nineteenth-century liberals would make strong objections to these propositions on the grounds that they were extrapolations from correct but narrowly conceived premises about the nature of man and society or that their implementation would be ruinously costly, impractical, or menacing to individual freedom. Lowe, himself, would have insisted that the rationalization of society was an abstract goal which would not and, indeed, should not be completely realized. And yet, if pressed, he would have conceded that the many reforms he advocated or initiated during nearly forty years of public life had all been deliberately pointed toward that objective.

The Rev. Robert Lowe

Robert Lowe, MP for Kidderminster

Georgiana Lowe

THE RIVAL CONJURORS.

Professor Bob. "THERE IS NO DECEPTION—THE BAG IS EMPTY. HEY, PRESTO, PASS! (*Produces the egg.*) **SURPLUS!!!**"
Professor Ben. "WHY, WE COU'D HA' DONE *THAT*— (*P. soce.*) IF WE'D ON'Y THOUGHT ON IT."

Robert Lowe

Acton Smee Ayrton

Robert Lowe

Viscount Sherbrooke

Robert Lowe

1

The
Open Arena
of Life

'I began my life,' wrote Robert Lowe in 1876, 'in fact, very much in the state of persons who have been couched for cataract.' One of his eyes was malformed and almost useless, the other was so sensitive to light that he had to peer out at the world through eyelids kept nearly closed. 'I have never been able,' he wrote, 'to enjoy the luxury of staring any-one full in the face.' His mother's instinct was to shelter him from the world, as she had sheltered his sister Elizabeth, also an albino; but his father, vicar of the Nottinghamshire parish of Bingham, was determined that his active, precociously intelligent son should learn to make his own way and sent him to school in nearby Southwell. When that experi-ment proved to be successful, the father decided, when 'Bobby' was fourteen, to submit him to a sterner test and packed him off to Win-chester School where he would need to compete in order to survive.[1]

Once again the son demonstrated that he could hold his own, but this achievement exacted a price. The defences he developed were to be his most characteristic personality traits. Looking back after fifty years, with a memory totally unaffected by old-boy sentiment, he described the crowded, spartan, negligent, often cruel life of the unreformed pub-lic school – his sense of outrage quite obviously undiminished. It was 'an ordeal which a boy so singular in appearance, and so helpless in some respects as I was, might have trembled to encounter.' 'No one was so dull as to be unable to say something rather smart on my peculiari-ties and my short sight offered almost complete immunity to my tor-mentors.'[2]

He soon discovered that one way of protecting himself was to excel as a scholar. He picked out his brightest schoolmate, Roundell Palmer, and set out to compete with him for the position of top boy. To com-pensate for his bad eyesight, Lowe trained his mind to remember Latin and Greek words and usages by memorizing and comparing passages that contained them. Later he was to astound scholarly friends by his ability immediately to connect a word or a figure of speech with an internal concordance of literary references. To a certain extent, his reputation as a debater and an intellectual depended on that remarkable talent. Palmer, in his memoirs, spoke of his rival's 'robust and tasteful talent, rather than minute and technical scholarship.' No doubt Palmer meant this kindly but nevertheless he managed to convey an implied criticism: even as a schoolboy Lowe was impressive for the wit and exuberance with which he could display his learning rather than for any deep academic attachment to classical languages.[3]

Palmer also managed delicately to convey the impression that the young Lowe was feared for his skill in inflicting pain. One of Lowe's fags, James D'Israeli, used to say that 'no one knew what a bully was till he knew *him*' – or so James's famous brother, whose dislike for Lowe was profound, took pleasure in reporting. Faced by an insurrection over a caning incident, the Winchester prefects, amongst them Lowe, first tried to intimidate the rebels and then, when terror did not seem to work, turned to appeasement. In his autobiographical note Lowe recalled, with a still palpable sense of injury, that he alone persisted in enforcing ('with infinitely more power, with infinitely less control, than I have ever had since') the full letter of schoolboy law. He claimed to have had no heart for the work or sympathy with the cause but had decided to persist in doing his duty, regardless of the unpopularity it brought him, and accept philosophically the abuse which poured in on him from both sides.[4]

Incidents of a similar kind kept recurring throughout his life. Again and again one notices this same self-righteousness and overtone of sadism while, at the same time, one is impressed by that same zeal, courage, and integrity. For reasons apparent to any armchair psychologist, this half-blind, pink-eyed adolescent, placed in a situation that could scar any sensitive person, made a fetish of toughness and of the virtues of persistence in unpopular but socially necessary actions. In this reflection about the Winchester School experience, these characteristics come through with almost startling clearness: 'It is usual for novelists and moralists to represent youth as the season of overweening confidence and self-estimation; that is not my experience. Some of the ablest men I have known have thrown themselves away for want of a manly confidence in themselves, from a sickly over-refinement, or from indolence concealing itself under the mask of humility. As far as I have been able to observe, the first step in life is greatly crowded with competitors, but this once passed, the scene entirely changes, and instead of a struggle for existence, the difficulty is to find men equal in any tolerable degree to the duties required of them.'[5]

This view that life is a struggle for existence he expressed in an essay called 'The Importance of Energy in Life,' composed, probably, during his Winchester days. One passage, while conventional for the period, is revealing: 'In some cases the force of circumstances absolutely compels persistence in a course once chosen, and habit is said to become second nature, and even if after all, not being native energy, it breaks down just at the critical moment, when the true characteristics of a man develop themselves spontaneously, the effort is worth making.'[6]

It is so obvious that this insistence on struggle and vigour was affected by the handicaps given him at birth that there is a temptation to place an exaggerated emphasis upon them. Lowe's competitiveness, his view that the world was an arena in which the Devil waited vigilantly to take the hindmost, was an attitude instilled by his father and not simply a defensive posture. Though there seems to have been little affection expressed between the two and much hostility, the younger Robert Lowe was, both in personality and outlook, almost a replica of the older; even their styles of handwriting seem nearly identical.

The Reverend Robert Lowe was a robust, black-haired man of strong and unsentimental opinions. He appears to have been one of those 'jack-booted parsons' whom George Eliot, in moments of nostalgia, professed to admire. He was remembered in county lore for his passionate attachment to angling and fox-hunting and his imperious bearing on the magistrate's bench; but he was more than simply a bluff countryman, he was also a cultivated gentleman, well connected through his family and his wife's family with London society. His sympathies were Whig, although far removed socially from that august cousinhood, and he seems to have taken an interest, at an early period, in the works of the political economists and the utilitarian reformers. His reputation as an innovator resulted from his attempts to solve the problem of what to do about the large numbers of farm labourers who, in the distressed period following the Napoleonic Wars, were kept alive with payments made out of the parish rates to supplement their starvation wages. The Rev. Lowe observed that this practice undermined the morals of the poor, made them 'idle, mischievous, and profuse,' and gave unfair advantages to the few farmers who benefited from employing this cheap, subsidized labour. His remedy was to devise means for 'rendering relief itself so irksome and disagreeable that none would consent to receive it who could possibly do without it.' The 'terror of a well-disciplined workhouse' would be the way to force 'independence on your paupers' – let the outdoor relief payments cease and let all who wish assistance submit themselves to the workhouse test. He tried the system out and was satisfied with the results. When sixteen years later he saw a similar solution adopted in the New Poor Law of 1834, he, not unjustly, claimed some of the credit of parenthood. Therefore he bristled when a fellow clerical innovator, the Rev. J.T. Becher, claimed to have done the pioneer work. The reason he had not troubled to publicize his own successes, Lowe wrote, was that his 'object was parochial utility not public applause ...' It is true, he added, that Becher's scheme was more elaborate, 'but I am so fond of simplicity and of acting by general rules in imitation of divine wisdom, that I hate exceptions, or anything which throws the principle upon which I stand into obscurity ...' His son was to make these values – the merit of simple, general rules which could be systematically applied to human activities, the stress on utility, the duty to act without thought of popular acclaim – the text of most of his public statements. Whether the son also learned of the theories of Bentham, Malthus, and the political economists first from his father is not certain, but there can be no doubt that when he did encounter them, either as a school-boy or at Oxford, he was prepared, emotionally and intellectually, to receive them. The second of three sons of a tough-minded provincial vicar, educated alongside the heirs of aristocratic titles and estates yet not himself a part of their circle, the younger Robert Lowe was conditioned to receive arguments in favour of improvement, rationalization, and the benefits of competition.[7]

At no time in his life was Lowe moved by nostalgia for the past or impressed by the argument from tradition. He luxuriated in the free atmosphere of Oxford after his Winchester ordeal and 'wasted' one whole year in glorious idleness, but he was decidedly unimpressed by the institutions of that ancient place. He claimed that his first impression on arriving at University College in June 1829 was disgust at the loose supervision of studies, the low standards of the university generally, the complacency and intellectual slovenliness of the faculty. And in the period before the mid-century reforms disturbed their repose, many Oxford dons did fill their days, as Gibbon observed a century earlier, 'with uniform employments; the Chapel and the Hall, the Coffee House, and the Common room, till they retired, weary and well satisfied to a long slumber.' Lowe manifestly lacked Gibbon's equanimity. The greatest and only service his college tutor did for him, he informed a committee of Parliament in 1852, was to excuse him from the 'unexpressibly tedious and disgusting' lectures, given by a man whose object in life was not to teach or learn but to wait for that moment when the 'unexpected living drops at last, and idle or diligent, learned or ignorant, he quits his college and is heard no more.' One of his fellow undergraduates remembered that occasionally 'Bob' Lowe would sit with Gladstone, Elgin, Dalhousie, and Cornwall Lewis to hear Briscoe's lectures on Aristotle, but only rarely, for he was seldom seen abroad before twilight. During the day he read or worked at mathematics. Since the only standards he respected were those he set for himself, he set them, in the total absence of guidance, impossibly high. He returned for his second year determined to achieve a double first – in classics and mathematics. The techniques he worked out at Winchester had given him a mastery of Latin and Greek, so the first in classics was no challenge; he won that prize after 'a scene of high jinks' with his examiners. Mathematics was a different matter. He spent his vacations pouring over figures and diagrams, work which must have cost him physical torture. One of the many Oxford legends he left behind was that he got only a high second in mathematics because he rubbed out with his nose what he had just written with his pen. Another difficulty with mathematics, he admitted, was that, 'like Macaulay,' he had an awkward desire to 'argue the point and to contend that what I was told was conclusive reasoning, was not conclusive at all.'[8]

Failure to get a double first kept him from receiving any major academic recognition. Despite that the fellows and students at Oxford marked him out as a leading figure among a remarkably talented group of contemporaries. One of them, a future dean of Westminster, recalled that University College was known at the time and for years after he took his degree as the college of Robert Lowe. Some of that fame came from a burlesque Latin poem he wrote on the occasion of a visit, one damp day, by the duchess of Kent and the Princess Victoria. It began, after a brief introduction, 'Rainy dies aderat.'[9]

But most of the attention he got was the result of his activities at the student debating society. The Oxford Union achieved, in his day, what the university scarcely attempted: the practical training of young men for the life they were most likely to lead. The 1830s were, as one of its presidents said, the union's 'palmy days.' Its library provided the only convenient place where an undergraduate could find books, newspapers, and journals dealing with contemporary issues, modern criticism and literature, and there debaters prepared their arguments on the subjects currently being discussed in Parliament. They carried on their proceedings and behind-the-scenes manœuvring in imitation of the tribunal most of them expected some day to enter. For them the affairs of the union were more than a game of pretence. It can be imagined what a heady experience it must have been for young men, who had been given a long training in esoteric subjects in a monastic atmosphere, to confront the real questions of the day. Many eminent statesmen, Gladstone being the most famous, moved almost without pause from the floor of the union onto the floor of the House of Commons. Roundell Palmer said that he and Lowe, after their rivalry at Winchester, went up to Oxford, had their interest in politics awakened at the union, debated there on opposite sides, and eventually moved to Parliament where, from opposite sides of the floor, they continued what they had begun as boys. At Oxford Palmer upheld the conservative, High Church, position while Lowe joined those hardy spirits who dared to uphold the cause of parliamentary reform and the other radical heresies which were disturbing the tranquility of the university in the period of the Great Reform bill.[10]

In the days when the urban centres were stirring with the debates and agitations which preceded the constitutional change of 1832, Oxford was a small city in the midst of an agricultural county. To be admitted as a student it was necessary to be at least a nominal Anglican. Fellows, even if laymen, were required to be celibate. A small oligarchy, made up largely of clergymen, controlled university government. It was a close-knit, insular society, agitated periodically by religious or fraternal disputes, and deeply out of sympathy with the economic and social forces at work in the outside world. As *The Times* wrote during the 1850s (in an unmistakeably Loweian style), Oxford cast the 'shadow of the Middle Ages far into the level lands of the nineteenth century'; in an industrial age, it remained 'a colony of the half-forgotten time before Melancthon wrote or Luther preached.' But, according to the great master of Balliol, Benjamin Jowett, the intense party feeling and popular excitement of the period did manage to penetrate into the 'mean and unattractive building' where the union met.[11]

One of Lowe's first actions there was to move that the king be urged to create enough Whig peers to move the Reform bill through the Lords. The fact that Lowe could find only four supporting votes shows how much in the minority he was, how far to the left of the limited range of Oxford opinion. Because of this and other challenges, he gained a reputation as a dangerous man, a reputation which was preserved for decades in many a rural parsonage and manor house. There can be no doubt that he enjoyed this notoriety; his position among the outsiders was suited to his talents as a satirical critic. Also he loved to cause a commotion. A contemporary, Francis Doyle, attended the union at boat-race time in 1831 when the Lords had, for the second time, blocked the Reform bill. This action had provoked threats and demonstrations and there was a tense feeling in the atmosphere on the night Doyle entered the crowded debating room. He said that he noticed a 'dear old boy' in the audience who listened intently while an 'earnest young Tory' denounced the Whig sponsors of revolutionary change, calling them a 'vile crew of traitors.' To Doyle's astonishment, the white-haired gentleman suddenly jumped to his feet and with ringing voice replied: 'The hon. Gentleman has called her Majesty's Ministers a crew. We accept the omen, a crew they are: and with Lord Grey for stroke, Lord Brougham for steerer, and the whole people of England hallooing on the banks, I can tell the hon. Gentleman they are pretty sure of winning their race.' Doyle was impressed, and on inquiring was surprised to learn that the speaker was an undergraduate named Bob Lowe, the radical champion, the composer of macaronic verse, and the number seven oarsman on the varsity crew.[12]

The passage of the Reform bill changed the character of British politics, although the change was much less drastic than its opponents had predicted. Men who had made their mark at Oxford and Cambridge, providing that they had a combination of wealth and influential connexions, could still assume after 1832 that positions would be found for them by the great magnates. Within a short time after taking their degrees, Lowe's schoolmates and debating partners, Cardwell and Palmer, had found seats, but Lowe knew he could not expect such effortless promotion. His father made it clear that in his opinion holy orders was the only sensible course; as a clergyman in a rural parish or with a comfortable college fellowship he would not be seriously hampered by being an albino. Lowe did have a taste for theological controversy, but it did not incline him towards joining the church ministry. He rejected his father's advice out of hand. 'Prudence,' he admitted, 'would have counselled me to take holy orders, get a Fellowship, and work my way through Oxford to whatever haven Fortune might open for me; but as I had decided objections to the Church, I determined to go to the Bar.' That determination would have to include self-support, replied the Reverend Lowe. Thus the only solution the son could see was to find a lay fellowship which would provide a living while he read the law. Magdalen offered one for a scholar from Nottingham, a provision which did not suit Lowe's principles but which ensured his election. Unfortunately it would not be vacant for another year, so Lowe decided to fill the interval by working as a private tutor at Oxford.[13]

In the spring of 1835 he got the fellowship and immediately enrolled at Lincoln's Inn. Shortly afterwards he proposed to a girl he had met while on a reading vacation in Wales and was accepted. Her name was Georgiana Orred, 'a clever and handsome lady of some fortune.' His father, thoroughly exasperated, threatened to break with his son completely if he even considered marriage before he was in a position to earn, at the very least, five hundred pounds. The younger Robert Lowe reacted to this threat with spirit; he promptly resigned his fellowship so that his brother, Frederick, might be sure of getting it, broke with most of the rest of his family, married Georgiana in the spring of 1836, and set out with his bride for a summer of hiking, poetry, and love in the Swiss Alps. He may have been an unsentimental man, but he was not passionless.

In the autumn, return to the drudgery of life as a private tutor on the periphery of academia was the only course open to him. Desire to prove his ability to live independently rather than the threat of poverty (Georgiana had a small income) drove him to take on the heaviest possible burden of pupils, 'selling my life-blood at 7s 6d the hour,' twelve hours a day, vacations included. The function of the private tutor was to supply the skilled coaching needed by an aspirant for honours, but which the colleges did not, in most cases, offer. Lowe found the work enormously wearing. He said that he nearly reached the limits of his energy and was only sustained by the satisfaction of contrasting his own great success with his pupils, outside the college walls, with the bumbling inadequacy of the 'academic gerontocracies' within. There is a quantity of evidence to support his claim of excellence. His students got far more than their share of firsts. They included a number of men who became prominent later and who testified to their tutor's skill. One of them, Gathorne Hardy, who became a Conservative minister, said that while Lowe was generally unpopular with the Oxford establishment, he was everywhere respected for his record as a teacher and for the fact that he refused to take money from any student who did not meet his high standards. Arthur Hugh Clough was another admirer. He served for a time as Lowe's private secretary at the Board of Trade and, despite a radical difference in temperament, had the kindest thoughts about his former tutor and employer. John Thaddeus Delane, the great editor of *The Times*, also passed through Lowe's hands. He paid his tribute of respect, as we shall see, in more than mere words.[14]

Eventually Lowe did manage to enter the ranks of the university establishment, if only part way, through appointment as a 'little go' examiner. His duties were to decide through questioning whether a student should be allowed to continue on and complete the formal requirements for a degree. Others might treat the assignment casually, Lowe did not. He used to the full this chance to expose the gross inefficiency he saw all around him. He proceeded to send down as many 'idle and dissipated young men' as possible. Asked how one examination was progressing he answered, 'Excellently, five men plucked already, and the sixth very shaky.' The growls this sort of behaviour provoked delighted his heart and compensated him, in part, for his resentment at having to make his living by supplying what the colleges were established to offer but failed to produce. He was to keep Oxford growling, on and off, for the next forty years.[15]

Lowe freely confessed that he had gone back to the tedium of drilling classical literature into the heads of students not out of any sense of dedication to the improvement of the young but because of a crass determination to make seven hundred pounds a year. He was not ashamed of this; he thought it made him a more successful teacher. He was ready to match his results with the cosily placed fellows in their 'feudal and monastic' sinecures. He believed with the political economists that men were keenest in pursuit of their own interests; experience had confirmed this assumption. It was 'a melancholy fact,' he wrote in 1877, that teaching is the profession to which this doctrine most strictly applies. The reason was that 'teaching, though a highly honourable, is also a highly irksome kind of labour.' Thus if a teacher receives any advantages, any favourable circumstances which 'enables him with impunity to retrench some part of the labour,' he will at once seek his own ease and comfort. That premise accepted, the remedy was obvious. Reform of higher education could rest on a clear and simple principle: put teacher into competition with teacher and student with student; that was the way to clear the path for merit and ability. More specifically, he would make Oxford and Cambridge national universities, 'co-extensive with the domain of human intellect itself.' Throw open prizes and fellowships to free competition; rid the system of all religious disabilities: this, he proclaimed in the 1870s, was the way out of the seemingly hopeless deadlock over university education in Ireland. Let the government offer attractive inducements in the form of scholarships tied to examinations and leave Catholics and Protestants to work out ways of meeting the demand such inducements would create. Even bigotry could not stand forever against the laws of the market place. Do something, he urged, about the deplorably low standards for most degrees at English universities by giving a committee of learned and independent persons the examining function. The colleges have a vested interest in the success of their students; therefore they treat their examination function 'with an amount of tenderness and consideration which cannot but be extremely gratifying to their pupils, as well as agreeable to themselves.' Make the system of private tuition regular. If you give the student a free choice of tutor, then competition will winnow out the incompetent and give the able incentives to work hard. Allow any holder of a master's degree who meets university requirements to open a hall of his own and compete with the colleges for residents; this would lower costs for impecunious students and compensate them for the expense of private tuition. And, finally, make promotion rational by opening the professorships to successful teachers so that university teaching can become a profession rather than remain merely a temporary sinecure; make the professorships attractive by freeing them from the triviality of undergraduate lecturing. Professorships, he wrote, should be 'archetectonic,' not 'catechetical.'[16]

He knew that free trade in education would never come to the two ancient universities without drastic reforms in their means of government and, of course, he had recommendations to make about that as well. In an exchange of letters with Gladstone in 1854, when that statesman was at work on legislation which did much to speed up the process of modernization in the universities, Lowe stressed that the object should be to simplify lines of responsibility. So long as conflicting jurisdictions were allowed, rival ecclesiastical interests would continue to intrigue and job. The correctives were obvious: free all fellows from the need to take holy orders and to remain celebate; make them members of convocation; let convocation elect one-third of the executive body every year; turn over responsibility to men who are interested in scholarship instead of religious controversy. Give Oxford a liberal government, he advised Gladstone, based on the rational model offered by the administrative system practised in the municipal corporations.[17]

The premises and prejudices contained in these recommendations underlay almost every speech Lowe ever made or any administrative act he ever attempted to carry out, no matter what the subject. They reflected the utilitarian, free trade outlook of most liberal reformers in the first three-quarters of the nineteenth century, differing only in the austerity, even audacity, with which it was elaborated. A summary of Lowe's recommendations on university reform must stretch over a long period of activity, from 1852, when he entered Parliament, to 1880, when he retired from the House of Commons. It also must include a formidable quantity of letters, speeches, leading articles in *The Times*, testimony before committees, and lengthy essays in journals. And such a summary need not make allowances for modification of position; what he advocated as a pugnacious 'little go' examiner in the mid-thirties he was still advocating as an old man in the House of Lords, frequently borrowing felicitous words and phrases from one era to use again in another. Occasionally he tried to restrain his impulse always to present the conclusion he made from his liberal premises in their logical nakedness. He knew, or at least he had pointed out to him often enough, that the technique of shock loses some of its value with repetition. But he was never able to restrain that impulse for long. He had the instinct of a journalist and the intellectual pride and impatience of an academic. Sometimes the combination produced tangible results although the consequences were not always what he intended.

In the case of university reform, it is difficult to assess the effect of his activities. He was only one critic among many. The Royal Commission report, which was the basis for the important act of 1854, cited Lowe's testimony to support its recommendations that the old oligarchical monopolies be replaced by a more representative system. Gladstone made a provision in his bill which would allow any member of convocation to open his residence to students, and this may have owed something to Lowe. But far more important than any direct influence was Lowe's friendship with Benjamin Jowett, the symbol of a changed and enlarged spirit that was moving in Oxford in the 1850s. Jowett supplied him with ideas and specific reform suggestions; Lowe passed these along to government leaders. In 1871, when Lowe was chancellor of the exchequer, he secured Jowett's appointment as master of Balliol. Together, that same year, they worked energetically to support Gladstone in his move to abolish the remaining religious tests. Lowe's speech to the House of Commons on that subject is an example of some of the more generous and admirable sides of the classical liberal tradition.[18]

Not surprisingly, Lowe was never in the least impressed by the university reforms that were put through; they were all too temporizing to suit him. He insisted that Oxford in the seventies was as deplorably deficient in free trade as it had been when he was an undergraduate and, therefore, just as remote from any 'leaning to and affinity with the future.' One indignant don accused him, not unjustly, of suffering from the 'Rip Van Winkle fallacy.' A Regius Professor of Medicine complained to Gladstone about Lowe's 'inveterate' and ignorant prejudice against his old university. To these and other similar complaints, Lowe made in 1877 an impudent public reply in a letter to *The Times*. As was his custom, he dwelt on the ingenuity teachers always showed in avoiding change and the corresponding skill needed by the reformer. One of his critics, a fellow of Lincoln College, was named Thomas Fowler. That gave Lowe an irresistible opportunity for a jab: 'But surely in vain is the net set in the sight of any bird.'[19]

It is important to notice one more distinctive feature of Lowe's approach to reform, a feature clearly revealed in his pronouncements on Oxford and Cambridge: his tendency always to base his proposals consciously and literally on the authority of some holy writ taken, for the most part, from the classical economists. On educational matters, as on so many other matters, his authority was Adam Smith. Smith was the first and only man to discover a real science of mankind, or so Lowe told the Political Economy Club during their centennial celebrations of the publication of *The Wealth of Nations*. Lowe thought Smith's special genius lay in his ability to anticipate what men would do under certain circumstances. He thought Smith's discovery of the fundamental laws of human behaviour placed him in the 'highest rank among those who have cultivated the more abstruse parts of knowledge.' He was the 'Plato of Political Economy,' in the same way that Ricardo 'had been its Aristotle.' No part of *The Wealth of Nations*, he announced, is more admirable than the treatment of educational institutions, yet no part is less read or has had less influence on the way men act. Lowe manifestly did not include himself in that generalization. Smith's radical extension of the principles of competition and individual liberty of choice to educational reform was an exact blueprint for Lowe's own programme. A poor Scot on a meagre scholarship, Smith had been decidedly unimpressed with the Oxford of the 1740s. Before riding his horse south to Balliol, he had spent several years at Glasgow College – an infinitely poorer and more modest place. But how much more relevant its curriculum, how much keener its teachers! The very richness of Oxford's endowments, he concluded, must explain why she had become the sanctuary for 'exploded systems and obsolete prejudices,' why her professors had long since 'given up altogether even the pretence of teaching.' Smith proposed the changes which Lowe used to build his reputation as an educational innovator. The pupil never thought to hide the fact that his ideas were borrowed from the great teacher. On the contrary, he constantly found comfort in the reflection that science as well as justice was on his side.[20]

After six years Adam Smith left Oxford to become professor of logic at Glasgow. Lowe almost found that same escape, only to see it slip, at the last moment, tantalizingly away – one of those minor tragedies which occasionally disturb the groves of academe. A professorship of classics fell vacant at Glasgow. University authorities first offered it to Archibald Cambell Tait, the future archbishop of Canterbury. He turned it down, because religious scruples prevented him from subscribing to the required confession of faith, and generously recommended Lowe, his arch-rival of union debating days. The salary was large, the duties light. Lowe's aversion to secure and privileged oligarchies did not prevent him from hurrying north to stay with a relative, a Glasgow banker with influence at the university, and plunging into a month of Levantine machinations to secure the necessary votes. His hopes were high: 'My testimonials were, as I believe testimonials always are, a splendid instance of what Bentham calls the fallacy of indiscriminate laudation.' On the day before election he counted seven professors on his side against only three for his rival, a man named Lushington. Those three, however, represented landowning interests who were out to suppress all radical elements. The three approached Lowe's chief supporter and menaced him with a threat to oppose his own promotion to a prized chair of moral philosophy. The very fact that Lushington was so 'objectionable in every way,' Lowe explained to a friend at Oxford, 'and my being so universally popular only made it more a punishment to their adversaries to bring in Lushington ... The turn of the straw rendered all my efforts futile.' The reflection that he owed his defeat 'to the miserable system of translation' did not soothe him. No failure, he confessed years afterwards, ever hurt so much as this one – 'the greatest disappointment that ever happened to me in my life ...'[21]

That disappointment came at a particularly discouraging moment. His stipend as an examiner had allowed him in 1837 to take time away from coaching to begin a new edition of Herodotus, a work that would establish him as a professional academic. Then came the capricious dashing of his hopes. Just then he had to admit to himself that his eyesight was rapidly deteriorating. Pains in his eyes forced him to give up reading by candle-light. He had to face the possibility that he might soon be severely incapacitated, and with a sense of desperation he began again to read law during the few spare day-time hours that he could find. He distracted himself by learning some Sanscrit, studying Icelandic, and reading Hegel. When a praelectorship of logic opened up at Oxford, he applied for it, but his reputation as a disturber of the peace put him out of the running. On top of all these reverses Georgiana lost the baby she was carrying. Apparently she was unable to have children. Oxford, Lowe said, is a 'triste place for a lady.' Frustrated and worried about the future, they decided to 'take the plunge into the great world.'[22]

All available resources they put into mining stock in hopes of a quick return and set out for London where Robert would learn the 'art of Special Pleading under the wings of a man called Peacock who is indeed covered with silver wings and his feathers with gold.' Happily, the Reverend Lowe softened and sent a hundred pounds. Soon Georgiana was cheerfully writing home that Robert, 'is reading law from morning to night; it seems quite a delightful occupation. I am so glad he appears to find the law so easy; from the constant cultivation to which he has subjected his mind, the difficulties of which others complain appear trivial to him. He has already, I assure you, from his memory been able to correct old lawyers on some law points. I look forward with the greatest assurance to his someday becoming a great man, he unites such rare industry with his abilities.'[23]

It would never have occurred to Georgiana to speculate about the feelings of those old lawyers thus corrected. Sensitivity to the feelings of others is no prerequisite for greatness, nevertheless it can be a valuable trait in a person who has to make his own way in the world. The few close friends who were able or willing to penetrate beneath his caustic exterior did find warmth, charm, and sensitivity. But even they were frequently put off by his apparent need to belittle others and to mock, sometimes playfully sometimes seriously, any show of sentiment.

He also had a tendency, they noticed, to disparage those activities which came easily to him – and law was one of these activities. His talent for logic, his precise use of words, made him an excellent practitioner; his taste for general principles earned him a reputation as a legal theoretician. Yet he claimed that he needed to give his mind a 'serious wrench' to master the sophistries of that 'wretched trade.' The most wretched part was special pleading. When he came to its 'mysteries,' he wrote, 'I stood aghast at its mingled iniquity and absurdity.' Worse than the law itself, were the lawyers. In the midst of a plea he made in the Legislative Council of New South Wales in favour of free trade in law, he announced that 'no man was too ignorant to be made a barrister of.'[24]

After two years of intensive study, the eating of the required thirty-six dinners at Lincoln's Inn, the payment of a hundred guineas, Lowe became a barrister early in 1842. Prospects could not have been bright; that year marked the economic nadir of the nineteenth century. Intensive reading had further weakened his eyes. He consulted London specialists – 'three Job's comforters,' he called them. They pronounced that in seven years he would probably be blind. They prescribed, Lowe claimed, outdoor employment, preferably in the Antipodes. Even allowing for the fact that early Victorian doctors often suggested eccentric remedies, the recommendation of bright sunlight for unpigmented eyes seems so bizarre that one is tempted to accuse Lowe of wanting to disguise the real reason for deciding to move to Australia. The reason was surely economic. Wealth and position were to be won at the English Bar, if at all, only by long apprenticeship; in a new community quick success was possible. It is likely that the enthusiastic lectures at Oxford by the political economist Herman Merivale on Australia's great promise gave Lowe the idea of securing wealth and independence there in the shortest possible time.[25]

The decision made, Lowe quickly settled his affairs. Georgiana practiced her skill with water-colours, so that she would be able to capture the sights of their adventure and send them home to relatives. On 8 June 1842 they set sail on the *Aden*. In the middle of June, John Delane sent his former tutor an invitation to become a contributor to *The Times*. 'Had it reached me in time,' Lowe wrote, '[it] would most probably have altered my destination, and with it my whole career in life.' But the letter followed in the wake of the *Aden*, bound for New South Wales.[26]

2

'On Australia's Olive Shore'

When Lowe arrived in New South Wales in 1842 he believed that he could not afford to wait for events but must force them with all his energy. That energy was prodigious and the opportunities to exercise it in the young colony were nearly unlimited. In 1850, seven years later, he returned a moderately wealthy man, rich enough to afford a country home in Surrey and a career in English politics. He also returned with a reputation as an educational reformer, a legal theorist, a crusader against convict transportation, and an ardent, though somewhat ambiguous, spokesman for popular causes, colonial autonomy, and responsible government. He left behind him in Sydney a number of admirers, a few friends, and swarms of enemies. Friends, admirers, and enemies agreed that his path of advancement in the colony had been full of dramatic turnings. Lowe agreed that he had changed his positions often yet maintained with the most sincere conviction that he had never compromised his integrity in his scramble for quick success. He admitted his inconsistencies and claimed they were the consequences of his steadfast loyalty to his principles.

It would be foolish to accept Lowe's version of the truth as an accurate description of reality. There was more tension between his personal ambitions and his principles than he was willing to admit or able to perceive. It would be strange if this were not so. He could never forget that the doctors had given him a sentence of blindness that fate might at any moment force him to serve. One way he learned to live with that anxiety was to stifle introspection and to assure himself that everything must at last yield to perseverance.

But it would be even more mistaken to dismiss his assertions of moral superiority as mere self-justification, totally at odds with the facts. Close examination of his behaviour in Sydney shows that underneath his

superficial inconsistencies there was a steady bond of principle. These
liberal principles, consciously developed by reading and argument, he
had brought along with him on the *Aden*. When he returned home his
presuppositions were the same, only greatly strengthened by experience.

The voyage out from England in mid-century was risky, uncomfortable,
and long. For Lowe, one of the greatest hazards was being forced to
endure, at close range, the company of an odd assortment of humanity.
There was, he tells us, the purser's daughter ('the very pink of vulgarity'), the 'uppish and snappish Irish-woman, who ate pig's fry, curry and
fat salted pork all together for breakfast,' and the 'very good country
gentleman-like' landowner whose religion was, unfortunately, 'tainted
with enthusiasm and illiberality.' As the *Aden* neared the tropics, Lowe
recalled, 'the coarser passion of greediness' gave way to 'the gentler influence of love,' until at last her passengers reached 'a state of absolute
vacuity,' broken for a few hours by a fire at sea and near shipwreck on
the 'desolate promontory' of Cape Otway. The ship touched briefly at
Melbourne, where Robert paid a call on Superintendent La Trobe while
Georgiana spent the day painting. Then finally, after nearly four months
of travel, the golden-coloured headlands of Port Jackson rose up like
the gates of paradise. Georgiana described their first view of the 'fantastic confusion' of bays, hills, and rocks of Sydney harbour, 'thrown in
every exquisite form together' – the white stone cottages along the shore
half-hidden by trees 'of strange leaf and form; the rock's white stone
stained with rich red and brown, strange and fantastic species ... of
cypress-trees and lignum vitae, and bright and lovely flowers.' They had
with them letters of introduction from family connexions and Oxford
friends to the governor, Sir George Gipps and his lady, and these produced a warm reception. The vice-regal couple were rowed out on their
eight-oared barge to welcome the new arrivals and carry them up the
river to their official lodge in the village of Paramatta. In that beautiful
setting they spent their first days ashore. It seemed delightfully dream-
like. Lady Gipps took Georgiana for rides through blooming orange
groves; they visited a women's prison and an orphan school while the
governor, an austere old soldier, made an unaccustomed effort to be
agreeable to her husband. Georgiana noted that this attention would
make them 'important in people's opinions which will be serviceable to
Robert.' The governor introduced them to Sydney society as it paid its
ritual calls. Prospects seemed in all respects sunny. They looked for a
place to live in the city so that they could move there before the opening of the courts and found an attractive terraced house with a view of
the harbour. It, miraculously, still stands on Macquarie Street facing
Government House and the Botanical Garden. 'To think of being able

to make money in such a place,' Georgiana wrote, 'one's idea of making money is confined to back streets and melancholy Holes.'[1]

This euphoria was delicious but transitory. Letters home reported that Robert's eyes were hurting him severely just when briefs were beginning to come in. William Bland, one of the doctors he consulted, thought he detected impending blindness and ordered a total halt to reading. According to his gloomy prognostications, Lowe was not to have even the seven years of sight promised him. 'This,' Lowe said many years later, 'was the lowest ebb of my fortunes.' The governor and his wife did what they could; they encouraged the Lowes to explore the beauties of Illawarra and the eucalyptus-lined canyons of the Blue Mountains, where Georgiana sketched and wrote poetic descriptions for her relatives in England. Then, mercifully, the pains in her husband's eyes began to ease. She joyfully sent the good news home, in the summer of 1843, that he had decided to ignore Bland's warnings and resume his practice. He hired clerks, gave his wife dictation, and listened to her read depositions in the evening. He was, in time, to forget his debt to Governor and Lady Gipps, but he never forgave Dr Bland, his 'Sydney Aesculapius,' for this false diagnosis. Fate had given him a reprieve. Those sudden dramatic shifts from bright prospects to desperate thoughts form the background to the frenzy of activity which marked his stay in the Antipodes.[2]

Australia had also reached its 'lowest ebb' in 1842. A depression in England, beginning in the late thirties, had spread around the world by 1841. A falling-off of demand from the mother country for wool brought disaster in that year to the Australian sheep graziers and therefore to the whole economy. Henry Parkes, a future prime minister who arrived as an immigrant in Sydney in the midst of the depression with three shillings in his pocket, described the pessimism and despair he encountered on landing. While he had been at sea, wages in the colony had dropped in half. 'Insolvency, like some fearful epidemic,' he wrote home in 1842, 'is daily discovering itself in some new place ...' The prevailing mood, Georgiana recorded that year, was most dismal: 'many say the colony will never live again.' She was shocked to see the fine peaches she had admired on landing being fed to the pigs. The graziers, she wrote, were boiling down their sheep for tallow or selling them to butchers for a ruinous five shillings.[3]

Trouble for the graziers meant trouble for the bankers and the rest of the business community. Several months before Lowe returned to his practice in 1843, a rash of bank failures culminated in the crash of the Bank of Australia. Credit for saving the finances of the colony from total collapse went to William Charles Wentworth, a great landowner and champion of colonial self-government, who, together with his associates, pressed the new Legislative Council to pass a bill allowing banks to advance credit on the forthcoming wool clip. His party also proposed to restrict bank interest rates to 5 per cent by law. Some representatives of the grazing and financial interests even began to talk about the necessity of a protective tariff.[4]

This financial crisis and the solutions that were being suggested worked in an indirect way to Lowe's advantage. He was, of course, scandalized by such heretical remedies. So was Governor Gipps, a strict, dogmatic free trader. That economic difficulties could be cured by governmental regulation of the bank rate and by tariffs seemed dangerous nonsense to him; moreover, he suspected that those who asked for this legislation had impure motives. These suspicions he shared with his brilliant new friend, who enthusiastically seconded them. Gipps assumed that he had acquired an ally against Wentworth and his followers. Therefore, when a vacancy occurred among the nominated members of the Legislative Council, he announced, in November 1843, that he had decided to appoint the recently arrived barrister, Robert Lowe.[5]

The news that the governor had named to the Council a junior member of the bar, a man who had lived in the colony for scarcely a year, caused a great deal of jealous comment. Georgiana, who expected prodigies from her husband, was apprehensive about the reaction she expected would follow the release of the news, although she was, of course, filled with joy and wonder at this sudden reversal of their fortunes. 'Now, my dearest mother,' she wrote, 'does not Robert overcome every obstacle and impediment?' As for the governor, he was not greatly concerned about colonial sensibilities; his main interest was in finding a strong man to help him resist the attacks he saw coming on the imperial interest. He explained to the Colonial Office that Lowe would be of great assistance because 'he is a man of first rate abilities and a forcible speaker.'[6]

No one was ever to question that judgment. But force and ability were not the only requirements. As Wentworth said, Lowe was a 'comparative stranger in the land, ignorant of its wants, ignorant of its history, ignorant, in short, of everything connected with it.' This ignorance Lowe probably did not apprehend and certainly never acknowledged. He had his complete intellectual framework; he could apply it to any point at issue no matter how abstruse; he had an extraordinary capacity to master and remember details. So equipped, he saw no reason to inquire into the anxieties of a rude community, undergoing the stress of adapting to significant social changes. This insensitivity, the reverse side of his strength, was a serious impediment to his effectiveness as a politician and the source of the hostility which bristled up around him wherever he went.[7]

The mails on the *Aden* brought a new constitution, conceived in the Colonial Office. It was Whitehall's response to persistent agitation from

Wentworth's Australian Patriotic Association. Peel's government decided to grant some of the concessions the association had been demanding. The most important was the replacement of an entirely nominated legislature by a Council made up of six crown officials, six crown nominees, and twenty-four elected members. This was a considerable victory for Wentworth and his fellow association leader, Dr Bland. In the twenties and thirties the colonial establishment had interpreted the cry for representative government as an attempt by the freed convicts and the lower and middle class free immigrants to gain social equality; by the time the new constitution arrived in 1842, this tension between 'emancipists' and 'exclusivists' had dampened down. One important reason for this relaxation was the decision, made in England, to stop transporting criminals to the colony. Members of the old, 'exclusivist' ruling circle disliked this action because it threatened to cut off the supply of cheap labour; accordingly, their emotional ties with the mother-country began to weaken and their appreciation of the advantages of self-government began to grow. This movement brought the large landowners and the urban professional men who were related to or dependent on them somewhat closer to the position of Wentworth and his 'emancipists.' At the same time that this was happening the emancipists had steadily been improving their social and legal status. Some of them had become rich graziers who, because they ranged their sheep on vast tracts of crown lands, came to be known by the deceptively homely name of 'squatters.' Others had gone into business and accumulated money and some of the symbols of respectability. This improvement in their position gave them a certain harmony of interest with the old élite. Both of these factions tended to close ranks against the emerging class of small arable farmers, self-employed craftsmen, and urban workers, many of whom were Irish and Roman Catholics. This lower middle class and proletarian element naturally resented the fact that landowners and graziers controlled so much political and economic power, particularly since the source of their wealth in many cases was the exploitation of what was meant to be public lands, set aside for the benefit of the whole community and its posterity. More specifically, they disliked the policy of keeping the price of crown land high, since expensive land virtually guaranteed that the great sheep graziers could retain what amounted to a monopoly over its use. Also the landowners and graziers favoured transportation of convicts and this meant that free wage earners would have to compete with servile labour. By the forties, this radical group was growing in size and becoming more articulate. In view of this development, it is not surprising that wealthy men, regardless of their social origin, who derived their incomes directly and indirectly from sheep and rents should tend to draw together for mutual protection.

William Wentworth's career illustrates this trend. He was born outside the aristocratic pale. His father was an Ulster physician who had dodged a conviction for highway robbery by agreeing to disappear into the colonies. The father had prospered by his exile, and the son grazed his sheep on vast tracts of crown land. He had not entirely forgotten his resentments against the aristocratic Macarthurs and their circle by 1842, but had come to recognize by then that all the wealthy and influential property owners had a common enemy in democracy; therefore he rallied both emancipists and exclusivists to stand behind the new constitution. He regretted that it had not granted full powers to the representatives of the wealthy interests in the colony but he did welcome the provisions for a franchise that was sufficiently high to keep the votes out of radical hands and for property qualifications which would make sure that elected members of Council be men of substance. These constitutional provisions, along with the high statuatory price of land (a minimum of a pound per acre), were to be the cornerstones on which to construct a secure oligarchy.[8]

Originally the high land price policy had come about because of the influence of Edward Gibbon Wakefield and his theory of systematic colonization. Successive colonial secretaries had been persuaded by the Wakefieldians that such a policy would force immigrants to work as agricultural or pastoral wage-labourers until they could accumulate sufficient capital to buy their own pieces of land. The intention was to encourage the early development of an open but stratified society on the English model and at the same time provide revenue from land sales to bring new immigrants from Britain.

Some Australians favoured high land prices and some did not, but almost everyone resented the way the new land regulations of 1842 provided for the use of land-sale revenues. The act directed that half go to the assistance fund and the other half to crown officials to be used by them for public services. Colonists understood that so long as the governor had independent sources of revenue the traditional means for achieving responsible government would be difficult to use. More odious still was the provision of a permanent civil list of £81,600 and provision for the setting up of district councils, charged with raising part of the funds needed to maintain police and jails. These would, of course, further increase the governor's autonomy by removing a considerable expenditure from the control of the legislature. All these grievances: appointed Council members, a permanent civil list, control by Whitehall over land policy and revenues, taxation without representation, had led to rebellion in Canada in 1837. Rebellion there had led eventually and gradually to the granting of responsible government. The elected representatives had the Canadian model in their minds when they assembled in 1843. Therefore it could be expected (and Governor Gipps did expect), that the majority of the Council would demand responsible government and colonial control over internal affairs.[9]

It was predictable that Peel's Tory ministry would resist those demands: the officials of the Colonial Office also had Canada in mind. They maintained that events there had proved that colonists would interpret any grant of internal sovereignty as broadly as they could, to the detriment of imperial interests. And the ministers of the crown had the responsibility to resist acts which might jeopardize the rights of future settlers who would want to claim their share of imperial resources. Further, the Colonial Office could see that more concessions to Wentworth and the association would probably put an end to 'systematic colonization.'[10]

Canada had an artful governor in Lord Sydenham and then a sympathetic governor in Sir Charles Bagot; between them they quieted extremists and allowed evolutionary change. New South Wales was not so fortunate. Governor Gipps's past experiences as a colonial administrator and his personal qualities, including his admirable ones, made it unlikely that he would be artful or flexible. Before coming to Australia in 1838 he had gone out to Lower Canada with Lord Gosford's commission of inquiry. He had concurred with the commission's advice that local autonomy which had been granted there be curtailed. When Gipps and the other commissioners had gone home, Papineau led his small band of French-Canadian patriots in a skirmish with British troops. Gipps observed that concession led to insurrection and concluded that self-government for colonial legislatures meant the end of the British Empire. He was the kind of man who acted on his conclusions; he was rigid, incorruptible, disdainful of public opinion, determined to do his duty. In many respects he was like Robert Lowe. He was a clergyman's son, had no aristocratic patrons, depended on his office and the income it provided for his social status, and, again like Lowe, he was a rigorous free-trade liberal and a staunch man of principle. In New South Wales he worked to extend the right of trial by jury and supported attempts to set up non-sectarian education. He guarded the royal prerogative, not because he was a conservative, but because he thought it a necessary protection, in his colony, against the narrow, selfish interests of the constitutional reformers. He had not the slightest doubt that the people who used rhetoric about responsible government were irresponsible hypocrites, and his scepticism was based on evidence, not simply prejudice. Soon after arriving in the colony he met with a band of Maori chiefs from New Zealand and got them to put their lands under the protection of the British crown. Then he discovered that Wentworth had, during the proceedings, duped the chiefs into selling a huge tract to a group of his associates. Gipps was furious. He asked for legislation to protect what was left from speculators. After that experience he could not stomach declamations by Wentworth and his squatter friends about the free-born rights of Englishmen.[11]

Lowe knew when he accepted a crown nomination to the Legislative Council that he was automatically taking sides in a dangerous duel although he could not have foreseen how dangerous it was or how his independence would be compromised. He recognized his philosophical affinities with the governor. The opportunity Gipps handed him was a miraculous escape from the anxieties he had been living with since his disappointment over the Glasgow professorship. A seat meant clients for his law practice; clients would bring him income; fortune was essential for a political career at home. Thus he was not inclined to search his conscience too thoroughly. Wentworth was, after all, a protectionist and an interventionist and, therefore, a heretic. So, scarcely pausing to reconnoitre, he marked out a suitable rival and rushed joyfully into action. Georgiana reported that, 'Robert will have to oppose a violent, clever Barrister, a Mr. Windeyer, an opposition member who was returned by a popular constituency and everyone is expecting that Robert will quite get the better of him.'[12]

The issue was Windeyer's bill to establish a Land Bank for the purpose of easing the currency shortage. Gipps directed his nominees to oppose it, believing the bill to be a ruse aimed at circumventing the exclusive power of the government to originate money bills. Lowe argued that confidence in a monetary system was a natural growth, 'not to be forced in the hot-bed of legislation.' But he did not get the better of Windeyer, who saw his bill pass. Lowe, however, was not in all respects the loser. The Sydney newspapers reported that Gipps had found a most intelligent spokesman who had a remarkable command of metaphor and a talent for making intrinsically dull subjects seem interesting. Parliamentarians in Australia and England were to be amused and annoyed by this talent for the next forty years.[13]

In the course of one session Lowe emerged as a leading figure in New South Wales. In the process he created an ambiguous image for himself in the public mind. He began as the champion of the government against the squatter opposition; he became, before the year was out, a recruit to Wentworth's side and a personal enemy of Gipps, his benefactor. There seemed to be solid evidence that he was a sincere, reforming liberal who cared for the poor and the unprivileged, and solid evidence that he was an opportunist and a class-conscious snob. When it came time for a review of the first phase of his public career, the *Sydney Morning Herald* warned the colony that a 'political Dick Swiveller' was in their midst, a trimmer who had got his start by 'infesting' Government House but who, after a falling out over a petty question of manners, had thrown over his position as 'Groom of the Stole' and promptly made the discovery that his liege lord was actually a tyrant, out to suppress the liberties of the Anglo-Saxon race: 'Thus does the learned chameleon change his beautiful prismatic hues – now bright and dazzling, now mild and subdued; now black as the raven's wing, now white as the mountain snow ... now glowing with the lustre of an humble Christian, now flaring up in the lurid blaze of Cerebral Physiology.'[14]

Lowe's answer to this attack was spirited: 'Let obloquy come. I dare it – I defy it.' He admitted that his path had been full of twists, but adamantly denied that he was a twister: 'I admit then my inconsistency; but if I have been inconsistent, I have yet been honest.' It will not do to accept his apology without question; he was a politician with extraordinary powers of rationalization. And yet it will be the contention here that he was honest, within the limits of human fallibility, and that he was even consistent, at least to the extent that his behaviour, seemingly so erratic, had a rational coherence. His allegiances changed dramatically but his principles remained, for the most part, the same. The causes he promoted in Australia he was to promote again in England; the arguments he used as a fledgling statesman he was to use again as a mature one – often to the extent of using the same words.[15]

One point which seems beyond dispute is that he stood behind or initiated most of the liberal reforms of the 1840s. The effect or the intention of these reforms was to rationalize laws and institutions. Not surprisingly he found himself opposed by the upholders of the Anglican establishment and by those elements in the colony who felt menaced by his anti-clericalism and his liberal secularism. Some attention needs to be paid to these reform activities because they show us how his mind worked and because they form a pattern. This pattern of responses and attitudes extends over his career in New South Wales and on a larger scale over his English career as well. The fact that this coherence runs through forty years of public life is an answer to the charges of opportunism and inconsistency which he continually faced.

Several of these causes he took up during his eight-month term as a crown nominee, a time when restraints were on him as an unofficial representative of the government. One of the causes was his successful campaign to change the law obliging a delinquent debtor either to declare himself insolvent or to go to prison. Lowe thought this law reflected an old-fashioned, punitive attitude towards social problems rather than a rational, utilitarian desire to make the workings of the economy efficient and honest. The existing statute, he insisted, would oblige the small landowner, who might have no ready cash on hand, to auction off his property in a depressed market. This put an unreasonable burden on one particular section of society and it punished the poor to the benefit of the rich. It gave the small holder the choice between selling his land at an artificially low price to the large landowner, in other words, allowing himself to be exploited, or accepting the 'barbarism' of a prison term for an action which might have been entirely outside of his control. Small farmers, many of whom faced disaster in 1843, hailed his speeches and actions on this subject as examples of humanitarianism. Lowe did not like that label; reason, not sentiment, should be the measuring stick, he believed. But that does not mean that he engaged himself in the subject dispassionately. In 1881, when he had been sent to the semi-retirement of the House of Lords, he made another vigorous plea for a rational law of bankruptcy in an essay for the *Nineteenth Century*. It had the same ring of indignation as his speeches in 1843. This suggests that he was not merely bidding for popularity in 1843 and trying to discredit the squatter opposition on orders from the governor, although there is no reason to rule these motives out.[16]

His eloquently expressed dislike of moralistic attitudes towards crime and punishment did not, on this occasion, shock or enrage the religious; his defence of the murderer, John Knatchbull, did. His arguments as counsel for the accused served notice on the Anglican establishment that they had a mortal enemy to contend with.

Knatchbull, a transported convict, at large on a form of parole called a 'ticket of leave,' entered a Sydney shop kept by the widow Jamieson, hit her repeatedly over the head with the sharp side of a tomahawk, and took eighteen pounds from her purse. A passer-by heard the sound of blows, 'as of a hammer breaking a cocoanut,' and summoned help. Neighbours rushed in, seized the blood-stained assailant, found the dying woman's two young children cowering in an upstairs bedroom.[17]

Aside from the clumsy brutality of the crime, there were some special features which focused the attention of the entire colony. The murderer was the son of a Kentish squire; his half-brother, Sir Edward Knatchbull, had served in Lord Grey's cabinet. During the Napoleonic Wars, John Knatchbull commanded a naval ship. After Waterloo he retired on half pay but was soon cashiered from the navy for failing to pay a bad debt. Then police caught him in the act of lifting a wallet from the trousers of a passer-by in Vauxhall Gardens. After a period of imprisonment in the hulks, the authorities transported him to Australia, but even in Australia he kept to his erratic course. A series of scrapes landed him in Van Diemen's Land and a special punishment camp. Eventually he made his way to Sydney with the comparative freedom of a ticket-of-leave man.[18]

Shortly before the murder he proposed marriage to a servant girl. According to one version of the events, he then decided to rob Mrs Jamieson in order to buy his fiancée a wedding dress, a detail which sent a stir of romantic sympathy through the female population of the colony. What caused the most interest in the crime was the rumour that influence and money from England was being used to cheat the gallows. It was widely supposed that Governor Gipps had, himself, hired Lowe

to defend Knatchbull and that Lowe was ready to accept the assignment because he and the accused had been at Winchester together. This
rumour probably had some substance. The part about Winchester was
false, but Lowe had been friendly with another member of the Knatchbull family at Oxford and had carried with him from England a letter of
introduction from Sir Edward.[19]

There could be little hope that any plea could save Knatchbull. Nevertheless, Lowe could be assured of an attentive audience for his first
major trial. He knew that his only chance was either to find a procedural error, one of 'the tricks of this wretched trade,' or to make a plea of
insanity, but when he did discover a technical loophole, the judge
quickly plugged it. Then when the defence made a request for postpone-
ment in order to gather witnesses who might make a case for Knatchbull's insanity, the motion was denied. Judge Burton, Georgiana noted,
had been the author of the Insolvency Act which Robert had just altered
and was on the look-out for a way to vent his 'long suppressed malice.'[20]

Such a combination of unfavourable circumstances: a hostile judge,
a blood-thirsty press, a public watchful for signs of favouritism, did, if
nothing else, give the defence scope for ingenuity. There is no doubt
that Lowe supplied that in full measure. He had not, he told the jury,
been allowed time to make a case that the defendant was insane in the
legal sense; he would agree that Knatchbull was sufficiently rational to
distinguish right from wrong. And yet it was possible, he argued, that a
person might not be a sufferer from 'frenzied delusions' of the intellect,
and still feel himself in the grip of an 'invincible and unavoidable necessity,' feel himself led by an 'internal impulse to evil' – evil which his intellect could understand but not control. He said that Knatchbull was
such a person. He was a monomaniac; his mind was rational but his will
was diseased. Why else would a man of gentle birth, with prospects of
high station, plunge repeatedly into 'self-created vicissitudes'? Here was
no common ruffian. Impulse, not calculation, must have forced him to
steal money he did not need, to murder without precaution, and then
make no effort to escape. 'The narrow imaginations of our forefathers,'
he told the jury, had simple notions about the motives of criminals.
They thought that justice was done when the facts were made clear.
Since, Lowe concluded, civilization had progressed far beyond this cru-
dity, 'I can only hope for a dawning of a brighter day, when your attention might be extended also to a full enquiry into the motives which
lead to crime.' But the imagination of the jurymen did not stir. Without
bothering to retire, they found the prisoner guilty. Judge Burton expressed his horror at hearing an argument which impeached 'the wisdom and goodness of Providence.' How monstrous it was to believe that
the 'Almighty Power had created beings whom he exposed wilfully to
temptations without giving them power of self-control. If wickedly dis-

posed men would yield step by step to the approaches of the Evil One, they must expect to be led at last by the Tempter to that precipice down which it was his desire to cast them, but in order to avoid this they must resist the temptation in its infancy, and they would resist it successfully.' Delivered of these verities, the judge ordered Knatchbull to be hanged. Shortly thereafter a clumsy executioner publicly did his duty.[21]

Georgiana probably was right in believing that the case would bring Robert forward. His legal business apparently flourished partly as a result of the publicity. Respectable Christians, of course, were shocked by his 'cerebral physiology.' Either he believed what he had said, and was dangerously unsound on the doctrine of free will, or he did not believe it and was using his ingenuity for base purposes. A man of circumspection would have pocketed his gains and said no more about disease of the will. But circumspection was not Lowe's style. He hugely enjoyed a public row with enthusiasts. Besides, he seems to have been sincerely convinced that Knatchbull was insane, but in a way that the primitive legal definition did not comprehend. The exaggerated argument Lowe had invented in a hopeless case had provoked an exaggerated response.

Once started down a line of thought, he could not rest until he had followed it down all of its byways. To save Knatchbull, he had cooked up a theory of insanity. When outraged philistines began to protest, he wondered if there might, after all, be substance to the theory. Having come to take the question seriously, he began to speculate about the existing definitions of legal insanity and to work on proposals for practical reform. Then his mind moved on to the question of punishment and its effect as a deterrent. He was sickened by the public spectacle of Knatchbull's execution. When, a year later, another murderer died slowly on the rope in front of an hilarious throng of spectators, Lowe printed this comment:

> To *them* 'tis sport – at worst a heartless whim,
> But 'tis the bitterness of death to *him.*

He denounced the use of the death penalty in the newspapers as contrary to the spirit of the age and argued that the circumstances surrounding violence were usually too complex to be influenced by public acts of deterrence. He thought it an eloquent comment on the effects of denominational education that mothers would wish to bring their children to watch those anti-Christian spectacles.[22]

While he was writing communications to the press about the inhumanity and, more importantly, he thought, the inexpediency of hangings, he received a copy of a curious English journal, the *Zoist.* Its editor was John Elliotson, a student of mesmerism who had become interested in phrenology. This theory, which originated, appropriately, in Vienna, held that the brain was not unitary but had within it localized organs, each of which controlled specific behavioural characteristics. There was an enormous interest in this pseudo-science in Britain and America during the 1840s and 1850s. Because the subject combined improvement with entertainment, clerks and upwardly mobile workers and their families flocked to Workingmen's Institutes to hear lecturers talk on such subjects as 'Mesmo-phrenology' or 'Phrenotypics.' It was, however, more than simply a popular fad; George Eliot, Harriet Martineau, and other intellectuals were attracted by the possibility that human behaviour might be scientifically diagnosed. If, as phrenologists claimed, both heredity and exercise affect the specialized organs of the brain to the extent that the skull shape conforms to enlargement or lack of development of these organs, then character might be measured, mankind might be liberated from the religious doctrine of original sin, and crime and all anti-social acts might be controlled and reformed.[23]

Lowe seems to have had this theory in mind while constructing Knatchbull's defence, for he explained to the jury that it was possible for one part of the brain to be healthy while another part was stunted or impaired. The *Zoist* noticed this argument when an account of the case reached England and was pleased with this evidence that phrenology was catching on around the world. It printed a long account of the trial, praising Lowe's logic and his courage in holding up the 'doctrine of philosophical necessity' against Judge Burton's 'barbarism.' Lowe reprinted this notice in the *Atlas*, a newspaper he anonymously edited. He expected that this re-opening of the subject would provoke his enemies into another round of furious absurdities. He was not disappointed. The *Sydney Morning Herald* immediately lashed out; it called him 'a Cerebral of the first water,' a man who dared, out of a spirit of 'impious ribaldry,' once again to spread the poison of his Godless determinism, to the detriment of all moral and civil government.[24]

Greatly pleased, Lowe swooped down. He wrote in a public letter that the newspapers had given an inaccurate report of his summation for the defence but that he had, at the time, thought it 'ridiculous egotism' to 'meddle' with it, especially since he was not in the habit of attaching 'much weight to what falls from counsel in argument.' But if ignorant sectarians felt the need to lecture him on free will, he felt he should remind them that the Church of England did not make the doctrine of man's free agency the 'foundation of the whole system of Divine Government.' He added, 'I ask you for Christianity and you give me Methodism.' He had printed the article from the *Zoist*, he claimed, for the sake of amusement. He did not think that journal a manual of scientific truth. But what of those who claim that the Bible is such a manual? 'We shall not go to Genesis for Geology, to Numbers for Arithmetic, to Joshua for Astronomy, nor to the New Testment for the Phys-

iology of the Brain ... Those are no friends to Revelation, who place it
continually, like Uriah the Hitite, in the front of the battle, and seek to
build upon this eternal foundation the transitory tabernacle of prejudice or opinion.'[25]

It must not be concluded from this exchange that Lowe was a positivist. He was a liberal intellectual who believed in the possibility of free
choice and the necessity of individual responsibility. He was aware that
crime was to a large extent the outcome of poverty; he agreed with the
Zoist that defective mental equipment and external circumstances acting upon that equipment might drive a man to do things for which he
could not be held morally responsible, but he was unwilling to accept
determinism. The reason he could not, he wrote in a public letter signed
'A Phrenologist,' was that the great majority of men could reason. Given
some education and relief from severely brutalizing circumstances, their
reason 'enables them to triumph over sin.' Thus he had neither the optimism of those who thought human nature to be infinitely malleable nor
the pessimism of those who thought men to be depraved at birth. He
believed that fresh air, exercise, and education could make most men
progressively amiable and rational. At the same time he was quite certain that all men were born with some limitations to their mental faculties so that perfection through social improvements and human engineering was impossible. He thought that even the best education that
society could afford would not make cultured gentlemen out of Anglo-
Saxon street arabs. He thought that some races could never be brought
up to civilized standards – the Aborigines were, to him, a case in point.
But that did not imply that the Aborigine should be shunned or exploited or that the slum children should be left in ignorance. Like all
those who accepted the conventions of classical liberalism, he believed
in progress, but progress circumscribed by unavoidable economic scarcity and by the limits nature would always place on the mental capacities of the general run of humanity. Thus, while most people thought
Lowe a profound pessimist, he always thought of himself as an optimist.[26]

The optimistic side of his liberal compromise he demonstrated, to his
own satisfaction if not to others, through his work, first in Australia
and then in England, to establish a system of national, non-sectarian
education for the children of the poor. In both places this work plunged
him into a bitter controversy with the upholders of the existing sectarian systems. These were, for the most part, clerics of the Anglican
church. Lowe's impulse to provoke outrage over cerebral physiology in
1844 and 1845 came during, and partly as a consequence of, his battle
to take the responsibility for elementary education out of the hands of
the church and put it into the hands of the state.

The battle began in 1843, not long after Lowe entered the Legislative Council, when he moved for a select committee to investigate the state of the colony's elementary schools. He chaired the committee, did most of the interrogating of witnesses, and wrote the report. During the questioning and in the report he took obvious relish in exposing alarming facts about the inadequacies of the state-assisted, denominational, voluntary societies that provided poor children with schooling. He followed his report up with a pamphlet dealing with the danger of illiteracy in a society like that of New South Wales where almost anyone had a fair chance to accumulate enough wealth to qualify for a vote. In both report and pamphlet he made the point that the existing system educated badly and perpetuated the crippling religious animosities of the old world. He announced to the council that the government was the only agency which could teach people to 'live in harmony, to enlighten them, to soften them – to teach them that religion is a blessing and not a curse ...'[27]

He believed that religion provided a practical ethical code. He thought that the contemplation of God's law in the workings of nature ought to inspire reverence and awe. Doctrine should be kept within the bounds of reason. This bluff, common-sense Latitudinarianism was strengthened by exposure to the heady religious atmosphere of Oxford in the 1830s and 1840s. Some of his undergraduate friends might hurry to St Mary's on Sunday to listen to Newman's exquisite sermons, but Lowe did not. He thought Anglo-Catholicism the enemy of candour and open-mindedness; he was convinced that its practitioners were casuists and frauds. Newman's attempt to find room for Catholic interpretation behind the Protestant words of the Thirty-Nine Articles brought Lowe into the pamphlet campaign against Tractarianism. Lowe's contribution got an answer from William George Ward, a rival at the Oxford Union and a former schoolmate at Winchester. The two carried on an acrimonious public exchange of opinions. As contributions to spiritual enlightenment, Lowe's efforts were negligible; he merely demonstrated the shallowness of his religious imagination. But they do demonstrate that as a young man he was firmly convinced that those who fix their eyes on 'ends instead of principles,' on 'final instead of formal causes,' are far gone on the road to authoritarianism and moral dishonesty. Such men, he thought, cease to be moral agents and become time-serving calculators of expediency – which is to say, they become conservatives. By this reasoning Anglo-Catholics would have to be political conservatives because, in their search for escape from personal moral responsibility, they had found dogmatic authority. The error of one position was the error of the other.[28]

Lowe always refused to grant that a rational person could ever deliberately choose to be dependent and he assumed that most conservative politicians and Tractarian clergy did not believe what they professed. Therefore he was not inclined to give any credit for sincerity to the many clerical voices crying out against his proposals for non-sectarian, public education. He was especially intolerant of the loud protests which came from William Grant Broughton, the crusty, authoritarian Anglican bishop of New South Wales. Broughton was a Puseyite. To Lowe that meant that he had joined with those whose historical role it was 'to keep the people in a state of darkness.' In England, Lowe informed the readers of the *Atlas*, people like Broughton had made the national church into a symbol of power and money. Clerical conservatives of his type had made the church the supporter of protectionism and every other abuse and delusion. He cited as evidence Broughton's statement that if he were forced to choose between secular education in remote, thinly-populated regions of the colony or no education, he would emphatically prefer the latter. This kind of obscurantism was what Lowe expected of 'creeping, crouching Puseyism,' but even he was shocked when Broughton deprived a pastor of his living, after a drum-head trial in 1848, on the grounds that the young cleric entertained Broad-Church sympathies. Lowe compared this action unfavourably with those of Judge Jeffreys and Pontius Pilate and moved a bill for church reform. The bill did not pass, but many of its provisions eventually found their way into the statute books. If Lowe did not win all of the rounds against the bishop, he did, at least, win his share. 'The man's malice is quite inexpungnable,' the bishop wrote. 'How Oxford came to breed such a disposition I cannot tell.'[29]

Unfortunately for education, Bishop Broughton, 'conservatism,' and clerical obscurantism were not the only obstacles in the way of state schools. The new constitution had given the district councils the responsibility to provide for education. Governor Gipps was no conservative and no Puseyite; he agreed in principle with Lowe's educational objectives; but he did believe it essential that he hold out against any encroachments from the squatter majority in the Legislative Council. During the summer of 1844, when Lowe's feud with the church was at its hottest and the Knatchbull trial still fresh in everyone's memory, Gipps decided that he needed Broughton's support. That meant throwing over Lowe, who was on the point of presenting his education report. This was no personal sacrifice, for by this time he and his former protege had reached a parting of the ways. The governor would have to sacrifice a principle, for he doubted the wisdom of administrative decentralization, yet in the circumstances he could see no alternative. At the beginning of the year the Colonial Office informed him that five thousand immigrants were on their way and directed him to provide one hundred thousand pounds worth of bounties. This expense, coming on top of an equally large amount still owing from previous calls on colonial resources, would force him to tax the occupiers of crown lands – a move certain to bring on a major confrontation with the squatters. He thought he might blunt that counter-attack if he could pass on education and police costs to the local districts. Therefore, when Lowe presented his education report in August, Gipps cited the Constitution Act, referred to the clerical displeasure, and refused the authorization of funds.[30]

Lowe and his supporters organized a pressure group, the National School Society, and held big public rallies. They got the Legislative Council to petition the governor to reconsider, but again ran into a veto. The bishop and the governor had made their bargain, Lowe announced, 'Ignorance for Oppression – Oppression for Ignorance.' This was unfair to Gipps if not to the bishop, but it was true that no progress towards national education was possible until New South Wales got a new governor. In 1847 Lowe persuaded Gipps's replacement, Sir Charles FitzRoy, to face up to Bishop Broughton and to place an item in the estimates for non-denominational schools. Nevertheless, it was not until 1866 that Lowe had the satisfaction of hearing that a workable system of state supported elementary education was securely established.[31]

In its power to arouse passions, controversy over education can scarcely be matched, especially when the lines are drawn, as they usually are, along religious lines. As spokesman for the 'friends of a General system of Education,' Lowe was bound to draw to himself the hatreds and anxieties of parents in the Anglican, Roman Catholic, and Hebrew communities. But only part of the acrimony that surrounded him was unavoidable. If enemies demanded explanations from him, he always explained, but in the most provoking way he could think of. If he noticed that flames were crackling around him, he reached out and fanned them. It was this seemingly arrogant behaviour as much as his willingness to undertake difficult and controversial causes that made people dislike him and question his motives. It is probably no accident that when the storm over the Knatchbull trial and the battle with the clerics were at their fiercest, he involved himself or allowed himself to be involved in a series of incidents which disconcerted even his few friends.

However, one of these personal quarrels came about as the result not of his cantankerousness but of his generosity. Georgiana asked that the two orphaned children of the murdered Mrs Jamieson be put under her husband's guardianship. This was after the widow's pastor, the Reverend John Dunmore Lang, had sponsored a subscription for Bobby and Polly Jamieson and arranged for them to be looked after by a schoolmaster member of his Presbyterian congregation. Lang had a violent and erratic temper. A member of council and a strong democrat, he looked on Lowe, the crown nominee, as a political enemy, and, on top of that, he was outraged by Lowe's 'monstrous' attempt to shield Knatchbull. Therefore he tried to prevent the court from sending innocents from his flock into the home of a moral leper. The court refused to listen and awarded the children to the Lowes, although not without protests from Lang and much public discussion.

The children remained in the Lowe household until late adolescence but their position in the household was ambiguous; they were not quite adopted children and not quite servants. At least while they were small Georgiana and her husband seem to have been fond of them and treated them as pets. Both of the Lowes, and especially Georgiana, were insecure about social position; they seem to have regulated their affection for the children by their sense of what was appropriate to children of such humble origin and unfortunate background. Although the facts are obscure, Polly seems to have married young and returned to Australia, probably to the relief of her guardians. Bobby may have been scarred by his gruesome experience in infancy, for he died young and in an asylum. Lowe's one recorded comment was a rueful epigram: 'What evil that I have done has ever been visited on me like this one good action.' Callous though this sounds, it should not be taken as proof that he lacked a heart but only that he was uneasy and suspicious about impulses which came from that direction.[32]

The feud with Lang did not end with the award of the court. Lowe heard that one of Lang's friends, an outspoken democrat and a popular Sydney alderman named Henry Macdermott, had been rejected by the Australian Subscription Library when he applied for membership. Lang mentioned the matter in the council chamber and attacked the library committee. Promptly Lowe submitted and passed a motion of confidence in the committee. Not content with that small measure of revenge, Lowe made a gratuitous remark concerning the 'blackballing' of Macdermott during an exchange with Lang in the council about the propriety of introducing private squabbles into the deliberations of the legislature. Macdermott immediately asked Lowe to explain. Lowe received Macdermott's emissaries but told them that he was not answerable to them for remarks made in the legislature. Upon being told that the alderman's intentions were peaceful, he laughed contemptuously and said that since his antagonist had come to the colony as a sergeant in the ranks, no other possibility could be contemplated. The enraged Macdermott sent a challenge. Lowe went to the magistrate and got an order binding all parties to keep the peace. But Macdermott got some vengeance at the police court hearings. To a large throng in attendance he explained, to the accompaniment of hoots and jeers, why he thought Lowe a coward and a poltroon, punctuating his points with: 'Well, Mr. Privilege Lowe, what have you got to say to that?'[33]

When this uncomfortable scene was over, Lowe assumed, as he was so often to do in the future, the air of an injured man of principle, bearing insult and calumny bravely in the interest of truth, duty, and justice. He asked for a select committee to discover if there was any threat to the freedom of speech of members of council. The committee met and discovered that, indeed, it did not have any clearly defined legal privilege and recommended that appropriate legislation was in order. Although no one in the council could have enjoyed the prospect of being involved in this pettiness, the opposition members did see that if they were to have a showdown with the governor over the tax on crown lands, then they would need to see to it that their legal position was as secure as possible. Accordingly they agreed to follow the advice of the committee and bring a test case against Macdermott before the Supreme Court.[34]

Edward Broadhurst agreed with the greatest pleasure to be counsel for the defendant. He was a neighbour of the Lowes on Horbury Terrace but had no neighbourly feelings towards them. On the contrary, no one in the colony was more eager to see the man behind the prosecution of Macdermott publicly humiliated. The reason was that Georgiana had heard some scandalous talk about Broadhurst and his two sisters, who lived with him, had collected a packet of letters containing evidence which supposedly proved that the Sydney barrister was unfit for polite society, and had sent the packet to the governor and other influential members of the community. Gipps indicated a month before the Macdermott affair that he would hear no evil; Lowe then pompously announced that if the Broadhursts could enter Government House, he and his wife would not. Broadhurst sent a challenge. Since he was a graduate of Cambridge and therefore, presumably, a gentleman, Lowe accepted without hesitation. As he was being rowed to the arranged spot near Woolloomooloo Bay, he was heard to mutter: 'They think because I can't see that I can't fight; but they will find that they are mistaken.' The tense party waited in the boat all night but Broadhurst did not appear. He had been arrested and bound over to keep the peace for one year.[35]

Now Broadhurst had the satisfaction of hearing his enemy proclaimed a slanderous coward. Equally satisfying, he had obtained a moral victory for his client, Macdermott. The verdict was that council members did have immunity for words uttered in debate; but the court then dismissed the action against the alderman on the grounds that Lowe had, by his own admission, shown that he would have been willing to wave his immunity and fight, had his challenger been of equal social station. The legal principle here may have been shaky but most people in the colony thought the decision could not have been more Solomon-like.[36]

Lowe affected to be indifferent to the uproar these tawdry brawls touched off. He had no difficulty convincing himself that he had been a martyr to the cause of free speech, which in a way he was. It could not be expected that a colonial community with an understandable sensitivity about matters of pedigree would honour him for his sacrifices on their behalf. Friends and acquaintances dropped away. Even those few who stayed loyal must have wondered whether his enthusiasm for secular education derived from his principles or from his contempt for the preachers and priests who assailed him for his cerebral physiology. Did he care about the constitutional issue of privilege, or was he worried about his own skin? Had he turned against the governor because he disliked his policies or because he disapproved of the guest list at Government House?

The answer cannot be entirely straightforward. Lowe was no coward, but he was, especially in the context of colonial society, a snob. He was also a virtuoso in the art of dressing up his vindictive and ambitious motives. He probably did believe that by his (or Georgiana's) snooping into a neighbour's private life he was saving 'Colonial Society from the most approbrious stigma which could be cast upon it.' He did not know how to win or lose graciously. But these unflattering traits must be kept in perspective. It would be a false diagnosis to conclude that he was a 'learned chameleon.' He had, as he claimed so often, 'fixed principles.' Free trade, rational religion, utilitarian standards of measurement, belief in the essential importance of education, the wish to create an aristocracy of the intellect – all these he testified to during his youthful Oxford days and pursued steadfastly into advanced old age. Ruth Knight, who has made the most recent and most careful study of his Australian career, comments on his love of contention, his tendency to allow personalities to dictate his choice of tactics, but rightly concludes that he was sincerely committed to the cause of self-government and that he was, fundamentally, a courageous man with a high degree of integrity.[37]

3

The
Cromwell of
the Antipodes

In 1843 Lowe sat as the governor's nominee in the Legislative Council. Early in 1844 he denounced his former benefactor as a tyrant and in August of that year resigned his seat to become the chief propagandist for the squatter opposition. In 1847 he turned against his new allies, stood for the popular constituency of Sydney in 1848, was elected as the champion of a working class franchise and hailed as the leader of the progressive interests in the colony. Then when his radical supporters asked him to assist their causes, he curtly refused them, saying that he was an independent liberal and therefore an anti-democrat. At each of these turnings he proclaimed his moral superiority. He called himself a 'sojourner,' a man passionately involved in the great constitutional issues being debated in Australia and yet detached from any personal interest in their outcome. Such professions almost demand a sceptical response. And yet, after all the necessary reservations are made, it must be admitted that, on balance, his claims were justified.

Within weeks of his appointment as crown nominee Lowe began to feel the difficulty of his position. He owed loyalty to Governor Gipps, shared his views about the squatters, yet found it difficult to resist the constitutional arguments of the elected representatives. The first sign of strain came when the governor interfered with the proposal to end imprisonment for debt on the grounds that the step was too drastic a departure from English practice. He thought colonials should take the lead in such matters from the imperial parliament. Lowe found the reasoning absurd but acquiesced. A more serious difference resulted from the decision Gipps made in March 1844 to act on advice from the Colonial Office and extract from the occupiers of crown land the revenue needed to pay for the passage of immigrants already on their way. Up to this point graziers needed only to pay a small licence fee and make a modest contribution for the maintenance of a border police. Gipps now proposed to extract a licence fee for every twenty square miles used or for every four thousand sheep or five hundred cattle put out to graze. He knew he could never get the change through council, so he simply gazetted his regulations, using the royal prerogative. In doing this he enabled the squatters to pose as the defenders of constitutional liberty and not merely defenders of their own pocketbooks. Lowe, who agreed with the governor that the rich squatters were greedy and monopolistic, immediately became a convert to their cause. He thought the invocation of the prerogative a dangerous, autocratic act. As for the purpose of the new tax, he thought that a betrayal of principles on which he and Gipps had wholeheartedly concurred. From the beginning they had agreed that the Wakefieldian system of colonial settlement was unsound; together they had damned the principle of keeping the price of crown lands artificially high. Lowe had amused Lady Gipps by writing verses on the subject. One of them, *The Woes of Australia*, she had copied out in her own hand. It ended:

> Hail! great panacea of many diseases
> Which makes us or marks us as Government pleases.
> Come Stanley extend thy beneficent hand
> And raise us by sinking the price of Crown Land.

The reason both Lowe and Gipps disliked that panacea was that it forced sheep graziers to become squatters and forced squatters to become self-interested politicians. Since the graziers' livelihood depended on the whim of the Colonial Office, they had no alternative. Moreover, high prices retarded the growth of a class of yeoman farmer who might have been a stable element in an unstable society. Equally bad in the eyes of Gipps and his nominee was the purpose to which the revenues from land sales were to be put. Assisted immigration brought to the colony a labour supply which had little relationship to the market demand for labour. Wakefieldianism violated fundamental economic laws and was the underlying evil which retarded the healthy growth of a balanced society. And yet here was Gipps himself agreeing to pay the costs of receiving immigrants which the bashaws in the Colonial Office, indifferent to all protests from the colonists, insisted on sending, and agreeing to impose a tax which would make it even more difficult for squatters, or anyone else, to secure a reasonably certain tenure.[1]

Lowe refused to accept the explanation that the governor was bound to follow orders. He concluded that Gipps wanted to hold the squatters up for ransom in order to have revenues which he could use at his own discretion, thus freeing himself from the restraints the legislature might want to put upon his tyrannous abuse of power. This conclusion made, Lowe clung to it with a convert's enthusiasm. During the conversion

process, and coincidentally to it, came the rift over the Broadhurst letters. This may explain why he lost all sense of proportion in his assessment of motives. His attacks on his former benefactor became slanderous and personal to an extraordinary degree.

To Gipp's frustrated annoyance, his nominee held on to his seat in
the council for almost five months after he had so vociferously joined
the enemy camp. During this time he carried on his feuds with Bishop
Broughton and Alderman Macdermott, thus mixing together his public
and personal affairs and gaining passionate self-righteous conviction in
the process. Inside and outside the council during those months he not
only joined but came near to leading the campaign of attack on the
governor's action. He became a member of the Pastoral Association, a
lobby formed to oppose the governor's regulations, and wrote most of
its propaganda. Gipps, of course, was livid. He tried to find a way to get
the traitor dismissed, and he wrote to Lord Stanley that the appointment of Robert Lowe 'is one of the acts of my government, which I
have reason to be sorry for.' Lowe hung on until he had finished his
education report, and then in August 1844 resigned.[2]

For the rest of that year and into the next Lowe shifted his arena of
combat from the council chamber to the press. In November some rich
men in the Pastoral Association sponsored a newspaper they called the
Atlas; Lowe was the obvious choice for editor. The position was offered
and he agreed, but insisted that they hire a front man so that he would
not be embarrassed on his return to the council (he had his eye on a
constituency) by too public an association with journalism. No one was
taken in by this. During his year of active management readers easily
recognized his strident voice. The unfortunate Gipps received broad-
sides from the leading articles and harassing fire from jokes and poems,
all, or mostly all, composed by the editor. Here is a brief sample:

> They say that if Governors choose to be skittish,
> To thwart them is Turkish, to bend them is British.[3]

To thwart rather than to bend was the aim of the *Atlas*. Its editor
announced his intention to trumpet and to irritate until, perhaps, he
could break through 'the desperate tenacity' of Mr Gardner, the Australian clerk at the Colonial Office. If that could be done then there was a
chance that Mr Gardner would alert 'Mr Oversecretary' Stephen. Then,
if talk of treason and rebellion were loud enough, word might penetrate
through to Lord Stanley and wake him up to the grievances of one of
the most remote of his forty colonies. But hope was slight, Lowe announced. 'If the Pacific Ocean were to sweep over this Continent ... the
labour of Her Majesty's Cabinet would not be lightened by a single
hour.' Stridency, he decided, was the only way to get attention from
these remote and indifferent bureaucrats. The only lasting remedy was

in the ultimate concession of responsible government combined with representation in an imperial parliament where knowledgeable men from the colonies could sit and call to account the 'freaks and misconducts' of a colonial secretary's clerk. Without these concessions, he told an excited audience at a dinner in Wentworth's honour, 'the bloody and expensive lesson [of America] would have to be read again in every quarter of the globe.' Grant responsible self-government and 'then indeed will England and her colonies be knit in an iron confederacy ...' Until that happened he would do everything in his power to shatter complacency.[4]

At this point he did not pause to consider what might happen if the squatters got their hands on the machinery of responsible self-government. Gipps, however, was aware that much of the high-flown talk of the Pastoral Association was a cover for less elevated objectives. He tried to buy them off with concessions. He offered squatters the chance to purchase at auction a three-hundred-and-twenty acre portion of their runs. This only increased the protests. Squatters complained that this would involve them in more expense and bring them no security of tenure. They petitioned for twenty-one year leases and the right to pre-empt their runs at a price set by the colonial legislature. This should have made Lowe suspicious, but he was now passionately committed to their cause, or what he believed to be their cause. The petition contained a strong protest against the unreasonably high upset price of land, and this put Lowe off the scent. The squatters, he explained to the *Atlas* readers, were moderate men; they wanted relief from uncertainty and relief from the arbitrary annual licensing power – a perpetual knife which the governor and the Colonial Office held to their throats. Fixity was not the same as permanence of tenure, he argued; fixity simply meant that a man could refuse to laugh at the land commissioner's jokes. Only gradually did he begin to realize that he had been naïve in thinking that all the squatters wanted was simple justice. 'The proposition was dexterously put,' and the subject was young then, he explained in an apology he made in 1847. This apology came after he had taken another dramatic about turn, this time away from the pastoralists. Once again he found himself explaining away an apparent inconsistency, but there seems to be no reason to reject the apology on that account. He was, as he said, 'in the hurry and eagerness of fear and anger.' And a great many other people were, in 1844 and 1845, in a similar state. In this period opposition to Government House united most of the factions in the colony behind Wentworth. Disillusionment with the squatter cause came later, not just for Lowe, but for practically everyone.[5]

Lowe's eyes began to be opened when he returned to the Legislative Council in April 1845. The sixty voters in the huge riding of St Vincent and Auckland ignored the *Sydney Morning Herald*'s warning that their candidate was 'not to be trusted'; they returned him unopposed. This was mildly depressing news to the governor who was otherwise in relatively good spirits. He had heard the good news that Whitehall had approved his land regulations. Even better, the home government had responded in a friendly way to requests for pre-emption and long leases passed on to them by agents which the Pastoral Association had sent to London. Gipps expected that this would cool the ardour for constitutional reform. It had that effect on the rank and file although Wentworth, Lowe, and a few others (including Lowe's old enemy, the Reverend Lang), tried to maintain pressure for constitutional reform. Lowe tried, and failed, to pass a bill providing for an audit to check the government's practice of spending more than the appropriations authorized or diverting money which had been voted for one purpose into other channels. Even had this measure passed, the governor would not have been seriously embarrassed, for economic recovery was bringing more revenues into the colonial treasury. The result was that the opposing forces reached a stand-off, broken only when Governor Gipps announced his intention to step down. He was exhausted and mortally ill but had put off his decision as long as he could believing himself to be the only safeguard in the colony against greed and democracy. He sailed away in August 1846, saying that for his own health's sake he had already stayed too long. Lowe was unmoved. He fired off this parting shot:

> Such is the mournful retribution,
> At which the courtiers groan –
> In ruining *our* constitution,
> Sir George has spoilt *his own*.[6]

To say the least, this was ungenerous and impolitic behaviour. Dr Charles Nicholson, for a long time Lowe's personal friend and political confederate, concluded by 1849 that the man was 'a sort of psychological monster – *all head*, and no heart.' It should be noted that he made this judgment after Lowe had, for perfectly honourable and responsible reasons, voted against Nicholson's re-election as speaker of the Legislative Council. Nicholson was not then disposed to recognize more amiable characteristics. And yet even when allowances are made for the difficult circumstances in which Lowe laboured and his ability to provoke his opponents into exaggerated rages, it has to be admitted that there was something peculiar about his emotional responses. He used his wit to fend off a world he felt to be hostile and then seemed to be genuinely surprised or offended when his victims struck back. He believed that sentiment should, as a general principle, be reserved for the contemplation of nature and the treatment of animals and children; in all other circumstances it clouded reason and therefore prevented, in the long run, the maximization of happiness. Sentiment must always, therefore, be treated ironically. His reaction to the death of Richard Windeyer illustrates the point. Windeyer had been Lowe's first political rival when he entered the council but soon became a close friend. Lowe felt the loss keenly and showed it by thoughtful actions towards the dead man's widow and son. And yet in the obituary notice he wrote for the *Atlas* there was a curious note of detachment. Windeyer, he wrote, was a success at the bar because his passionate nature so distorted his judgment that he could earnestly believe that the horse-stealer he was defending was worthy of sainthood. The departed was indulgent with his family, but humourless, immodest, coarse of speech, sarcastic but unable to bear sarcasm – 'a man in whom, to speak in phrenological phrase, the faculties of self-esteem and of benevolence were largely developed.' This was a strangely candid eulogy. Obviously Lowe believed honesty was the best tribute he could make to his friend's memory. But in this as on so many occasions Lowe seemed to be insensitive to the effect honesty might have on others.[7]

As her husband's unpopularity grew, Georgiana's letters home, initially so rapturous, gradually became critical and, finally, bravely forlorn. By 1845 the Lowes had closed themselves off from most of Sydney society. His enemies exercised their ingenuity to discover new insults. In April of that year, in the midst of the hubbub over the *Zoist* article, Broadhurst pasted notices on prominent walls around the city reading: 'I hereby proclaim Robert Lowe, Esq., M.C. to be a coward.' Lowe complained to the court and Broadhurst gladly paid a small fine. A move to expel Lowe from the Australian Club failed by the chairman's deciding vote. Georgiana announced that she would no longer accept invitations to mixed parties. With doors and drawing rooms closing against them, they looked for a place in the country and found a stone house, only partly finished, above a golden beach, a long horse-back ride from the centre of Sydney. It had a small turret at each corner, probably intended to give a romantic effect rather than, as some people thought, to withstand siege from bushrangers. It was a bastion both literally and figuratively. One night Georgiana sallied forth, a poncho over her nightgown, firing off a rifle and loosing bloodhounds when she heard sounds from suspected intruders. This and other stories went the rounds. Georgiana manifestly did not fit the stereotype of upper class Victorian femininity. Proper colonial ladies found her either amusing or impossible. But for a while she was blissfully happy, cutting trees, helping start an orchard and kitchen garden. A deep stream bank near the house she made into a picturesque grotto with a small waterfall, a rosery, a lover's walk. Her face became unfashionably tanned. Neighbouring settlers watched her jump horses over ditches and tree stumps and called her 'The Black Angel.' Totally disdaining convention, she would supervise the loading each Sunday morning of a cart full of vegetables and butter, and then she would follow the cart on horse-back to the George Street Market so she could make sure nothing got lost on the way. Several years later an officer's wife who had watched these scenes moved to London and into a house opposite the Lowes. She gossiped to friends back home in Sydney: 'You cannot think *how much worse* Mrs. Lowe looks dressed not very fine and grown very red and fat, *even* than she did when I saw her last, riding from Sydney to Cugee with a *basket of mutton* in her arms. Which fact I am afraid I maliciously stated to some of Mr. Lowe's patrons.'[8]

The house at Nelson's Bay was a tonic to Georgiana's flagging spirits and a sanctuary for her embattled husband. While they were happily engaged in finishing it, they heard that a new and promising governor was on his way. Sir Charles FitzRoy arrived in Sydney in August 1846. He was an urbane aristocrat who, like Gipps, had formed his views about colonial administration in British North America; but there the similarity stopped. Where Gipps had upheld the imperial interest in Lower Canada, FitzRoy had done what he could to advance responsible government in Prince Edward Island. As chief administrator in New South Wales he proved to be an ally of the colonists in their attempts to stretch or circumvent laws restricting local autonomy. He watched approvingly while the council moved to secure effective control over expenditures and money bills. He willingly conceded the right of the legislature to control how the money provided by the Civil List should be used. Although it would be premature to say that the campaign for responsible government was won by 1848, it was clear to everyone that the focus of controversy in the colony had shifted by that date. The various conflicting interests could no longer unite in a common cause against Whitehall and its minions. Now the crucial issue was an internal one: how the power which was in the process of being given to the colony was to be divided.

Lowe described this change to the British House of Commons in 1855: the period of controversy over the constitution had been an heroic phase, he said, but after 1847 there had been a 'decline of public spirit and patriotism in the colony.' He claimed that while Sir George Gipps had been governor, the great squatters had, like Pisistratus, cried out that they were in danger from the enemies of the people, and, like the ancient tyrant, they had turned the instruments given them for their protection into instruments of enslavement. He then explained that the bodyguard in this analogy was the Waste Lands Act which reached Sydney in December 1846. It did give the squatters the protection they sought: fourteen-year leases, the right of pre-emption, retention of the one pound per acre minimum price, a high price which insured them against competition for land from small-scale agriculturists. The act did retain imperial control over the revenues of land sales, but everyone expected that the British government would eventually concede even that. Thus the squatters had been given far more than mere protection; they now had before them the prospect of gaining what amounted to permanent tenure over a territory larger than all of the British Isles put together, a prospect they could seize as soon as they could get their hands on sufficient political power.[9]

Lowe's suspicions about the intentions of Wentworth and his party began before the provisions of the Waste Lands Act were made known. While Gipps had been at Government House, Wentworth had proven a reliable leader in the war of oratory and manœuvre. He had become a symbol to his Sydney constituents and to most colonists of Australian patriotism and desire for self-rule. 'Love of my country has been the master-passion of my life,' he had declared and few had doubted him. He treasured the esteem his countrymen extended to him. But he had no use for popular government. He sincerely believed that the way to make self-government secure and workable was to create an aristocracy out of the great landed proprietor class, men like himself who were durable elements in the community and could afford leisure and culture. These views had not been incompatible with popular leadership so long as his adversaries had been Governor Gipps and the Colonial Office. But when that struggle began to diminish in importance, it occurred to the radical leaders of the urban middle and working classes that Wentworth's objects and their own did not converge. If Wentworth were to establish his aristocracy he would need to maintain the monopoly over the crown lands for his class; that could be secured by maintaining the high price of land. If, as it seemed, the squatters wanted responsible self-government in order to get for themselves permanency of tenure, then the old cause could no longer bind patriots of all classes together. Thus when the Land Act became the central issue, Wentworth's popularity began to diminish.[10]

Correspondingly, Lowe's began to rise. Wentworth had no enthusiasm for national education nor any passion for free trade. By 1846 he could see that Lowe, despite the hatred felt for him in some circles, was potentially a serious rival. The two began to do some subtle jockeying for position. Then came the disclosure of the new land act; after that, no more co-operation was possible. Lowe was greatly alarmed at its implications and indignant that he had been used to help create a sheep-grazing oligarchy. He saw that if anyone was now to become the leader of an opposition to that oligarchy, he was the man. This realization forced him to consider his personal objectives. He would need to decide whether to make Australia his permanent home and reach for the prize in that provincial but accessible arena or to continue according to the schedule he had set for himself when he had decided to make the voyage out.

The decision to return to England seems not to have been a difficult one to make. His eyes were now free from spasms and getting stronger. Georgiana was complaining of severe pains in her legs and talking about home. In a few years, if the economic recovery continued, they could count on a sufficient income to make an English career feasible. The real estate speculations Lowe had made with his wife's money and with a small bequest his father had left him when he died were beginning to show fat profits. He wrote to a friend that his 'expedition' was turning out to be satisfactory after all, and he had hopes that he should be able to bring it to a close in several years. In the meantime he would take advantage of his freedom to fight without concern for compromise. He would do all he could to frustrate the Australian Pisistratus. He was perfectly open about his intentions. 'I am,' he told the council in 1847, 'only a sojourner.'[11]

Being a sojourner did not seem to diminish his zest for fighting for Australian causes although it did liberate him from any need to win friends or suffer fools, inclinations he never experienced compellingly in any case. In 1847 he made a series of speeches with the intention of stirring up a protest loud enough to catch the attention of Lord John Russell's Whig government in London. He told audiences of working men and tradesmen how Wentworth, in his greed, and the Colonial Office, in its ignorance, were about to turn New South Wales into 'one vast job.' He warned that permanency of tenure for the graziers would plunge the colony into class war; the result would be to turn the fields and villages into a great, permanent sheep walk, where 'man is to be penned within narrow limits, that sheep and cattle may have leave to roam at large.' The answer from Wentworth and most of the press was that the new tribune of the people had done still another flip-flop, one more act of treachery. Lowe told a cheering crowd that for all the errors of the past, he had at least been consistent to his 'abstract feeling for liberty,' which was more than his opponents could say. Sydney radicals who had once hissed Mr Privilege Lowe were not this time prone to be critical. They could find no other powerful champion. Where Wentworth had expressed his antipathy to democracy, Lowe had urged a lower franchise to protect society from a self-interested oligarchy; where Wentworth had defended the importation of Polynesian labour, Lowe had denounced it as 'a new form of slave trade,' a trade practiced by men who first want to people the stations with convicts and then 'inundate the country with cannibals.'[12]

So wide did the rift become between the two rivals that not even a shared dislike for a new constitution, in the process of being served up to them by Russell's doctrinaire Colonial Secretary, Earl Grey, could bring them together in effective opposition. Grey had envisaged a symmetrical pyramid. At its base would be a reformed system of elected district councils. The councils would elect members from their own ranks to the lower chamber of a bicameral legislature; this body would, in turn, send representatives to an all-Australian assembly. Grey thought the federal assembly should have limited powers and act mainly as a guarantor of free trade throughout the continent. James Stephen worked out the scheme in his orderly brain, and Grey presented it in a spirit of liberal, if paternalistic, goodwill. Grey believed that colonies had the right to govern themselves up to the point where their actions impinged on the rights of other colonies or the imperial interest. He thought that decentralization of power would make it easier to preserve the public domain in trust for future generations. The federal assembly would prevent the colonies from ruining each other with wasteful economic nationalism. Having worked out this formula, Grey and Stephen could see no reason why they should not implement it. They were not indifferent to colonial opinion and they had no wish to override differences in local conditions or traditions; it simply did not occur to them that a careful investigation of these factors was necessary. Had they more than a flicker of imagination they might have foreseen that men who had fought so long for responsible government and against district councils would react to these constitutional proposals with angry frustration. Even Grey's gentle nudge in the direction of colonial federation produced resistance. Lowe was one of those who had at one time expressed a mild interest, but on reflection he changed his mind. Systems providing for decentralization of power, he decided, had many intrinsic weaknesses, and the more he thought about the question the stronger his reservations grew. In 1857 he warned the Colonial Office that premature federalism would lead to civil war. This was one of his typical exaggerations. What caused most leaders in New South Wales to hold back was the possibility that a federal assembly would not recognize the predominance of that colony.[13]

Opponents to Grey's constitution held protest meetings, newspapers fulminated, politicians made fervent speeches. The British constitution, Lowe reminded an appreciative gathering in a Sydney theatre, 'was not founded by closet politicians, scheming experimentalists, speculative emperics or crack-brained philosophers.' The difficulty was, however, that Lowe and Wentworth were only united in their rhetoric. When it came to specifics, they disagreed. Lowe and his friend, Charles Cowper, wanted a bicameral assembly; Wentworth favoured a unicameral system. Both sides therefore presented rival resolutions about Grey's proposals, and Dr Bland complicated things still more by bringing in a plan of his own. The object of each of these factions was to embarrass one another. They succeeded at this, with the result that Grey received no clear guidance from the Legislative Council.[14]

While this excited bickering was going on, word came of the February Revolution of 1848 in France and of the revival of Chartist militancy at home in England. Alarmed officials decided that it would be dangerous to give radicals time to agitate and moved the colonial elections ahead a month. They sensed that the working men in Sydney were beginning to gain confidence and political unity. This was correct. What the radicals lacked was an influential spokesman in the Legislative Council. Therefore conservatives in the colony became greatly alarmed when they detected signs that the urban radical leaders were making approaches to Lowe, the man who had warned that a contest over the future of the waste lands might end in class war. Conservative men thought Lowe capable of any turn. He had first been Gipps's pet, then the darling of the pastoralists; could he not become tomorrow a democrat and a tyrannous demagogue?[15]

These fears were unfounded. Liberalism, not sympathy with democracy, made Lowe agree to be the leader of the popular cause. He welcomed the advances of a group of young Sydney merchants, some of whom were to have distinguished political careers, not because he wished to see their class in power but because he wished to see no class in power. He thought that if the urban middle class joined with the farmers and skilled workingmen there was a chance that they might balance off the sheep-grazing interest. He perceived that the threat to the balance of interests came, at that stage, from a self-appointed oligarchy and would-be aristocracy, people who were indifferent to the 'noble ultimatum of all government and all legislation, the greatest happiness of the greatest number.' Years later, in a leading article for *The Times*, he spoke of Australia as a 'working man's paradise – a democratic society where everything is open to talent and industry.' Yet it is clear from everything he said in the last two years of his stay in New South Wales that he admired the open society but not democracy. In 1848 he believed democracy was the enemy of liberty, although that belief was not so fervent as it was to be in 1866. He went to considerable lengths to demonstrate his independence from his Sydney backers in 1848, even while he was asserting the rights of the common man and courting the favour of the working class and lower middle class voter. His subsequent behaviour as member for Sydney showed, frequently to the consternation of his constituents, that his support for their political and social advancement was decidedly conditional.[16]

His entry into the race for a Sydney seat against the two incumbants, Wentworth and Bland, proceeded in gradual stages. Knowing that Henry Parkes and other radical leaders would probably invite him to run, he nevertheless assured his St Vincent and Auckland constituents that he intended to canvass their votes. When a Liberal businessman named John Lamb announced that he would stand for a seat in Sydney, Lowe pledged his support. But Parkes and the other radical leaders were not easily put off. They hired a hall and filled it to overflowing with artisans and tradesmen who gave groans for Wentworth and cheers for Lowe. Parkes collected signatures to a petition, approached Lowe again with an offer to defray all expenses, but received another refusal. This time, however, Lowe agreed, under pressure, that he might accept a draft. He would not, he announced, solicit votes and would continue to support Lamb, but if the citizens were really set on having a triumph for the principles they cared so strongly about, then he would not insult them with a refusal. There was shrewd calculation behind this coyness. A draft would give him a position of almost total liberty to act as he pleased and to depart when he pleased. Parkes immediately sent the machinery rolling. The unhappy Lamb found himself sidetracked as Bland and Wentworth turned their attention to a more formidable rival. On nomination day Wentworth expressed thanks to 'your own idol, Mr. Lowe' for doing so much to help squatters get fixity of tenure. No one, he said, had 'half so much weight with the Home Government,' in moving it to act on the petitions of 1844, as this 'parasite of the moment.'[17]

Tensions were high on polling day, 28 July 1848. Late in the afternoon it became obvious that Lowe's backers had brought about a major upset. Wentworth topped the poll but enough skilled workmen had turned out to put Lowe only some one hundred and fifty votes behind, securing for him the second seat without his having given a speech or spent a penny. His acceptance address flattered those who had worked for him, although it contained a significant reservation. He said that rich businessmen and sheep graziers, presuming to be aristocrats, offered no firm social base on which to build a bright future; the workingman and the free immigrant embodied that future. That promise could only come true, however, if the masses could be educated. 'I do not fear to entrust ample unrestrained power into the hands of the people, so long as they possess the knowledge which can teach them how to wield it.' It is probable that at this stage in his life he was optimistic about the possibilities of mass enlightenment, but any of his listeners who knew his mind would have been aware that this qualification was fundamental. An educated mass electorate did not exist in 1848, and if Bishop Broughton had his way, might not exist for many years. It is unlikely, however, that most of his listeners on that July day were interested in qualifications; they were out to celebrate what they believed to be their great democratic victory. They unhitched horses from a carriage and, cheering lustily, pulled their new representative through the streets.[18]

It was not long before the Sydney working and merchant classes discovered that although they had won a victory by electing Lowe, they had not elected an egalitarian. Parkes wanted to follow up the success by forming a political organization to continue the agitation for popular rights. Lowe warned them that such a move, at a time when all of Europe was trembling with revolution, would frighten away all respectable and influential supporters. Undeterred, the Sydney radical group formed their association and used it to press for the extension of the

franchise and for public works to relieve the distress caused by the re-
cession of 1848. They asked Lowe to speak at a rally and received a lecture on the wickedness of governmental interference in the natural law
of the market place. He would not attend 'because I do not think the
mechanics of Sydney ought to put themselves in the position of paupers receiving charitable relief at the expense of their equally distressed
fellow-colonists.' This abruptly ended the one-sided romance between
the working class and Robert Lowe. Disillusionment deepened when he
explained that no remarks he had made during his acceptance speech or
at any other time implied that he believed in universal suffrage. Asked
to second a series of resolutions on the franchise which were to be presented at a public meeting, he agreed, but only after Parkes had deleted
a clause claiming the right to vote for all tax-payers. He told Parkes he
could agree that more voters needed to be added to the rolls so that a
balance of interests could be reached and that he would speak for a significant reduction, but he would not speak for democracy or the rights
of man. He was candid in his private communications with Parkes and
equally forthright when the public meeting took place. When a heckler
interrupted with a shout of 'Paupers!' Lowe shouted back that he had
supported franchise reform, 'not to enable them to put money in their
pockets, but to prevent its being taken out.' This frankness won a cheer,
but disappointed radicals felt betrayed. Perhaps Dr Bland had been
right when he said that their candidate would prove to be a man of ter-
giversation.

But Lowe's conscience was clear. Some seventeen years later he was
to have his previous record on the franchise thrown back into his face.
He was to answer, correctly, that he had never varied from his classical
liberal tradition although, being an empiricist, he had adapted that position to the radically different conditions which existed on the other
side of the world. What inconsistency there was between his behaviour
in 1849 and in 1866 was, he maintained, in the eyes of the beholders.[19]

Lowe's notion of how best to serve the interests of those who voted
for him lay in a different direction. He could not agree to bread and cir-
cuses, but he could see to it that their city was honestly managed, that
their streets were lighted and cleaned of filth, that their water was pure,
and that their open drains were covered. He got a select committee appointed to investigate the City Corporation. It uncovered an unsavoury
mess of corruption. Lowe's solution was drastic: abolish corporations,
'relics of a past age,' and turn over supervision of drainage, water supply, and lighting to an appointed commission. He knew that this would
be to surrender the elective principle; he was ready for a flood of 'pot-
house rhetoric' about no taxation without representation, but he said
that he still agreed with Edmund Burke that elections were in themselves evils to be endured only when they 'work out a greater good.' In

feudal times when central governments were incompetent municipal corporations had served some purpose, but times had changed. How ab-absurd it was to preserve an outmoded custom in order to uphold 'this flimsy shadow of constitutional right.'[20]

To thoughtful conservatives this kind of primitive utilitarianism appeared dangerously radical; to Sydney radicals, it seemed dangerously reactionary. His brief experience with popularity slipped quickly away, but he hardly missed it. He was, as he put it, 'like a cork floating on the surface of colonial society.' His investments had continued to prosper. Whenever he chose he could leave this den of iniquity behind. In the few months that were left he would see to it that there was at least one man left capable of denouncing cupidity and speaking the unvarnished truth.

One last episode remained. On 7 June 1849 watchers sighted the transport, *Hashemy*, laden with two hundred convicts, on its way to Port Jackson – tangible evidence that transportation had begun again. Before the Lowes had arrived in the colony Whig ministers had decided that the shipment of criminals to New South Wales was expensive and out of keeping with their theories about planned colonization. Free immigrants had been glad to have the importation of convicts cease; emancipists could look forward to an improvement of their social status once the colony ceased to be a prison camp; patriots welcomed the decision as an essential prerequisite to self-government. But not every-one was pleased. Employers of labour, and particularly the large graz-iers, hated to lose a cheap and necessarily tractable work force. Some British officials also regretted the curtailment of this alternative to do-mestic imprisonment. The depression years had filled the prisons at home and at the convict settlements in Van Dieman's Land and Norfolk Island. Feeling these pressures, Gladstone, who was for a few months in 1845 colonial secretary in Peel's ministry, marked out a new area of convict settlement in northern New South Wales and offered to send convicts to the rest of the colony, should the people there want them, to engage in public works. He also proposed that those who had served a period of confinement in the penal colonies be permitted to enter New South Wales as free labourers. Peel's government fell before it could get a reaction to these proposals. Nevertheless, Gladstone's succes-sor, Earl Grey, took over the Tory plan and added, as an inducement, an offer to balance the inflow of parolees with an equal number of free immigrants, provided at the imperial expense. Grey did not make much of an effort to find out the attitudes of the colonists although he did send a request for an expression of opinion from the Legislative Coun-cil. It did not respond with a single voice. Wentworth chaired a commit-tee, on which Lowe also sat, to consider Gladstone's plan. The commit-tee gave a favourable report in October 1846 and on hearing this Grey moved ahead with his modified scheme. But while communications were slowly moving across vast distances, church and labour union groups complained so noisily that the council reversed the findings of the committee. Immediately afterwards they proceeded to reverse their reversal, and at this Grey lost patience. Although he knew that a tight budget made it impossible to keep his promise about sending the free immigrants, he gave the order to begin the shipments – hence the appearance of the *Hashemy* in Sydney harbour that June day in 1849, and hence the demonstrations of protest which followed. Anti-trans-portationists were exasperated by this high-handedness. Organized by Parkes's Constitutional Association, they decided to have a direct con-frontation. Association members called for people to mass at noon on 9 June on Circular Quay. They called on Lowe to preside.[21]

Despite his refusal to be the spokesman for radical causes, Lowe was the logical choice. He was still leader of the movement to curb the power of the squatters and, by 1849, transportation and the squatter interest had become closely linked in the public mind. Up to this time Lowe had not taken a strong position on the issue. He had agreed with the judgment of Wentworth's committee and written in the *Atlas* his opinion that the colony had progressed sufficiently since 1840 to be able to absorb another round of transportation. So long as the British government respected the wishes of the colonists, he thought no harm would be done; England could relieve the crowding in her prisons and the colony would get needed bridges and roads. In addition to these practical advantages, there was the chance that transportation to a land of opportunity might, for some of the convicts, break the cycle of bit-terness and poverty that had trapped them in the old world. But he had written this before his disillusionment with the squatter cause. After that, everything they favoured was automatically suspect. He reasoned that if they were to have their oligarchy they would need to maintain high land prices; land sales would be sluggish with high prices and there-fore there would be little money to assist the bringing in of free labour. Transportation must be their solution. It followed that opposition to transportation must be a way to check their ambitions. This conclusion he reached well before the election of 1848 and before the radical group first approached him to accept the Sydney candidacy. He had made his conclusions public. Thus when the association approached him to lead the demonstration, there seemed no way to refuse, much as he disliked the prospect. After some negotiation on the phrasing of resolutions he agreed to chair the meeting at Circular Quay. 'Bob Lowe has taken an-other *turnabout* and wheelabout,' wrote one of Parkes's confederates, 'in this case for the better.'[22]

There could be no more turning about once the *Hashemy* demonstra-tions were begun, although Lowe did manage to arrive an hour late, after the proceedings were already underway. The crowd roared approval when he appeared. As he climbed to the top of an omnibus, named 'Defiance,' an elderly woman called out, 'Ah! bless this dear old white head.' Once into his speech his diffidence evaporated. He began: 'the stately presence of your city, the beautiful waters of your harbour are this day again polluted with the presence of that floating hell – a convict ship.' And why so? To benefit a privileged class, an oppressive tyranny sends the 'worst and most degrading slavery.' From that vigorous beginning he proceeded to an inflammatory ending. He must have had the following in mind years later when he remarked that there was a moment in his life when he might justly have been hung for treason:

> As in America, oppression was the parent of independence, so shall it be in the colony. The tea which the Americans flung into the water rather than pay the tax upon it, was not the cause of the revolt of the American States; it was the unrighteousness of the tax – it was the degradation of submission to an unrighteous demand. And so sure as the seed will grow into the plant, and the plant into the tree, in all times and in all nations, so will injustice and tyranny ripen into rebellion, and rebellion into independence. (Immense cheering.)[23]

The next day the alarmed governor filled the stables of Government House with soldiers, doubled the guard, and stationed police in the kitchen. So prepared, he received Lowe and a small delegation when they called to deliver a petition. Sir Charles promised to forward the petition but brusquely refused to send the convicts home. While the demonstrations and negotiations were going on, graziers were bidding for the *Hashemy*'s cargo so that by the time the second, and bigger, rally took place on 18 June, half the convicts were already on shore and at work. At this second demonstration Lowe mounted the 'Defiance' again and described to the crowd how the governor had received his delegation. 'I behaved much more civilly than usual. (Great laughter) ... But I chose, on behalf of those who sent me there, to assert the right of a cat to look at a king.' Again he reminded the Colonial Office of America and 1776. He asked his hearers to reflect that even the arrogance of British officialdom had not dared to offer a gift of criminals to those three colonies with truly independent government: Canada, New Brunswick, and Nova Scotia.[24]

The results of this excitement ('one of the few heroic moments of Australian history,' one chronicler called it) were unspectacular. FitzRoy dismissed the incident in his despatch as merely a gathering of rabble. The respectable parts of the community had not joined in, he noted, and advised Grey to take comfort in the fact that all of the convicts had been quickly taken up by employers. On the other hand, he did acknowledge that many of the colonists seemed to have been in a rebellious temper. When he heard that the Legislative Council had, before the oratory on Circular Quay, condemned his action, he suspended shipments until such a time that the council might change its mind again. That did not content anti-transportationists; so long as the Order-in-Council remained in effect, the threat was there and so, on a smaller scale, the demonstrations continued. Radical groups and sympathizers in the council joined to form a colony-wide association with a lobby in London. Lowe worked as one of the association's agents after his return to England and in that work and through his influence with *The Times* contributed more to the cause than he did by his performances on top of the 'Defiance.' Public opinion in England moved in the anti-transportationists' favour when the discovery of gold stimulated a new interest in Australia. The Colonial Office did not repeal the offending Order-in-Council until 1852, when Russell's resignation forced Lord Grey from his secretaryship, and Grey resisted to the last. Parliament, he declared, need not feel itself bound to 'listen to every clamour' from the colonies, 'reasonable or unreasonable.' Lowe did not let readers of *The Times* forget those words; he stood on guard for a decade against any move to revive transportation or extend it in Australia, although he did soften his position on transportation to other places. In 1862 and 1863, after a commission had recommended the opening up of Western Australia to convict shipments, he wrote that hardened criminals must not be sent to enjoyable climates, 'where a bright sun and an exhilarating climate raise the spirits and deaden the sense of guilt and of misery.' He recommended instead places where 'the climate is healthy but rough, and nature is more repulsive'; Labrador or the territory of the Hudson's Bay Company might do nicely. There would be no danger in those places that convicts would turn into millionaires![25]

The cheers Lowe heard on Circular Quay were the last he was to receive during his Australian adventure. Then the newspapers had referred to him sarcastically as the 'Cromwell of the Antipodes.' He did not intend to remain a Cromwell long nor remain in the Antipodes. While the demonstrations were underway he was making preparations to depart. He had a few accounts to settle: there was Bishop Broughton's arrogance to be given one more check; the laws governing real property needed looking into, the Sydney Corporation remained steeped in sin; the working men of the city needed further education in self-reliance. He would teach that lesson by taking a tougher line about subsidies to assisted immigrants. He proposed that any man who had accepted assistance should be forced to refund the cost of his passage to Australia before being allowed to move on to the gold fields of California. He added that he thought it a sound proposition that all immigrants be forced to rid themselves of the taint of subsidy even if they settled permanently. One further matter urgently needed attending to:

Lord Grey, if reports were true, was getting ready another of his constitutional idiocies. That he would see to when he arrived in London.[26]

Thus up to the last minute he kept the pot vigorously boiling. During
these last days he heard that the governor had named Dr Bland, an ex-
convict, to the Senate of the proposed new University of Sydney. This
was an insult to the colony and to higher education, Lowe proclaimed,
and proclaimed it loudly. Bland sent a challenge, Lowe cited him for
breach of privilege, and Sydney was treated to a repeat performance of
the Macdermott comedy, complete with the same exaggerated postur-
ings and crude insults.[27]

Controversy followed Lowe all the way to the gangplank of the *Kate*.
When the ship sailed for England in November 1849 no cheers sped the
travellers on their way – no speeches, no testimonial dinners. In his
diary, Sir Alfred Stephen, the chief justice, one of the few prominent
men who had not broken with the Lowes socially, noted their going
with a mixture of regret and relief. 'Probably no man ever made so
many bitter foes in so short a time or acquired such little influence with
such commanding abilities.' Still, he concluded, 'one deeply laments'
the loss of one whose 'opinions on *very* many topics were so hostile to
the ... dishonesties or stupidities of the day.' Others were to make similar comments at the end of Lowe's life, for his Australian career-within-
a-career was a rehearsal for most of what came later. In 1875 the positivist Frederick Harrison remarked to Henry Parkes that while he was
no admirer of many of the things Lowe stood for, he did admire his
candour and his courage: 'he told our people some home truths, and he
had learned them in the colony.'[28]

Lowe did learn things in the colony, but his home truths he brought
along with him from England. Few English statesmen in the Victorian
period had so thorough a theoretical grounding, fewer still had in their
early years such an opportunity to put theories into practice over so
wide a range of subjects. In six years in the Legislative Council, at the
colonial bar, as editor of the *Atlas*, he had plunged, with great energy,
into almost every matter of central concern to a mid-nineteenth century statesman. Wherever he found himself in the years ahead – as an
official in four ministries, as a participant in innumerable committees,
as a parliamentarian, as a leader-writer for *The Times* – he could usually
remind himself that he had been there before. His forced schooling gave
him many advantages, but some disadvantages as well. He was sometimes so confident of his principles and so in command of the details of
a particular issue or piece of legislation that he was blind to the special
circumstances or the reaction of those who needed more time to learn
and digest. Conflict, misunderstanding, and dislike were the inevitable
consequences of his insensitive precocity. Despite his show of indifference and scorn, this hostility was frequently a severe trial to his spirit.

He had learned at Winchester, at Oxford, and now in Australia how to contend with hostility. He had perfected his powers of attack. If they proved insufficient to overcome some obstacle he found consolation in telling himself and others that he was a just and independent man, a truly liberal Liberal, surrounded by a world teeming with avarice, privilege, stupidity, and intolerance.

4

New Men
with
New Ideas

The Lowes left for New South Wales in 1842, a grim year in a troubled decade. The *Kate* brought them home again in the spring of 1850, when the comparatively prosperous and socially peaceful mid-Victorian period was beginning. Lowe found the England he returned to much more to his liking than the England he had left. 'The times,' he once smugly remarked, 'have come to me instead of my being compelled to go to the times.' Oxford associates had thought him 'a very advanced and somewhat bitter liberal'; by 1850 the free-trade principles he had upheld at the union were on their way to becoming orthodoxy. In 1846 signs of a growing demand in Western Europe for central and east European grain combined with a disastrous potato blight in Ireland had moved Peel to risk repeal of the Corn Laws. Reform-minded Liberals believed this victory to be the completion of a quiet revolution which had begun with the Reform Act of 1832. They were sure that a great progressive force had been loosed which would work to free people from dependence on irrational institutions and ways of thinking, a force which would allow individuals to be masters over their own persons and capacities. They believed that it would be their function to implement the logic of the revolution by removing artificial barriers to merit, putting the administration of government on a business-like basis, placing the wealth of the nation in the hands of enterprising individuals, and allowing English-speaking colonists to become masters of their own houses. The repeal of the Corn Laws, Lowe wrote not long after his return, 'overleaps the ordinary achievements of legislation as the Arc de Triomphe towers over the low-lying buildings at its feet.' He believed that the structure was now secure. It remained for men like himself who had an architect's vision of what the completed liberal city should be like to make sure that the side streets and subsidiary buildings, yet to be constructed, were made to conform with the master plan.[1]

'Advanced' but 'moderate' liberals in the 1850s were not, however, complacent about the future of their country. They did not believe that once the constitutional and economic underpinnings for a free-enterprise society were in place England's institutions would necessarily become rational or her industry efficient. Crucial to that transformation was the action of government and, they were impatiently aware, the administrative and executive arms of government were still firmly in the grasp of the traditional ruling élite. New men who lacked inherited wealth and aristocratic connections found that it took extraordinary ability and luck to break into the charmed circle. In the confusion of parties which lasted for a dozen years after Peel's resignation, young men found themselves becoming middle-aged while the Gowers, Stanleys, Temples, Fitzwilliams, and their like danced their exclusive, though not always stately, combinations and permutations. Lowe and others longed to join in so that they could change the entry rules. But how, lacking influence and great wealth, could they put themselves into a position to make intelligence and expert knowledge the avenue to high office?

In 1850 Lowe was nearly forty. He had gained a certain reputation among the country's leaders although not the sort of reputation that would dispose many of them in his favour. He now had an income nearly big enough to make him independent. The gold discoveries at Ballarat, Bendigo, and the revival of the Bathurst fields of New South Wales in 1854 increased the value of his Sydney real estate. 'They pay up to 60%,' Georgiana told a visiting Australian, 'and we made our fortune.' They were able to buy a country house at Caterham, near Warlingham, in Surrey. But, by the standards of the time, his estate and fortune were modest. Until the late 1860s he needed to supplement his income with earnings from writing in order to maintain the standard of living expected of a public man. Later in his life he remarked on how ridiculous it had been for him to have pledged at his wedding to endow his bride with all his worldly goods, when he had none. Georgiana reminded him that he had his brains – 'Well all the world knows I did not endow you with them,' was his unkind reply. And it was true that his brains were his great asset. His intelligence and energy had taken him near to the top of colonial politics in a remarkably short space of time. In the 1850s it appeared possible that he might, in spite of formidable handicaps, be able to repeat that experience in a much more challenging 'arena of life,' to use his metaphor. Since this accomplishment had come through the application of his own personal resources, it might be well to say something more, at this point, about those resources.[2]

People who knew him in this first mid-Victorian decade invariably mentioned his eccentric appearance. After that they would often comment with some awe about his physical and intellectual energy. They described how 'this strange uncouth man' would walk through the streets of the West End, 'the swift, nervous, incessant blinking of his eyeballs' keeping pace with his quick short steps. He would sing and talk quietly to himself and roll his large white head from side to side as he walked, reminding passers-by of 'a bear at a zoo.' He had a burly muscular body, loved exercise of all kinds, and only recognized the handicap of defective eyesight when invited to hunt grouse. He entertained, and terrified, his guests at Caterham by taking them for high-speed drives down narrow country lanes in his one-horse shay. Next to hiking, cycling was the sport he loved best. Once, when asked to present prizes at a bicycle race, he became almost lyrical about the virtues of this 'means of locomotion': it was 'the best antidote for gout,' it was cheap to operate, inflicted no cruelty on animals, was propelled by one's own strength (thereby teaching a moral lesson), and reduced delinquency by occupying the idle hours of adolescent boys. Pedestrians along the roads connecting Lownes Square and Westminster Palace often were startled to see a white-headed figure astride a huge tricycle, an Inverness wrapper streaming out behind him, skimming through traffic as though totally oblivious of the dim shadows of vehicles that rushed past him.[3]

His deliberate disregard for the intransigence of natural objects led, as one might expect, to a succession of accidents. The most spectacular occurred on a walking trip in Scotland with a party of Oxford pupils when he slipped on a mossy bank by a waterfall, shot over the edge, rolled over several times in the air and landed uninjured in a deep pool. Letters between his friends not infrequently contained such items as: 'Lowe is supposed to have fallen down a Highland precipice' or 'Lowe had not only a heavy fall but his portmanteau followed him and fell on his back.' He was determined to live fully, regardless of the consequences. Lady Monkswell recorded, with almost an audible sniff, that her white-haired dinner companion had attempted to entertain her by boasting of having ridden 'dead drunk' through the streets of Sydney, 'after a ride of fifty miles in the burning heat and half a bottle of port wine, etc. ...' Her disapproving tone would have greatly amused him; he loved to shock the puritanical. He had, he confessed, an admiration for the bawdy and was delighted with a nickname, invented by a friend, 'Rabellaise au lait.'[4]

He could with almost equal facility enrage or charm. On one occasion, accompanied by Goldwin Smith, then Regius Professor of History at Oxford, and the dignified Lord Chancellor Cranworth, he made an expedition into the Irish countryside. Waiting for a return train, Lowe said, 'Let's have a row with the carmen about the fare.' A row there was, recounted Smith. 'The Lord Chancellor looked the picture of dismay.' It is difficult not to share this dismay. If Lowe considered anyone unworthy of his respect (Irishmen were to him intrinsically comical, although savage when aroused), he took a sadistic pleasure in being rude, but in the company of educated men and women and in an atmosphere where bright talk was expected and appreciated, he was gentle, considerate, and good humoured in an almost boyish way. Most people who travelled with him (the acid test of friendship) were invariably won by his companionableness. Above all it was his brilliant conversation which attracted intelligent men and women to him. Unlike many famous Victorian talkers he was always ready to listen and to engage in genuine dialogue. Goldwin Smith said that he was 'as likely to say a good thing to you as you sat by him on the driving box than to say it to the most appreciative circle. Touch him when you would, he gave out the electric spark.' Jowett testified that 'he was the life of a country house'; Antonio Panizzi, the great director of the British Museum, used the promise of Lowe as bait to attract interesting guests to his intimate, literary-political dinner parties. George Cornewall Lewis, Palmerston's scholarly and unassuming chancellor of the exchequer, chose Lowe as the companion he would prefer on a desert island. Justin McCarthy, on first entering the House of Commons as an MP, spoke of his surprise at the cordial greeting he received from the supposedly disagreeable Lowe. Arthur Hugh Clough's wife was also surprised by his warmth and kindness when her husband was forced to quit his post at the Board of Trade. She wrote to the ailing poet that Lowe was 'a very good card and a very trusty friend.' Even the queen warmed to him. She had been shy of inviting him for a weekend after his appointment to the Exchequer in 1868 because Clarendon and others had warned her that he had a sharp tongue and an unkind heart. When the inevitable visit did take place she asked Lord Granville to sit close by at dinner and act as a shield. To her relief she discovered that no protection was necessary. The formidable man turned out to be 'extremely agreeable.' She wrote in her journal that he spoke with such 'extreme clearness and admirable language ... [that] I could have listened long to him, he was so interesting.' Caroline Norton's response was similar but more poetic. It was, she remarked, 'as good for the mind to be with Robert Lowe as for the lungs to walk among pines.'[5]

These social graces partially compensated for his dearth of influential relations. In time, invitations to dinners and weekend parties came from aristocratic houses, even from the Whig mecca, Holland House. Disraeli had already demonstrated how a genius for dinner party conversation and the patronage of great ladies could break through if not overcome aristocratic exclusiveness. But Georgiana was a decided liability in any attempt to conquer by means of charm and wit. Her eccentricities were annoying as well as entertaining, particularly her compulsive need to talk incessantly. Lowe's intimate friends joked about her and sent preparatory warnings to prospective hosts. Lowe's more tolerant friends did speak about her good nature and admired her extravagant devotion to 'Bobby.' On one occasion Sir Charles Dilke was a fellow guest at a country home and spent part of a Sunday afternoon helping her experiment, using a burning glass, to see if ants could communicate with each other. He noted in his diary her comment that ants were 'half way between radicals and men.' Dilke found her highly amusing and clever. Nevertheless, there seems to be no doubt that Georgiana's 'social enormities' were major impediments. Lowe bore her complaints, her constant illnesses, her ludicrous and sometimes public squabbles with servants, for the most part, with patience, although he could not resist the impulse, occasionally, to throw some of his barbs in her direction. Turning to hand her considerable bulk down from a jaunting cart on one social occasion, he gave a mock bow and exclaimed, 'Descend ye nine!'[6]

His connection with *The Times* was another impediment to acceptance by Whig society although it was a crucial factor in his rapid rise within the Liberal party ranks. John Thaddeus Delane, the young editor of *The Times*, had, as we have seen, been interested in recruiting his former tutor to the newspaper as early as 1842. He seems to have had second thoughts when he read reports of some of Lowe's inflammatory speeches in Sydney in 1849. A *Times* leading article, written while the *Kate* was still on its way home, spoke about the eccentric 'Bob Lowe of Oxford fame' as an example of a type of ambitious colonial who was willing to use any kind of demagogy to get total independence for Australia. The article called him the 'O'Connell of the Southern Hemisphere.' But those fears disappeared when Lowe returned. Sir William Molesworth, one of Delane's close friends, welcomed the new arrival as a recruit to the cause of colonial reform. *The Times* had been giving Molesworth strong support in his criticisms of Grey and Russell; therefore, in August 1850 Lowe received a second invitation to write leading articles, reviews, and occasional pieces and this time was able to accept. As we shall see this connection was to be of the greatest consequence to Lowe the politician, but its first effect was to bring Lowe, through Delane, into a circle of friends, men who influenced Lowe's outlook on many issues and who used their inconspicuous but extensive influence over public affairs to advance Lowe's interest.[7]

Two of Delane's most intimate friends were Edward Ellice and Joseph Parkes. Like Delane, these two did not fit neatly into generally recognized social categories. Ellice was a great trader, but not 'in trade.' His position as governor and one of the principle shareholders of the Hudson's Bay Company lifted him to the very top of the upper middle class; his landed estate in Scotland and his marriage to the sister of the Whig prime minister, Lord Grey, put him over the top, into the ranks of the untitled aristocracy. Parkes came from a manufacturing family and, after school, instead of attending a university, had been articled to a solicitor. He did not become, however, an ordinary middle class solicitor. The Whig party employed him to manage their intricate domestic affairs. Factions of the Whig party used his house to meet and work out agreements. Thus Parkes knew everyone of importance in the party, if the loose and shifting coalitions of interests can be called that before the 1860s. He moved easily in many social circles: radical intellectual, Birmingham trade, landed aristocracy.

Parkes, Ellice, and Delane were secure within the traditional social orders and, at the same time, independent from them. None of them aspired to political office; they were all three more interested in influence than in authority. Neither Parkes nor Delane contemplated standing for the House of Commons and Ellice, though in Parliament, was not really a parliamentarian. They were practical men of affairs: willing compromisers – not without opinions and genuine liberal aspirations, but with eyes accustomed to searching out the possible. Free trade they accepted as revealed truth (so long as it did not affect in an adverse way *The Times* or the Hudson's Bay Company). They were distressed to observe at the middle of the century that the aristocrats who occupied the front benches seemed not to be aware that the nation was in need of modernization or, if aware, seemed to be unwilling to act forcefully. The three friends worried that in the confusion of parties in the 1850s Whig and Tory magnates were involving themselves totally in the scramble for office and were not allowing new men with new ideas to come forward. In 1852 Parkes wrote to Delane about the anxiety he and all 'reflecting people' were feeling: 'All parties of the Aristocracy are playing with edged tools. If they don't take care they will among them unhoop the old Constitution, and call in a third and less governable Party – the out of doors Democracy. I see no safe leader among all, for the present state of political elements.'[8]

When Delane introduced Lowe to Ellice and Parkes there was an immediate recognition of affinity. Lowe became a regular guest at Glenquoich in Invernesshire, where Ellice dispensed hospitality lavishly during the summer and autumn months. If anyone was the centre of this group of 'reflecting' liberals, it was Ellice. Everyone called him 'The Bear,' not because he resembled one but because he was England's leading fur trader. As a young man he had been a disciple of the Benthamite reformer, Joseph Hume. His brother-in-law, Lord Grey, had made him patronage secretary of the Treasury where, during the 1832 Reform bill struggle, he gained a reputation for his skill at applying gentle persuasions where they did most good. Grey rewarded him with a cabinet appointment, but he soon resigned it; he much preferred to act as back-stage manager, the man to come to for advice about appointments or matters of policy. Because he persistently refused honours and avoided centre stage, he had a reputation for disinterested altruism. Cabinet ministers discovered that he had, through his business connections, contacts and informants on the continent, in India, and all over North America, an information network which most governments would envy. As Lowe wrote at the time of his death, 'he was above all things, a citizen of the world.' English Liberals consulted him on trade and foreign policy and used him as a clearing house for messages, hints, and ideas. For his own part he was glad to use his influence quietly to promote the policies he cared about and, incidentally, the interests of the Hudson's Bay Company.[9]

When Ellice wanted to find a seat for a promising young man or to discover the temper and preoccupations of a critical constituency, he almost always contacted Parkes. The two men were an harmonious team. Parkes had, like Ellice, been impressed in his youth by Bentham's ideas. Marriage with Joseph Priestley's daughter also brought him directly into connexion with the late eighteenth- and early nineteenth-century radical tradition. Municipal and legal reform were his specialities. As a parliamentary solicitor he gave advice on legislation concerning these matters and helped to draft bills. (It is no accident that some of the first leaders Lowe wrote for *The Times* were on chancery reform.) His memory was a great storehouse of information on the intricacies of how to get legislation through Parliament; no one, except, perhaps, Ellice, knew more political lore or gossip.[10]

'The Bear' provided the Scottish retreat for the circle of friends; Bernal Osborne, the chief jester of the House of Commons, provided the Irish one. Born Ralph Bernal, the eldest son of a distinguished family of Sephardic Jews, he was brought up a Christian, married into the Irish aristocracy, and took his wife's family name. Endless supplies of money from the West Indies allowed him to be a dilettante all of his life. Politics was something more than a pastime to him but not much more. His position on the great issues of the day changed with his whims, but in the 1840s and 1850s he usually sided with the advanced reformers. Aberdeen found him a position at the Admiralty and for a short while there was speculation that he might be the rising star among the parliamentary radicals. But he quickly tired of office. He was too full of boisterous fun to be taken seriously. When dropped from his post in 1858 he admitted that he had 'laughed himself down.' In his thirty years in Parliament he won and promptly lost a succession of seats. His constituents invariably objected to his casual indifference to local issues and refused to re-elect him, but he was so accomplished at amusing crowds and parrying the shouts of hecklers that he somehow always managed to find another constituency. Members of Parliament from all parties were always glad to welcome him back; news that Osborne was about to speak brought them hurrying from the lobby and coffee room. Lowe especially enjoyed his irreverence. Eventually Lowe too was to receive thrusts from what Gladstone called 'the light javelins of his sarcastic rhetoric,' but until the mid-1860s the two men were intimate friends. Lowe, frequently accompanied by Delane, visited him in Tipparary and formed his opinions about Irish problems during those visits.[11]

George Cornewall Lewis was another man who befriended and influenced Lowe. They had been acquaintances during their student days at Oxford; Parkes and Ellice brought them more closely together. Lewis was not a frequent visitor at Glenquoich or part of that informal circle, but he was greatly admired by all of them as a model of what a public servant should be in the modern age. He was an aristocrat; he inherited a baronetcy from his father and married Lord Clarendon's sister. But he did not regard public service as merely a duty which followed from his position. Before Lowe began visiting and corresponding with him, he had done the exacting work of a Poor Law commissioner and a Treasury official. Underneath this practical experience lay an intellectual framework constructed out of careful reading in Bentham, Adam Smith, and the classical economists. In addition, he had a European reputation as a classical scholar. This unusual combination of talents and experience caused him to be selected editor in 1852 of the prestigious *Edinburgh Review*. Three years later Palmerston made him chancellor of the exchequer. Lowe, Delane, and their friends hoped that Lewis might become the leader of 'some future coalition,' but his premature death in 1863 put an end to that hope. He was proof, Lowe wrote in *The Times*, that a classical education need not always stunt the growth of 'practical good sense.' Lewis, Lowe wrote, knew 'better than any other how to conciliate theory with practice, and to play the part of Statesman without forgetting the principles of the philosopher.' Lowe doubted if there was another politician in the nation about whom the same could be said.[12]

Through Parkes and Ellice, Lowe did, however, meet another man who seemed to be able to think like a philosopher and act like a practical man of good sense and experience – George Grote, the utilitarian theorist and historian of the Roman Empire. The sad irony was, Lowe once remarked to a gathering of Grote admirers, that their friend was 'like Rob Roy,' born an age too soon. If merit were ever allowed to prevail, Lowe thought, society would place the Grotes and Lewises of the world in charge of public administration. Their scholarly detachment would help to preserve them from the corruption of power and their practical knowledge of how to get things done would insure that they were efficient.[13]

The Grotes lived only a few miles from Caterham and would occasionally pick up Lewis, 'the learned fish,' and pay a visit, enduring 'Frau

Georgiana's chatter about her pigs' for the sake of Robert's conversation. But most frequently Lowe and the old historian met over the dinner table at meetings of the Political Economy Club. Grote had been an early member. In the 1820s he had attended the club's monthly meetings, meetings which had grown out of gatherings around David Ricardo's dinner table. Ricardo and his guests wanted to bring into their informal discussions of economics people who were making decisions, so they found a suitable tavern, arranged dinners, and invited educated businessmen, politicians, civil servants, lawyers as well as university fellows and professors. They decreed that the occasions be informal, the atmosphere relaxed. After food and wine members read papers on topics of current importance and then took part in general discussion. They invited Lowe to be a member as soon as he entered Parliament in 1852; he attended, more regularly than any other prominant public official, until his health began to fail in the 1880s. In the sympathetic companionship of men who would appreciate his literary allusions and understand the point of his theoretical digressions, Lowe found an atmosphere much more closely attuned to his temperament than Legislative Council or Parliament. At these monthly meetings he could practice the lessons he was attempting to teach himself in monetary and tax theory and profit by the reactions of many of the leading intellectuals of the day. Undoubtedly this experience enhanced his reputation in some circles, but it probably did not make him a better parliamentarian. As it was, his taste for the abstract and attenuated was already overdeveloped to suit the tastes of most members of the House of Commons. Walter Bagehot once wisely observed that if Lowe could learn to leave 'these remote principles in their remote unintelligibility, he would not suffer so much.' After those evenings at the Thatched House Tavern on St James Street, he found it doubly trying to 'dress up a case for Parliament.'[14]

While he was in the process of making these fortunate connections with *The Times* and with men who were in positions to advance his interests, Lowe made a start as a practicing barrister by joining the Northern Circuit. He did not enjoy the experience. With his years in Australia behind him, he could not bring himself to behave with the meekness expected of a newcomer. The established members of the circuit were not inclined to make allowances for an upstart from a place like New South Wales. They boycotted him. One young man who had not yet been initiated made the mistake of being civil. A veteran afterwards took him aside and told him that such familiarity would not do: 'the man comes here and on the ground of colonial experience acts as if he were a senior, and the circuit will have nothing to do with him.'[15]

But his reputation as a colonial had its advantages also. Metropolitan newspapers had noticed the flamboyant speeches he made in Sydney in 1848 and 1849. For the most part these notices had been uncomplimentary but they had made the leading Whigs painfully aware that he existed and had returned. Critics of Russell's colonial policies were glad to recruit a man who could speak with the authority of first-hand experience. And it was Lowe's good luck, perhaps his good planning, that Australian affairs were unusually prominent at the moment of his arrival in London. Russell had announced his intention in 1850 to put into the statute books an amended version of Grey's Australian Colonies bill. This had provoked Sir William Molesworth, a philosophical radical and an outspoken foe of transportation, into forming a Society for Colonial Reform to organize opposition to the proposed bill. Naturally, he immediately sought the newcomer out and recruited him to the cause, with the result that, within weeks of his return to London, Lowe found himself on a platform addressing a well-organized and well-reported public meeting on the subject of Earl Grey's manifold sins of omission and commission.

In his total ignorance of actual conditions, Lowe said, the colonial secretary had not thought to make clear distinctions between those domestic affairs which would be handed over to colonial legislatures and imperial affairs which the home government would continue to reserve to itself. Such ambiguity would work against colonial responsibility – 'one single dispatch from a governor will outweigh volumes of the most elaborate evidence,' causing the rebellious spirit, presently being kindled, to smoulder on. In their own defence, supporters of self-government would 'turn agitators, and stir up all the elements of the community, which, if we had a free government, everyone would wish should lie dormant.' Undoubtedly Lowe intended this not merely to be a warning but also an explanation for his own past extravagances, but the nub of his speech was his statement that the proposed constitution ignored the central question: how was gift of power to be divided up among the colonial factions? So long as this question was left vague the government could expect 'anarchy, discord, and ultimately ... revolution.' He explained that Grey had left the franchise in its existing state, with the vote restricted to those who owned £200 worth of land or a house with the annual value of £20, thereby excluding all leaseholders and those free immigrants who could not afford so expensive a house. Emancipated convicts who happened to be around when there was money to be made would vote while the urban middle class and the respectable working man would be unenfranchised. In his ignorance, Lowe said, Grey had not grasped the essential point that the gift of responsible government would have disastrous consequences for the majority of colonists if it were not accompanied by an extension of the

franchise. To invite the unrepresentative colonial legislatures, now domi-
nated by the sheep-grazing minority, to remodel their new constitutions
in any way they might choose would be an invitation to establish an oligarchy. What every colonist understood, but what the Colonial Office
refused to recognize, was that the first priority must be the settlement
of the Crown Land issue. Until that happened, colonial politics would
be beset by factionalism and class conflict. If, Lowe concluded, Grey
and Russell sought the path of least resistance and backed away from
their responsibilities to prepare the ground for responsible government,
they would expose Australia to decades of instability.[16]

These trenchant warnings had no effect on Russell nor on the majority of Parliament. The bill passed easily through a bored and sparsely
attended House of Commons and an even more apathetic House of
Lords. But if Lowe did his former homeland little good by his speech,
he greatly improved his own fortunes. The press gave his remarks wide
and respectful attention and colonial reformers in Parliament frequently
referred to Lowe's argument. Molesworth's society printed the speech
and distributed it widely. Undoubtedly Molesworth also called Delane's
attention to Lowe's effectiveness as a critic of Russell. Delane, in turn,
suggested to John Walter, the proprietor of *The Times*, that the newspaper could use a man who could put his opinions so forcefully. The
invitation was made; Lowe soon became known as a *Times* man. That
association was to lead, in a remarkably short time, not only to a seat in
the House of Commons, but to a post in government.

After Lowe had been writing leading articles for only a few months,
Delane asked Parkes if they would look for a suitable constituency for
their friend – a seat that would not bind him too closely to Russell's
sinking fortunes. This was not a difficult assignment for a man like
Parkes. He knew that Lord Ward (later the earl of Dudley) could deliver
the Liberal vote in the Worcestershire town of Kidderminster and was
looking for a man who was not closely associated with either the Palmerston or Russell factions. Ward had the agreement of some of the
Kidderminster Tories and even most of the radical shopkeepers that
they would not oppose such a man if he could be found. Parkes told
him that he had located the perfect candidate, an experienced liberal,
with sound free-trade views, who had just returned from Australia and
was entirely independent of any of the Whig networks. Late in 1851 a
meeting was arranged; Lord Ward liked what he heard and saw to it that
Lowe became MP for Kidderminster, without a contest, in time for the
autumn sitting of 1852. Parkes carefully coached the candidate on how
to act and what to say. His main worry was Lowe's tendency to put
cases strongly. Lack of tact might be fatal with such an odd assortment
of supporters. Besides it would be well if Lowe did not put his policies
on the record at the moment. Parkes did not think 'Jonnie Russell's

rotten old tub' could stay afloat much longer. The time to make a bid for prominence would be when the tub finally sank; then 'reflecting' Liberals who cared about good government and not simply office might be able to put together some workable combination. In the meantime, he told Delane, they should both do their best to keep 'our fair friend of Eaton Square' from compromising himself with some strong statement of conviction.[17]

Lowe heeded this advice and chose a neutral subject, Irish law reform, for his maiden speech. Since rumours about his connection with Delane had got around there was considerable interest in finding out what he was like. When he rose to speak there were whispers of 'Times, Times.' The House doorkeeper heard one old Tory mutter, 'I am told we've got an Albanian now amongst us; I wonder what we shall have next – a nigger, I suppose.' But in spite of resentment at seeing their club invaded by journalism, members agreed that Lowe seemed cool and professional. They were more impressed by some impromptu remarks he made a week later about a proposal to deny the privilege of limited liability to a shipping company intending to enter the trans-Atlantic trade. Spokesmen for the companies already carrying goods and passengers to America tried to explain why competition would suffer if people were encouraged to invest, with limited risk, in new steamship companies. Lowe was irritated by this perverse logic; he predicted that the day was not far off when the march of progress would push aside all restraints on how individuals chose to invest. Limited liability had, he said, already covered the land with railroads and should be allowed to cover the seas with ships. The only protection the investor needed or should have from the government was regulations which forced companies to make their affairs public; after that, let the investor beware. In a few years Lowe was to take a leading part in bringing that prediction closer to fact. In 1852 this first short, lively, discourse on a subject which most MPs found dull or obscure served notice that the new member, only just returned from the other side of the world, was no novice.[18]

Henry Bruce, another freshman member, wrote to his wife at the end of 1852: 'I was at the House today and made acquaintance with Bob Lowe, far the most successful debutant of the season.' Bruce did not have limited liability in mind when he made that compliment. It was Lowe's first great confrontation with Disraeli that had impressed him. The occasion was the debate on Disraeli's budget in December 1852. The Tory chancellor of the exchequer had attempted nothing spectacular. Lord Derby's 'Who, Who?' ministry was in power only because the opposition was divided into Palmerstonians, Russellites, Peelites, and Radicals – each group peevish or disillusioned with the others. Disraeli had a small surplus to dispose of and no need to make enemies, so he decided to please the brewers by reducing the tax on malt, lowering duties on sugar and shipping, and to make up the loss by a small increase in the house tax and by an extension of incomes subject to tax in order that more people on the lower end of the scale would have to pay. During a curious informal conversation with Bright, he said that he would not mind if the details of his proposals were altered; all he really cared about was approval in principle.[19]

Opposition was stronger than Disraeli anticipated. Free traders of all descriptions thought that the Tories were trying to please protectionists by making concessions to grain growers and shippers and by squeezing the urban middle class to pay the bill. Sir James Graham, on behalf of the Peelites, gave the budget a pounding; then Lowe had a turn. He declared that consumers of champagne would pocket all the tax relief while beer drinkers would pay as much as they always had for their pints. Since the brewers controlled most of the pubs they would see to it that nothing was passed on to the consumer. Free trade in beer was the only remedy for that, he thought. He stressed the point that this opportunistic feature of the budget was only one symptom of a general Tory irresponsibility in economic affairs. Disraeli was innocent of 'financial considerations,' he said; his budget was like 'the reveries of Alnaschar with his basket of glass.' A procession of similar jibes and unflattering metaphors followed, printed in full, as one might expect, in the next morning's *Times*. And in case the lazy reader might pass over the small print, a leading article on the same page gave a summary of what it called a 'lucid and interesting' speech by a hitherto little known but rising star in the House of Commons.[20]

Those who did take time to read the speech discovered no profundities. Lowe had worked hard at gathering information about the malt market and the technology of brewing and had served it up pedantically and not particularly accurately. It was a good speech only because it irritated Disraeli – and a great many members on both sides of the House enjoyed the spectacle of Disraeli irritated. It provoked the chancellor of the exchequer into giving a taunting, personal, reply, which put the House into a hooting, shouting passion. The division that took place that night defeated the budget and brought Derby's government down. Lowe could take credit for having been in at the kill. Even Disraeli handed him a back-handed compliment. Turning to the new member he congratulated the House for having acquired from the colonies a man of such 'ostentatious learning.' He was, he said, 'glad to find him here among us; but all the opinions I have heard from him yet appear to be anything but sound.'[21]

It did Lowe no harm with his party to be singled out for abuse on this important occasion. Nevertheless, Disraeli had, in his unerring way, found exactly the tender spot to make his jab. Lowe's carefully wrought set speeches did 'smell of the lamp.' They were written by lamplight, memorized, and delivered, word for word. Few English politicians could have spoken more spontaneously in private or more mechanically in public. There were times when he could move the House with his oratory. In 1866 during the great debate over parliamentary reform the *Spectator* said that the low, sardonic ring of his voice sent a 'shiver of half-mocking intelligence' vibrating 'like a glass bell through the House.' But these times seldom occurred during his first decade in Parliament. When his turn came to speak he would shoot straight up from his seat, spill out his carefully chosen words in a torrent, sometimes hanging his head when he came to the stinging tails of his most crucial sentences, and then trailing off in broken tones, scarcely audible to any but his immediate neighbours. At the end of the performance, without an instant's pause, down he would drop, as suddenly as he had appeared, as though intensely relieved to have brought a painful experience to an end. Observers noticed that when one of his sallies did bring a laugh or a cheer, he would start with surprise and pleasure, slow his pace and lift his voice. Except on those rare occasions his speeches in Parliament sounded like lectures given by a brilliant but shy professor who had reconciled himself to being unpopular and misunderstood. Thus when Disraeli spoke of Lowe's 'ostentatious knowledge' and, a decade later, called him 'an inspired schoolboy,' he gave expression to a sense of vague irritation many members of the House had been feeling. It was the beginning of one of the longest and most bitter feuds in Victorian political history. Disraeli usually observed the formal civilities with his opponents, even with Gladstone. But when asked toward the end of his life if there were any of his political enemies whose hand he would refuse to shake, he paused and replied, 'only one – Robert Lowe.'[22]

The next spring, in 1853, Disraeli remarked, with a sneer, that Lowe had received 'a memorable reward' for his contribution to the Tory defeat. The reward he referred to was an offer to join Lord Aberdeen's coalition government as a joint secretary of the Board of Control for India. Aberdeen informed him that this promotion, after only some six months as a private member, was in recognition of his services in Australia. This could hardly be the real reason. Distribution of offices, always a ticklish matter, was especially so this time because there were so many factional interests to consider. Aberdeen concerned himself with cabinet appointments and gave Sir James Graham the task of finding people for the lesser posts. Russell wanted Graham to give a joint secretaryship to one of his few Irish Catholic supporters. Circumstantial evidence suggests that Lowe got the position instead in recognition of the support Aberdeen had received from *The Times*. Cornewall Lewis noticed one morning, while the secondary posts were still being distributed, that unusually kind things were being said about Graham on the

Times leader-page. He sent Graham a note asking, 'What did you do to the Times?' He meant this as a joke, but in fact Graham did send advice to Delane, by way of Ellice, about the tone he thought the newspaper should adopt toward Grey and Russell. He was afraid that these two favourite victims of *The Times* might make trouble for Aberdeen if unduly riled. The selection of Lowe was most likely a signal to Delane that his support had been and would be appreciated.[23]

Graham's selection of the Board of Control for Lowe was not haphazard. One of the first items of business the new government would have to deal with was the question of what to do with the East India Company whose charter would be up for renewal in 1854. Lowe's close connexion with the colonial reformers would be sure to prove valuable, and of course it would be a great assistance if *The Times* could be induced to speak softly on one of its favourite topics. Also Lowe was quick-witted and good with details; these would be valuable assets to Sir Charles Wood, the president of the Board of Control, who was a competent administrator but a notoriously muddled speaker.

Colonial reformers had started their campaign to end or drastically change the way India was administered well before Aberdeen came to office. During the previous seventy years legislation had increased the administrative jurisdiction of the East India Company's Court of Directors but decreased the company's economic privileges and its policy-making authority. The British government, through the Board of Control, had by 1853 become the dominant partner in a dual arrangement. It alone made decisions about external affairs; it also had a supervisory control over internal affairs. This was an awkward, irrational structure, favoured by some politicians and civil servants not in spite of but because of its anomalies on the ground that imprecise jurisdictions were the best protections against the misuse of Britain's despotic power over the subcontinent. They feared the consequences of turning over an enormous pork barrel to the politicians. These Indian experts had, for the most part, no particular love for the East India Company but nevertheless wanted to see the contract renewed until ways could be worked out to make direct rule safe. They were opposed by the middle class radicals led by John Bright who had been working for several years to end, at the earliest opportunity, the company's special position. Lord Dalhousie, the prestigious governor general, pressed for a compromise. He would retain 'double government' for a while longer but move at once further to increase the authority of Her Majesty's representatives by, among other things, appointing crown nominees to the company Court of Directors and increasing the power of the governor general.[24]

Wood agreed, in general, with Dalhousie. He and a cabinet committee prepared a bill calling for the renewal of the charter for an unspecified period and the reduction of the Court of Directors from twenty-four to eighteen, six to be appointed by the crown. The bill was short of what Dalhousie wanted since it left the machinery of the government in India unaltered. Bright and his 'Young India' followers said the bill was cowardly. A large minority of the cabinet wished to postpone action of any kind until political conditions at home and in Eastern Europe became more stable. Wood got his bill introduced in the spring of 1853 only because Aberdeen pressed hard for action.[25]

Lowe thought Wood an obstinate bumbler – a man 'predestined to ruin himself and everybody connected with him.' Delane had decreed that *The Times* should press for 'a really sweeping measure' which would end the rule and patronage of the company's directors once and for all. Lowe agreed. He openly criticized Wood to friends and acquaintances and let it be known that he was thinking of resigning. He gave Delane full and pessimistic accounts of what was being discussed by the ministry and urged him to use his eloquence on Wood 'for verily are we in a scrape.' He hoped that Delane would not force him to 'shipwreck' his character by agreeing to identify himself with Wood's 'incapacity' should the cabinet decide to go ahead.[26]

But when the time for decision came he elected to stay with the ship even though that meant standing by his chief in the House and blasting away at him from another great tribunal. He did both with spirit. When Wood stupefied a half-empty House with a five-hour introduction of his bill ('the dullest that ever was heard,' said Greville), Lowe sat directly behind him, 'putting him right every ten minutes.' In the course of his supporting speech Lowe had to explain how he, of all people, could think the appointment of crown nominees to the Court of Directors a good idea. Lowe managed it, but not without pain. Five years later, when he spoke in favour of the act which ended dual authority, a Tory asked him if he was able to recollect his defence of that arrangement in 1853. He had taken the trouble to re-read his speech on that occasion, Lowe confessed, and had discovered that it did not make a particularly favourable impression on him. His real views he had kept for the leader page of *The Times*, although he naturally did not make that excuse in public. The morning after Wood had made his 'laboured apology,' the paper chastised him for fearing to 'lay a sacreligious hand on the golden image in Leadenhall Street.' Another leading article pronounced 'unworkable' the plan of combining crown nominees with functionaries 'elected by some 2,000 ladies and gentlemen.' Whether or not Lowe wrote these articles cannot be verified; everyone, however, who knew of his connections suspected that he had done so.[27]

Annoyed as he was with his government's timidity, he did wholeheartedly agree with one feature of the 1853 India Act – a provision to open the Indian Civil Service to competitive examination. Thomas Macaulay, and other Indian experts, had been advocating this reform for years. During the debate Lowe identified himself with the examination clause and boasted afterwards that the opening of appointments to 'full, free and fair competition' had been the one great accomplishment of the Board of Control and one of the few positive accomplishments of Aberdeen's ministry. During the debate Lord Stanley, the Tory leader's son, had defended the patronage system in one of his first speeches after entering the House. Stanley had a speech impediment and used peculiar gestures to emphasize his points; nevertheless, he managed to compensate by making his points intelligently. On this occasion, he made a reasoned case for the superiority of character and breeding over pedantry and mere knowledge. Lowe congratulated the new member for the eloquence and ingenuity with which he had pleaded the 'cause of ignorance,' and then proceeded to plead the cause of intellect: 'When an ignorant and stupid man is brought in contact with people differing in manner, dress, and language, he regards them with contempt, treats them as inferiors, and rejoices in his own superiority, small as they might be; whereas a man of talent, accustomed to reason and think, regards them as an object of curiosity, interest, and sympathy, and makes it his business to study them as another variety of the human race; and those habits of familiarity induce a kindly feeling on both sides, which is of enormous advantage in a country like India.' He might as easily have said 'in a country like England.'[28]

This reply to Stanley greatly pleased the cabinet members present, especially Wood, who 'chuckled, spluttered and suggested, and pulled by the coat tails, gleefully.' The parliamentary reporter who described the scene commented that the duel between character and intellect had been an odd, but an interesting one – a near blind speaker who used a microscope to read his notes 'replying to a speaker with a cleft palate.' He thought Lowe had come off well; he had said more in less than an hour than his chief had managed in five.[29]

This success gave people the impression that Lowe was the author of the examination clauses. Gladstone, who had directed Northcote and Trevelyan to prepare a report on ways to reform the British civil service and was, therefore, moving along a similar (though apparently a separate) path, gave Lowe full credit for this significant step in the process of changing the character of the public service. However, recent scholarship has shown that Thomas Macaulay and Benjamin Jowett were really the ones responsible for the form the examination clause took. It was Jowett, then a fellow at Balliol, who first recognized that with a few alterations in the examination clause in Wood's bill, the Indian Civil Service might be made into a preserve for Oxford and Cambridge graduates; at the same time he saw that reform of the public service could be made into a lever for university reform. This had been in the minds of neither Lowe nor Wood when they had the bill drafted. It had been their understanding that the examinations would be for admission into the East India Company's Haileybury College, where boys as young as seventeen could enter to be prepared for the company's service. Jowett approached Charles Trevelyan, Wood, Gladstone, and Lowe, after the bill had gone to the Lords, with the suggestion that the examinations be opened to candidates who held BAs. He argued that if this were done first-class graduates who had no important family connections might have an alternative to the church or the bar. The universities would then be under pressure to make some adaptations to their curricula. The effect, he thought, would be to 'give us another root striking into a new soil of society.' Lowe and the others saw the point immediately and the changes were made before the bill became law. The new law provided for a committee to work out the details of the examination. Macaulay was its chairman and with the greatest ingenuity he manipulated the committee into agreeing that the subjects examined be adjusted to a level of attainment which only the cream of the university graduates would be able to reach. Wood, who did not detect Macaulay's sleight of hand, then agreed that Haileybury had become redundant and authorized that it no longer be the prescribed preparing ground for the Indian Civil Service.[30]

When Lowe discovered what Jowett and Macaulay had done, he was greatly impressed. He made Jowett his life-long friend and adviser and adopted his programme for wedding together the two reform causes. Lowe was not an innovator but he did learn lessons quickly and well. His important Civil Service reform of 1870 applied the principle that positions involving policy decisions be staffed not, as he had originally advocated, by 'full, free, and fair' competition, but only by those highly intelligent people who had been refined by the great universities. He expected, as Jowett did, that a carefully selected programme of examinations would force the universities to react to the pressure of demand and provide training in the fields the examiners offered. In this way ancient institutions could be rationalized without the need for a drastic revolution in the social structure.

There was one more ramification of the India Act which had a long-term effect on Lowe's development as a liberal, utilitarian, reformer: this was a provision which established commissions to codify the Indian civil and criminal law and the penal procedure. Once again Macaulay had been a pioneer. He had begun twenty years earlier to attempt to make order out of the anarchic blend of royal and company jurisdictions and of Eastern and Western customs. In 1853 a committee in India was still considering how to unravel the tangle. Wood removed the process from Calcutta to London and turned it over to his appointees, men who were either interested in English law reform or who had experience in India. He named Lowe, Sir John Romilly, and the chief justice of the Court of Common Pleas, Sir John Jervis, to ensure that 'sound and liberal principles' were applied. They would keep the old India hands 'on the right track,' Wood hoped. But he reminded the commissioners that they were to design legal codes for people with different tradition, and, while retaining the framework of English law, make the appropriate adjustments to a different conception of what justice was and how it should be applied. The commissioners did make an honest effort to consider that reservation but could not escape from their cultural insularity. The codes which they produced and saw enacted in the late 1850s and early 1860s furthered the process of 'assimilation' – the attempt to refashion India in England's image. Eric Stokes, a modern scholar, while agreeing that the codes simplified the Indian system and made it more logical and better organized than anything prevailing in England, nevertheless thinks it 'perhaps a debateable issue' whether this process of rationalization was worth the damage it caused to the integrity of Indian culture. Lowe had no such modern, relativistic, doubts. He had made an eloquent claim that intelligence promotes sympathy for the varieties of human experience, but his own intelligence did not work that way. In 1855 he and Jervis dissented from the first report of the commission on civil procedure because they did not agree with the majority on the necessity to begin the work afresh. They stated that since English civil procedures were already being applied in the King's Courts in Calcutta, Madras, and Bombay, it would be simple and time-saving to extend those procedures, so far as possible, into the more primitive areas where the company courts had been using their odd mixture of Hindu, Moslem, and English practices. Native practitioners might have trouble understanding English law in those places, they agreed, but that would also be true of any code which the commission might eventually produce.[31]

Therefore if the other Victorian gentleman on the commission were locked into their own culture, Lowe was locked even more hermetically. His imagination was limited by the fact that he understood and believed so completely in his liberal, utilitarian presuppositions. At the Board of Control for India he learned enough about the complexities of Indian administration to understand that it might not always be expedient to act as though Indian peasants were English farm labourers and factory workers. But he did assume that the truths of political economy were the objective standards which needed to be regarded, even when departed from, and that any departure must be justified in the end by its practical effect in producing a rational, free trade, society. He was quite explicit about his belief that the whole world would benefit to the degree that it became like the liberal England he envisaged for the future, impossible though the quest might prove to be in certain insalubrious regions. During the 1853 debate a Conservative introduced an amendment instructing the Legislative Council in India to consult and recognize Indian customs and wishes. Lowe answered that it was the duty of the council to abolish evil customs; he gave as an example the inevitable suttee. 'Instead of Hindooising our own Government, we should,' he asserted, 'be able to Europeanize theirs.' Another amendment called for provision of one-third of the places at Haileybury for native Indians. Lowe pointed out that there were no barriers to their entry save their educational deficiencies. He agreed that this was a formidable barrier, but he maintained that it was not the duty of government to see that Indians got places, only that they be governed well. The principle at issue was not Indian feelings but open competition: 'When I take up a principle I like to carry it out to its utmost extent.' Obviously, he did not for a moment doubt that this principle was universally valid and more important to achieve than any interest or value with which it might collide. He could not even admit that those who raised these conservative objections might be sincere. This narrowness was a characteristic fault of Lowe's social outlook as it was a fundamental fault in the classical liberal outlook on the world.[32]

5

The 'Crusade Against Nepotism'

While Parliament was considering the India bill, its attention was shifting away from domestic and colonial questions and toward the gradual building up of tensions in Turkey and Eastern Europe. In the spring of 1853 the Russians sent an ultimatum to Turkey; in the summer they occupied the Principalities; in November their fleet sank twelve Turkish ships in the harbour of Sinope. Britain responded to this supposed challenge to her naval supremacy and the European balance of power by ordering the fleet to Constantinople, but it was not until March 1854 that England with her French allies entered the war and sent an expedition off to the Crimea. Englishmen were to die on a remote peninsula in the Black Sea because of a dispute that was obscure to all participants. Scandalous mismanagement of the expedition by Aberdeen's ministers ruined the reputation of the coalition and, for a while, called into serious doubt the capability of the aristocracy to govern the country. No war of the century was more freely and rationally denounced while it was being fought and no war was more popular. Cobden and Bright, cogent and fluent critics though they were, could not even persuade the main body of their fellow Radicals that the idiocy of the war itself should be the object of attack and not merely the conduct of it. The nation believed the war to be a test of their free institutions; it was thrilled by the reports of reckless valour in the newspapers and impressed by the myth of the Russian menace.

As soon as war was declared Lowe became a passionate advocate of war to the finish. He had no doubts that the cause was just; like the powerful newspaper he wrote for he was sure that England's armies were struggling to save European civilization from the tsar's reactionary dominance. He told a cheering crowd at Kidderminster that it was Russia's 'wanton and inordinate ambition' to seize control of the Black Sea and command the Dardanelles, gather in Austria, eat 'like a canker into the heart of Germany,' seize the great arterial river the Danube, reach out to the Rhine, and thus extend a 'ruthless tyranny' over the continent.[1]

He and Delane also shared in the apprehension that England's institutions might not stand up to the test of war unless they were revitalized by a fundamental change in the administration of government. They and the other 'reflecting liberals' were dismayed but not surprised when Aberdeen's ministers dithered and fumbled. The 'vice of public patronage,' Lowe said, 'pervades every department of the civil and military service.' Gross inefficiency is to be expected where 'merit is not promoted' and where 'the only thing considered is personal connexion and favour.' If the present system were allowed to continue, titled incompetents would lead ill-supplied soldiers into still more brave and senseless charges. Incompetence would give Russian despotism the victory. If that disaster happened, there would be the most profound discontent at home. Agitators would demand and receive an 'organic change in our institutions,' and then hopes for the achievement of the liberal society would be dashed forever. Therefore a way must be found within the existing system to put the direction of affairs into competent hands.[2]

In February 1855 Lowe announced to his constituents that he was now free to plead the cause of merit, unhampered by the demands of ministerial loyalty. Aberdeen had resigned when John Arthur Roebuck successfully moved for a committee of inquiry into the conduct of the Sebastopol campaign. The queen first asked Lord Derby to form a new government but eventually bowed to public opinion and called in Lord Palmerston. He offered to keep Lowe at the Board of Control but received an immediate refusal. Lowe was bored with his duties there; also he found the contradiction of his situation, if not intolerable, certainly uncomfortable.

That he wrote leading articles for a newspaper which had come out vociferously against the Aberdeen coalition and at the same time held a position in that government deepened suspicions that he was a double agent. Lord John Russell maintained that he was Delane's paid spy and tormentor. Alexander Russell, editor of the *Scotsman*, was sure he detected the hand of the secretary of the Board of Control in some of the 'liveliest' diatribes on the leader page, and, while it cannot be demonstrated conclusively, it is more than likely that he had been a responsible official during the day and had gone home to dictate in the evening thunderblasts against Aberdeen and all his works. But on the important issue of the Roebuck motion Lowe did stand apart from Delane in support of the prime minister. While *The Times* was drumming up support for the inquiry committee, Lowe was voting and speaking against it. He said that if Parliament tried to seize the direction of affairs from the slack hold of the aristocracy and place the administration of the country in committee, then it would be applying a remedy that was even worse than the disease. All history showed what would then follow: committees, responsible to no one, would appoint a junta, and the junta, acting under the cover of its emergency powers, would proceed to destroy the liberties which England had acquired over the centuries.[3]

Once the Roebuck issue was out of the way, shortly after Lowe's resignation, Delane and his most trusted leader-writer worked together to 'shout the government out of office.' 'What the Tsar is in Russia or the mob in America, the Jupiter is in England,' wrote Anthony Trollope in *The Warden*, published while the campaign was underway. Lord John Russell, who had received more than his share of the abuse, announced, during the grim 'Sebastopol winter' of 1854-5, that England had acquired a new estate in her constitution. And when he complained to Granville that Delane 'seems to be drunk with insolence and vanity,' he spoke the sentiments of a great many members of his class. Even those aristocrats who agreed with most of Delane's views on the war were concerned about the extraconstitutional power he seemed to be gaining over the political life of the nation. It was true that Delane was vain and that he did have power without accountability, except to the owner, John Walter, who generally gave his editor freedom to set policy. Delane's ego was large. Lord Elcho called him a 'social octopus,' who insinuated himself into the dining-rooms and drawing-rooms of the great. He was, as his enemies claimed, a pompous man who made oracular pronouncements and habitually projected an air of infallibility and condescension. This sense of self-importance appears even when he expounded on his own selflessness and humility as this letter, written in 1854 to a former leader-writer, demonstrates: 'Of late years the connexion of Ministers and heads of parties with the press has become more intimate and more avowed and one's position has become more that of a Parisian journalist than it used to be. To many the change would be agreeable but I have the bad taste not to greatly admire the society of Dukes and Duchesses and a nearer acquaintance with the stuff out of which "great men" are made certainly does not raise my opinion either of their honesty or capacity. So though I go more among Swells than heretofore I *live* just as much in my own coterie and shall be rejoiced to welcome you back to it.'[4]

People who knew him would be inclined to doubt his claim that he could separate his private from his public self. His ego and the newspaper he edited were inextricably confused with each other. If found at a duchess's soirée or if observed buttering up a cabinet minister at a country weekend, it could safely be assumed that he was in those places and doing those things for professional as well as social reasons. The success of *The Times* was for its editor an end in itself. He was seldom guilty of using the paper to promote his own ideas if those ideas proved unpopular with readers. Most people agreed that, in fact, he had few ideas of his own beyond a bluff John Bullism and a generalized sympathy for free-trade liberalism. Palmerston, who in 1855 was still coming in for his share of brickbats from *The Times*, assured Queen Victoria that there was no danger in his receiving Delane socially: '*The Times* both does and intends to do mischief, yet that mischief is often very temporary and much limited. That paper often takes a Line in Hopes of being followed by public opinion, but when it finds that public opinion goes the other way, it changes its course and follows public opinion.' Delane did believe in his campaign against aristocratic exclusiveness, and yet he was continually testing public opinion. As Palmerston indicated he was ready to adjust this course or any other to a strong change in the winds.[5]

While the country was still at peace *The Times* had praised Aberdeen's moderation and questioned the need for involvement. Once the war was on and once the reports began to come in from William Howard Russell, the paper's great correspondent at the front, the tone of the paper turned intensely bellicose. Delane visited the scene of the fighting in the spring of 1854 and was appalled at the administrative confusion, the stupidities of the army and naval commanders, and the suffering that resulted. While still on the way home he ordered his paper to sound the tocsin for a decisive victory and to begin a crusade for administrative reform. From that point restoration of the balance of power and the ending of 'shameless nepotism' became the two texts for sermons preached from the leader page. By December 1854 the government could count *The Times* among their most formidable opponents; any minister suspected of trafficking with that enemy risked being accused of treason, not only against Aberdeen but against the constitution itself. On one occasion the duke of Newcastle, the secretary for war and a prime target for *The Times*, warned the affable Lord Granville that his intimacy with Delane was widely resented. Granville admitted that his wife did invite the editor to her parties but claimed that he always was careful in conversation to keep to innocuous subjects. Newcastle, Russell, and many other Whig aristocrats believed that it was the intention of Delane and his friends to 'throw everything into confusion' and destroy the constitution. Therefore when Aberdeen resigned under bombardment from *The Times* as well as from the parliamentary opposition, members of the traditional ruling class were worried about the consequences of making concessions to demands from *The Times* – demands that all vacancies in the new government be filled with people of merit from outside the 'exclusive circle of Brookes's,' outside that old 'narrow coterie.' They were afraid that to do so would only increase Delane's arrogance.[6]

Palmerston, however, remained, as always, confident and unperturbed. His main concern in forming his government was to get Russell back into the ministry, and he knew that involved paying attention to Lord John's nominees. Within weeks of Aberdeen's fall it was obvious that the reign of efficiency was not about to begin. Molesworth was given his old post as first commissioner of works and public buildings, in spite of Delane's insistence that he receive something more important. At Delane's suggestion Molesworth, Granville, and Cornewall Lewis 'moved heaven and earth to get Lowe a place.' But, noted Greville, 'Palmerston and others set their faces against him.' Delane thought he had a commitment from the prime minister to make Austen Henry Layard, the excavator of Nineveh and Delane's companion on the trip to the Crimea, Newcastle's replacement at the War Office; Palmerston only came through with a lowly under-secretaryship which Layard refused. Particularly galling to the 'new men' was the announcement that the well-born but, according to Greville, 'totally useless' Vernon Smith had got a seat in the cabinet. This news put *The Times* into a dudgeon. Palmerston, it concluded, had determined to ignore the storm of indignation sweeping the country against the ineptitude of men who supposedly ruled the seas but could not supply the horses around Sebastopol with properly dried hay. It appeared a sad fact, the paper concluded, that even in a time of greatest national peril the prime minister had chosen to regard 'a powerful patron as more important than a clear head or a strong mind.' Aberdeen had experienced the consequences of that storm; now Palmerston must experience it for himself.[7]

The storm metaphor was not simply exaggerated rhetoric in the days before the French captured the Malakoff redoubt and the Russians abandoned Sebastopol. During the first six months of the new administration the winds of discontent continued to rise. The feeling was widespread that the nation's constitutional system was not standing up to the test of war. For a relatively brief period large numbers of Englishmen, and especially middle class Englishmen, rejected the call from their traditional leaders for unity in time of peril; many of them concluded that clamorous discord was the most positive way to respond to what seemed to them to be national bankruptcy. Thus the strident tone *The Times* adopted matched the mood of a large number of its predominantly middle class readers. At the same time the paper intensified the passions it responded to.[8]

The Administrative Reform Association, the most important pressure group in the movement for businesslike methods in government, received short-lived but powerful backing from Delane during the spring of 1855. His protegé, Layard, was his direct link with the organization. It was predominantly an association of business and professional people who believed that the only way England stood a chance of restoring her effectiveness as a world power was to substitute 'scientific' administration for the old system, based on deference and privilege. Their motto was, 'the right man in the right place' – right being one who had managerial experience and knowledge of business methods. Samuel Morley headed the association. He was a wealthy, Nonconformist, hosiery manufacturer who wanted to start a moral revival among voters so that they would elect, for pure rather than selfish motives, independent, knowledgeable, representatives. Not all who joined with him shared his moral fervour, but most members did believe in the 'mystique of business' and wanted to assert the social and economic importance of the entreprenurial and professional members of the community. The tone of moral uplift did greatly appeal to literary men from the same class, most prominent among them Charles Dickens, John Ruskin, William Makepeace Thackeray, and the Christian Socialist F.D. Maurice.[9]

Others supported administrative reform (although not necessarily the association) because they believed it to be the way to carry out a safe, evolutionary reconstruction of the machinery of government. Lowe was one of these. He had no use for sentimental notions about moral revival and he emphatically did not want to hand over the direction of the nation to Congregational bankers or Methodist linen-drapers. He asked his Kidderminster constituents to appreciate the irony of the fact that England supplied the world with engineering skill but seemed to lack the administrative talent to move guns and fodder the few miles from Balaklava inlet to the front lines outside the fortress of Sebastopol. The immense reserves of skill in the nation could be released, he maintained, if leadership talent, already available, could be moved forward and allowed to work, free from the harassment of Parliamentary commissions of inquiry or other such clumsy contrivances. Britain's ancient constitution was her most precious asset, 'but Russia has the advantage in war of having only one head, whose interest and that of the public, so far as the success of his armies are concerned, are entirely at one.' England's statesmen, by contrast, 'are not identified with the public interest.' While the people look to them to supply the best men to do the necessary work, they are looking 'rather to their own profits or that of their friends, or their parliamentary influences, than to the interests of the people.' Until you get this altered, he said, 'it is no use in talking of any kind of reform.' Merit must be allowed to rise through the ranks of the army; talent must prevail in the Civil Service; representatives must act independently and resist pressures from special interest. In all these things he was at one with Morley and the Administrative Reform Association, but he did not share in the faith that the middle classes embodied some special virtue. He admired the hard-headed, rationalizing approach of engineers and businessmen, but he did not think businessmen and engineers were capable of grasping broad philosophical issues. He was enormously impressed by the energies free enterprise and technology could release, but he never confused entrepreneurship with statecraft. He would recruit most of his intellectual élite from the middle class; he would not, however, allow them to become the guardians and administrators of the state until they had passed through the universities, widened their perspectives, gained a strong moral sense of responsibility for the general welfare, and learned to behave like gentlemen.[10]

While the Crimean War went badly the Administrative Reform Association flourished and its heterogeneous elements held together. In April 1855, when the Roebuck Commission was airing the frightful statistics from Scutari, respectably dressed men filled the Drury Lane Theatre on several occasions to hear rousing condemnations of the 'System.' One evening Charles Dickens denounced 'our English tuft-hunting, toad-eating, and other manifestations of accursed gentility.' On another afternoon three hundred commercial men boarded a clipper ship in Liverpool to hear Layard describe (not entirely accurately) the blunders of the generals and the admirals. He told them of his expectations that Palmerston would begin to clean up the mess and of his disillusionment: the government had been formed and here were 'all the old Whig scum again to the top of the pot.' In more moderate but determined language a meeting in April resolved: 'That the true remedy for the system of mal-administration which has caused such wanton waste of labour, money, and human life, – is to be sought in the infusion of practical experience and business ability into every department of executive rule.'[11]

From April until late June *The Times* applauded these sentiments, including the ones which equated talent with business ability. It noted approvingly the attitude of 'City people,' who believed 'that if the public business were to be managed in the same way as a good private business it might be found to answer at last.' And then, gradually, the leader-writers began to slip in a qualification here and there. One leading article suggested (in a style distinctly Lowean) that native ability alone does not constitute merit or qualify a person to decide and command. Admiral Boxer, the manager of transport service, and Major Sillery, supervisor of hospitals at Scutari, had both risen through the ranks because of their abilities and yet had proven to be dreadful administrators. The article went on to point the moral that education must be added to ability or else that ability will be buried under routine and minutiae. The shrewdness and drive which might lead a man to success in commerce was a kind of merit, but not the kind needed for government. The nation would not be improved if 'stockbrokers, railway directors and "Heaven knows who"' were made the ruling class. Ultimately, the writer thought, the fate of the nation depended on the universities; the way out of the confused morass that substituted for a public service was to identify the undergraduates who had proven their ability to deal with abstract ideas and then place before them a clear prospect of advancement in politics and the bureaucracy.[12] This qualification came in mid-June; during the month of July the paper ignored the subject of administrative reform entirely. In August two leading articles noted that the Administrative Reform Association, progressive though its general aims were, had come up with few practical suggestions and those that they had generated were totally unworkable. Public support for the association melted away at the same time that *The Times* withdrew its support. Although there was no necessary link between the collapse of the movement and the behaviour of the newspaper, association leaders were inclined to make that connexion and to blame, in particular, the influence of 'Bob Lowe.' They did not take a flattering view of his motives. Lord Goderich, Layard's closest associate, wrote in August: 'Lowe as you will have seen, got his reward and dodged himself into a Privy Councillorship. He has certainly played his cards well for *his* purposes – how far that has been a high one I will not pronounce.'[13]

The Times had made a suspiciously dramatic switch of policy in August. Not only had it abandoned the administrative reformers but it had announced, after a quarter century of criticism, that Palmerston was that long-sought-for phenomenon, 'The Right Man in the Right Place.' Careful readers concluded that this switch had been made between the composition of one leading article for the 14 August edition and another. One leader warned the prime minister that the great fund of patriotism sustaining him in office would run dry if he did not begin to match deeds with words. This was familiar fare. But on the same page was a 'Summary of the Session,' which Lowe had dashed off the previous day before leaving for Osborne House to be sworn into the Privy Council. This article praised Palmerston for having, by his speech on Disraeli's no-confidence motion, restored leadership to the governmental party. The prime minister was now, the article proclaimed, 'an exponent of the popular will.' Why the editor thought one speech could work so great a change was a question which may have puzzled many, but it did not puzzle Lord John Russell. Three weeks before 14 August he had written to his confidants that *The Times*, with its 'rascally motives,' had undertaken to prop up Palmerston and would receive a place for Lowe in partial payment.[14]

An examination of the motives of Delane does not show anything rascally, although self-interest was not absent. Charles Greville had written in January 1855 that *The Times* was 'rampant' and 'insolent' and would continue to be so 'as long as its circulation is undiminished.' Not long afterwards Palmerston's government repealed the Stamp Duty, a move which Delane interpreted as an attack on his vital circulation. This legislation had placed a penny stamp on every copy of a newspaper and had then permitted free mailing. This gave *The Times* a virtual monopoly in the country, since a provincial press could not compete with a great metropolitan newspaper, shipped quickly by rail through the kingdom. For almost a decade radicals had been complaining about this and talking about declaring 'a war on ignorance.' England's rulers had not appreciated the excellence of this radical argument until the Thunderer began its 'Crusade against Nepotism'; but when Cobden brought in a repeal bill in the spring of 1855, Palmerston's ministers, and Russell most enthusiastically, supported it. The bill called for the abolition of the penny stamp and the fixing of postal charges according to weight. Amendments modified this so that the act, when passed, gave a cheaper rate to papers weighing four ounces or less. *The Times* was the only paper that weighed more. Supporters of the measure argued that they did not intend to punish *The Times* but to make the nation more literate and informed. Repeal fulfilled their expectations; the provincial press became a force in the nation and *The Times* for the first time faced serious competition from less expensive rivals in the metropolis. The official *History of The Times* argues that this was the major factor in causing Delane to seek a rapproachment with Palmerston. The editor recognized that continued independence might be fatal to the paper's reputation as a semi-official authority. So long as his newspaper enjoyed a monopoly it could vilify ministers and still expect to get information from them. With competition this might no longer be the case. Thus, according to this interpretation, Delane ceased to be Palmerston's critic and became his confederate. Palmerston was receptive because his government was in trouble in July. Russell had made concessions at the peace conference in Vienna, concessions which his government had subsequently repudiated. Russell had been forced to speak against these concessions in Parliament. When this contradiction was made public there was a great outcry in the press and Lowe got a group of junior ministers to sign a statement condemning Russell. Palmerston then decided that the time had come to 'throw Johnny overboard.' Russell, feeling betrayed, immediately began to work to bring Palmerston down. Therefore when Delane's friends sent out feelers, Palmerston's friends responded and the seconds arranged social occasions. In quick succession Palmerston announced the promotion of Molesworth to the Colonial Office and offered Lowe an important sub-cabinet post at the Board of Trade and a Privy Councillorship. Thus by the end of the year Delane and the prime minister had established their mutually convenient special relationship; Palmerston got assistance from Delane in making the unpopular peace treaty palatable; in return, Delane got advance notice of its terms. This relationship lasted for ten years – until Palmerston's death in 1865 – and, among other things, maintained, according to the paper's historian, the journalistic predominance of *The Times* during this 'highly competitive period.'[15]

Presented this way the actions of Delane and Lowe seem opportunistic if not unprincipled. A closer look shows that journalistic calculations were not the only things going through their minds in the early summer of 1855. Delane did not throw over the Administrative Reform Association, abandon Layard, and begin what Lord Clarendon called his 'devil worship' with Palmerston, and Lowe did not first subvert the junior ministers and then 'dodge' his way back into office simply because some Whig aristocrats threatened *The Times*'s monopoly. Delane does not appear to have been desperately worried by the repeal of the penny stamp; he had a project under way for delivering papers by rail. Of course, he did not like the bill. He got Lowe to make a speech advocating a uniform rate regardless of size and weight; but there is no evidence to show that he believed his paper to be in serious danger.[16]

Changes in public opinion and in the military situation offer a more convincing explanation for why Lowe stopped talking so loudly about nepotism and began speaking of Palmerston as the 'exponent of the popular will.' The improving performance of the army in the Crimea relieved anxieties; once that happened, the differences within the association came to the surface. Layard's feverish exaggerations produced a negative reaction, especially in Parliament. These factors, and not the withdrawal of support by *The Times* sent the administrative reform movement into a rapid decline. Delane may have been stirred by Layard's enthusiasm for the movement, but Lowe never was. The 'Crusade Against Nepotism' had always been linked in their minds with winning a decisive victory over Russia. While *The Times* was blasting away at the 'system' in May, Lowe was lambasting the 'peace party' in the Commons. When the government declared that it would prefer to break off negotiations rather than concede to Russia the right to station her naval forces in the Black Sea, Lowe made several ringing speeches upholding that stand. When it was disclosed that Russell had, in fact, made that concession in Vienna and when as a consequence Russell resigned, Delane and his advisers at Printing House Square were presented with the choice of keeping up their barrage against ministerial inefficiency and further weakening the one man who seemed capable of prosecuting the war vigorously or quietly shifting its line and bringing the paper around behind the beleaguered prime minister. During July and early August they gradually brought the paper around to what they considered the patriotic course. The seemingly contradictory leading articles on 14 August were probably a part of that manœuvre.[17]

There is no reason to doubt that Lowe's appointment to the Board of Trade was part of a deal. It is unlikely that Palmerston would have brought him in out of eagerness for his services. The prime minister respected Lowe. According to one report he was supposed to have said that Lord Blachford (an eminent jurist), Gladstone, and Lowe were the three cleverest men he had known. But he did not trust Lowe's judgment. Nevertheless, he had no objection to giving him an important secondary office and, in July, with Russell out of the way, the deed was easily done. A month before *The Times* made its public change of front he wrote to the queen: 'Mr. Lowe has shown himself by his late speeches in the House of Commons to be a man of considerable talent. He is well disposed to the Government and has intirely [sic] quitted the other three Ls [Layard; W.S. Linsay, a shipping magnate; and, probably, Bulwer Lytton] and he would be an acquisition as Vice President of the Board of Trade.'[18]

The ending of the Crimean War, the rapid dissipation of middle class support for radicalism, the demonstrated willingness of the new prime minister to bend to pressure and invite 'reflecting liberals' into the government raised Lowe's hopes for the future of liberalism in England, if not elsewhere. He was not complacent; the crisis was passed but England had not emerged from it a modern state. The nation's aristocratic rulers had not yet been forced to substitute merit for 'connexion and favour.' Forces generated by industrial capitalism and the rapid growth of technology were making the old ways of doing things irrelevant, but those forces did not make the liberal society inevitable. On the contrary, the process of urbanization and the revolution brought by the railway were bringing people together physically and mentally but they were also working in the opposite direction; they were tending to harden class lines and divide segments of society into interest groups with mutually incompatible social and economic objectives. Only through timely political action could free enterprise and social harmony be reconciled. If, as now seemed likely, the aristocracy could be induced to modernize the administration and demonstrate to the increasingly alert masses a capacity of the existing system to manage the affairs of the nation efficiently, then 'organic change,' in other words, 'democracy,' could be averted.

By 1856 Lowe was reasonably sure that the liberal state had weathered the crisis of war, but he was pessimistic about its prospects in his former homeland. At the same time that he was doing his best to educate the English aristocracy in the realities of the modern technological world he was battling to prevent the rise of a selfish, materialistic 'squattocracy' in Australia. There, as everywhere, he believed political action to be the only way to avert social catastrophe. Had the ministers in Whitehall the will and the wit to make constitutions for the colonies designed to allow the development of balanced interests, then liberalism might survive, but he was sure they had not. Nevertheless, he would use his opportunities while he was an independent member of Parliament, between offices, to sound the alarm about the evils of class war and its inevitable consequences: tyranny and democracy. Australians would not pay heed nor would the Colonial Office, but the wealthy and educated citizens of England might be able to profit from the example of Australia and force their leaders to take preventive action in time to stop erosion of liberal institutions in the perilous future.

Back in 1850, during the debate over the constitutions for Victoria and New South Wales, he, like many opponents of the squatter interests, had felt himself pulled in two directions: he wanted a large extension of responsible self-government and yet was afraid that a premature or carelessly constructed extension might hand the graziers a monopoly of land and power. The leading Australian colonies would then appear to be moving forward when in fact they would be moving backward. They would be saddled with pastoral rulers just at the point when they were becoming urban, agrarian economies. His solution in 1850 was to give countervailing constitutional power to the skilled workers, shopkeepers, professionals, and businessmen. He had not wanted to attack the squatters openly at that time because he saw the need for a united front in the effort to get a generous grant of self-government. This explains why he introduced his curious argument that to preserve the existing high franchise qualification would be to give political predominance to the ex-convict element. He could safely count on the ignorance or bored indifference of most English parliamentarians to shield him from close questioning about this assertion. But at least one leading Sydney pastoralist, Charles Nicholson, noticed that Lowe was trying to lay a cunning trap for the innocents in the British government. The Conservative Nicholson was distressed to see the sponsors of constitutional changes accept Lowe's advice and insert an amendment cutting the franchise qualification in half. The amendors believed, Nicholson said, that they were saving Victoria and New South Wales from semi-reformed cut-throats when, in fact, they were giving 'all political power into the hands of the population of the towns.' Events between 1852 and 1855, however, showed that Nicholson's fears were unnecessary. As Lowe and the other anti-squatters had predicted, the pastoralists were able to use gerrymandering to maintain their control over the legislative councils. In Victoria they tightened their control over crown lands in spite of the fact that the gold rush prosperity was causing a demand for access to land for growing food and building houses and shops. In New South Wales Wentworth and his party acted on the permission the Colonial Office had given the Legislative Council to suggest further constitutional revisions. They submitted to Whitehall draft constitutions calling for an upper chamber made up of crown nominees, appointed for life,

and for a two-thirds majority rule in both chambers for future constitutional amendments. They sensed that these 'safeguards' against democracy would go down well with the members of Parliament in England –
men who knew almost nothing about conditions in the colonies and
who would be disinclined, in any event, to oppose any reasonable demands coming from what would appear to them to be the elected representatives of majority colonial opinion.[19]

Lowe did what he could in 1853, first in *The Times* and then in the
Commons, to frustrate the designs of the would-be oligarchs. How 'ludicrous,' he wrote, 'is the suggestion of the union of those two rather incongruous terms, Botany Bay and an hereditary order of nobility.' English peers, he pointed out, have instinctive good taste and have a feeling,
supported by an ancient tradition, of responsibility to future generations. By contrast the great sheep graziers had no 'pretension to merit
of any kind, martial or forensic,' except the claim of an 'entirely for-
tuitous acquisition of wealth.' They were not, he tried to make clear to
English readers, representatives of public opinion. They had got their
legislative majority by devious means and in an election held before the
gold rush drastically changed the nature of the population. True to
form, he ended his presentations with dire warnings of what would happen should Australia be given over, as Canada had been, to rule by family compact. 'Let no one suppose that ... the present apathy would continue. The passing of this act would be the signal for a struggle which
would never cease till every vestige of these undue privileges had been
swept away, and that democratic equality which these parvenue aristocrats dread so much had been pushed to that violent extreme which
ever follows a reaction.' Wentworth expressed confidence that 'our
friend Lowe' would get nowhere with this kind of talk. Government
leaders would be bound to accept the local legislatures as valid spokesmen and as for the rest, they are 'too occupied with the war to think
much about it.' Nicholson was more inclined to be wary; Lowe's 'organs
of *mischief* and *destruction* are so irrepressible, that I am sure there is
nothing he would like better than to hack down any machinery we
might set up.'[20]

Lowe hacked away but to little effect. Russell's Constitution bill
passed through a thinly attended House. The resulting act embodied
most of the provisions of the colonial draft constitutions, although Russell did make a concession allowing the New South Wales legislature to
set aside the two-thirds majority rule – a provision which the legislature
acted on in 1857. Many of the formal attributes of democracy followed
in the next decade as a consequence of this constitutional change and in
response to changes in the nature of the economy and society. Lowe
waited expectantly for the attendant evils to appear. He was not disappointed. Reports of corruption, governmental instability, the news that

protectionists were increasing in political strength he received with satisfaction. By the early sixties he convinced himself that all his predictions had come true: Australia had escaped oligarchy but in doing so had brought on herself an equally dismal fate – for which he blamed the 'narrowness and incapacity' of his two former allies, Joseph Parkes and Stuart Alexander Donaldson, who had both risen in New South Wales to the premiership. Mediocre leadership of the kind these men provided was to be expected, he told Charles Gavin Duffy, now that educated men from England no longer thought of Australia as a congenial place. In 1855 he had given Duffy glowing reports about Australia and urged him to emigrate. By 1866, when Duffy visited him in London, Lowe was profoundly pessimistic.[21]

That visit took place while Parliament was debating the Reform bill of 1866. Duffy had been asked to speak at a dinner in London about the public pronouncements Lowe had been making on the failure of democracy in Australia. Some rebuttal was called for, since Lowe had been holding up Victoria and New South Wales as object lessons in what England might expect should she allow herself to follow the example of her children. Lowe's speeches in Parliament that year had been peppered with uncomplimentary anecdotes or, as one indignant commentator called them, 'his *ad captandum* sketches designed to support his rhetoric exaggerations.' Duffy was not the only one to remonstrate with him about the slurs he was making on Australia's reputation. Supporters of the Reform bill had given Hugh Childers, another old Australian hand, the assignment of defending the honour of the colonies in the House of Commons. Should New South Wales and Victoria be maligned, Childers asked, when their finances were healthy, their credit excellent, their indebtedness low, their ministries staffed with such distinguished former associates of Lowe's as Charles Cowper and Archibald Mitchie, and when the democratically elected legislatures of those two colonies had done far more to advance public education than had the mother parliament? Then turning to the offensive, Childers called the attention of the House to Lowe's past record in Sydney. Had he not advised the citizens of that city in years gone by to keep the 'example of America before their eyes'?[22]

This was not the only reference made during the debate in 1866 to the alleged inconsistencies in Lowe's past. An Irish member referred to 'a wild shriek in favour of democracy,' which the former member for Kidderminster had supposedly made in front of his constituents in 1852. On that occasion Lowe had denounced the Tories for their 'perverse opposition to public opinion,' their obtuse blindness to 'an obvious tendency in this country towards democracy,' their inability to adapt themselves to changes, so that those changes might be effected 'with the least loss of that which we would gladly preserve.' At the end of these remarks Lowe had observed that thirty-five families from Kidderminster were about to emigrate to Australia and that when they arrived, the heads of those families would be able to vote for the first time in their lives. 'Gentlemen,' he had added, 'they owe that to myself.'[23]

Careful reading of that speech shows that he took pains to make distinctions between what he believed to be happening and what he desired to happen. It was obvious that when he said that 'a great growing feeling in favour of household suffrage is spreading in Great Britain,' he took no pleasure in the prediction. In an election broadside he wrote in praise of himself during the 1848 election in Sydney, Lowe talked of a 'new era' which was coming, an era when people would see themselves 'a mighty and self-acting power, thinking for itself, judging for itself, and working, through honest and independent representatives, for the real end of all good government – the greatest happiness for the greatest number.'[24]

He did not elaborate on what he meant by 'self-acting,' but it is safe to assume that he was asserting the liberal ideal of a populace able to stand on its own feet, free of servility and superstitious awe of its betters. In a speech he gave in 1858 to a predominantly working class audience (including a delegation of Chartists who stationed themselves in a corner of the hall), he repeated his conviction that honesty, independence, and respectability were advancing among the populace. He admitted that these advances deserved to be recognized, but then flatly stated that he saw no way to include that growing store of wealth and virtue in the political balance of interests without destroying that balance. In 1848, and at least up to 1855, he had used the balance theory to justify a franchise reduction in Australia. Presumably he wished that reduction to stop as soon as a balance was achieved there. Wentworth had used the argument that once one concession of the franchise was made to the working class there would be no logical stopping place short of equalitarian democracy. Universal suffrage or even household suffrage would 'swamp' all other elements in the polity and subject the minority to the tyranny of the majority. Lowe used that time-worn reasoning in his 1858 speech in Kidderminster and elaborated on it at great length in 1866. In the 1850s he was too engaged in the battle with the squatters to work out a solution to that liberal dilemma in Australia. For a while he seemed to put his hopes in the creation of a sturdy Australian yeomanry capable of standing between the rapacious grazier and the excitable and easily deluded urban worker. But by 1866 he had convinced himself that the clumsy Australian politicians had missed whatever chance they had to hold their constitutions at the balance point and had allowed the irretrievable downhill slide to start. 'My teeth which long chewed colonial beef and mutton,' he remarked to a visiting Australian, 'now positively refuse to chew any longer.'[25]

Most Liberals believed that they alone could be trusted to find a pragmatic way to adjust the balance of the constitution in a constantly changing social environment. They knew it would be difficult to accommodate the interests of an increasingly literate and disciplined working class without tipping the balance in its favour. Lord John Russell and people who thought like him believed, by mid-century, that intransigent resistance to any adjustments would produce the democracy which most of the Victorian upper classes, including most of the liberal intelligentsia, so anxiously wished to avoid. The Tories, these liberals were convinced, could not be trusted to make the necessary adjustments: their back benches were so backward-looking and their front benches were so office hungry that any Conservative government could be expected to make ill-considered, unprincipled, opportunistic concessions and thereby wreck the delicate mechanisms in the political scales. Lowe shared, with vehemence, that distrust of the Tory leaders and, before 1865 at any rate, also shared Russell's belief that the Liberal party must remain flexible and make modest adjustments from time to time in the franchise. The important thing to note, however, in the decade after 1855, is the gradual hardening of his position against the extension of the franchise to the lower middle classes and the working men. In 1854 he sat quietly in his seat and made no public objection when Russell brought in his abortive franchise extension bill. When, in 1859, Russell opposed Disraeli's bill by a wrecking resolution criticizing the Tory measure as insufficiently generous, Lowe voted with Russell, although he later explained that he disliked having to do so and merely 'gave a party vote.' He also kept his peace in the Commons in 1860, when Russell had yet another try, but this time worked energetically behind the scenes to kill the bill. He cautioned in *The Times* about the folly of risking a 'leap in the dark.' While serving as a member of the government he drummed up opposition within the Liberal party and attended clandestine meetings with the opposition to plot ways to defeat his own party's measure. Disraeli reminded him of this subversion in 1867, then said: 'And yet this is the right hon. Gentleman who talks of infamy!' If subversion was infamous in 1860, many others beside Lowe were guilty. A large majority of the Liberal party gave party votes, while grumbling more or less openly about Russell's mania. Lowe's progression away from parliamentary reform was part of a general movement of the late fifties and early sixties.[26]

What distinguished Lowe so markedly from most of his like-minded colleagues was his willingness, finally, to come out openly and vociferously against any concessions to the unenfranchised, no matter how moderate the bill or how hedged with safeguards. The progression of his attitude from 1852, when he expressed his impatience with the inability of Tories to grasp the advantages of making adjustments, to 1860, when he did everything except come out in open rebellion to stop Russell's modest proposals, was not entirely an intellectual progression. As we will see, his frustration over the failure of the Whigs to promote him or even to stand behind him while he did their dirty work precipitated his rash action in 1865 and 1866. The example of Australia, the feeling that all had been lost there because his warnings had not been heeded, confirmed rather than formed his outlook. The same can be said for his experiences in the United States and his observation of the deterioration of their federal union. It would be wrong, however, to leave the influence of his liberal ideology out of a summary of the causes which brought him into open warfare against what most liberal politicians and many conservative ones had decided was inevitable. It was not simply his fear of democracy which filled him with such passionate alarm but his conviction that parliamentary reform would jeopardize, on the verge of attainment, the creation of a meritocracy – a rational, peaceful society where talented administrators would protect men from the excesses of their own creative energies and at the same time allow those energies the freest possible expression.

In 1855, when he began work at his office at the Board of Trade, those frustrations and disappointments lay ahead of him. Association with *The Times* seemed to have lifted him forward and through the difficulties in the way of a returned colonist, without family patronage and with serious physical handicaps. He was aware that the special relationship between the newspaper and the prime minister made him unpopular with Palmerston's rivals in the Whig cousinhood. Russell, in particular, would do what he could to keep this 'able but unsafe man' in his place. He also sensed that he was not popular in the House of Commons. A man who could (as Russell claimed) punish 'by fifty lies, 300 invectives and 900 lashes from *The Times*' any one who crossed him, should not expect popularity. But Lowe never expected to be liked. He had shown that he was willing to take on difficult assignments; he had impressed even his enemies with the force of his intelligence; he had demonstrated his destructive force as a critic. It was on these terms that he wanted to be recognized. Palmerston had found it advisable to bring him forward to the edge of the inner circle; Lowe was confident that one or two hard pushes more, and the dispensers of power would widen their circle and invite him in.[27]

6

Among the True Votaries

In March 1856, seven months after Lowe took up his duties at the Board of Trade, Lord Overstone, a banker and financial adviser to Liberal governments, told Lord Granville of his strong disapproval of the Limited Liability bill which the vice-president was sponsoring; moreover, he disapproved of the admiring accompaniment the performance was receiving in *The Times*. He warned: 'Lowe is a dangerous Man to a Government. Very clever - a ready writer - a ready speaker, with great logical acuteness and dialectic power. But he is an abstract reasoner, with no practical experience nor any respect for it - with no diffidence nor any self-mistrust to keep him in order. He will drag a Government into difficulties similar to those in which the French Philosophers would have involved Bonaparte; had he not been a man of such extraordinary strong sense, practical sagacity and resolute purpose.'

Overstone proved to be a reliable prophet. Lowe did endanger the Palmerston ministry by his indulgence in abstract reasoning. And yet, paradoxically, he gained, during his stay at the Board of Trade, a great respect for practical sagacity - indeed, he made that virtue into something like an abstract theory. While at the board he was constantly in contact with intelligent public servants, expert at their complicated work and filled with a sense of mission about the public service. Like most reforming liberals, Lowe feared the growth of the bureaucracy because he believed it to be inefficient and corruptible. The permanent officials at his new post, however, were efficient, incorruptible. They were capable of making rational and pragmatic policy decisions and had the skill and 'resolute purpose' to carry it through. If the whole of the administration could be filled with such 'true votaries,' then it might be possible to extend the work of the government within limits recognized by the administrators and at the same time preserve and improve the free enterprise system.[1]

There is irony in the fact that the Board of Trade, this model for Lowe in administrative procedure, had been organized and staffed under the old, pre-reform, 'system,' that system which he and *The Times* had so recently been roundly damning. Lucy Brown, in her study of the Board of Trade in the early Victorian period, shows how markedly the personnel and traditions of this department differed from the stereotype. Civil servants were thought to be protectionist (because security-minded and appointed through the influence of landed magnates); the permanent officials at the Board of Trade were ardent free traders. William Huskisson in the 1820s and Poulett Thomson in the 1830s had established a tradition of Ricardian orthodoxy so strong that any new recruits who might not be perfectly 'sound' on the question in the beginning, quickly came around. Instead of being lovers of routine and avoiders of responsibility, these officials were accustomed to making decisions and encouraged to be innovative. The work the department did, especially the gathering of statistics, attracted to its service men with Benthamite tastes. Unlike the Foreign Office, where younger sons of earls abounded, Board of Trade officials tended to come from outside the aristocracy and to be unsympathetic towards aristocratic government. It was a congenial environment for Lowe.[2]

Two men in particular seemed to Lowe to be examples of the near perfect public servant. One was Henry Thring, undoubtedly the most accomplished drafter of bills in mid-Victorian England. Although not officially posted to the Board of Trade, he was invariably chosen by that department to convert the more complex and important proposals into specific bills. Between the conception and the execution of much of the reform legislation of the period lies the shadow of Thring's singular talent for ordering detail. The other model civil servant was Thomas Farrer, who had served the department for forty-three years and had prepared the Merchant Shipping bill of 1849, a measure that had greatly increased the business of his office. Politicians who came to depend on his awesome knowledge of administrative affairs commonly referred to him as 'That most meritorious public servant.' In the tradition of the department he had strong and doctrinaire views about the importance of extending the free trade principle, reducing estimates, and spending as little as possible of the public's money. In the 1890s he became president of the Cobden Club – a testimony to his economic orthodoxy. Yet at the same time he was enough of a utilitarian to wish the activities of his own department expanded. Like so many reformers of the era he had passion for economy. Yet, at the same time, he wanted to expand the departmental staff and enlarge its area of supervision and regulation.[3]

Pressures for expansion from civil servants like Farrer acted to increase and diversify the work done by the department in the early Victorian period. By 1855, when Lowe became, in practice if not formally, the responsible official at the Board of Trade, not only the amount but the nature of the work had changed from what it had been a decade earlier. Before Peel came to office in 1842, Huskisson, Thomson, and others had made the Board of Trade into what Lowe once called 'the grave of protection and the cradle of free trade.' Under the presidencies of Gladstone and Cardwell it continued to serve as the base from which the dismantling of the mercantilist system was carried out. After the victory of free trade in 1846, as tariffs came to be looked on merely as sources of revenue, their supervision gradually fell to the Treasury. While that was happening the Board of Trade began to take a prominent part in the rapid growth in activities of the central government. Because the officials and secretariat of the department had experience in collecting statistics and in giving advice about commercial activities, legislators found it convenient to make them agents for supervising new laws regulating the conduct of financial and commercial enterprises. By 1855 the board's administrative duties had become more important than its advisory ones, although the department did continue to serve as the collector of trade and industrial statistics. By then it had acquired four distinct divisions with specialized and professional staffs who were almost floundering under the weight of their miscellaneous functions. They investigated railway accidents, registered new joint stock companies and friendly societies, supervised lighthouses and harbours, watched to see that ships were not overloaded and their crews debauched or defrauded, and, for a brief period, supervised the training of science teachers, managed museums, and ran a school of industrial design. Those who directed policy at the Board of Trade not only had to deal with the internal confusion these heterogeneous activities were bound to generate but also to fend off business and commercial men and their numerous representatives in Parliament who felt menaced or inhibited by the board's inquisitions. Departmental traditions and careful recruiting practices had insured that the men who attended Lowe's frequent board meetings were dedicated public servants; the nature of the work they did required that they be knowledgeable.[4]

Lowe admired his subordinates and was admired by them. Veteran officials soon began to look forward to the regular discussions around a table in the vice-president's office. Those discussions, Farrer recalled, were 'most interesting' and 'certainly most amusing.' 'It was possible,' he said, 'to sit later and longer with Lowe than with any other man I have served, because every point was illustrated by some apt quotation, some good story, some flash of wit.'[5]

The subject of their discussions in the winter of 1855-6 was the revision of the laws governing joint stock companies and partnerships. The object of the reform was to simplify and extend the principle of limited liability. Early in 1856 Thring drew up bills, based on the ideas put forward at these meetings, and in February the vice-president introduced them. One of them, the Joint Stock Companies bill, was the most significant achievement during Lowe's stay at the Board of Trade. In his lively, even entertaining, introductory speech he claimed that he was proposing not merely some changes in company law but a reform which would work 'in favour of human liberty.' Those who listened to him apparently did not find that statement overblown; unusually generous applause and congratulations came from politicians and financial experts from all the political factions.[6]

This measure was not the first to give a British corporation the right to act as a legal person and to limit the liability of shareholders to the amount of their investment. In 1844 Parliament passed a bill giving associations with twenty-five or more shareholders the right to register as limited liability companies so long as they satisfied an elaborate set of conditions and regulations laid down and supervised by the Board of Trade. Laws passed in the eighteenth and early nineteenth centuries during, as Lowe put it, 'the first paroxysm produced by the busting of the memorable South Sea Bubble,' had virtually withdrawn the right of traders and businessmen to form joint stock companies except by securing an expensive royal charter or getting a special act of Parliament. Relaxation of these controls had still left investors in joint stock companies exposed to the danger, under certain circumstances, of being responsible for the debts of the company to the full extent of their personal wealth and property. This had not inhibited the expansion of British industry in any serious way; until the 1870s and 1880s partnerships were adequate for all but such huge undertakings as the construction of canals and railways.[7]

Lowe over-dramatised the economic disadvantages of unlimited liability, but he did not rest his case on utility alone. Supporters of the 1844 Act had made the point that it was illiberal in principle to extend privileges to great enterprises and deny them to others. The growing demand for individual freedom, they argued, conflicted with restrictions which the very wealthy could overcome by special legislation. Lowe carried this theoretical debate further by asserting that the rules governing personal morality – the feeling that fairness, honour, and 'eternal justice' decreed that a man should accept a risk proportionate to his chance of profit – were irrelevant in a modern world where economic transactions were understood to be governed by the laws of the market place. The 1844 law had done much, Lowe said, to overcome this moral attitude towards speculation, although it had not, itself, been entirely free from the personal and paternalistic outlook of the previous century. The sponsors of that bill had made the Board of Trade into a bumbling investigator who, in the process of catching one fraudulent venture, penalized a hundred honest ones. He told the Commons that paternalism of any kind infringes individual liberty, hampers the working of economic laws ('planned by infinite sagacity'), and undermines the self-reliance of individuals by 'lulling their vigilance to sleep.' He would correct this by removing all restriction and allowing any seven or more persons, merely by registering a memorandum of association, to become a corporation with their personal liability limited to the amount of their investment. The only protection a rational public needed was the requirement of full publicity. Therefore he proposed that the government require that proposers of a venture declare publicly their aims and disclose their financial particulars, that it require such companies to include 'Limited' in their title, and that it then trust individual investors to be the best judges of their own interests. Human beings were, he thought, generally rational about their own cupidity, so long as they knew the facts.[8]

It sometimes takes an effort to recall that in the mid-nineteenth century such arguments as these had behind them a conviction that opportunities for freer association would tend to promote the just society, not by making men more equal but by extending to most individuals the possibility of sharings in the supposed blessings of free enterprise capitalism. Despite all their talk about the irrelevance of personal morality in the field of economic relationships, mid-Victorian liberals usually expressed their reform convictions in moral terms. Lowe, in his testimony and speeches, and Thring, in a pamphlet on the subject of limited liability, stressed the desirability of directing all available savings, great or small, into productive (meaning 'private') channels. They believed the effect of that would be to advance the national prosperity and to involve the small tradesman and provident artisan in a common endeavour. If the effect of free trade policies on company law was to encourage the formation of worker co-operatives, so much the better. In this way the poor could experience the tonic of self-help and develop cultural affinities with the better-off. Though Lowe had the tact, for once, not to say so directly, he suspected that opposition to his bill came from large capitalists who wished to protect their virtual monopoly on the privilege of limited liability. Government could end that monopoly by making the formation of joint stock companies simple and cheap. Government should, by ceasing to coddle the investor, make him fully responsible for his decisions. Lowe believed his limited liability bill would show how the state, by refusing to protect the individual from his own greed and folly, could advance the moral education of the nation, promote prosperity by decreasing fraud, direct more savings into productive investments, and, in the process of doing these things, make more people conscious of their common interests.[9]

Of all his many accomplishments as a politician, Lowe took greatest pride in this one. Many of the acts he sponsored were worked out and presented to him by others; the essential principles of the Limited Liability Act he designed himself. Almost forty years after the bill was passed, when he was blind and his memory was dim, Farrer brought a smile of delight to his face by telling him the Act 'had been one of the most efficient ... useful laws which had been passed in our lifetime.' Gladstone heard about Farrer's compliment and said, with some asperity, that while most acts of modern, liberal legislation had proven useful, he had many reservations about that one.[10]

Gladstone had good reason to doubt. The number of joint stock companies increased but at a slow rate; no rapid change in company organization took place until the 1880s. There was a gradual widening of the investing public, but no large class of worker-capitalists emerged. In fact, as Gladstone sensed, the act of 1856 and its elaboration and codification in 1862 did nothing to stay the steady movement away from the small, personal, relatively competitive economic organizations towards the large, complex, impersonal amalgamations – a process which tended eventually to weaken faith in the existence of an automatic economic regulator, or, as Lowe described it, that 'infinite sagacity' which, without human direction, does its work of 'correction and compensating errors – one extreme invariably producing another – dearness producing cheapness, and cheapness dearness; and thus the great machine of society is constantly left oscillating to its centre.' It is ironic that Lowe's bill, in an indirect way, did something to promote scepticism about the beneficent workings of this Divine oscillation. A merciful Providence spared Lowe the realization that he had helped to create an economic environment inhospitable to the mid-Victorian liberal pieties he held to so steadfastly.[11]

Lowe was not allowed to enjoy his success over the Joint Stock Companies bill. Submitted concurrently with it was a bill to extend limited liability to partnerships. Palmerston strongly supported the principle of limited liability but quickly sensed that to extend it to partnerships as well as to corporations would be too much for conservative men in both parties. Several of the government's chief legal advisers fought a rearguard campaign before the Partnerships bill was put forward. They were afraid, and not without reason, that the recommended provisions of immunity for some investors in partnerships would endanger England's world-wide reputation for open, honest, and fair dealing. Others expressed the fear that partnerships with small amounts of capital and numerous partners might induce unsuspecting and innocent workingmen to gamble away savings they could not afford to lose.[12]

Lowe thought these objections were nonsense and fought back pugnaciously. If it is the duty of the state to save men from their own improvidence, he said, then we might as well 'begin by burning haystacks lest people should draw straws out of them, and bet on lengths.' Besides, provisions for liberalizing partnership law almost identical to his own were, he pointed out, common practice in France and the United States. It would have been wiser had he avoided that tack; admiration for France was not at its peak in February of 1856, and the appeal to American precedent was not likely to be widely popular. Lord Grey asked if Englishmen, famous for their commercial probity, needed to learn lessons in morality from the 'Yankee system of doing business.' Tempers did not improve among those who heard Lowe's speech on 1 February when they discovered an admiring resumé of his arguments on the leader-page of the next morning's *Times*. They concluded sourly, and probably correctly, that Lowe was rather overdoing it. If anyone dares to question the imperious junior minister's proposal, even in private, grumbled Lord John Russell, he can expect to find himself 'gibbetted in the next day's *Times*.' This reaction, not only against the partnership bill but against the rhetorical excesses and tactics of its advocate, was widespread. Concluding that half a loaf was better than none, Palmerston ordered that the partnership reform be dropped. Since Lowe had made such exaggerated claims for the benefits that would result from his reform and the evils of retaining the existing partnership laws, there was no way for him to execute a face-saving retreat. So closely did this humiliation follow on his triumphant success in extending limited liability to joint stock companies that it would be difficult to say which feeling predominated at the end of the debate: admiration for the vice-president's cleverness or pleasure in seeing him trip.[13]

Failure with the partnership bill was an embarrassment but not a fatal reverse; the Joint Stock Company Act was only the partnership bill under another name, Lowe claimed. He denied that the withdrawal was, as Disraeli had said, 'a very unfortunate catastrophe for the Minister of any public department to experience.' The manner in which Lowe had handled the department's business may have left much to be desired, but so far he had annoyed rather than alarmed conservative people. But his next proposal, a Local Dues for Shipping bill, was undeniably a catastrophe. When he sat down after introducing that measure, little was left of his reputation as a parliamentarian. Equally damaging, he had made statements which caused men of property to conclude he was a dangerous man.[14]

The purpose of the bill seemed straightforward and reasonable. It sought to do away with the rights of several seaports to levy tolls on ships passing near or entering their harbours – rights which had once benefited the public by providing refuges for storm-blown mariners and by providing funds for improving docks. But these tolls had ceased to perform these functions long ago; they were, in most cases, used for purposes completely disconnected from their original intent. A notorious example was the toll purchased in the seventeenth century by the Corporation of Liverpool from its noble owner. The corporation made collections from the throng of ships on the Mersyside (even those not using docks but unloading into lighters) and used the revenue to relieve citizens of rates, to build an impressive concert hall, and, according to one charge, even to purchase the portraits of Russian Tzars! These tolls were, as Lowe claimed, a flagrant violation of the principles of free trade since they taxed foreign ships at a higher rate than domestic; also they were a conspicuous example of how particular interests sought to serve themselves at the expense of the public in general. Well in advance of the debate, Lowe told Palmerston to expect trouble from Liverpool and Newcastle; their representatives would use all their influence, inside Parliament and out, to protect their ill-gotten gains. The Board of Trade could expect no support from the English shipping companies; they were glad to comply with a system which put foreign competitors at a disadvantage. Ultimately, it would be the English consumer who paid for Liverpool's concert hall, Lowe explained to the Commons. But who would speak for the consumer? Not the House of Commons, certainly! Its members were sensitive to pressures and bribes from the powerful interests. Only the rectitude of the Board of Trade could protect the public from the pettiness, selfishness, and moral frailty which lay all about.[15]

How he expected to win votes with such a sermon cannot be explained. When he sat down after delivering his homilies, the cause was clearly lost. 'Bob Lowe, who is disliked by many in the House,' Lord Granville noted, 'made a rattling speech ... showed a great want of knowledge of the House, and either disgusted many, or at all events, gave them a pretence for voting as they wished, viz. against the Bill.' Farrer, who had helped to draft the measure, said that his chief had given 'one of the ablest and most injudicious speeches ever made in Parliament.'[16]

Farrer exaggerated, but only slightly. Some of the pages of Hansard for 4 February 1856 would make a useful manual on how not to succeed in Parliament. Unfortunately Lowe could not be content with a simple statement of charges against Liverpool's tolls; he went out of his way to trample on her civic pride. How curious it was, he observed, that Liverpool, Hull, and Newcastle could tax the whole world and yet have such dismal records for urban improvements. When the representatives for the three cities finished spluttering out their protests, Lowe added sneer to insult by agreeing that his words had been unfortunate; he had only meant to say that conditions in those favoured localities were not 'placed exactly in that ornate state which one might have expected.' Portsmouth also came in for a kick later in the month when Sir Francis Baring, a prominent Liberal and the city's representative, chastized

Lowe for failing to respect the rights of local government. Could Baring's concern be related, Lowe asked, to the £3800 worth of tolls which Portsmouth received last year?[17]

Worse even than these gratuitous insults were his digressions into the nature of corporate property – and, to the country gentlemen on the opposite benches and the board chairmen on his own side, harrowing digressions they were! Individual property, Lowe said, was one thing, corporate property another. The individual is an element, not a creation, of society and carries into society sacred rights, among them property; whereas corporations are the 'creatures of public utility, and when they cease to subserve the public utility, they may and ought to be abolished.' Sir Frederick Thesiger, MP for Liverpool, expressed shock at the boldness of this statement and warned that any tampering with corporate property made compensation compulsory. Not so, Lowe replied; a charter which allows Liverpool to tax every bale and board which enters the Mersy is merely property in another man's property. Why should Thesiger's constituents be compensated for some 'musty parchments' which supposedly give them the right to treat the rest of us like serfs?[18]

His listeners reacted to this lecture on property, Sir James Graham said, with a mixture of 'amazement and alarm.' Landed gentlemen could not be expected to relish the phrase 'dusty parchments'; railway directors (not an inconsiderable group in the mid-Victorian Parliament) wondered how the vice-president of the Board of Trade planned to apply this dangerous-sounding doctrine to their own semi-public enterprises. Some radicals cheered Lowe's advice to send this 'intolerable abuse' to the 'same limbo of departed acts of iniquity which has already received within the last thirty years, rotten boroughs, rotten corporations, and a rotten commercial system.' Cobden spoke of the 'signal ability' of Lowe's performance, but praise from an opponent of the Crimean War in 1856 was cold comfort. Palmerston sensed the ugly temper on both sides of the House, and, as Cobden noted, abandoned both Lowe and the bill. No governmental law officer and no important minister came to his aid. Thus within weeks of putting through one of the most important economic reforms of the mid-Victorian period, Lowe had suffered a stunning defeat. Politicians generally, Cobden included, looked on Lowe as the most conspicuous failure of the day. It became a fixed convention that Lowe was too clever by half, a brilliant man who had insufficient control over his powers and too little sense of how things were done. In mid-March he had to preside over the interment ceremonies for the bill. 'Yes,' said Thesiger when it had been safely disposed of, 'Lowe and I have thrown it out.'[19]

The only solace Lowe could find was in the reflection that his was only one failure among many in the session of 1856. Palmerston did have the Peace of Paris to his credit, but the treaty was not popular in Parliament or the country. Englishmen believed that the deviousness of Louis Napoleon and the weak complicity of the British government had cheated them of a decisive victory. Palmerston, deprived of the support of what remained of the small but talented band of Peelites, depended on the Irish and the radicals for his majority and was sustained in power more by the incapacity of the Tory opposition than by any parliamentary strength of his own. Disraeli stood almost alone as an effective voice in opposition. Unlike most Tories, he supported Palmerston's peacemaking but did his best to implant the idea that in domestic affairs the Liberals were bent on destroying the props of the constitution – and Disraeli's best was, of course, superb. In his review of the session he gave Lowe's humiliations a thorough treatment. In a tone of ironical sympathy he commiserated with the luckless man, left to face catastrophe by ministers who were themselves almost Lowe's 'equals in mischance' and so filled with defeatism that they neglected 'that scrupulous exactitude, that fineness, that finish, and that completeness of detail with which a confident government goes about its business.'[20]

To be lectured by Disraeli on the virtues of scrupulous exactitude was a severe trial for any Liberal to endure. On top of that, the Peelites who had abandoned Palmerston could not suppress a temptation to gloat. 'I doubt,' wrote Graham to Cardwell, 'whether so many flagrant Follies ever were committed by any one Administration in the short space of a single Fortnight.' Graham was referring to the simultaneous 'juncture' of Lowe's alarming views on property and the 'war on the House of Lords.' He had in mind the attempt by Palmerston's law ministers to get an eminent jurist, Sir James Parke, made a life peer and seated in the House of Lords, an attempt which failed amidst charges that the ministry was out to subvert the hereditary principle. At the same time that Lowe was laying his impious hands on 'sacred property,' the Tory Peers were accusing his colleagues of wanting to destroy the foundation-stone of aristocracy. Palmerston did not want to complicate his difficulties over the treaty with Russia by a confrontation with the landed magnates. This, rather than any personal reason, probably explains why he did not come to the rescue of the Board of Trade and its spokesman in the House of Commons.[21]

Lowe saw that his ambitions had received a major check. After his defeat he could not mount any new campaigns from the Board of Trade office in the cause of freedom and utility. He was in low spirits and reconciled to the necessity for retreat. When an opening appeared at the Treasury some months later he expected to be moved to that less exposed office and was prepared to accept, until Ellice advised him that he would not be 'au fait' at the Treasury because his zeal in his present office had made him unpopular with the City. Besides, Ellice warned prophetically, the Treasury was no place for a man too blind to deal with detailed correspondence. Since there seemed to be no escape, he decided to soldier on patiently and to show his superiors that he could be discreet and useful.[22]

It seems likely that Lowe's desire to see Palmerston survive as the leader of the government explains why he spoke with such ardour in the Commons and on the hustings in 1857 in defence of one of the prime minister's more outrageous acts of jingoism. In that year Palmerston had ordered the bombardment of Canton in reprisal for the seizure by Chinese officials of twelve Hong Kong Chinese sailors from a ship, the *Arrow*, illegally flying the Union Jack. In the 1860s and afterwards Lowe gained a reputation for being an out-spoken enemy of direct, imperialist expansion and all forms of gunboat diplomacy, yet in 1857 he supported Palmerston's rash actions without qualification and rhapsodized about the flag which brave Englishmen in savage climes gathered to their breasts and 'glued there with their best heart's blood.' Possibly his views altered with the passing of time and the general reaction against the foolishness of the Crimean adventure, but it is also possible that he spoke up for Palmerston because he disliked the hypocrisy of his critics and feared that his defeat might advance the cause of Lord John Russell.[23]

Lowe did not support the prime minister only because he feared the alternatives; he had a positive admiration for Palmerston's capacity for work, his leadership qualities, his pragmatic form of liberalism. This admiration seemed to be independent of personal considerations. The rebuff Lowe suffered on the Partnership bill was not the last he received from Palmerston, nor the worst. Yet never, privately or publicly, did he turn his sarcastic wit against the Liberal leader. In 1868, when Lowe was out of office, when his prospects of ever being offered another one were not bright, and therefore when he had no personal reason to hide his real opinions, he attended the unveiling of a statue to the dead statesman in a market place near Broadlands. Lowe had expected to be asked merely to sit on the platform, but during the ceremony was called upon to say a few words to the small gathering of people, stretched out on the grass in warm sunshine. He surprised some of his friends and perhaps himself by the warmth of the eulogy he gave. In these extemporaneous remarks he returned to themes from an anonymous article he had written in 1857. In speech and article he referred to Palmerston's 'inexhaustible and indomitable industry and perseverance,' his light touch, perfect manners, generous forbearance, and sensitivity to the emotional currents running in the country. He was not, Lowe admitted, a sincere reformer, but he had the ever-fresh intelligence to perceive the changing needs of the country and the strength to act when those needs became clear and urgent. Lowe thought this pragmatism would not have been sufficient to cope with the revolutionary spirit of the thirties and forties, when structural changes needed to be made in the constitution, local government, religious institutions, commercial policy, and the relationship between mother country and colonies. Once those changes had been made, once the liberal foundations had been laid, then the time became right for a leader who could act efficiently whenever popular opinion unmistakably demanded some further application of established principles. Lowe did not claim that the Palmerstonian decade had been a progressive era; his own reform attempts in 1856 and 1857 had failed in spite of a clear need and obvious demand. Palmerstonian pragmatism had not aided him on those occasions but he did not blame the prime minister or his form of moderate liberalism.[24]

Lowe thought the reason for the virtual paralysis of the government's capacity to act lay somewhere else. In his 1857 *Edinburgh Review* article, 'The Past Session and the New Parliament,' he searched for, and discovered, to his own satisfaction, the basic fault. The article deserves more than passing attention because it is a highly personal exploration by an intelligent mid-Victorian into the reasons why the reform impulse seemed to slacken in the fifties. The solution he suggests there shows the influence the experience at the Board of Trade had on his attitude towards government and administration. Also, and incidentally, the article was an important episode in the history of the *Edinburgh Review*. The editor, Henry Reeve, called Lowe's submission 'a model of vituperation.' It raised one of the angriest storms in Reeve's journalistic experience, and the storm produced brisk sales. Purchasers apparently enjoyed seeing the sins and foibles of Liberals mercilessly probed in the leading Liberal journal.[25]

According to Lowe's analysis, liberalism had ceased to be effective because of several interrelated factors. The election of 1852 was one of them. Parliament emerged from that election, he thought, in a state of near paralysis. On one side of the Commons sat ranks of honest, slow-witted squires, led from on high by a Tory lord who continued to hang on to economic and social theories which any clear-headed man could see were untenable, and led, lower down, by a shifty, tricky assistant who substituted for policies the 'best concocted phrases of the most disastrous political thaumaturge.' Over in a corner of the House sat a small group of Manchester School radicals, clever and eloquent men, for the most part, but without party allegiance and, after the beginning of the Eastern Crisis, without popular support. Whenever the ship of state had to sail close-hauled, the radicals could be expected to throw themselves onto the lee side. Because Bright, Cobden, and their followers were, in the political sense of the word, 'irresponsible,' and because the Tories were obscurantist, Liberals found they scarcely needed to exert themselves to get elected. All they needed to do was mouth free trade slogans and they would usually head the poll. Thus the average man who sat on one of the Liberal benches had 'limited intelligence.' Whenever he was faced with the practical implications of his undigested free trade slogans, that so-called Liberal's true conservative instincts surfaced, and he began vigorously to defend the vested rights of all manner of traditional, local, and special interests. Lowe wrote that the success of liberalism after 1846 had dissipated the already scarce reserves of ideological commitment among the rank and file. Prosperity increased complacency still more. By becoming the dominant creed, liberalism, like the Established church, included within it an increasing number of smug, prosperous, occasional worshippers. With the Tories ready for 'insolvency court,' with the back-bench Liberals repeating the rhetoric of freedom and tolerance while voting to shore up Ecclesiastical Courts, threatening to withdraw support from the Irish Catholic seminary at Maynooth, turning their backs on justice for Jews, and with the radicals doing their best to make any government impossible, it was small wonder, Lowe thought, that the party system ceased to respond to the demands of the changing times.[26]

After establishing this background Lowe proceeded to deplore the vacuum of leadership in the nation. As might be expected, he gave careful attention to the two mortal sins of Lord John Russell: pride and faithlessness. Gladstone fared no better. Lowe thought him an anachronism. In an age which called for pragmatism he was the abstract reasoner, the ultimate casuist. For a while Peel had held to earth his 'soaring reveries' about the Church Visible and the Platonic Ideal, but now there was no one to keep him from 'luxuriating' in the 'metaphysics of finance': his 'additions are performed in a species of oratorical ecstacy, and his subtractions are made with the violence of a paroxyism.' Only one man remained above this chaos of faction, this vanity, this violent, misplaced idealism, and that was Palmerston. He alone emerged from Lowe's portrait gallery with a semblance of patriotism and common sense. If Palmerston could only manage to strengthen the executive with Liberals who believed in free trade and were able to apply it courageously but pragmatically to every facet of English life, then, Lowe thought, a new era of moderate, practical, non-organic, improvement might begin. But for the moment, the radical and Peelite splinter groups, the dishonest Conservatives, the factious Liberal rivals prevented that bright day from dawning. The Crimean War had forced the factions into a semblance of co-operation, but now that the emergency was passed, these promoters of political anarchy were once again 'like Milton's fallen Angels,' raising their heads 'from the oblivious pool, to plot anew ...'[27]

This analysis of what had gone wrong with liberalism is not profound. What it shows is how completely Lowe was convinced that modern life had rational well-springs. He believed that if something happened to break up the even flow of politics then the physical and spiritual substance of the nation would decay. It is also obvious that he believed the least crucial part of the political system was the legislature. Most of the men whom people or interests sent to Parliament were, he thought, venal or superficial. Deprive them of strong leadership and lull them with prosperity and security and they will quickly revert to their natural conservatism and conventionality. Like municipal aldermen, shipping magnates, school and university instructors – people with great power within narrow confines – members of Parliament needed always to be controlled by institutional checks and by firm direction so that they would devote their energies to the public good. At the same time he shared the fear most liberals felt that the necessary regulatory controls might be used to jeopardize free expression and action. His solution was to find an executive leader with the strength to enforce party discipline and resist pressure from special interests in Parliament and elsewhere but also with the pragmatic sense to see that the reforms which needed to be carried out should be left to the initiative of specialists within the administration. Palmerston, himself a hard-working, demanding administrator, did not feel compelled to put forward new programmes of legislation but was content to leave the adjustments in the existing laws and regulations to the silent workings of the central bureaucracy. It is not surprising, therefore, that Lowe, through all his disappointments as a minister in Palmerston's governments, always considered himself a Palmerstonian.

The positive theme of Lowe's *Edinburgh Review* article was his statement that regulation and freedom could be reconciled if the central regulatory agencies could be staffed with 'true votaries,' consecrated public servants like Thring and Farrer, men who were enlightened by liberal education, schooled in the practical, technical problems of administration, thoroughly versed in the science of political economy, and disciplined by that knowledge to restrict governmental activity to an efficient minimum. He did not believe that the power of the idea alone would keep even the best and most dedicated men perpetually honest and eternally consistent to the free trade faith. A parliament, responsible to the balanced interests of the community, must keep a watchful eye, aided by an alert and courageous press. There was, he recognized, danger that true votaries might become not too weak but too zealous in the faith. Liberalism was in danger not only from those who had lost their sense of mission but from those who had become 'crotchety and useless,' useless because they had not learned that 'an habitual sacrifice of individual conviction' was essential to the progress of practical, evolutionary reform in this imperfect world. Once again he returned to his reliance on checks and balances to keep enthusiasts from turning into cranks. The administrative élite must remain responsible to the passive but strong and vigilant executive. The lines of responsibility from civil servant to ministerial department head to tough-minded, even ruthless, prime minister must never be muddled or confused. In this respect, as in the others, he thought Palmerston the perfect model. In 1857 Lowe feared that this intricate political instrument was a long way from realization. When, in the sixties, he believed the instrument had just begun to work, he was incensed when parliamentary reformers proposed to tamper with its fragile, painfully constructed mechanisms.[28]

This view that departmental experts were the best, if not the only, protectors of the public interest comes out clearly in a spirited defence Lowe made of his department several months after the *Edinburgh Review* article appeared. Thomas Horsfall, Conservative MP for Liverpool, tried to follow up his city's victory over the Board of Trade by moving for a select committee to inquire into the history of the growth in that department's powers. His complaint was that the board had become a poll-pry into every nook and cranny of the seaports. He ended his bad-tempered speech by saying that the whole business community was in rebellion against the ever-growing interference of a peer and a lawyer (meaning Stanley of Alderley, the board's titular chief, and Lowe) in the every-day commercial activity of the country. Lowe's answer was in his best style and did something to improve his position in the House. He began by giving a graphic, though not meticulously accurate, history of the department and its relentless war against incompetent merchant marine officers, against ship owners who deliberately wrecked their vessels to collect insurance, against city officials who made cosy deals with railway promoters, and against dock trusts which sent their parliamentary agents to lobby against proposals to improve the facilities of their rivals. Each victory for the public meant a growth in the department's work, but, he added, that work was directed towards an object which no other agency of the community had so exclusively at heart: the greatest happiness for the greatest number.[29]

There were limits, he thought, not to what governments could do, but what they should do to further this end. In each case officials should use common sense and prefer the practical solution to the theoretical one. For example, he admitted that a railway, being a natural monopoly and in a twilight zone between the private and public sector, might, in theory, be owned and managed by the state. But for historical reasons England had not taken that course. To nationalize the system now would involve the government in huge expense and in negotiations which, given the size of the railway lobby in Parliament, were likely to be stained with jobbery and graft. He once advised Gladstone, during a discussion of the fate of Irish railways, that a serious accident on a nationalized line might bring a ministry down. Asked if he did not think the Board of Trade should have power to prosecute a company that neglects safety rules and allows serious accidents to happen, he answered that, perhaps, in theory, it should; but experience had shown such interference to be unwise. He thought the board should have the right to inspect, summon witnesses, and publicize but should not be asked to enforce, for that would encourage the companies to hand over to the state the legal responsibility for safe maintenance. Even so desirable a regulation as uniform signals ought not to be decreed. It would be enough, he thought, to warn the public and then leave the imposition of penalties to the courts; any partnership between government and private ownership, in such a semi-political enterprise as a railway, would guarantee that the country lose the advantages of either form of management.[30]

Used in so flexible a way as this, the argument from utility was too easy a way out of any difficulty or inconsistency. He believed that only the expert central bureaucracy could regulate efficiently; he also believed that every penny spent by the state was a penny taken out of productive use. But efficiency did not come cheaply. He did not deny the paradox but had no difficulty finding his way around it. If he found ship owners sending over-laden vessels to sea with unlicenced masters he could use the greatest happiness argument to justify asking for more inspectors and more regulatory powers. Efficiency, he could say, brought more benefit to the public than the increased estimates for the department brought pain. If, on the other hand, he found a railway company asleep at the switch, he could refuse to become involved and argue that extra expenditure for regulation would produce insufficient benefit to compensate for the cost. Without being conscious that he was doing so he always put his weight on one side or the other of the efficiency-economy scale – depending on whether he happened to be in an office which was engaged in regulating private functions or one which was mainly concerned with cutting back expenditures. Had he explored the paradox in more depth he might have been impelled to examine more critically his classical liberal premises. Matthew Arnold, John Stuart Mill, T.H. Green, and other liberal intellectuals did begin that re-examination in the sixties and seventies; but Lowe never deviated.

Palmerston discovered in 1858 that not even a popular mandate could protect his government from the effect of faction. Faction had caused his defeat in 1857, over the bombardment of the forts on the Canton River; an election had returned him with a larger statistical majority. Faction brought him down again and caused the resignation of his government early in 1858, this time over his attempt to placate Frenchmen who were outraged by the discovery that a bomb, thrown at Napoleon III, had been manufactured in Birmingham and sold to an Italian refugee.

In 1857 Palmerston's rivals had accused him of immorality and high-handedness; in 1858 they accused him of truckling to an inferior. Observers of these radical changes of line might well wonder how this unstable political system could be improved and the government of the country carried on efficiently and in the public interest. Lord Derby's acceptance of office in 1858 certainly gave no promise of solution; for the next year and a half the Tories were sustained in power only by the divisions among the opposition.

Thus, in 1858 Lowe ended his stay at the Board of Trade. The events during the three years he had spent in Palmerston's first ministry had been instructive. While political anarchy prevailed in Parliament and in the executive arm of government, Lowe had sat in the midst of a group of dedicated public servants, working amicably and productively in the public interest. He was surer now than he had even been that that government is best which is administered best. He had believed in an intellectual élite before 1855, he had now observed one in action. One result of that experience was to confirm his belief that it would be a risky thing to tamper with the constitution in any way that would strengthen the legislative branch at the expense of the executive, for a weak executive could not protect the true votaries from the harrassment of special interests. Indeed, confirmation of his anti-democratic convictions seemed to come from every quarter in the latter half of the fifties. During the summer parliamentary recess of 1856 he had gone to the United States and experienced at first hand the troubles that were tearing that republic apart. Australia he believed to be deteriorating into a dull, protectionist democracy. None of these observations caused him any surprise. At the age of forty-seven his verities were the same as they had been at twenty-seven; earlier he had held them as theories, now he believed he had experienced them as realities.

He must have found it difficult to assess what those three years had done to his personal fortunes. He had demonstrated, now convincingly, that he had a great talent both for administering creatively and for making enemies. After the Shipping Dues fiasco the Whig leaders found it harder than ever to decide which was worse – to exclude Lowe and feel his wrath or to include him and feel the wrath of the people he irritated. Lowe seems to have been aware that he was as far as ever from his goal. Lord Stanley, who had joined his father's Conservative government as colonial secretary, offered a solution. He informed Lowe that an opening had occurred in the Governor General's Council in India and asked if he would consider becoming the legislative member. Lowe asked for time to consider. Expecting an acceptance, Stanley wrote to Governor General Canning, putting the candidate's situation in the best possible light: 'If he consents to go out ... you will gain the assistance of a very varied experience and remarkable talent. The bar, the House of Commons, the Indian Board, the Board of Trade, the Law Commission, to say nothing of Australia and journalism, have given Mr. Lowe a training such as few have enjoyed; and having sat opposite him in Parliament for six years, I can vouch that only his physical deficiencies have prevented him from taking a much higher place than he has taken. I know scarcely anyone of more acute intellect. The offer was made him yesterday. It is possible that some of the political friends of Government may not be pleased, but that is my affair.'[31]

Lowe decided to decline. He had already spent his years of colonial exile and was not yet prepared to abandon his hope that perseverance would lead to a place in the cabinet – an ambition which had, ever since his Oxford days, been a dominating force in his life.

7

North America

In mid-July 1856 Edward Ellice informed his Hudson's Bay Company agent in Canada, John Rose, that he should expect a visit from the leading men of *The Times*, Delane and Lowe. These two 'very special friends,' Ellice wrote, had decided to make a tour through the United States in order to see with their own eyes how well the experiment with democracy was working and to form impressions about American habits and character traits. No other men in England, he said, had so much power to impress on the public the opinions they formed. It was probable that they would be making an excursion north of the border and if they arrived in Toronto or Montreal, 'Pray initiate them in the mysteries of Canadian parties,' Ellice instructed Rose. 'They may be of great use to Canada.'[1]

Shortly before their ship, the *Canada*, left for Halifax, Nova Scotia, and Boston, Massachusetts, on 2 August, Delane announced that the press of business would force him to postpone his trip for several weeks. He urged Lowe to go on without him. Ellice had convinced both of them that America was on the point of explosion. The dissolution of the federal Union would be a momentous event, not simply for America but for England as well, since democracy itself would be on trial. Therefore it would be a great advantage to *The Times* if some of its editorial staff could speak from first-hand experience.

Lowe spent the ten day crossing preparing himself for that experience. He read *Democracy in America*, de Tocqueville's great inquiry into the nature of the republic in the era of President Andrew Jackson. Lowe had the good luck to find that one of his fellow passengers was the distinguished Bostonian man of letters, James Russell Lowell ('a most agreeable gentleman; one might almost take him for an Englishman'). Lowell was glad to talk about the changes that had taken place in America since Jackson's day. Lowe questioned him about the 'peculiar institution' of slavery and heard, in reply, an abolitionist sermon. Another passenger, an Episcopalian bishop in the Southern state of Alabama, argued the other side ('the Bishop has a weakness for niggerdrivers,' Lowe noted). Between them, the two Americans gave the English visitor a foretaste of the passion with which the great national debate was being conducted. They also filled him with anecdotes about the crude energy of their homeland. It is doubtful if many travellers have received so concentrated and excellent an education during their first passage across the Atlantic.[2]

Lowe found a substitute travelling companion for Delane: a railway expert at the Board of Trade named Captain Douglas Galton. Because Galton wanted to see as much as he could of the rapidly spreading rail network of North America, the travellers were almost constantly on the move. Halifax, the first stop, did not impress them favourably; they found the city mean and the inhabitants leaden and lymphatic. Boston was an improvement. Lowell had given them an introduction to Emerson; they met young Henry Adams, but, on discovering that most of the other interesting people were away on holiday trips, they boarded a train for Niagara Falls. Lowe found that spectacle 'emblematic' of the two nations over which the water flowed: 'the American broad, prominent, glittering, and without much depth of water, the English retiring, massive, and grand.' Pausing momentarily they moved on into Upper and Lower Canada. Writing from Cumberland, Maryland, Lowe gives this sketch: 'Boston Albany Niagara Toronto Montreal Quebec Portland Boston (again) Providence Newport New York Niagara (again by the Erie Railroad) Toronto (stay with Sir E. Head) (a very good fellow I think) Detroit Chicago (most wonderful) Galena and Dubuque (a little excursion with Iowa) (there is no water in any of the rivers) ... St. Louis, Terre Haute Indianapolis Cincinatti Wheeling Cumberland. A pretty good months work I calculate.'[3]

From Cumberland, Maryland, he went to Baltimore, then Washington and finally back to New York. Wherever he went in that wide swing he listened to a constant flow of political talk. Railway porters, waiters, fellow passengers on railway coaches and steamboats – the whole nation it seemed – was intent on the approaching national election and on its great issue: the future of the 'peculiar institution.' Only a short time before Lowe and Galton arrived pro-slavery 'border ruffians' had sacked Lawrence, Kansas, and John Brown had responded with his appalling little massacre at Pottawatomie Creek. Parties and factions within parties were taking positions on the battleground of 'Bleeding Kansas' that summer and autumn. Everywhere, except perhaps in booming Chicago, where the citizens were totally absorbed in building and making money, the travellers noted an undertone of impending violence. 'North and

South are rapidly becoming two nations,' Lowe informed Ellice, 'all other political divisions are rapidly being merged in this.' For a joke, Lowe wrote his letter home on notepaper engraved with the luxuriantly flowing beard of Colonel John C. Fremont, the noted explorer, whom the newly-formed Republican party had chosen as their presidential candidate. He would be their leader in the stand against the spread of slavery into the west. Lowe believed (wrongly) that he stood an excellent chance of upsetting the Democratic candidate, James Buchanan, because the nativist, anti-Catholic, Know Nothing party would, he thought, draw votes away from the Democrats. The Know Nothings were gathering for their convention in Baltimore when Lowe got there; they provided the visiting Englishmen with entertainment of a peculiarly American kind. Lowe and Galton got their fill of Southern oratory, torchlight parades, wild-eyed argument, and street brawls. The newspaper which announced the arrival of distinguished English visitors was given over almost entirely to accounts of five riots which had just disrupted the city – one, a massive fracas, involved three gangs, the 'Rip Raps,' the 'Plug Uglies,' and the 'New Market Runners.'[4]

It was also in Baltimore that Lowe had his first direct exposure to slavery. He had a letter of introduction to a Colonel Carroll who owned a huge plantation north of Baltimore. The colonel gave him a tour and explained the economics of farming with slave labour. Lowe thought the instruction interesting but found that after another week in Baltimore he had absorbed as much of Southern customs and bombast as he could stand and cancelled a planned excursion to Virginia. After several days in 'melancholy and half-finished' Washington, he hurried on to New York where, on 1 October, he boarded a ship for the homeward voyage. He brought back a large collection of anecdotes, folk ballads, and electioneering songs to amuse his friends. The American writer, George Ticknor, heard some of these anecdotes at Lord Palmerston's dinner table and assured his correspondents back home that the vice-president of the Board of Trade had looked at their homeland 'with an eye both very acute and very intelligent.'[5]

That acute eye had discovered nothing that might challenge élitist predispositions; Lowe was a convinced anti-democrat when he sailed on the *Canada* in August and returned home even more convinced. But in one important respect his seven weeks of rapid movement through the eastern half of North America had altered his perspective on the world. In Chicago and in the American heartland he had sensed the enormous potential for development. He became convinced that despite her serious internal contradictions, the American republic, perhaps altered in form and extent by the breakdown of the federal system, would emerge in the near future as the dominant power in North America and a force to be seriously reckoned with in the western hemisphere. After his return home he used his influence as a journalist and a politician to alert England to the consequences, both domestic and imperial, of that inescapable and, in some respects, menacing fact. Owing to that influence and also to certain fortuitious circumstances, his activities did have significant effects on the relationships between Britain, her North American colonies, and the United States. Therefore those circumstances and activities need to be examined with some care.

Everywhere on his tour Lowe had been received as a distinguished visitor and not merely as a casual tourist. His association with *The Times* was well known and that alone insured special treatment. Also the fact that Lowe was a member of Palmerston's government (American newspapers frequently reported that he was a cabinet member) meant that the press would notice his arrival and report his comments. The *Toronto Globe* thought he might be in training for the governor generalship. *The New York Daily Times* announced that he had been sent to negotiate a settlement of the dispute then simmering between England and the United States over Nicaragua. The editors commented that from all reports they had heard diplomacy was not in Lowe's line. 'He would,' they wrote, 'much rather cut the Gordian Knot than endeavour to unravel it.'[6]

Although none of these speculations were accurate, it was a fact that Lowe did have an unofficial commission, not to conduct any negotiations, but to make certain soundings for the Colonial Office. In July Labouchere, the colonial secretary, had discussed with Ellice some of the outstanding problems facing British North America and had involved Lowe in them either directly or indirectly. Ellice told Labouchere that Lowe would bring a report '*de omnibus rebus*' and that it would be available to the Colonial Office. Apparently Lowe was asked to raise certain questions with the Canadians he met and record his general impressions.[7]

These impressions were almost uniformly unfavourable. 'Canada politically is in a bad way,' Lowe wrote to Ellice during the journey. Not only was the colony in peril from the Yankees, but in peril from its own politicians. 'The Ministry (all of whom I saw) appear to me to be quite impares negotes and to have no other idea than compromising and jobbing.' The only official he met who seemed honest and knowledgeable about the fundamental problems was the governor general, Sir Edmund Head, who was, of course, not a Canadian.[8]

In his usual fashion, Lowe concluded, within days after his arrival in Toronto, that he had mastered all the important things about the country that an informed man needed to know. His main source of information was John Rose, the chief solicitor for the Hudson's Bay Company, who, on Ellice's instructions, had offered to entertain the visitors during their stay. Lowe almost immediately began sending home disquisitions on Canadian politics. As he saw it, the 'mischief' at the bottom of domestic affairs in the colony arose from changing conditions since the settlement of 1842. Then Upper and Lower Canada had received parity of representation in the legislature – an advantage to English Canadians, since they were, at that time, a minority. But in the intervening fourteen years the demographic ratio shifted; Upper Canadians, who had gained control of a disproportionate share of the wealth and now outnumbered the French Catholics, found that the constitution no longer worked to their advantage. Serious tension had grown between extremists in both of the Canadas, and to keep these tensions from becoming explosive, moderates on both sides had formed a coalition whose main purpose was to dampen down any potentially devisive issue. Three months before Lowe got to Toronto this ungainly combination of conflicting personal, regional, ethnic, and religious interests had broken up over a dispute about where to locate a permanent capital. After a short period of readjustment the coalition reformed around John A. Macdonald, who at this point began his long stewardship over Canadian politics. Radical anti-Catholics in Canada West were agitating against a political arrangement which they believed stood in the way of westward expansion and healthy economic development. In the summer of 1856 Macdonald seemed to be capable of controlling these elements but Lowe doubted that the delicate balance could be kept for long. He was unpleasantly reminded of his past experience in New South Wales, so much so that he advised his host to steer clear, at all costs, from any involvement in colonial politics – advice which Rose, probably to his regret, did not heed.[9]

Lowe repaid his host by giving him a précis of Colonial Office attitudes and some predictions about likely future policy. The interest of the Palmerston ministry was, he explained, to protect the North American colonies from American expansionists but to do so in such a way that the citizens of the raucous republic to the south would not be provoked into taking hostile action. Defence which was too strong and obvious, Lowe pointed out, was as dangerous as no defence at all. What Rose thought of this rather unreassuring analysis is not known. Probably he, like many other Canadians, was beginning to wonder if England would try to appease the United States by sacrificing her North American subjects. The worry was legitimate; the mother country loved her children in British North America conditionally and not, it seemed, too well.

At the time of Lowe's visit the Colonial Office was in a moderately optimistic frame of mind about Canada. In 1856 there were signs that this colony, at least, might prove to be an economic success. The Crimean War had helped to start an era of prosperity, enhanced by a railway boom. Success for Canada would serve to reassure the English governing class that British institutions were superior to republican ones. Labouchere sounded this note in a letter he sent to Delane in August: 'I am in hopes that you will find Canada as prospering and enjoying as much political freedom as any part of the United States but without some of the scandals and evils which have of late been so flagrant among their neighbours.'[10]

The difficulty was that prosperity and expansion would make Canada attractive to American adventurers. The United States might not enjoy the advantages of the English connexion but it was incomparably the richer and more promising region. If the Union remained intact, it was bound to improve its already enormous preponderance on the continent; if it threatened to fall apart, its leaders might decide to invade Canada in order to draw discordant factions together. Either way the future of British North America seemed precarious. War with the United States would not only involve England in an almost impossible military operation but would endanger her position in the European power balance.

British and Canadian leaders had been reminded of these dangers during the Crimean War. Attempts by England to recruit in the United States had caused spread-eagle American politicians to bluster about the possibility of an invasion of Canada. By the spring of 1856 this crisis had largely passed but American nationalists had worked themselves into a new passion, this time about Britain's supposed faithlessness over the Nicaraguan settlement. Canadians felt themselves to be in real danger. Their small volunteer force was half-trained and virtually unarmed; with the St Lawrence frozen solid, the only way of shipping arms to them quickly was to use the harbour at Portland, Maine – clearly an impossible situation. The War Office did dispatch five regiments from the Crimea to Halifax and then overland to Canada and they were there when Lowe arrived. By August the tensions had eased, but the threat and the consciousness of Canada's vulnerability were still at the forefront of everyone's mind. Governor Head was especially impressed with the need to work out a solution; not only was he fearful about Canada's safety but he recognized that a war with the United States would be disastrous for the British empire. He knew that Yankee jingoes, in a passion to twist the lion's tail, had only to make an almost effortless reach north across their border and give a twist. England might bluster and threaten to use her fleet but could do nothing effective to protect British North America.[11]

Many liberal free-traders believed that the way out of the dilemma was to stop over-protecting the English-speaking colonists and force them to accept responsibility for their own safety, yet most of these liberals were unwilling to carry through that logic to the extent of advocating the withdrawal of all British troops. By the 1860s Lowe was one of the few anti-expansionists who was ready to accept that drastic position. In 1856, however, he seems not to have advanced quite that far with his colonial self-help logic. In his talks with Rose in Toronto he urged the adoption of a bold plan for combining effective military protection from Britain with the promotion of colonial self-reliance. He suggested that Canada might construct at her own expense a railway from Halifax to Quebec; this would give her an outlet to Europe during the winter months and give the British government a way to send in soldiers and supplies. This railway would at the same time bring Canada into closer relationship with the other British colonies in the eastern half of the continent. Canada might then be compensated for the expense by being permitted to annex the vast region of Rupert's Land. He thought the Hudson's Bay Company would be willing to relinquish its rights there for a million pounds. If these arrangements were made, Lowe argued, the British colonies in America might, in time, cease to be a provocation to the United States because they would be more self-contained and less dependent on English military establishments and English governors. As a consequence, the empire might be relieved of the economic burden, and the federation of all British North America might then take place without antagonizing the Americans.[12]

When the governor general heard that Lowe had been in Toronto and had been advocating these comprehensive moves, he immediately sent an urgent request for a meeting. Lowe had gone back to New York, after having narrowly missed Head during their first visit to Montreal and Toronto. On receiving Head's message, the two travellers hurried back to Toronto where Lowe and the governor had protracted conversations. It was obvious that Head interpreted, or chose to interpret, the visit by the vice-president of the Board of Trade as an invitation from Palmerston's government to open far-reaching discussions about colonial reorganization. Lowe's specific proposals could not have interested the governor general much. He did not give the idea of an intercolonial railway, built by colonial initiative, serious consideration. He knew that Canadian politicians could not be persuaded to build and then subsidize a railway through hundreds of miles of wilderness or to police and develop the great expanses of the North-West Territories.[13]

The conversations between Lowe and Head in 1856 deserve a place in the history of Canada, not because they produced any practical solutions to the problems of national integrity and unity, but because they set in train a series of events which led, in 1867, to Confederation. Lowe did suggest to the punctilious Head that the Colonial Office would be receptive to communications from the governor general. Assuming that after his talks with a government minister it would not be improper to put forward his own ideas for comprehensive constitutional reform,

Head began his fruitful negotiations with Whitehall. But Canadians have no cause to honour Lowe for his contribution. After his return home and for the rest of his active life he did his best to raise doubts about the future of Canadian confederation, to oppose subsidies for Canadian railways, to discourage hopes for a rapid and successful spread of settlement into the Red River country and into the wilderness west of the Rockies. John A. Macdonald listed Lowe along with Bright and Gladstone as the three most dangerous enemies, in 1870, of imperial unity and Canadian safety.[14]

Macdonald had cause to fear Lowe's intentions and activities. In 1865 Delane asked Lowe to write an article on the Confederation negotiations and asked if he would try not to 'throw too much cold water' on the subject. Lowe, who had insisted from the beginning of his association with the paper that he be allowed to refuse assignments that conflicted with his own views, reminded Delane of that fact: 'We have always been against the defence scheme, against guarantees, against Railways, against compelling the lesser colonies to confederate, how on earth can we chop around on a vague intimation like this – at any rate I can't.'[15]

The water which he, by means of *The Times*, had been throwing on confederation had been cold, but not icy cold. He warned that this step would lead eventually to separation from the Motherland, but thought this a natural progression in any event. What distressed him most about the British North America Act was that the federal system it established appeared to leave the powers of the central government weak and ill-defined. Lowe had opposed federation for Australia in 1857 on the grounds that 'history teaches nothing with more uniformity than the failure of federations, and their failure precisely in the point in which this federation is weakest, the power of enforcing federal resolutions against individual states.' History would, he was sure, pronounce against Canada as well. Since Canadians appeared to want confederation, then they should have it, but no one should expect it to solve any fundamental problems: nature had not endowed that region of the world with suitable geography for constructing a vital nation, and no amount of constitutional tinkering would repair that act of fate.[16]

Pessimism about Canada's future developed in the course of his summer visit in 1856 and steadily ripened afterwards. When, for example, Lowe was in Toronto, he seems to have agreed with Head that the best way out of the problem of where to locate the centre of government was to pass over all of the leading cities, on the grounds that the selection of one would stir up all the fundamental cultural and economic rivalries of the country, and to settle on a small town, in a 'wild position,' near the boundary between Upper and Lower Canada. Therefore, when the queen, on the advice of her ministers, proposed Ottawa, Head assumed that Lowe would be well disposed and inclined 'to do a job,' and wrote requesting favourable publicity in *The Times*. That newspaper did respond with a few tepid but favourable words. But two years later, after having written many uncomplimentary things about Canada's prospects, Lowe exposed, in a scathing leading article, the folly of having placed the capital in the 'Ultima Thule of Canada ... the abode of a rough and disorderly population of lumberers.'[17]

His position on the disposal of the territories of the Hudson's Bay Company shows how deep-seated this pessimism had become by the early sixties. When he proposed the annexation of Rupert's Land to Canada in 1856, he knew that the company's charter would soon be up for renewal. In his briefing about Canadian politics, Rose must have given him an account of the activities of George Brown, the editor of the *Toronto Globe*, who had been organizing a campaign against renewal. Edward Ellice and the company's governor, George Simpson, knew that stiff-backed resistance would only give this agitation force. Upheaval among settlers in the Red River settlements, the widening criticism of the company's monopoly on free-trade grounds, along with declining fur trade profits, convinced them that it would be wise to surrender part of their holdings (preferably for a generous compensation), so that the company would be able to retain as much of its monopoly as possible.[18]

In September 1856 Labouchere proposed to Ellice a compromise whereby the company would relinquish only those areas necessary to settlement and communication. Lowe would be home soon, the colonial secretary said; he would be full of the subject and could bring them up to date on the attitudes of Canadian politicians and officers of the company. Ellice replied that the company was anxious to be accommodating to changing conditions but cautioned that a sudden and drastic curtailment of its rule would bring anarchy to the settlement within its territories, would cause the rapid extermination of wild life, and would lead to exploitation of the native populations. His refrain was, 'Above all things do not weaken your instrument of Govt. unless you can dispense with it.' This was a shrewd line to take; Ellice knew better than any colonial secretary how reluctant the Canadians would be to pay for the roads, police, and government of remote regions, therefore he would be reasonable and conciliatory and wait for the time when critics of the company's rule would have to come forward with practical substitutes. Until then he would confine his statements to reminders about the hazards of settlement and development in a bleak and frozen land. Lowe's proposal about annexation of Rupert's Land to Canada, if taken up by John Roebuck, Charles Fitzwilliam, and their fellow colonial reformers, would force the company into making a public stand in defence of its interests. Ellice warned Labouchere that Lowe had picked up some 'delusive notions' in Canada and, when his friend returned, he tried to persuade him that such a drastic solution was unworkable and that monopoly had its uses in the primitive environment of the north and west.[19]

Ellice had complete success with his mission of conversion. Early in 1857 the House of Commons appointed a committee to make recommendations about the future of the Hudson's Bay Company in British North America. Lowe was a member, and it was obvious from the kind of questions he asked witnesses that he was acting as a friend of the company and was being coached by Ellice. When Ellice had his turn in the witness chair, Roebuck and other members of the committee asked him to explain how a free-trade liberal could defend monopoly. Ellice answered that monopoly could never be defended where an alternative existed. Looking over his company's holdings, he named Vancouver Island as a place where an alternative did exist. He thought Rupert's Land a different situation entirely. Responding to questions which Lowe conveniently supplied him, he gave a dismal account of the present state and the future prospects of the settlement along the Red River. He said that settlers would never flock in great numbers to the lands south of Lake Winnepeg so long as better land remained unclaimed in Minnesota to the south or Upper Canada to the east. Hardy souls who did venture into company territory along the Red River would find that their only practical route of communication with the outside world would be through the United States. He warned that if Canada undertook to administer the region, she would soon tire of the expense and ask to be relieved. If Britain decided instead to set the region up as a separate colony, then the taxpayers of Britain would be asked to make an unprofitable and dangerous investment. A military garrison would have to be established to prevent a gradual American encroachment, but that would do more harm than good; for the presence of British troops would be a provocation to American expansionists. Guided by Lowe's questioning, Ellice drew the conclusion that however much the continuance of the company's monopoly might violate the abstract doctrines of political economy, that monopoly did, nevertheless, protect the interests of British subjects and keep the peace in British North America.[20]

Before the committee made public its report in 1859, Lowe had anticipated all of its conclusions in a series of *Times* editorials and in an anonymous article for the *Edinburgh Review*. Report, editorials, and journal article all made the same point: company land should be transferred to Canada when, but not before, the colonial government demonstrated its willingness to administer the settlements made upon that land and to open communications with those settlements. This was the line Ellice wanted the government to take. He was confident that the

Macdonald coalition government in Canada would move slowly. The post-Crimean prosperity had ended in 1857, drying up revenues which might be used for territorial expansion. Thus both company officials and anti-expansionist Liberal politicians concluded that peace with the United States as well as the cause of economic retrenchment would best be served if Canada learned to recognize and come to terms with the limitations which nature had imposed on her destiny. Ellice did not explicitly point that moral although Lowe did do so on this and numerous other occasions.[21]

Once he had arrived at the premise that geography made British North America a risky investment, it was not difficult for Lowe to justify, on familiar pragmatic, utilitarian grounds, the retention of the company's special position in the western part of British North America. The question remains: how did he arrive at that premise? Friendship with Ellice must be part of the explanation. He trusted Ellice's judgment completely. He believed Ellice to be not merely a merchant prince, but 'a citizen of the world,' a man who knew more about the American continent than any other Englishman, someone who could see beyond the narrow confines of his business interests. Lowe distrusted the motives of most people but tended to exempt Ellice from the general rule about human selfishness. He was glad to assist Ellice by making inquiries during his stay in Montreal into the activities of one of the company's factors, but he never considered himself to be a company agent. Had he been acting on Ellice's instructions he would not have made the suggestion about the annexation of Rupert's Land to Canada. It seems clear that he was susceptible to Ellice's negativism about the future of British North America partly because travel through the rich lands of trans-Appelachian America had convinced him that the United States, or at least the area below the Great Lakes, was bound to become the centre of power on the continent. After his swing through what he, in 1856, considered to be the western frontier of America, he became, like Ellice, a geographical determinist.[22]

It was his stay in Chicago that convinced him that the United States would emerge as a tremendous world power. He agreed with Ellice that this would happen whether or not the economic and social tensions between north and south, east and west eventually destroyed the federal union as it then existed. What he observed on his swing through Illinois and Iowa filled him with enthusiasm. There on the frontier he thought he had found the true heart of America; there the simple, thrifty, energetic, honest people seemed free from the corruption and bigotry of the east. Open to their enterprise was a land so rich that they could expect wealth, 'like the Laird of Dimbedikes's trees, to grow while we sleep.'[23]

He must have conveyed some of this enthusiasm to the citizens of Chicago; for Delane, who followed him to that bustling, young city two months later, reported, 'Lowe seems to have created an immense sensation here. They have not done writing about him yet.' Lowe showed his sincerity by investing a large sum in the Illinois Central Railroad. That particular attempt to participate in the growth of the American heartland was not a success, but his enthusiasm for the potential greatness of this region did not weaken. When he returned home his friends could not be sure which impressed him more: the folly of America's democratic politics or the magnificent destiny which lay before her people.[24]

What chance did the British colonies of North America have to compete successfully with such a rude, exuberant giant? Little or none, Lowe thought. Canadians had most of the faults of their neighbours to the south and few of their virtues. Canadian businessmen were as scheming as Yankees, but schemed on a meaner, narrower scale. When Lord Monck, an 'innocent lamb,' left England to replace Head as governor general, Lowe predicted that the 'men of Canada would know how to put his simplicity to good account'; posting him there was like 'sending a cat into Hell without claws.' Not one single member of the Canadian government, he told Sir George Grey, could be trusted with money – so accustomed were they to fattening themselves on railway swindles. He thought that one had only to observe the history of the Grand Trunk Railway (in the process of construction during his visit) to grasp the total depravity of Canadian officialdom. The project was an 'inexpressible mess,' one vast sink of watered stock, insanely incompetent planning, scamped construction, shocking mismanagement. So long as colonial politicians could 'job and plunder ad bibitum,' so long as they could perpetuate a system as 'gross' as any ever imagined by a Walpole or a Newcastle, the public must be prepared to see railways pushed through desolate wastes, connecting nothing with nothing, to find electorates bribed with their own money, to watch tariff walls being erected against the produce of those English people who paid the bills for defences and public works. He granted that Canadian institutions had been spared by the imperial connexion from the worst absurdities of the American republic, but he thought the Canadians who worked those institutions were as petty, corrupt, and self-seeking a lot as could be found anywhere on earth.[25]

Lowe could not admit that the future might be brighter than the present. British North America also had a western frontier, but he did not think greatness lay in that direction. In many of the forty-odd leading articles he wrote on Canadian affairs during the decade after his visit and in his article on the Hudson's Bay Company for the *Edinburgh Review*, he warned Englishmen not to be optimistic about the development of the North-West Territories nor about the settlement of the forests on the far side of the Rocky Mountains. These wastes, so well looked after by the Hudson's Bay Company, constituted, he wrote, an

'American Siberia,' where dour exiles from Aberdeenshire and the Ork-
neys, 'men trained in poverty and self-denial,' extract hard-earned profits from the 'swamps, the stunted forests, the icy plains, the dreary
lakes, the obstructed rivers, and the inhospitable climate ...' There was
no reason, he thought, to offer congratulations on the birth of British
Columbia in 1858: 'Cast the horoscope of the new born infant, set the
probabilities of disease against those of health, the chances of disgrace
and misfortune against those of honour and prosperity, and who shall
say that it is a good thing that that child was born into the world; and,
still more, who shall say that it is an auspicious event for its parents.'
The timber and gold to be had there would bring no compensations to
the parent country; those resources would attract exploiters, 'trained in
the rough school of California.' These 'dregs of society' would work
their way up through the Fraser's menacing cliffs to find waiting for
them the 'crafty, bloodthirsty, and implacable savage.'[26]

Reports about Vancouver Island, 'the last and most remote of England's colonial dependencies,' did, he admitted, make it seem a gentle,
smiling place. In its capital city of Victoria, he noted approvingly, settlers could eat locally cured Yarmouth bloaters and enjoy an English
climate. But even that remote retreat, that 'picture of harmless and con-
tented industry,' could not retain her virginal innocence forever. He
warned that the light of civilization, which illumines, sooner or later,
every corner of the globe, will reach that spot and then a rush will begin
of immigrants from the American Pacific coast, people who will have
no taste for tranquility or old-country delicacies. The conclusion he expected his readers to draw from all of this was clear: what little there
was that was worth having in that great stretch of geography from the
pre-Cambrian Shield to the Pacific would go some day to the aggressive
Americans. Once the light of civilization was allowed to penetrate,
those regions would soon be lost to the British empire. Contemplation
of that loss did not give him pleasure but neither did it give him great
pain.[27]

A second conclusion followed from that first one: the Hudson's Bay
Company was a 'perfect Godsend.' Monopoly was an anachronism in
most of the civilized world, including India, but not in British North
America. In some areas settlement was possible; wherever settlers could
construct a physical base on which to construct a self-governing community, then the company should immediately relinquish control. But
until that happened, this particular monopoly was indispensable. Doctrine must stand the test of utility, Lowe maintained; the physical obstacles in the way of a continental union of British North America were
insurmountable. The project ('so much talked of and so little really believed in') for connecting the British colonies by rail and canal from sea
to sea was simply a pipe dream. Americans were entitled to dream of

manifest destiny because they had the climate, geography, and wealth to make continental union a reality. American rails would not run through thousands of miles of howling wilderness but through a settled, fertile, hinterland. Canadians might share with the people of the United States a feeling for the wide open spaces, the lure of the 'mystery of the Far West,' but rails could not rest on sentimental affinities for the 'remote and the magnificent,' or run 'where the land is bad' and where 'existence can only be supplied by the chase of a few wild animals, and by a nauseous and poisonous lichen, known by the name of Tripe de la Roche.'[28]

Lowe did not trim his free-trade convictions merely to fit the interests of the Hudson's Bay Company. If he used arguments based on geographical determinism to escape the logical conclusions of his liberal hypotheses, he at least did so consistently in all his actions and declarations having to do with North America. And in doing this he was far from unique. The writers and politicians who used geographical arguments to explain their pessimism about the future of the British empire on the North American continent were large in number and lived on both sides of the Atlantic. To a considerable extent this pessimistic school established the image in European minds of a splendid and vast, but cheerless and frozen country, an image still not entirely dissipated. Lowe was not the creator of this image, but he did make, through his journalism, a considerable contribution to it.

It was not his journalism, however, which gave Lowe a reputation for extreme Little Englandism and anti-Canadianism; since his editorials were unsigned, Canadians could only guess at their authorship. It was his public stand on the issue of Canadian defence that showed the colonists that they had a dangerous enemy in high places. The subject of defence had tended to fade into the background after the improvement in English-American relations during the later 1850s, but it returned to the centre of public attention with the outbreak of hostilities between the Federal Union and the Southern Confederacy in April 1861. Palmerston's immediate reaction to the news of General Beauregard's attack on Fort Sumter was to send reinforcements to the tiny, four-thousand-man complement of regulars who were guarding the Canadian cities. Radicals and Gladstonian economizers protested and demanded a committee for the purpose of investigating colonial expenditures. Since Australia as well as Canada would be involved in any policy changes, it was natural that the committee should ask Lowe to testify. Some of the military experts called as witnesses explained the strategic disadvantages of dispersing soldiers and naval ships all around the world at a time when affairs in Europe were dangerously unsettled; Gladstone complained of the cost; but of all those who spoke against increased military expenditures for colonial defence, Lowe was the most direct and categorical. The real question, he said, was how much England was willing to sacrifice to retain her self-governing colonies and how much these colonies were willing to sacrifice for their own self-protection. He thought it unreasonable that British taxpayers should be asked to maintain garrisons in wealthy colonies or be asked to subscribe, on the basis of some emotional appeal to honour or duty, to the defence of some indefensible spot. 'Duties,' he declared on another occasion, 'are limited by possibilities.' Naval defence, he thought a different matter. Without the promise of protection by the world's most powerful navy the colonies would soon discover that there was no 'practical utility' in retaining an imperial connexion. On the other hand, if colonists were unwilling to make any sacrifice in return for that naval protection, then they would not be worth retaining. He hoped that his questioners were 'above the vulgar notion that the mere extent of territory over which our flag waves is any increase in our strength.' Should a colony be sufficiently mature to wish to stand alone, then everything should be done to make sure that the separation be 'amicable.' Nothing, he thought, would be more certain to stand in the way of a friendly parting than the notion that British troops must be stationed on colonial territory in order to demonstrate Britain's prestige to the rest of the world. He could not help looking forward, he added, to the time when some of Britain's offspring would arrive at an independent maturity, but until such a time arrived, he believed that the home government should do everything possible to teach her colonial children to stand on their own feet. In the case of Canada, this education in maturity would be hastened by an immediate withdrawal of all British garrisons. Such a move would break no trusts; Britain had made no 'federal compact' with her colonies and was therefore free to take as hard-headed a position as Canada would surely take someday when she decided it was to her interest. 'If we go on in the present system,' he concluded, 'there is risk of reducing the Colonies to the same position to which Britons were reduced by the Romans, when they left them to the mercy of the Picts and Scots.'[29]

These forthright opinions, first expressed to the Parliamentary Committee, reappeared, only slightly toned down, on the leader page of *The Times*. The democrats of the American Northern Union, he wrote, had taken it into their heads to 'empty all the vials of their wrath on the English nation.' Fire-breathing demagogues there will almost certainly wish to heal internal discord by turning northward towards Canada. Canada would be easy prey since it had weakened itself by political corruption, the Grand Trunk fiasco, ethnic disharmony, and protectionist economic policies. But Canada's weakness was not an argument, he thought, for rushing in troops. Quite the contrary, such an action would only be a pointless challenge which the American hyper-patriots would use to their advantage. As for the British troops, they might not, after experiencing the 'monotony of Canadian life,' be entirely trustworthy; they might, he suggested, desert in large numbers, slip south across the border, and enlist under the Stars and Stripes.[30]

He made this testimony and its editorial elaboration in the spring of 1861. During that spring, *The Times* was trying to decide which side of the American struggle it should support. Four years later, when the Civil War had ended, Leslie Stephen performed a skilful autopsy on the policy of *The Times* and demonstrated how England's leading news-paper, 'like Dogberry giving judgment in a Chancery suit,' had gone about transmitting the 'popular ignorance' about American affairs into the 'language of political philosophy.' Stephen thought that *The Times* had not misled its readers deliberately but had merely stated authorita-tively what was really 'random ignorance.'[31]

Delane came eventually to agree with Stephen's judgment. He tried to pass the blame for his newspaper's wrong-headedness onto the shoul-ders of Charles Mackay and Francis Lawley, his correspondents in the field. They had, he said, 'shamefully deceived us.' Delane blamed Lin-coln's government for depriving *The Times* of a perceptive reporter. He had sent out his best man, William Howard Russell, at the beginning of the war, and this great reporter had sent home balanced accounts of what was happening. The trouble was that Russell was too accurate; his reports of the Northern disaster at Bull Run in 1861 had caused the Union government to send him packing. Mackay, who replaced him, sent out reports which were heavily biased in favour of the Confederacy. In time Delane began to detect that bias but not until the war was all but over. To leave Mackay in New York, Delane advised his assistant editor in 1865, would be 'almost a *casus belli* in itself.'[32]

John Walter, the newspaper's proprietor, also made this same excuse. Shortly after the end of the war, he wrote to Delane from New York: 'whenever I hear a remark made about the line wh a certain journal took in the war, I always reply, "Why did you send Russell away? He always stood up for the North" – which generally shuts them up.' But Walter must have known that the policy-makers at *The Times* could not be got off as easily as that. An effective reply to Walter would have been to point out that Russell had been 'tabooed' from writing on American matters after his expulsion from the United States because his belief in the eventual victory of the North did not coincide with the prejudices of the men who dictated policy at Printing House Square.[33]

Lowe was one of those prejudiced policy-makers. He shared with seven other leader writers the task of interpreting for the readers of *The Times* the course the war was taking and what the news from America meant. Between 1860 and 1865 he wrote approximately one hundred articles on the political and economic implications of the news from the correspondents in America. Delane gave Lowe and his other writers general directions about what lines to take, but it is safe to assume that the opinions Lowe expressed were his own. He and the editor had no differences of opinion on this question.

Editor and leader-writer agreed that the federal system was fundamentally faulty and could not be repaired, no matter how the fortunes of war turned. Therefore they believed the determination of the Washington government to restore the Union by force was irrational and its perseverance in that impossible attempt was perverse. But they, like all English supporters of the Confederate cause, were unsure about how to reconcile this position with their distaste for the institution of slavery. Lowe was often assigned the task of explaining to readers how liberal-minded people could at the same time abhor slavery and admire the Southern cause. This explanation called for unusual dexterity, particularly since *The Times* had taken a guardedly pro-Northern position at the commencement of hostilities. In January 1861 Lowe had written that slavery was the issue that was threatening the Union and that the South, 'enamoured of her shame,' had instigated the conflict by insisting on her right to extend slavery into the frontier regions. But when it became obvious that the opening skirmishes had settled into a full-scale civil war, the paper decided that the Federal cause was hopeless and the continuation of the war nonsensical. Therefore, in mid-March Lowe asserted that it had not, after all, been the slave owners who were responsible for the civil strife, but the 'ironmasters of Pennsylvania and the cotton-spinners of Lowell.' Northern protectionism was the real issue, he declared, not slavery. By May Lowe and *The Times* had moved one more step away from the North and towards the South. Now that the fighting had grown so intense and savage, Lowe wrote, even the economic issues had become obscured. The forces of the Federal Union were now motivated by the spirit of vengeance. In their war to the knife, Lincoln's armies had lost all sense of restraint and were even planning to loose 'millions of Negroes on their proprietors.' This was the line the paper maintained through much of the war: the South may have brought on the crisis, but the bloody-minded Northerners had provoked the holocaust of savage war. Gradually the interpretation was simplified into a formula: slavery was irrelevant; the North was fighting for empire and the South was fighting for independence and against the degradation of mob-democracy.[34]

Until Captain Wilkes pirated two Confederate diplomats, J.M. Mason and John Slidell, from a British ship, *The Times* had counselled neutrality, but when Lincoln's government refused to release the prisoners and pushed England to the brink of war, the newspaper worked to keep feelings at the boiling point. Even before the American secretary of state rejected Palmerston's stiff protest about the boarding of the *Trent*, Lowe announced his readiness to see England throw 'the whole weight of the Empire' onto the 'vibrating scales.' Privately, he was, if possible, even more bellicose. 'I agree with you in thinking that the Yankee black guards won't fight. I heartily wish they would,' he wrote to Ellice. But they did not. With the aid of the dying Prince Albert, a way was found to save American face and avert war. Lowe could scarcely conceal his disappointment. He gave the 'spoilt children of democracy' a pompous lecture on their inability 'either to persist with dignity or to yield with courtesy.'[35]

The fortunes of the Northern Union sank to their lowest point in August 1862, when General Lee overwhelmed a much larger Federal army, once again at Bull Run; after that the superior material resources of the North began to tell. By the spring of 1864, when General Sherman began his march through Georgia, most observers could see that the war must end in a victory for the Union. But Lowe was undeterred by these events. He had been demonstrating how the inflationary policies of Lincoln's ministers had necessarily to lead to ruin, and he stuck to his predictions: 'America might as well expect the law of gravitation to be suspended in her favour as to escape the inexorable Nemesis which overtakes every nation and every individual who believe in the creation of wealth from any source except honest and persevering labour.'[36]

But these demonstrations that the North was pursuing dishonourable ends by ruthless and self-defeating means could not remove the unease which pro-Southern Englishmen felt over the subject of slavery. So long as Lincoln proclaimed that the purpose of the war was to preserve the Union, not end slavery, *The Times* could argue, not unreasonably, that the points at contention were too confused to allow for clear moral judgments. But when the president issued the Emancipation Proclamation, the newspaper's writers were faced with a difficult task. That task was, more often than not, given to Lowe, the American expert. He announced that the proclamation was a cynical manœuvre made by a desperate man. He argued that since Lincoln freed only the slaves in the Confederacy, he was, in effect, making abolition a punishment and the retention of slaves a reward. Lowe refused to admit that the Northern leaders could be sincere: for all their talk about equality, they were no more willing than Southerners to sit with black men in a theatre, eat with them at table, or travel next to them in the same railway carriage. The Southern planter exploits the Negro, treats him like a domestic animal, but, Lowe asserted, feels no aversion for him. 'No the Negro has no friend. The South, which likes him best likes him only on the condition of his fulfilling the duties of a beast of burden. The North, which hates him most, is willing, indeed, to preserve him from involuntary servitude, but only on the condition of a degradation just as intolerable ...' Lincoln's true aim, he concluded, was to unleash on his enemies 'the execrable expedient of a servile insurrection.'[37]

The stereotype of the Negro found in these leading articles was typical of the period. Lowe said that experience in the West Indies showed that the black man has an 'invincible disposition to idleness' – not, perhaps, an innate quality, but the product of a long conditioning which amounted to much the same thing. But, though lazy, the Negro had a happy nature and a strong sense of loyalty and if treated decently bore towards his master a 'very hearty good will.' Lowe claimed to be impressed that the Confederates had the restraint and 'pride of race' to refuse to arm their slaves and use them against the Federal armies, for, he claimed, the slave would fight as bravely in support of servility as of liberty.[38]

This expression of admiration for Southern pride and restraint was made only five months before Lee surrendered at Appomattox in April 1865. Several weeks before that final act of the Civil War *The Times* finally conceded that the Confederacy was doomed. Delane directed Lowe and Thomas Mozley, who occasionally wrote articles on American affairs, to answer the criticisms which were pouring in from all sides. The two writers made no apologies for having misled their readers. *The Times*, they stated, had always known the North would win; the paper's only error was the tendency to underestimate the ability of the South to resist. And just possibly, they added, that brave resistance might continue after the formal end of hostilities, and the 'real contest' which might then follow could prove *The Times* right after all.[39]

When the fighting did actually stop several weeks later, the editors began searching for some more graceful means of retreat. The outpouring of sympathy at the news of Lincoln's assassination gave them a chance to make amends. Once again, Lowe was given the assignment. All through the war he had written about the president's cruelty and economic foolishness. In 1863 he said, 'Experience shows that a man who has steered a barge or split a rail may be as inveterate a foe to private liberty and public law as the descendant of a hundred Earls or a hundred Emperors.' But in May 1865 he wrote of the simple man whose 'quaint humour' and 'sterling rectitude' had touched the hearts of all the realm. Lowe called attention to the outpouring of grief that greeted the report of Lincoln's martyrdom; it showed that a substratum of good will had always existed between the two nations. England's policy in the future, he concluded, must follow the direction of that feeling and recognize that the destinies of Britain and America were inextricably tied together.[40]

It would be interesting to know if Lowe experienced any qualms of conscience at writing this. Probably not. Introspection was not his outstanding characteristic. His failure, and the failure of so many liberal politicians, to understand the issues and feelings in America resulted from the limitations of rationalist presuppositions. Lowe supposed that the federal union would break apart as soon as people came to see that their regional interests were being sacrificed in the struggle with the South. As others have pointed out, what most of the Southern sympathizers in Britain failed to comprehend was the mystical feelings Americans had about the union. Disraeli, on the Tory side, and the duke of Argyll, on the Liberal, had the imagination to understand these feelings; Lowe, manifestly, did not. To him the federal union was merely a matter of convenience, a useful *Zollverein*, a valuable 'counterpoise to democracy.' Patriotic passions occasionally worked through him and distorted his own calculations of interests and advantages; as we have seen, he lusted for blood during the *Trent* affair. But in appraising the behaviour of others he invariably fell back on his supposition that the enduring ties between men are those of practical calculation of interest and that such things as nostalgia and belief in national myths are not enduring.[41]

While the Americans were fighting each other, these assumptions led him to entertain some passing hopes that Canada might survive and prosper. His nationalistic paroxysm over the capture of Mason and Slidell produced several *Times* leaders predicting that those Yankees who marched north of the border would be met with Canadian fortitude, bred of the severe, bracing climate. But a more considered reason for optimism was his calculation that once fratricidal blood began to flow, the separate, conflicting regional interests would assert themselves and rend the union not merely into two confederacies but into three and perhaps four. He believed that the grain-growers of the West, like the Southern planters, had everything to lose and nothing to gain by the high tariffs imposed during the war by the government in Washington. Perhaps the people of the Great Lakes region would in time recognize that they could escape the exploitation and protectionism of the East by sending their raw materials out to England and continental Europe through Canada's system of lakes, railways, and rivers. If interests were indeed what brought and held groups of people together, then what undreamed-of possibilities might lie ahead for Britain's empire in North America![42]

Until a year before the war's end Lowe wrote repeatedly about this great possibility in *The Times*'s leader pages. When conflict between England and America seemed near in 1861, he explained to Ellice how essential it was to have a trained diplomatist on hand in Canada. It should not be difficult for him to arrange, in case Palmerston declared war on Lincoln's government, for England to remain at peace with New England and with the western states. If that could be done, the stage would be set to put together a mighty 'Northern Confederacy.' Settlement of the *Trent* affair did not completely destroy Lowe's hopes. He looked expectantly for signs of an 'awakening' in Illinois and Indiana. He believed that General McClellan, the Democratic candidate for president in 1864, might win those states and, perhaps, lead them out of the war and into a new alignment. But McClellan went down to overwhelming defeat. Lowe then wrote that the American democracy had passed that transition stage in history, 'through which Republics pass on their way from democracy to tyranny.' After that disappointment he said no more about the possibility of a union between Canada and the great American heartland.[43]

When it became clear to most observers in 1864 that the North would win and the Union would be reconstructed, English statesmen began, once again, to think seriously about the problem of Canadian defence. In the early days of the war Palmerston thought it 'very probable' that 'vapouring, blustering, ignorant men' like Secretary Seward might pick a quarrel with Canada to 'make up for ill success against the South.' In 1864 there was the fear that the formidable Federal army might be turned northward as a means for healing the wounds of civil war. At the urging of de Grey, the secretary for war, the British government sent Col. William Jervois, a fortification specialist, to investigate. He brought back several schemes; the second, submitted late in 1864, called for the construction of fortified 'nuclei' at Quebec, Montreal, and Kingston, around which resistance could gather. Palmerston decided to adopt this plan but to implement it cautiously. He asked Parliament to vote two hundred thousand pounds, a tiny sum in the eyes of the Canadians but far too large for the economizers. Gladstone, the chancellor of the exchequer, complained loudly in the cabinet, but was forced by ministerial discipline to keep his peace in public.[44]

Lowe was not under that constraint in 1864; he had quit his post at the Privy Council several months before the prime minister brought in his bill. He plainly stated that Britain should pull all of her troops immediately out of Canada and should make no attempt to defend the Canadian border in case of attack. Jervois's 'nucleus' would, he said, 'gather to itself a sort of vapouring mass' – the Canadian militia. And then, if colonial defenders had their way, the British government would rush in reinforcements by way of Halifax and over a ruinously expensive railway which the English public would be asked to subsidize. The British army might, if it hurried, arrive in Quebec in time to be overwhelmed by a huge invasion of American veterans and be paraded through the streets of New York and Washington as captive spoils of a Yankee triumph. He thought it time to tell Canada the truth; tell her that 'if, after well-weighed consideration, she thinks it more to her interest to join the great American Republic itself [No, no!] – it is the duty of Canada to deliberate for her own interests and her own happiness.' It was England's duty, he said, to present her with the facts, 'not as seen through the illusion of dignity and glory, and things of that sort.'[45]

If blunt words were what England owed Canada, then Lowe had been uncommonly generous. Lord Elcho praised his courageous common sense; John Bright, who had never before exchanged civilities with Lowe, spoke of the powerful effect the speech had made on the House. But government and opposition leaders expressed shock. Palmerston, excusing himself for using a play on words, said that his former minister had 'taken very low ground.' Disraeli chided Lowe for having marched the American army, over and over again, 'like the hosts of Xerxes,' through the debate. Others spoke of the chill winds that would be blowing across Canadian hearts when reports of the speech reached them, and on this occasion, at least, 'chill' was the appropriate word. George Brown wrote in his *Toronto Globe* of 'the changed feeling of England,' and urged the leaders of all the North American colonies to consider closer unity. Canadians did not rejoice at the announcement that Parliament had given Palmerston the money to build some redoubts at Quebec and send a few cannon. The speeches of Lowe and Bright, the criticisms in *The Times* and other English newspapers against the waste of money warned them that sympathy for their plight seemed to be fast diminishing in Britain. This sense of apprehension which Lowe, perhaps more than any other Englishman, helped to create was his real contribution to the realization of Canadian confederation.[46]

When the Confederation bill came up for debate in 1867, Lowe did not oppose it directly but confined himself to criticisms of the provision which would give Canada a loan guaranteed by the English government to build a transcontinental railway. If Canada wished to set herself up as a rival to the United States, Lowe said, that was no reason why Britain should insist on facilitating such an absurdity. He stressed the essential importance of peaceful relations between England and the United States. As for Canada, he trusted that the natural restraint of her people and the frigid climate (but not 'this charming railway') would protect her from invasion.[47]

Parliament approved the guarantee. When the time came for the implementation of the loan clause, two years had passed and Lowe was no longer a parliamentary independent but chancellor of the exchequer. That meant that he would be responsible for administering what he had denounced. No doubt it was more in sorrow than surprise that he discovered his former host and travelling companion, Sir John Rose, now the Canadian minister of finance, had 'misappropriated' funds sent to him from England by temporarily diverting the money to pay off high-interest debts which had been incurred for reasons entirely separate from railway building. Thus, when Rose asked for a guarantee on loans needed to reimburse the Hudson's Bay Company for surrendering their rights, the permanent officials at the Treasury, fearing a major explosion from their chief, side-tracked the request to the Colonial Office and the gentler eyes of Lord Granville.[48]

Still another request followed shortly thereafter, and this time Lowe could not be spared the unpleasantness of dealing with it. The Canadians had asked the British government to guarantee a loan for the purpose of building fortifications – Lowe's special abomination. The cabinet approved and Lowe was bound by the rules to let it go through as a Treasury measure. Opposition members, remembering Lowe's ringing denunciations of investments in 'vapouring masses,' took pleasure in inquiring into the views of the chancellor of the exchequer – who had made it a point to be absent from the House that evening. That experience did not sweeten his temper. His parting words to the marquis of Dufferin, about to embark for Canada to become the governor general, were: 'now you ought to make it your business to get rid of the Dominion.'[49]

It is likely that Lowe's doctrinaire, free-trade liberalism would have led him to this extreme Little Englandism even if he had never seen the dominion. But it does not follow that because he went to North America with a set of unshakable preconceptions he therefore learned nothing during the summer and autumn of 1856. His travels through Upper and Lower Canada, his observation of Canadian politicians, and his talks with Rose and Head sharpened his perception of the obstacles which would impede the growth of a Canadian national entity. He predicted that regionalism, the impossibility of constructing east-west communications and trade patterns, the threat of American penetration, the divisive effect of ethnic suspicions and hostilities would prevent the formation of a unified state. These predictions were exaggeratedly pessimistic, and yet they did point to questions which subsequent history has not yet satisfactorily answered.

It also seems likely that direct contact with the enormous latent power of America explains why he became, in the later 1860s and through the 1870s, one of the most outspoken advocates, outside the radical circle, of the necessity of establishing a special relationship with the United States. In one respect he was, to use an ambiguous term, profoundly anti-American. He believed Americanization to be, in the decade and a half after the Crimean War, the greatest threat to liberalism and meritocracy. His blindness to the meaning of events during the Civil War was due to his wish to see the American experiment with democracy fail. When he finally had to admit that the Union had endured its trial, he refused to concede that the victory of the Federal armies demonstrated the virtues of the democratic system. 'I never doubted its terrible warlike power,' he said. What he did doubt was the capability of its leaders to exercise a wise guardianship over the power at their command. On the other hand, he accepted that power as an inescapable fact. He believed, even while the states were torn by civil strife, that the destiny of all North America lay in the American heartland and in the hands of its energetic people. After reading de Tocqueville's interpretation and then immediately experiencing the actuality, he came away impressed with the positive as well as the negative features of American society. He admired the remarkable organizational ability of Americans at every level. He was impressed by the wisdom of the American founding fathers who had built into the constitution barriers against the direct expression of popular opinion and on several occasions shocked conservative men in all parties by recommending that England adopt some of these checks and balances.[50]

'Travel,' wrote Joseph Parkes, after welcoming Delane and Lowe back from their tour, 'puts bow windows in men's minds.' He was not sure, however, that the 'White Man' had really broadened his outlook much. This was true. Travel had not broadened him but it had, in some important respects, deepened his awareness of the forces which liberalism would have to contend with in the future.[51]

8

The Member for Kidderminster

Lowe returned from his tour in October 1856, deeply impressed by the energy of the American people and the enormous resources they could command. Earlier than most English politicians, he sensed that the United States would eventually become a great, perhaps the greatest, power in the world and that her democratic ideology would extend with her power. There were other reminders closer to home that he would have to strive for his liberal society against the tide of events. In his own constituency of Kidderminster, democracy was becoming an issue. Shortly before he started out for North America and then soon after he came back he found himself in the focus of a furious class conflict in that troubled industrial town. The missiles thrown at him by the hungry and frustrated weavers were painful reminders that the latent power of demos was beginning to awaken inside as well as outside Great Britain. The brickbats of Battery Road as well as the exuberant vitality of Chicago convinced him that a critical period was beginning for English liberalism. If, during the decade or so ahead, the logic of free trade could be applied everywhere and if the administration of government could be made efficient and modern, then it might be possible to withstand the movement of the times towards equalitarianism; but if that opportunity was missed, history, he was sure, would never provide liberals with a second chance.

In the 1920s an American scholar, Frances Gillespie, offered convincing evidence that the period immediately after the Crimean War was, as Lowe suspected, the beginning of a conscious movement on the part of the working class to achieve political democracy. She showed that there were clear indications in the election of 1857 that the period of comparative apathy which followed the failure of Chartism was at an end. In Bradford, Leeds, Liverpool, Salford, Bolton, Manchester, and many other industrial centres unenfranchised workers either induced middle class radicals to oppose the Liberal party establishment or tempted Conservatives into becoming spokesmen for the aroused workers. In many of these boroughs the radical or Conservative candidates appealed directly to the unenfranchised. They advocated more or less democratic reforms of the franchise and denounced manufacturers who broke unions and substituted machines for men in their factories. In all but a few instances the embattled conservative-liberals were elected by the ten-pound householders. Nevertheless, the price of their victories was often schism within the local Liberal organizations and a legacy of class hostility. And Kidderminster was, to a heightened degree, a case in point.[1]

It would be difficult to find a town whose history illustrates more graphically the disruption caused by the change from hand to machine industry. In the eighteenth century carpet weaving became the major occupation of this Worcestershire town. The introduction of this enterprise and the hand-loom weavers to work it was resented by the traditional town oligarchy. Proponents of the old and the new battled for political control. Violence and open corruption became so common that the town gained national notoriety. The people of Kidderminster were easily provoked to riot because their livelihoods were dependent on an industry which was particularly sensitive to any fluctuations in the economy. The depression following the Napoleonic Wars struck the town immediately and devastatingly, and competition from Scotland, where capitalists were introducing power looms, made recovery slow and sporadic even during periods of upturn in the economy. With so much capital invested in the older techniques of production and with an over-supply of desperate hand-loom weavers, it is not surprising that the Kidderminster employers were slow to follow the Scottish example and tried instead to survive by squeezing wages. Unemployed and semi-employed workers were bound together by shared miseries and a shared consciousness of who their oppressors were.[2]

It was often during the rituals of election day that these anxieties and hostilities found outlet. Experience had shown the poor that disciplined means of making their feelings known were ineffectual. In 1828 the carpet weavers and the boatmen and carpenters who served the industry went out on strike, a strike which was long, violent, and unsuccessful. Workers concluded that indirect methods might succeed better than direct ones. Accordingly they developed boycotting and intimidation into a fine art. Shopkeepers, publicans, and beer-sellers who displeased them were subjected to a custom known as 'blocking up shops.' A greengrocer or a public-house keeper who had voted on the side of the employers might find his premises surrounded and have his customers ordered out, abused, and warned not to return.[3]

Because the employers, their agents and dependents, and the regional magnate were all Liberals, it was to be expected that some of the local Conservatives – prominent among them certain barristers and solicitors who felt themselves to be excluded from the ruling clique – should try to organize and use the unenfranchised poor. In the thirties a barrister named Godson got himself elected to Parliament by saving some weavers arrested for rioting from, as a Liberal partisan put it, 'well merited punishment.' With the failure of Chartism and the victory of free trade in the late forties, Whig interests in Kidderminster saw a chance to curb this turbulence and secure the seat for their faction. They were led by the county's principal magnate, Lord Ward, who had a strong interest in law and order since he had invested heavily in a new, steam-powered, carpet works. His plan was to form a coalition of Whigs and those Tories who were worried about the effects of corruption and appeals to working class militancy. His hope was to find a candidate who had a reputation as an ardent free trader and a friend of parliamentary reform and thus recruit the radical shopkeepers into the coalition. He got in touch with Joseph Parkes in 1851. Parkes, as it happened, knew just the man to fit their requirements. Lowe's free trade credentials were impeccable, his long absence in Australia had separated him from any of the Whig factions, and his reputation as a popular candidate in Sydney would go down well with the radicals. This last point did, however, worry Parkes; he knew his friend was no democrat. All would be well if the candidate could be induced to say as little as possible on that point. But Parkes knew that sooner or later Lowe was certain to 'hoist his exact, true colours,' at which time his constituency would be likely to give trouble. Naturally, he did not pass on these reservations to Lord Ward.[4]

For the first few years as member for Kidderminster Lowe did manage to disguise his true position on franchise reform. On nomination day in 1852, his Conservative opponent expressed mock surprise that Lord Ward's nominee did not come dressed in a tricolour. He warned the radicals that their favourite would not remain true to their interest; in Australia he had changed his principles three times. Lowe answered by saying that sixty thousand voters in Sydney had shown their belief in him. This was a safe formula; Lowe could avoid commitment to parliamentary reform in England and yet preserve his standing in Kidderminster by referring to his record as a friend of franchise reform in New South Wales. Unless pressed, he need not mention that the reasons which made him a reformer on one side of the world made him cool towards parliamentary reform at home. He could not, however, keep up that deception. For one thing it was impossible for him to hide for long his true opinions; he had an irrepressible expostulatory urge. Also, his silence during the debate on Lord John Russell's Reform bill of 1852 was noticed by his radical constituents. His acceptance of office under Aberdeen, his subsequent criticism of the way the coalition had managed the war, and then his acceptance of office under Palmerston annoyed other elements – so much so that Delane was worried about his chances when he submitted himself for re-election in 1855. He feared that troublemakers might unleash the 'drunken carpet weavers,' made desperate by the threat to their jobs from Lord Ward's steam looms. For the moment, however, concern about the angry temper of the workers held the coalition together, but there were signs that peace would not last much longer. A solicitor named William Boycott, son of one of the county's leading Tories, had attempted to contest the seat. He contributed generously and publicly to relief collections for the unemployed, denounced the high price of bread, and told the weavers, who had come to his meetings in large numbers, that they deserved to have the franchise. Lowe was equally forthright. 'If you want money, beer, flattery, mob oratory, and clap-trap,' he shouted above the jeers of an unfriendly crowd, 'you must go to another shop.' Fearing trouble, Mayor Kiteley hired special constables to back up the borough police on polling day, but the danger passed when Boycott decided at the last moment to withdraw. Although Lowe was re-elected without contest, everyone in Kidderminster knew that they had not heard the last of Boycott.[5]

1855 had been a bad year for the carpet trade; 1857 brought some improvement, although not enough to relieve the chronic distress. The factories were open but, thanks to Lord Ward's improvements, needed fewer hands. Where steam looms had not been installed, the operatives found that they had to compete for wages with an ever increasing reservoir of unemployed. The largest factory in town, managed by James Pardoe, still used the old methods and had kept going by steadily applying the squeeze. Trade was unusually brisk in February, yet the mayor's charitable fund was keeping 290 weavers and their families alive. Given these conditions, it is not surprising that by 1857 William Boycott had become the hero of the poor and that Pardoe had become the most unpopular man in town. It should be noted that Pardoe was the local Liberal leader and Lowe's parliamentary agent.[6]

Boycott knew how to exploit the wide-spread hatred of Pardoe and the other mill owners. In the interval between Lowe's election in 1855 and the general election of 1857, the Tory solicitor had run successfully for the town council and, as alderman, had repeatedly denounced the evils of the poor law and proposed a graduated income tax with exemptions for wage-earners with small incomes. He spoke feelingly of the growing estrangement between rich and poor in the community and the indifference of masters to the life of their workmen once the factory doors were closed. He explained that it was this indifference to the obligations imposed by wealth and privilege which allowed the majority of Conservatives to form an unholy alliance with radical shopkeepers, Unitarian businessmen, and heartless mill owners. The selfish had joined together with the frightened, he said, to keep in Westminster a man whom almost everyone disliked, a man who had contempt for charity, and a man who was indifferent to local issues.[7]

In all of these charges against Lowe, Boycott was correct. When approached in his Whitehall office for a contribution to the mayor's relief fund, the member for Kidderminster had made several small, grudging donations, accompanied with a lecture on the futility and wastefulness of charity and the observation that the length of a politician's purse was no measure of his usefulness to the poor. No one found this gesture endearing, especially since Lowe had not bothered to visit his riding and make a show of personal interest. He must, however, have kept sufficiently in touch with local feelings to know that he was in for an ordeal at the next election.[8]

He could have avoided it had he chose. A group of wealthy businessmen in Manchester decided to overthrow Bright and Milner Gibson and collected £16,000 for the purpose. They approached Lowe and offered to pay all of his expenses if he would agree to oust Bright and his clique of pacifists and democrats. They were attracted to Lowe because of his campaign to take the collection of port dues away from Liverpool and because of his well-known antipathy to Manchester School radicalism. Had he accepted he probably would have been elected, since Bright and Gibson went down to defeat on a wave of patriotic indignation against their opposition to the Crimean War. Why he refused this opportunity is not clear. He told the delegation that he was 'bound in gratitude' to his present constituents, 'from whom he had always received the utmost kindness and confidence,' but that could not have been the reason. Obviously he did not relish the prospect of contesting a large borough and suffering the indignities of active campaigning; he had not enjoyed the restrictions which his Sydney constituents had tried to put on his independence during his last year in Australia. The non-electors in Kidderminster might give him some unpleasant hours on the hustings but after that necessary inconvenience he could safely go on about his business as a statesman.[9]

When he boarded his train for Kidderminster in mid-March 1857, Lowe knew that he would return the elected representative. There were some five hundred voters in the borough of whom all but one hundred and sixty were perfectly safe. Like other good Palmerstonians, he would make speeches in defence of England's honour against those hypocritical moralists who were denouncing the prime minister for his high-handedness in China. 'The sword,' Lowe shouted to a large audience assembled in the Music Hall, and not 'Quaker counsels' had won the empire and only by the sword would it be maintained – words he could not have remembered in later years with pleasure. He did refer briefly to the main issue, unemployment, but only to offer a comfortless nostrum: increase the flow of emigration to Australia.[10]

In front of the Junction Inn thousands of excited workingmen, accompanied by their wives and children, were cheering for Boycott and the right to work and strike. Prominent on the platform were representatives of Kidderminster's one hundred and fifty public houses and beer shops. One reason why they were on Boycott's side was that the Licensed Victuallers had sent out an appeal calling on publicans to oppose government supporters. The Victuallers were apprehensive that Palmerston's ministers might approve a committee recommendation that the liquor trade be thrown open to anyone, without need of licences. In fact there was no chance that Palmerston would act on the report but there was substance to the suspicion that Lowe would like to see free trade established in beer and gin, as in everything else. When the Victuallers had approached him with a request to support their petition to extend Sunday closing hours, they were coldly told that as a government minister and an MP he was a public servant, not a beer lobbyist. The result was that, except in the more respectable places of refreshment where Lord Ward's discipline could reach, the pubs of Kidderminster were rallying grounds for Boycott. Publicans could deliver seventy votes from among their own number for the popular candidate and they could dispense with their beer accounts of the miserly heartlessness of Pardoe and his candidate.[11]

Seeing how things were going and assuming that Boycott would not retire this time, Mayor Kiteley once again hired seventy or eighty 'specials' to bolster the regular police force of twenty. These precautions were clearly necessary. Several days before the two candidates were to be presented for nomination Lowe had lost his temper when a shouting, pushing crowd of two thousand had prevented him from speaking. He had told them to mind their manners and had called them 'children.' Thus when he climbed onto the hustings to be nominated, there were angry shouts of 'children, children' from the throng gathered around the semicircle of police. The mayor had ruled that no brass bands could be present, but the crowd, according to a witness, made its own 'discordant sounds' and roared like 'a powerful organ, with all the stops open, all the keys down, and a steam engine at work at the bellows.' Only occasionally did the voices of Lowe and Boycott break through the din, but when the crowd sensed that they had been asked to express their preference, they raised their hands for the friend of the workingmen. The mayor then called for a poll the following day, to be held on Blakeway Green. A small scuffle ensued, after which the two camps retired to their respective pubs to prepare for the next day's ceremony. That night men milled through the streets shouting 'Boycott for ever' or 'Lowe for ever.' They overturned tables and landed blows. After midnight, when Boycott's forces heard that some of their voters had been imprisoned in the enemy headquarters at the Swan Inn, they sent a band of weavers to break in the door and smash the windows.[12]

When the polls opened the next morning, most of the factory operatives were at work, so all was quiet. By noon Lowe had a comfortable lead. There could be no doubt that he would win by a wide margin. Had it been a full working day it is likely that the polls would have closed without incident; but it was a Saturday, and the mills shut down at 2:00 PM. When the closing whistles blew, a ring of workingmen and their families began to form around the tent in the middle of the green. Late voters who wore 'decent coats' and were taken to be Lowe supporters had to walk a gauntlet of threats and insults. Although constables had cleared the grounds of stones, some of the more aggressive members of the crowd brought their own supply and began pelting the tent. One of Boycott's men asked the hooligans to stop but provoked instead a heavy volley. This, Lowe's supporters later charged, had been his intention. A few minutes before the polls closed, Boycott offered to provide Lowe's party with an escort so that they could retire in safety, but Pardoe, who was certain that the demonstration had been well rehearsed, proudly and unwisely refused. At that the defeated candidate, bowing and smiling, departed, leaving the victor, as *The Times* put it, to the mob's 'deadliest vengeance.'[13]

At 4:00 PM Mayor Kiteley closed the poll and read the result, to the accompaniment of hisses and groans. Then Lowe and his party linked arms and led by the mayor and the chief constable began their retreat down the two hundred and fifty yards of Battery Road. On all sides there were shouts of 'Kill the bastard; kill the pink-eye!' But for the first fifty yards they advanced without great difficulty. The fusillade began when they came to the spot where the road cut through a ten-foot-high embankment, lined twenty deep with furious men and women. Stones and pieces of brick rattled off top hats like 'hailstones on a roof.' Every step of the way men were falling to the pavement. Young boys raced along beside the procession throwing rocks up into the downturned faces. The 'specials' quickly faded away into the rear while the 'regulars' stumbled ahead, all of them streaming with blood. When they fell they were savagely kicked.[14]

Fortunately, the Reverend John Sheppard, headmaster of the grammar school and a staunch Liberal, lived in a house at the end of the cut. An iron gate, surrounded by a high wall, opened onto Battery Road. Sheppard opened the gate and helped to drag Lowe inside, his hat riddled with holes 'from which the blood flowed down the brim and then ran out like rain.' Someone summoned a physician who managed to get through to the patient because the mob heard that their prey had escaped through a back way to the Albert Inn and had stormed off to 'do for him.' Lowe was safe but his skull was fractured and he was covered with bruises. When darkness came friends spirited him away and out of town. Frustrated in their attempt to kill Lowe, the rioters poured through the streets, 'bonnetting' all the well-dressed pedestrians whom they discovered in the open and assaulting anyone who did not respond to cries of 'Boycott for ever.' At midnight a train from Birmingham brought part of a troop of the 10th Hussars. Protected by soldiers, the mayor read the riot act to gangs of men who were smashing the windows of Lion's Hotel, but even this show of force did not immediately quell the anger of the men in the streets. It was not until the early hours of Sunday morning that quiet finally came to the town. By then hundreds of rioters and citizens who had got in the way were cut and bruised about the head and face. None of the town police escaped injury. Constable Jukes, who suffered a broken nose and a severe skull fracture, died in hospital.[15]

Newspaper readers on Monday morning learned that the wicked old days of election day violence were not quite over. The queen wrote to King Leopold that her Kidderminster subjects had 'behaved shockingly' and had come near to taking Lowe's life. The Liberal press called the incident a 'Tory riot,' blaming Boycott and his backers for having incited the weavers to murder. No one, not even the radicals, bothered to ask themselves why the people of Kidderminster had behaved so furiously and savagely.[16]

Lowe recovered quickly and tried to make light of the incident; the Kidderminster Liberals, however, were not in a mood to forgive and benefit from the inevitable reaction of sympathy in their favour. The police had arrested most of the more conspicuous rioters – mainly weavers, bargemen, and bricklayers. They were brought before the magistrate who, wishing to give the town a chance to cool down, held over the trials until the next spring's assizes, but Pardoe, who had also had his head broken, was determined not to let matters rest. He formed a committee to raise money to collect evidence and to bring an indictment against two of Boycott's more respectable supporters on the charge that they had deliberately planned the murderous attack on 28 March. In reply, a defence committee covered the town with placards calling on workers to give subscriptions in support of their persecuted brothers. As it turned out Pardoe was cheated of his revenge. Witnesses against Boycott's associates were, in some cases, jeered at in the streets, threatened, and beaten up, and when the case came to trial, the prosecutors discovered that they had insufficient evidence to make a case. By the time the arrested workingmen came before the judges in 1858, the mood of the citizens had set so strongly against Pardoe that the counsel for the defence, a Mr Huddlestone, was able to get suspended sentences for all the rioters.[17]

Lowe did receive an address of sympathy, signed by three hundred leading citizens, and replied by stoutly pledging that no threat of physical violence could deter him from their service so long as it was required. Yet when the next election took place, following Lord Derby's defeat in 1859, he decided not to contest Kidderminster. His explanation, expressed in a private letter, was that his agents had done a canvass of the voters and could not promise him an easy victory. Pardoe's vindictiveness had caused the coalition to break up. Even the Tory clergy preferred to return to the corruption and disturbances of the past rather than ally themselves with the prosecution committee. When, only two weeks before polling day, Lowe announced his decision to withdraw, he tried to find some consolation. 'I have at any rate,' he wrote to a friend, 'baulked them of the saturnalia which they promised themselves, and I hope exonerated Mr. Huddlestone, the Conservative candidate, from the payment of the eighty-four bribes which I am told he promised.'[18]

Loss of support cannot be entirely blamed on the Kidderminster Liberals; Lowe, himself, alienated the radicals by speaking openly against franchise reform. It is significant that on his first visit to Kidderminster after the riot, in December 1858, he deliberately chose to 'hoist his exact, true colours' on a question that a more circumspect politician, dependent on an uneasy coalition, would have avoided. The progress of civilization since the passage of the Reform Act of 1832 had, he declared to another gathering at the Music Hall, made reform less, not more, necessary. A network of telegraph and rails had, since then, drawn England together into one metropolis. A consequence of this had been to focus and increase the power of public opinion. In 1832 the sponsors of franchise reform had desired to break down aristocratic monopolies, an objective the intervening years had brought within reach of being realized; now the constitution must perform a different function: it must prevent the abuse of this continually expanding and increasingly articulate popular power. A few modest changes – the disfranchisement of the remaining pocket boroughs, the equalization of the county and borough franchises – might prove useful, so long as they did not give encouragement to those dangerous men like Bright who wished to Americanize England. He perhaps knew more of the realities of America than did Bright, Lowe reminded his audience: Bright had never been to the United States, while he had, himself, only recently returned from a visit there. He could testify that the American experience proved conclusively that liberal progress and democratic passion were antithetical. A group of Chartists in the rear of the hall had been making disturbances throughout this part of the speech so he turned to them and said: 'I know the hostility that I ... provoke, and am prepared to meet the consequences, for those are principles that I cannot and dare not trifle with.'[19]

The consequences he had in mind on that occasion were most likely the loss of the support of more Liberal electors and certain defeat at the next contest. Two weeks before the election in April 1859 it became clear that some Liberals would put a higher priority on the national issue of reform than on a local party victory. Lowe withdrew when he recognized that fact. This left Pardoe in an awkward position. He finally persuaded an election agent named Alfred Bristow to stand against Huddlestone. After Bristow made a speech to the weavers, promising to work for franchise reform and a secret ballot, five hundred non-voters signed a document of support and a committee of workingmen canvassed sympathetic voters. The result surprised everyone. Bristow won the election by eight votes and held the seat for the Liberal party.[20]

This victory was a minor humiliation for Lowe. He affected to interpret this turn of events to the power of mendacity over honest virtue, but he must have known better. If the voters of Kidderminster were to be swayed by the organized public opinion of the majority of the citizens of the town, then that constituency and places like it were unsuitable for a man of liberal rectitude. He looked for a refuge and found one. Lord Lansdowne offered him the borough of Calne, a Wiltshire town which had entirely escaped from the attacks on pocket boroughs in 1832. To accept a sinecure from the hands of its noble owner would be bound to cause a certain amount of embarrassment to someone who prided himself on being a crusader against privilege. He could expect jibes to be made. As Bright was later to remark, Lansdowne might, if he chose, have sent to Parliament his butler or his groom. But jibes could be borne more easily than brickbats and intimidation, and Lansdowne would impose no restraints on his freedom except the necessity of acting intelligently and forthrightly in the public service. Lowe had learned by the experience of the last two years that the threat to his independence would come from below, not above. That being so, he accepted the offer gratefully. 'Fortune,' he wrote to a friend, 'has not wholly forgotten me.'[21]

Calne proved to be less of a quiet bower than he had supposed. When he mounted the hustings as Lord Lansdowne's nominee, a clergyman asked him whether he believed a widower should be allowed to marry his deceased wife's sister. Since there was no contest, the mayor ruled that awkward question out of order. The vicar then made a contest by nominating the proprietor of a local flax factory. The nominee accepted, the show of hands went in his favour, and, therefore, a poll had to be taken. Under the watchful eyes of Lord Lansdowne's agents, Lowe won easily. When they heard the announcement, the mob chased the constable into the town hall and ransacked the police station. As Bright took pleasure in remarking, it seemed that 'there are men who make discord wherever they appear.'[22]

Discord at Calne and Kidderminster Lowe took to be signs, not of any personal failings, but of significant changes in the temper of the nation. In a *Times* leading article he expressed his concern that the political process was breaking down in this new atmosphere: 'A contested election is a glorious thing while it lasts, but everybody knows that it bequeaths unpleasant legacies in the shape of broken heads, personal animosities, and a very long account to settle.' He concluded that politicians who wished to be representatives rather than delegates and who had the courage and character to risk unpopularity for the general good would in the future find themselves subjected to the same indignities he had recently endured. This conclusion had not come to him suddenly. The ordeal in Battery Road was, nevertheless, a painful reminder that liberalism's period of crisis was beginning. This sense of urgency as well as the move from boisterous Kidderminster to the dignified patronage of the Lansdowne circle prepared the way for his rebellion against his party on the reform issue in 1866. But that feeling and that change of circumstance did not make rebellion inevitable. He did not reject his party's leadership until they had, in his eyes, first used and then rejected him.[23]

9

The Era of 'Practical Liberality'

When Lowe returned to Parliament in 1859 as member for Calne he was optimistic about the chances of creating a liberal society strong enough to withstand the challenge of democracy. By drawing together the conflicting elements of his party during that year, Palmerston had provided what 'moderate men of progressive views' believed to be essential: an executive arm of government strong enough to override the self-interested factionalisms, the aristocratic arrogance and obscurantism, and the radical dogmatism which had impeded the progress of the nation since Peel's death. Practical liberals were by definition opposed to fundamental or organic reform in the future because they believed all of the prerequisites for the construction of a modern society had been achieved with the reform of the old constitution and the acceptance of the principle of free trade in the first half of the century. They were convinced that the factories, the railways, the telegraph, the advance of science, the awakened intelligence of the previously inert masses were rapidly making snobbery, deference, traditionalism, and sentimentality obsolete and irrelevant. But they feared that the political system might prove to be too sluggish or too faction-ridden to react to the facts of change. Because of short-sightedness or the stupidity which traditionalism engenders, those with power might hang on too long to their monopolies, privileges, and cosy family arrangements. Aristocratic politicians might be so obsessed by the right of property that they would resist the modification of those inheritance laws which prevented efficient management; they might continue to allow endowments made by mediaeval burgers, in fear of their souls, to set the curriculum of the nation's schools; they might, out of love for the archaic, permit the youth of the governing class to grow up entirely innocent of the world of technology and specialization. Worst of all, they might permit the socialists, the

democrats, and the Manchester School dogmatists to become the natural leaders of the lower middle classes and of the masses. Lowe, Ellice,
Parkes, and Cornewall Lewis had met often on country weekends to
discuss these matters. Occasionally they invited Lowe's patron, Lord
Lansdowne, to meet with them. But before Palmerston began to assert
his affable, pragmatic leadership over the political life of the nation, the
men of the Ellice circle had met to deplore as much as to plan. Now
that the great liberal mechanism had, at last, found its driver, those
with moderate progressive views could look forward to an era of 'practical' reform.

Lowe's optimism was generalized; when he came to assess his own
position, he could see nothing but a kind of distinguished apprenticeship stretching ahead of him. Because the prime minister had to give the
Peelites, the radicals, and the followers of Lord John Russell their due,
he could not spare offices for those whose only claim was efficient and
loyal past service. As Lowe ruefully noted in a *Times* leading article,
this ship of state, 'like a first rate American yacht,' has been built to
win a race, at the sacrifice of 'symmetry, beauty, comfort, everything ...'
Lowe's own sacrifice was to accept the vice-presidency of the Board of
Education at the Privy Council, a subordinate office in a hard working
and non-glamorous branch of the administration. Chichester Fortescue
was amused to hear Lowe fume at the dinner table that he had heard
nothing from Palmerston and would certainly not take the Education
Office and then to learn the next day that he had taken it. Merit, it
seemed, like symmetry, had once more to give way to the 'domination
of cliques and coteries.' Angrily, Lowe reflected that the group of Whigs
who controlled his fate was ready to grant him almost anything so long
as it was out of England. Had he been a radical he might have been
co-opted, 'but for a man of moderate views the Cabinet was closed.'
They would be sure to call him in if they had some complicated bill to
shove through, some tedious committee work to do, or some particularly unpleasant assignment to perform. 'My kind friends seem ready to
give me anything in the world,' he wrote to Ellice, 'except what I want.'
When, on another occasion, Delane reported that the government leaders had spoken well of him but regretted that they had no promotion to
offer him at the moment, Lowe replied, bitterly: 'It is very pleasant to
me who am never hardly mentioned but to be abused to hear any good
of myself. Only I hope they will consider this – I have no great friends
to oblige no party to please by my promotion. If I am worth putting
in at all it is to do work too hard or too dangerous for aristocratic
hands.'[1]

Hard and dangerous work was certain to be the lot of any man who
accepted the vice-presidency in the mid-Victorian period. The Privy
Council had become a dumping ground during the first half of the cen-

tury for any newly-developed governmental function which did not fit neatly into a traditional category. Russell had used an Order-in-Council to establish Kay-Shuttleworth's Privy Council Committee of Education in 1839. When parliamentary reactionaries struck down Edwin Chadwick's General Board of Health, many of its functions submerged to appear again in the late fifties in the Privy Council. Lord Granville, who had accepted Palmerston's offer to be the Lord President, was one aristocrat who was willing to soil his hands with hard work, but he had also undertaken to be the majority leader in the House of Lords and therefore was glad to turn most of the responsibilities of his department over to his subordinates. For all his protests to the contrary, this suited Lowe perfectly, especially when he discovered that the permanent officials he would be associated with in the Privy Council were the same kind of 'true votaries' he had worked with so harmoniously at the Board of Trade. One of them, Henry Cole, the energetic head of the Department of Science and Art, noted in his diary: 'first Board with Mr. Lowe who was very intelligent indeed.' One of Cole's inspectors commented: 'Mr. Lowe differs greatly from our late sub-chief, Mr. Adderley; Mr. Lowe is very shrewd, sees the real point at once, and decides on principle and not on detail.' The other important secretaries, Ralph Lingen and John Simon, were also relieved and delighted to find that they had a new superior who seemed ready to act decisively on matters they brought to him. Lowe, while insisting that he knew nothing about teacher training, pottery design, cattle diseases, or sewage disposal, immediately commenced searching for ways to simplify and enlarge his duties. In some ways the vice-presidency was the perfect place for a person who believed that the heroic period of liberalism was past and the commonplace, practical work of extending its principles was beginning.[2]

Lowe's activities at the Board of Trade had already proved to him that the old administrative system as it existed before the introduction of a competitive civil service could do impressive amounts of constructive work and attract men who were not only highly educated but filled with confidence in the universal applicability of their nostrums. He probably would have been willing to admit privately that the irrational organization and jurisdictional confusion characteristic of the old system provided positive advantages to clever, dedicated public servants. The best illustration of the truth of this is the impressive expansion of the national health services which took place because Lowe gave John Simon protection and room to innovate. This chapter will attempt to show that Lowe's contempt for red tape and his respect for expert knowledge and individual initiative greatly improved the general welfare; a later chapter will give comfort to those who argue that the public can be injured as well as served by a disdain for procedures.

Towards the end of his career Sir John Simon published an account of how the government came to accept an ever widening responsibility for the nation's health. In his *English Sanitary Institutions* and in a short tribute, included in A.P. Martin's biography of Lowe, Simon spoke of the debt he owed his political superior and champion. Not only the Privy Council staff but a great many of the leading members of the medical profession were repeatedly impressed, Simon wrote, by Lowe's ability 'almost intuitively' to see what was needed and by his 'generous indignation' on behalf of the poor, weak, and ignorant. Had Simon said 'sympathy,' he would have aroused our scepticism; 'generous indignation' gives his tribute the authentic touch. Lowe's sympathies were seldom with the weak. But he could be roused by what he took to be injustice and irrationality.[3]

Like most educated mid-Victorians, Lowe was respectful towards science, so long as it kept within its own preserve. As a young man he had once gone for a walk with Charles Darwin and had been exhilarated by the experience. As soon as the *Origin of Species* came out he and Georgiana read it and wrote about it to their friends. Another naturalist, William Sharp Macleay, Lowe's closest friend in Sydney, revealed to him a world which Winchester and Oxford had ignored. He came to resent this snobbish prejudice against scientists, nevertheless he did retain a classicist's disdain for the idea that science could usefully be applied to human behaviour. Some months after coming to the Privy Council he wrote to Cole: 'Of Art and Science I know very little and for the pretensions of the so called Social Sciences I have the greatest contempt.' His experience with physicians who had prescribed such strange remedies for his eyes and who had sentenced him to blindness inclined him to extend that contempt to medicine as well. He confessed to his fellow classicist, Cornewall Lewis, that he had 'imbibed' most of his notions about doctors and their arts from Moliere's *Malade Imaginaire*. He asked Lewis to reflect on how many lives must be sacrificed each day by 'men acting upon that as a Science which is really no Science at all.'[4]

When he wrote this he was in the process of preparing himself to introduce the Public Health bill of 1859. Pro-forma advocacy changed into enthusiastic conversion as soon as he encountered the obscurantist tactic of the bill's opponents. Under the tutelage of Simon, he became the leading exponent in the House of Commons of the need to utilize the findings of medical science in the framing of new laws. Some of the legislation he put through, compelling mothers to vaccinate their children and empowering health officials to take drastic action when epidemics struck, would seem draconic if enacted in a twentieth-century welfare state. Once involved with Simon in the struggle to purify the water, dispose of urban waste, eliminate smallpox, and control the sale and labelling of poisons, Lowe entirely lost his anti-statist inhibitions. 'Sheridan,' he once remarked, 'when he saw a Highlander in a very large pair of trousers, said that converts were always enthusiastic.'[5]

Simon believed that the 1859 bill marked a turning-point in the history of public health in Britain. During the previous Derby ministry Simon had managed to persuade the government to put through several bills which the ministers responsible apparently only dimly understood. By their provisions the medical officer and his staff were moved over to the Privy Council with extended powers of inquiry and report. On the surface these measures seemed to be concessions to the anti-bureaucrats for they abolished the Board of Health (the 'Board of Pelf,' its fanatical critic, Tom Duncombe, called it) and left to the local Poor Law guardians the option of deciding which regulations they would apply in their communities. The guardians were now to be the ones who initiated prosecution proceedings against people who did not comply with stringent, nearly unenforceable, compulsory vaccination regulations. These concessions pleased but did not disarm the anti-centralists, most of whom were radical representatives of large municipalities with slum landlords and rate-payers' associations to placate. When the Tory government tried to give the medical officer permanent status and permanent emergency epidemic powers, Tom Duncombe and his allies set up such a howl that the sponsors made a 'grotesque compromise' and agreed that the office and its powers would come under annual review. Simon knew that before he could make any progress in setting up systematic proceedings, he would need to secure relief from this handicap. Thus he looked on the fall of the Conservatives in 1859 and the appointment of Lowe as a godsend. His new chief agreed at once that permanency was essential and promptly sent the appropriate bill to the Commons. This he did before Simon had even begun to convert him to a belief in the wonders of state medicine. What appealed to him was Simon's plea for freedom from red tape and a degree of immunity from harassment by politicians and interest groups. Lowe saw that Simon was an admirable professional who knew how to get things done and determined to clear his path. There could be 'no parsimony more miserable, and no jealousy of power more displaced,' he told the House of Commons, than to shackle detached and expert men to 'the many local elements of prejudice, ignorance, and self-interest.'[6]

Lowe got the bill through although the margin was narrow. On the surface at least the Tories divided against the bill because they did not wish the state to interfere in areas where individual liberties might often be trampled on. But that could not have been the only consideration. Few of them had made any protest when Spencer Walpole, the Conservative home secretary in 1858, had asked that the Medical Office be made permanent. Walpole had withdrawn his request as a concession to the big city Liberals and not in response to opposition from his own party. Therefore it is probable that the party leaders decided, at the last minute, to send their followers into the lobby against the bill in order to humiliate Lowe and embarrass the government. No one had forgotten how Palmerston had abandoned his unpopular junior minister only a few years previously over the issue of the shipping dues. Another chance to remind the rural squirearchy of 'musty parchments' seemed to be at hand. They noticed that Palmerston, who had been an energetic home secretary during the Aberdeen coalition and had been keen about sanitary reform, had shown no interest in the Privy Council bill. There is no reason to suppose that the prime minister intended any disloyalty; he was distracted by the exciting events taking place in Italy. But Lowe could sense that he was exposed and in for trouble before the division took place. As a result he made an effort to be polite and conciliatory, to the extent that Acton Smee Ayrton, radical member for the Tower Hamlets and a ferocious economiser, complimented the vice-president on his 'exceedingly temperate manner' – an implied sneer which brought a laugh. Possibly this unaccustomed effort to be agreeable (a severe trial whenever Ayrton took part in a debate) saved Lowe from another defeat and saved the Medical Office. As it was, the bill survived only because the Liberal whip was able, after the division bell had rung, to round up six members who had been chatting outside the chamber. Had the bill not passed by that six-vote majority, Lowe might have been remembered by his permanent officials not as the successful expeditor of legislation to control epidemics and remove sewage, but as the unfortunate politician who inadvertently caused the temporary breakdown of the public health service.[7]

That close call greatly increased Lowe's ardour. He gave consistent and vital support to Simon in his successful attempts to enlarge the functions of his office and to gain for it a remarkable degree of autonomy. One of the reasons why Lowe trusted Simon so completely was that they both shared the same minimalist assumptions about the place of government. Since they agreed on the general proposition that the least government is best, they thought they could, in good conscience, depart from that hypothesis when it came to specific exceptions. And they had the authority of Adam Smith and other classical economists to support them in their contention that health was an exception to the general rule; it was one of those fields in which private enterprise could not be expected to harmonize private greed and public good. A leader Lowe wrote for The Times in 1865 asked why medical science had not kept step with progress in other branches of science and in other professions. He concluded that the reason was that the physicians had been allowed to 'go their own way without attention.' The profession would become healthy and medicine would begin not merely to observe but to 'interrogate' nature only when doctors and medical scientist were forced by government action to look outside the narrow confines of private practice and to see health as a national and a political as well as a clinical problem. Lowe and Simon believed that liberals could be trusted to guide this extension of the government's welfare role because they alone understood why they were departing from a general principle and therefore could be trusted not to confuse the exception with the rule. Tories, they were sure, could not be trusted. Disraeli had made *Sanitas*, *sanitatum, omnia Sanitas* his motto, but Lowe did not grant for a moment that he might be sincere. When a Tory administration began in the later seventies to restrain the growth of the Medical Office, Lowe quipped that what Disraeli had really meant was not *Sanitas*, but *Vanitas*, or, perhaps, *Vanus*, meaning 'empty.'[8]

In their campaign against smallpox, Simon and Lowe demonstrated how far they were willing to go in promoting state intervention. The 1859 bill contained a clause which would have given Poor Law guardians authorization to pay for the prosecution of those who refused to co-operate with compulsory vaccination laws. This came under heavy attack in Parliament and Lowe, saying that he was 'no friend of compulsory vaccination,' dropped it. A smallpox epidemic broke out several months later. Local authorities proved unwilling and unable to compel parents in infected areas to take their children to the often untrained vaccinators. Simon's professional inspectors brought in statistics, showing these shortcomings and giving estimates of the lives that might have been saved had the clause, which had been dropped as a gesture of conciliation, been carried into law. The statistics made Lowe a friend of compulsion. In 1861 he took the initiative in reinstating the clause, saying that it was a bitter reflection that had he been less tractable in 1859, thousands of children would not have died. He delivered a stern lecture to Duncombe and Ayrton: 'It would be profaning liberty, self-government, and independence to say that any man has a right to set up his own sordid or brutal prejudices against such opinions as those I have quoted to the exposure of his child to disease and death.' When he finished, the House approved the clause without difficulty.[9]

As might be expected, the officials of the Privy Council soon came to the conclusion that it did little good to increase the powers of the local authorities without at the same time increasing the supervisory and enforcement powers of the central government. Simon supplied statistics to show that this was true and convinced all but the most obdurate. Impressed by the power of numbers to overcome prejudices, Lowe moved that data on the causes of death be laid before Parliament once a year. This action considerably enlarged the scope of the department's work; the annual document the statisticians prepared came to be known as 'Lowe's Return.'[10]

Lowe's assistance did not cease when he left the Privy Council in 1864. In 1866 he persuaded a Select Committee to recommend that subsidies be paid to the vaccinators according to the number of successful vaccinations they performed. This 'payment by results' principle, then dear to Lowe's heart, proved to be a way to expand the department's influence; by employing it, the central authority could issue regulations and administer examinations and yet not appear to be responsible for the means by which the grants could be earned. Lowe also got behind a bill which stemmed from this same Select Committee report, calling for a consolidation of the provisions of the many vaccination acts passed over the years. The surprising feature of this act was a clause requiring magistrates to jail vaccination defaulters and to prosecute them again should they fail to comply on release – a measure similar to the notorious 'cat and mouse' provision used against suffragettes before the First World War. Like many other mid-Victorian liberals, Lowe was perfectly willing to force people to be free so long as the subjects of the action were poor and presumably incapable of helping themselves and so long as free economic enterprise did not seem to be endangered.[11]

Lowe also made sure that Simon received friendly treatment from *The Times*. The first great champion of public health, Edwin Chadwick, had to endure years of unrelenting abuse from that newspaper; Simon was never mentioned without words of praise. A favourable press was, of course, a great advantage to his cause. But Simon needed a powerful political sponsor even more than friendly publicity if he were to achieve his main object: a separate, professional, and semi-autonomous ministry of health. It was good luck for him, therefore, that Lowe was chancellor of the exchequer from 1868 to 1873. During those years most applicants for new appropriations trembled at the thought of confronting the terrible Lowe and his even more terrible subordinate, Ralph Lingen. But all was cordiality where Sir John Simon was concerned. Repeatedly the chancellor of the exchequer overruled the fanatical Lingen over Medical Office requests. Simon got in instalments most of what he wanted: more staff, more money, and more independence. By 1869 Lowe could note with satisfaction: 'Mr. Simon's department consists of himself.' To Simon, Lowe was an extraordinary phenomenon: a politician who knew how to trust and use his permanent staff, a classicist who had come to believe that science 'was henceforth to be the chief helper of man.' To Lowe, Simon was the model civil servant, an expert with enough political sense to ingraft 'a highly scientific department, upon what had been a most unhappy and unintelligent order.'[12]

Lowe's conversion to the cause of national health had an unexpected consequence for himself – it saved his political life. As a result of the

Reform Act of 1867, Calne, or more accurately, Lord Lansdowne, lost the right to send a member to Parliament. Because of his reputation as the nation's foremost opponent of franchise reform, Lowe had no chance of winning in any constituency where the newly enfranchised had any weight and he could expect no favours from the Liberal party he had so recently helped dislodge from office. Had he not been able to win the seat for the University of London, his public career would have ended with the election of 1868. Because the Conservative reform act had given London its seat, Disraeli greatly enjoyed recalling that had he not saved his enemy from oblivion, Parliament would have lost its melancholy prophet. But Lowe did not receive the seat as a gift; he had to work hard to win the academic voters away from a number of other attractive candidates, among them Walter Bagehot, Edwin Chadwick, and John Lubbock. Bagehot was the most dangerous rival since he was one of the university's most distinguished graduates. Nevertheless, Lowe wrote confidently to a friend: 'They will take the better man ... My burning blushes hide the rest,' as Heloise says.' He felt that he had earned their support. Disraeli's original intention had been to give a joint seat to the University of London and to Durham University. Lowe, who had sat for a number of years on the University of London Senate, thought Durham a prime example of the evils of endowment: 'all salaries and no work, all teachers and no taught.' Accordingly, he spoke against Disraeli's proposal and got the revision, excluding Durham. Naturally, the fellows of London felt gratitude. But more important in getting him the seat was the support of the medical profession. A large and influential group of medical graduates campaigned hard for the politician who, according to Dr Buchannon, his nominator, 'has done more than any other member, often working alone, to forward measures of Public Health.' A third of the names on the petition calling for his nomination were from the medical faculty.[13]

This strong backing gave him the seat without a contest. He was profoundly relieved. He began his acceptance speech by saying: 'If ever a candidate ... had grounds to be grateful to a constituency, surely I am the man.' He then flattered the audience by explaining why he considered London University to be in many respects superior to the institution of higher learning he had endured: 'Your degree is a more difficult and more searching test, and therefore confers more honour on its recipient, than the ordinary degrees of either Oxford or Cambridge.' This superiority he thought due, not to money or 'deference to class prejudices,' but to a structure which separated teaching from examination and thus secured impartiality of standards. How fortunate they were, he told the assembled academics, to have no endowments to use for bribing students into attending, no religious tests 'to conciliate the bigotry or prejudices of any religious body,' no 'long, storied memories, no ancient chronicles in which you have been recorded.' He ended with earnest discussion of what he thought was the leading issue of the day: the need to 'adapt ourselves and our institutions' to meet, as the University of London had so successfully done, the exigencies of the democratic era that had, he was sure, now begun. The future would depend, he thought, on how well the educational institutions of the nation at all levels adapted themselves.[14]

10

Education for the Modern World

One of Lowe's more astute perceptions was that the structure of the nation's educational system might be the means by which a meritocracy could be maintained within a political democracy. During a crucial period in the development of elementary education, he was the Victorian equivalent of a minister of education. He had access to important people both in the worlds of politics and academia and he could influence opinion through the leader page of the most powerful newspaper in the land. For these reasons he was able to command attention for his reform ideas and put some of them into effect. His Revised Code of Education caused a storm of controversy during Palmerston's last ministry; even now, more than a hundred years afterwards, he has his critics and apologists.

Before entering into that controversy, it is essential, for the sake of perspective, to examine his views on secondary education, for without some idea of his reform programme for middle class education it is impossible to judge fairly his treatment of education for the children of the poor.

What to do about education in a democratic age was the question occupying his mind when he went up to Edinburgh in November 1867 to receive an LLD from the university. His speeches against franchise reform in the parliamentary session of that spring and the year before had given him a national reputation as a cantankerous, brilliant Jeremiah. The educated classes respected the courage with which he had clung to his views despite the sacrifice, or so it seemed at that moment, of his political future. They were prepared to pay him tribute, especially now that Disraeli had managed to dispose of the tiresome issue. Lowe appreciated the compliment, for he had felt himself to be something of a pariah. He reported to a confidante, Lady Salisbury, that the Edinburgh ceremonies had included a church service where he had been preached at from Proverbs 6:18, on 'feet that be swift in running to mischief' and on 'he that soweth discord among brethren,' but that the audience at the conferring of degrees had given him a much better reception than it had given Disraeli, who had also been on hand to receive a degree. While in Edinburgh he had appeared before the Philosophical Institution and spoken his piece about classical education. He was relieved to find that it 'struck a cord to which popular sentiment here at least heartily responds.' He was also pleased when the press reported his remarks and fulminated against him on their editorial pages. He had produced another hubbub, had sown even more discord among his brethren, and was, on the whole, well pleased with the results of his visit. However he did confess, in a postscript to Lady Salisbury, 'I am beginning to wonder what the rest of mankind will think of me.'[1]

He had gone to Edinburgh with the intention of awakening the educated to the alarming consequences of what they and their representatives had allowed to happen the previous spring. He had said that so long as the political power remained in the hands of an intelligent minority, it had been possible to get by with patchwork mending of the educational fabric; but now, after the Reform Act of 1867, it had become necessary to make a thorough-going re-examination of the whole of the educational establishment: 'Now it is a question of self-preservation – it is a question of existence, even of the existence of our Constitution.' He recommended that immediate attention be given to education of the newly enfranchised; religious scruples, he warned, must no longer be allowed to deprive the country of a national, state-assisted and inspected system of elementary education for the poor – 'our future masters.' To bring that about every parish without a voluntary school must be made to found a school of its own and support it. A conscience clause must be enforced in the existing Anglican schools so that Nonconformists and Catholics may attend them. Once these things were done then it might be possible, though perhaps not politically desirable, to consider compulsory education. In accomplishing these tasks, religious zeal and private enterprise must be subordinated, since the survival of the 'whole community' was at stake: 'There is no effort we should not make – there is no sacrifice, either of money or prejudice, or feeling, we should not submit to – rather than allow a generation to grow up in ignorance, in whose hands are reposed the destinies of all of us, the destinies of the nation.' Lowe's clerical enemies assumed, of course, that the former education minister was now openly admitting to his wish to impose secular schools upon a Christian country.[2]

Many people who shared Lowe's sense of urgency about the need to create a state-sponsored, secular, system were alarmed by his statement of educational objectives and by the specific inferences he drew from them. 'After all, gentlemen,' he had said, 'education is a preparation for actual life,' and yet, 'our education does not communicate to us knowledge ... it does not communicate to us the means of obtaining knowledge, and ... it does not communicate to us the means of communicating knowledge.' All that education provides the upper classes and a large proportion of the middle classes is a smattering of phrases from dead languages. Greek and Latin and ancient history, the staples of public school and university curricula, in so far as they communicate any information about how men live, do so about men who 'knew only monarch and municipality' and knew nothing of the concept of progress and the principles of representation. Boys at public schools who are chastized for 'the slightest slip in the name or history of the innumerable children of the geneology of Jupiter and Mars' make gross errors about the contents of the Bible without fear of the birch. Oxford undergraduates receive a smattering of Greek and Latin grammar, most of which they forget before they are thirty, but are not likely to know anything about their own bodies, are largely oblivious to physics, biology, and their own great national literature, and have not the slightest grasp of mediaeval history, even though 'great schisms have arisen in the Church of England from absurdly exaggerated ideas of the perfection of everything in that dreadful period.' The Englishman seems almost to 'worship inutility'; he cannot even order a dinner in a French cafe and 'squabble over the bill without making himself a laughing stock to every one present.' 'I submit,' Lowe said, to an amused and applauding gathering of Scots, 'that we have too much Latin and Greek and that if we are to have it, it ought to be taught on a very different system.'[3]

He thought the classics had some limited uses for the sons of the élite who were headed for the church, law, or statecraft, but none for the sons of the middle and lower ranks of the middle class who leave school at fourteen or fifteen. Their time for schooling being necessarily limited, they needed to be given studies directly useful to them. He acknowledged that he had acquired the reputation of a person who looked at education 'from a mean and sordid point of view.' It would have been to his advantage, he said, to have done what he could to correct that impression. He could have made everyone happy by 'quoting Cicero in praise of study and learning': 'But, gentlemen, among my sins cant has never been included (cheers). I have no idea of sending people ruffles when they want a shirt (laughter), and if you can succeed in teaching boys in this rank of life things which will be useful to them in their future career you ought to be well satisfied (hear, hear).'[4]

At a dinner given by the Philomatic Society at the Town Hall in Liverpool several months later, he expanded on what he thought useful knowledge to be. But first he explained what it was not. It was not the same knowledge required by the people who made national policy and guided the national institutions. That being so, it followed that the middle classes (defined as those who would not send their children to the state-supported schools and who could not send them to public schools or the universities) would be making a tragic mistake if they modelled the curricula of their secondary schools on Eton and Winchester. He said that he was all too aware that middle class parents might choose this wrong model. The English shopkeepers had, earlier that year, sat back unprotestingly and watched Disraeli steal their political power away from them. They were as supine now as they had been in the eighteenth century, when they had allowed the endowed schools, originally founded for their benefit, to slip into the pockets of the landowners.[5]

Because middle class people lacked confidence in themselves, they might ignore reality; or they might make the error of the opposite extreme and offer subjects tied to the immediate requirements of the market-place. He observed that many of their private schools merely taught indifferently what was offered in the voluntary primary schools for the poor or else supplied nothing but technical training in such things as accounting, book-keeping, or other subjects which might better be learned in the shop. What the boy who left school at fourteen or fifteen needed was intellectual discipline, a critical turn of mind, an awareness of the world 'as it really is.' He would learn those things best from the sciences, so long as they were taught by experiment and not by rote. He would learn to think and communicate properly if he were given a composition in his own, living, tongue, if he were taught 'synthetical,' as opposed to 'analytical' mathematics, and if he were supplied with a good grounding in English literature and modern European languages. Memorization drills, grammar exercises, improving tracts written by 'insipid moralists,' the stock-in-trade of most private schoolmasters, were mind-deadening and totally irrelevant to a boy headed for an active life in the practical world.[6]

What Lowe failed to explain satisfactorily on this occasion or any other was how a class supposedly lacking a cohesive culture could be expected to institute a curriculum appropriate to itself. He was, however, aware of the problem. He had read Matthew Arnold's long essay, *A French Eton*, which named the state as the only conceivable authority for bringing about a reform. Arnold had argued that it would be unreasonable to expect people whose most conspicuous fault was an inability to see further than the counting house to be able to constitute the authority for their own improvement. Lowe had tried to answer Arnold in a speech made in Nottingham in 1864, not long after the essay had been published in *Macmillians*. Lowe thought that the idea of setting up English lycées, patterned on the French, would be impracticable; the enfranchised poor could not be asked to pay taxes to educate the relatively well-off. Also, the clerical lobby would be certain to denounce a non-sectarian system, the only conceivable state system, as 'Godless.' Furthermore, it would be wrong to ask the state to stand between the duty of parent to child. He did allow that there was one constructive thing the state could do without corrupting the family or unfairly taxing the poor and that was to set standards, to inspect, and to report. Hard-headed businessmen might not know what education was best for their children but they did know when they were not getting their money's worth. If the state would only tell them what education was available and how good it was, demand and supply could be counted on to do the rest. He made his Nottingham audience laugh by describing the horrified reaction of the public school headmasters to a proposal, made by the Public Schools Commission, to send inspectors on a tour of examination of the ancient public schools. The headmasters knew, Lowe said, that a report of their findings 'would terrify the papas and mammas of England out of their wits.' Presumably if similar reports were made available to middle class papas and mammas, there would be revolution in the private schools led by infuriated merchants who knew what it was to get value for money.[7]

Understandably these attempts to apply a free trade analogy to education were denounced as superficial and false. Men like Sir James Kay Shuttleworth, who believed that the state-supported schools had a civilizing mission, wrote angry rebuttals, pointing out that few schools and schoolteachers were activated by the profit motive. The supply of education, they insisted, must create its own demand, since ignorance could not be expected of itself to desire the enlightenment it lacked. But Lowe shrugged off such criticisms as sentimental and self-interested. So wedded was he to his dogmatic position that he even repudiated the suggestion that the public repossess the endowments appropriated by the Church of England after the reformation and use them to subsidize modern subjects at secondary schools. He had, he said, 'not the slightest objection' to confiscations and redirections, but he could not agree to their being reapplied to support a new curriculum orthodoxy. Reading of Adam Smith and three years on the Charity Commission had convinced him that all educational endowments were, in themselves, evil. They were the 'opium that puts all exertions to sleep.' Subjects considered modern now would soon be superseded. Thus to perpetuate endowments by confiscating and redirecting them would be to perpetuate the evil of monopoly.[8]

He repeated his objections to endowments but modified his position on the function of the state before a Royal Commission on the endowed schools, struck in 1864 and chaired by Lord Taunton. Granville had asked Lowe to serve on the commission. Lowe had refused, saying that its members were poorly chosen (W.E. Forster 'wants educating himself,' Stafford Northcote was a 'hypocrite,' Lord Lyttleton was 'a bigot'), and, besides, he would 'never join a commission he could not control.' Nevertheless, he took full advantage of his invitation to appear before them to state his views. Endowments, he said, no matter how wise in their intentions at the time of donation, must inevitably, with the advance of civilization, 'put a premium on obsolete knowledge.' Were he an autocrat he would abolish them and turn all educational institutions into private enterprises, free to supply whatever subjects parents demanded, free to hire the best teachers available on the market whether clerical or lay, and free to go to the wall if examinations demonstrated to the parents that a particular school was not giving satisfaction. This, of course, was impossible in a country like England, but it might be approximated if the courts of equity would interpret the provisions of the endowments broadly. The Privy Council might then attempt to counteract the deadening influence of these revised endowments by paying subsidies to schools that prepared their pupils to pass standardized examinations in modern subjects. He emphasized that the state should not dictate but neither should it shirk its responsibility 'to know what is being done with those children on whom the welfare of the State depends.'[9]

This was hardly a straightforward statement of position. Obviously if the state encouraged the teaching of non-classical subjects it was interfering with the free play of supply and demand and doing far more than merely informing itself about the condition of its citizens. Whenever faced with the necessity of reconciling self-regulating mechanisms with the right of the community to protect itself and provide direction, Lowe always fell back on a utilitarian compromise. Arnold was much more courageous about recognizing the paramount authority of the state, but even he was constrained by his liberalism. When he turned from theory to practical suggestions for implementation, his recommendations seem nearly as minimal and compromising as Lowe's. Arnold thought that as a first step in the process of exercising its authority, the state should make a provision of twenty thousand pounds a year for scholarships to secondary schools in return for the right to inspect and report. His English lycées, or 'Royal Schools,' would receive only part of their support from government subsidies and get the rest from school fees and from endowments appropriated to them by a commission. In one of its features, then, Lowe's recommendations for state action went further than Arnold's: Arnold might favour a slightly higher rate of financial support from the central authority but Lowe would use the resources of the state to influence, but not to dictate, the subject matter offered to all students in secondary education. Arnold wanted to civilize the nation and Lowe wanted to modernize it. To the extent that he wanted to alter drastically the curriculum, Lowe's was the more radical proposal.[10]

The Taunton Commission did recommend some of the inspection and examination schemes which Lowe had urged upon it. Forster, when he became vice-president of the Board of Education in 1868, set up a commission to encourage the teaching of sciences and modern languages. When the Conservatives came to office in 1874, they tried to slow the movement to open up endowments and got roundly denounced by Lowe. Yet he had to admit that the cause of modernization seemed doomed and that only rearguard action was open to him. Nevertheless, he persisted. When a Public Schools bill came up for debate in 1868, he moved an amendment requiring that every boy in the seven great public schools be examined annually in reading, writing, arithmetic, English history and literature, and world geography – the results to be made public. 'Of course I shall not carry it,' he wrote to Lady Salisbury, 'but it will be amusing to see the reasons that will be given against it.' John Stuart Mill was one of the few who appreciated the ploy. He said that Lowe's proposal to examine the élite of the nation in subjects that any pupil in a National School should know 'might be an extremely good joke against the schools'; nevertheless, he 'hoped no one would vote for it seriously.' His point made, Lowe then withdrew his amendment.[11]

By these gestures as well as in his public addresses in Edinburgh in 1867 and in Liverpool early the following year he had intended to stir up a public debate and in this respect, if in no other, he succeeded. Editorial writers in the daily press, essayists in the monthly journals, and clerical headmasters in numerous pamphlets expressed their shock and sense of outrage. *The Times*, of course, did not join the irate chorus. On one occasion Delane allowed Lowe to write a leading article in praise of 'practical education,' but, after that, steered him on to other, less provoking subjects. When Lowe gave a speech in praise of the engineering profession, a speech eloquent with warnings about the consequences of falling behind the United States, France, and Germany in provisions for scientific education, Delane directed two regular writers, Thomas Chenery and Thomas Mozley, to write a commentary balancing praise with caution. They noted that of all the critics of education in the land, Lowe was the 'most vigorous, the most eloquent, and perhaps the most extreme.' They thought he was right to praise science, wrong to advocate a special education for the middle class, and wrong, as a distinguished classicist, to preach against the muses he once worshipped. 'We are rather inclined,' observed *The Times*, 'to hold that what is the best education for the one class is the best for another, so far as it goes.' Lowe's other critics said much the same thing but in far less temperate language: they called him a vulgarian, an enemy of religion, a worshipper of things, a fomenter of class disharmony.[12]

Matthew Arnold used satire rather than vituperation when he came to deal with Lowe. The charge he levelled was philistinism. In 1866 the

Pall Mall Gazette began to print Arnold's 'Arminious Letters' in serial form; they were published later as *Friendship's Garland*. The hero of the story is Arminious von Thunder-ten-Tronckh, a linial descendent of Candide. The point of the satire was to expose the poverty of English liberalism: its middle class narrowness, its obsession with machinery, its disregard of spiritual ends. Occasionally Lowe appears in the role of a nineteenth-century Dr Pangloss, obsessively bent on proving that the middle class, business, culture, and the liberal political constitution which reflects its values was the ultimate perfection of human civilization. Lowe appears again as a Pangloss in *Culture and Anarchy*. There Arnold accuses Lowe of having debauched the middle classes by praising them for their worship of bigness and worship of energy for energy's sake. What, Arnold asked, was one to make of a man who would elevate the middle classes by teaching them 'to fight the battle of life with the waiters in foreign hotels ...?'[13]

Arnold deliberately distorted Lowe's position because he found it served his polemics to do so. In fact, the two men had more affinities with each other than either was prepared to admit in public. They met at least once and that was in Paris in 1865. Arnold wrote to his sister, Francis, that he had been agreeably impressed and had found a 'side in him I did not know was there.' For his part, Lowe paid Arnold the tribute of plagarism. In his 1868 Liverpool speech he said that the middle classes, 'want culture, they want refinement, compared with the same classes in other countries. They want elevation of mind, and they want to be taught that money is not to be the all-and-end-all of life. They want to have their morale raised, their sense of honour developed.' This discloses, to say the least, a careful reading of *Culture and Anarchy* and suggests the possibility that, despite their disagreement about the function of the state, they shared a number of similar assumptions.[14]

Both Arnold and Lowe stated emphatically that the middle classes, whatever their faults, were bound in the near future at least to provide the model of behaviour for the emerging working class. They both thought it crucial that the middle classes be elevated out of their narrowness so that they might see the world dispassionately and realistically. The judaizing cast of mind, both agreed, was the chief barrier to the nurture of a dispassionate, critical, intelligence. Even their difference about the worth of science as an instrument of education was less deep than Arnold imagined. Lowe did not hold, as Arnold and a writer for the *Saturday Review* charged, that 'matter is everything and mind nothing.' Lowe was never a high priest of the 'steam intellect.' He insisted that science was an essential part of a modern liberal education. Technicians needed to master scientific rules and information; most men, however, could make little use of these details. Science, he told the Taunton Commission, has a more general function: it instills a sensitivity to the natural world around us and, equally important, it instills habits of thinking that tend to counteract the most common defect of the popular mentality – the habit of generalizing on the basis of unexamined assumptions. In this respect, he said, the 'human mind needs the rein rather than the spur.' The inductive method leads a person to take nothing on trust that can be objectively verified; it causes him to sift evidence, compare, and estimate probabilities. For those reasons he recommended that science, taught by means of experiment, become the backbone of the curriculum in middle class schools. If administered correctly, it would be sure to undermine that ignorant and bigoted sense of assurance that was so unattractive and conspicuous a part of the bourgeois personality. 'There is nothing,' he said, 'so valuable for man as to avoid credulity.'[15]

Arnold might not agree entirely with that categorical statement but he would agree with Lowe's assessment of the problem of middle class education and with his insistence on the importance of finding a solution before political democracy fully developed. Arnold did not hold that science was the best means for developing the sensitive and critical faculties and yet he would emphatically agree that the end of education was to produce a harmonious balance between the various parts of the human personality. Both men believed that learning for its own sake was the best reward of leisure and that sweetness was wanted as well as light. Where they differed most profoundly was over the way this Platonic ideal could be realized and the feasibility of extending this kind of liberal education to the nation at large. Arnold, the poet, counselled perfection. He did so on the premise that it was possible through the agency of the state to reintegrate society and the human soul and by means of mass education to counteract the disintegrating effects of an atomizing, industrial, environment. Lowe, the utilitarian, thought that human beings, though capable of nobility, were basically selfish and pleasure seeking. Culturally nurtured habits of altruism, patriotism, co-operation might curb this natural grasping instinct, especially if the various institutions of education trained people to make distinctions, observe systematically, and act dispassionately. But no amount of careful nurture could destroy the old Adam within. And careful nurture was expensive. It required leisure and leisure depended on specialization and the productive labour of the great majority. Thus no society could provide sweetness and light for any but a tiny élite. Even if a society could find the resources to exempt most of its youth from productive labour it would find that only a minority would be equipped to respond. It was, he believed, the rare man or woman in any class who was capable of undertaking speculative philosophy or formal logic, and rarer still the person who was equipped to experience the arcane joys of classical philology or gain wisdom from the study of history, the most inexact and subjective of the disciplines. He was prepared to believe that the march of technology and the process of evolution might make it easier sometime in the distant future to create a common culture and a more rational citizenry, but utopia would never exist on earth and utopian thought was therefore harmful. Everyone did, indeed, require sweetness as well as light for a fully human life; but educational reformers would produce neither if they tried to supply both simultaneously. He agreed with Arnold that the lower strata of the middle class lacked taste and would profit from acquiring some. But, he asked, how was one to set about institutionalizing the dissemination of such a nebulous thing as taste? Some products of Eton lack it and some self-taught people have it. Cobden and Bright, he pointed out, were not sent to school to study words, and yet spoke the English language with consummate taste. Given the necessity of making a choice between virtues – and those who make decisions must always husband resources and assign priorities – then it was a clear duty for practical reformers to prefer those subjects where the methods of instruction and examination are well understood over 'spectacular things,' which were difficult to define and measure. A child from the lower middle class who is sent to school to study words rather than things will emerge from school unaware of the economic and social realities that will govern his life; he will not even be recognized as a gentleman, although his desire to be so recognized will be greatly stimulated. On the other hand, a practical education in how to think for himself and to understand the workings of the modern world could give him a solid base for self-improvement and social mobility.[16]

Lowe rejected as impossible and undesirable Arnold's vision of a society where everyone would be treated as if they were of equal worth. This was hardly surprising; equalitarians did not abound in the ranks of mid-Victorian liberalism. Where Lowe departed from conventionality was in his unquestioning belief in the existence of objective examination procedures by means of which the capability of people could be exactly graded. He had the deepest contempt for 'socialists' and do-gooders who objected to this approach to their fellow humans. Those who opposed the application of objective standards, tested by examination, did so, he believed, on woolly-minded, compassionate, grounds. They were warm-hearted people who held their belief in the perfectability of human nature on trust. Lowe was certain that such people would lose the race in a world growing ever more competitive, unless, of course, they happened to inherit wealth and have a head start. 'All of life,' he maintained, 'is not a formal but an actual examination.' And education was a preparation for life, not as it should be but as it was.[17]

Some idealists and humanitarians who entered the lists against this hard-headed position refused to grant that Lowe's motives were liberal ones. A pamphleteer named A.C. Weir vigorously denied that Lowe was interested in liberating people or in adjusting the subject matter of the schools to the realities of a competitive, industrial age. What those who talked about free trade in education really intended, Weir charged, was to make schools into instruments of social control. In the hands of men of this type, educational reform would become a weapon to protect the old social constitution from the 'destructive assaults of the untaught'; it would be a knife to be turned in the 'hands of the masses against the masses themselves.'[18]

There was a passage in Lowe's Edinburgh speech in 1867 which seems to substantiate Weir's suspicions:

> Is it not better that gentlemen should know the things which the workingmen know, only know them infinitely better in their details, so that they may be able, in their intercourse and their commerce with them, to assert the superiority over them which greater intelligence and leisure is sure to give, and to conquer back by means of a wider and more enlightened cultivation some of the influences which they have lost by political change ... The lower classes ought to be educated to discharge the duties cast upon them. They should also be educated that they may appreciate and defer to higher cultivation when they meet it; and the higher classes ought to be educated in a very different manner, in order that they may exhibit to the lower classes that higher education to which, if it were shown to them, they would bow down and defer.[19]

Such a statement as this, coming from a man who had just spoken out against franchise reform and had recently worked to pare down the curriculum of the primary schools, does appear to have been directed at keeping the ignorant ignorant and deferential. He seemed to have been saying that the primary purpose of education is not to attempt 'moral rescue' nor to bring the nation together in a common culture, nor even to turn villagers into efficient and tractable industrial workers, but instead to condition the poor to accept their inferior position in the social spectrum and to persuade them not to use their political power. This is the meaning which many people, at the time and since, have read into these words. But to examine the passage in context gives it quite a different slant. Before he came to these often-quoted lines he said that the time had passed when property, rank, and other 'indirect influences' could continue to hold society together. He said that in the future those who sought to 'direct the course of public affairs' would need to do so 'by the influence of mind over mind.' He then asked how this was to be done: 'Is it by confining the attention of the sons of the wealthier classes of the country to the history of these old languages and these Pagan republics, of which working men have never heard, with which they are never brought into contact in any of their affairs, and of which, from the necessity of the case, they know nothing?'[20]

Obviously, his point was that the élite must respond to the challenge of democracy by changing their education, not for the purpose of creating a monopoly of enlightenment but for the opposite reason. He was aware that the classical languages had served in the past to maintain that monopoly for the privileged caste; he was equally aware that the ruling élite wished to maintain the classical curriculum for that purpose. It distressed him to observe a revival of classically oriented secondary education at a time when he believed the advance of knowledge was making such a course ultimately disastrous. If the process continued, he feared that the ruling class would become ineffectual and obsolete, or perhaps worse: it might corrupt the middle classes into sharing its obsolescence, and in that case the march of progress might soon leave England standing on the sidelines. If the country were to develop the skills and institutions appropriate to the historical forces moving in the world, then it was essential that people at all levels be trained to perform their specialized functions by educational institutions. He was conscious of the fact that spreading literacy and awakening intelligence would make the task more difficult. The masses of people in the lower strata would have to be persuaded to give their assent to a community where wealth and status was unevenly distributed. They would have to be made to see that this was in the interest, not merely of the privileged, but of everyone. Lowe had the insight to grasp that education might be a way to produce this assent. If status could be closely associated with the various levels of education, then the majority of people, who necessarily would not be able to advance beyond the lowest levels, might recognize that their low status had some rational justification. He also saw that those at the bottom of the pyramid must receive the best education the nation could afford so that the poor would be capable of appreciating rational demonstrations of the general utility of inequality. He understood that the education of the élite must be intelligible to the common man; if the worker were to be made to respect and defer to merit, then it must be the kind of merit he could recognize and appreciate. Lowe was not an obscurantist who wished to keep the masses in darkness nor was he a conservative who wanted to maintain a deferent society. To a remarkable extent he was able to see that the logic of his premises led to the creation of a meritocracy closely linked to a radically revised educational system.[21]

The logic of his position did, however, extend into areas where even he was not willing to follow. If natural intelligence existed, as he knew it did, in all classes and in both sexes, then wealth, birth, or sex should not be criteria for admission to any stage in the educational apparatus. The bright from every group should be identified by tests and moved ahead, by scholarships and free tuition if necessary, as far as their abilities might take them. Lowe was not entirely unsympathetic to this idea. He believed, for example, that the virtual exclusion of women from higher education and from the higher professions was 'most harsh and unjust.' We treat the 'fair and better half of humanity,' he said on one occasion, with a veneer of compliments and precedence which serves to hide a substratum of 'cruelty and contempt.' His consistent efforts to strike down the educational barriers against those outside the Anglican community we have already noticed. Also he was ready and eager to cut off the duller sons of the upper classes, if not at Eton's door, then not long after they got inside. But further than that he would not go. Class bias, ignorance of what workingmen were like, his conviction that scarcity was a permanent fact of life, his belief in the virtue of retrenchment, his fear of big government, his 'practical liberality' prevented him from advocating a general opening up of secondary and university education to all classes. However, he did propose to the Taunton Commission that endowment funds be used to provide scholarships to universities and secondary schools for the most gifted sons of the poor.[22]

It is not surprising that few appreciated the boldness and the intent of his recommendations as an educational reformer. No one could forget that as the official in charge of revising the code for elementary education he had appeared to be interested in curbing, not expanding or improving, the educational system for the poor. Perhaps the greatest trial he had to endure as vice-president of the Board of Education was the experience of being abused for what he considered to be the wrong reasons.

11

Payment
by Results

Lowe knew when he accepted the vice-presidency of the Committee of the Privy Council on Education that he had been picked by Granville and Palmerston because they thought him sufficiently courageous and tough to do a necessary but thankless task. By 1858 all political leaders could see that something had to be done about the Education Department, about the way it spent its money and the seemingly inexorable increase in its rate of spending. Yet politicians also agreed that it would be impossible to change the system which produced so much waste and inefficiency. Most schools for the poor were managed by denominational societies, partly supported by state subsidies. The state could not act to rationalize the system without increasing its supervisory powers and threatening the autonomy of the voluntary school societies. Any significant movement towards reform must, therefore, go in the direction of secularism, but that way danger lay. In the sixties any discussion of education reform was certain to arouse religious passions, and those passions were certain to be immediately translated into politics. Thus no reformer could expect to have his proposals considered on their merits. No one was more aware of this trap than Lowe. His work to get a national system of elementary education in New South Wales had been frustrated by the bargain the governor had struck with the bishop: 'Ignorance for Oppression – Oppression for Ignorance.' As vice-president he would have to go into battle a second time and be met by similar bargains. He had considerable enthusiasm for the cause and no uncertainty about objectives. But experience had taught him that there was no chance whatever of winning a decisive victory and every chance that casualties among the general staff would be extremely high.

The new Liberal ministers were determined to act, not because they (with the honourable exceptions of Russell and Granville) cared deeply about the state of public education, but because they were committed to the great cause of economy in government. Retrenchers had been looking covetously at the Education Department since the end of the Crimean War. This was to be expected: the Education Department accounted for nearly one fifth of the entire civil expenditure in 1860. Also there was concern that unless the subsidy system was altered expenditure might continue to increase without either the Treasury or the House of Commons being able to do anything to control it. In 1833 Parliament had voted a paltry twenty thousand pounds in aid of the National Society, an Anglican body in charge of all but a fraction of the schools, and the British and Foreign Society, a non-sectarian body patronized mainly by Nonconformists. Six years later Lord John Russell performed a sleight-of-hand and, by means of an Order-in-Council, established a committee to distribute what had become annual grants. He chose as the secretary a Manchester physician named Dr James Kay Shuttleworth. Under his dedicated guidance the apparatus of central inspection and teacher training expanded and, with it, the costs. The thirty thousand pounds available to the Education Department in 1839 rose to $663,000 in 1858. Each year more schools applied for and obtained the grants offered for buildings, for employing certified teachers, for undertaking to train pupil teachers. Parliament faced the prospect, by 1858, of being forced to increase estimates by a hundred thousand pounds each year, a prospect which chilled the hearts of economizers. In 1860 even Russell thought the 'progress of the grant system must be slackened.'[1]

Lord Derby's ministry appointed a Royal Commission in 1858 to collect information about the workings of Kay Shuttleworth's system and to make suggestions for ways the grant-awarding process might be made more efficient and more responsive to state control. Chaired by the Duke of Newcastle, the commissioners sent investigators and solicited testimony. They published their recommendations and collection of testimony, packed into six heavy volumes, in 1861. Although they were not in agreement about much else, all the commissioners accepted the proposition that they were to find ways to cut costs and simplify a cumbersome administrative procedure. They tended to listen attentively to evidence which supported this preconception. Historians of British education have pointed out that the commission used vague and subjective criteria for measuring the quality of education being dispensed and that they were highly selective about the testimony they chose to cite. The Newcastle commissioners were partial to statements showing that teachers were over-educated for their humble tasks, that they tended to spend their time with the brightest pupils and neglected children most in need of attention. They listened sympathetically to claims that the rate of attrition among the children who entered the schools was disgracefully high and that many of those who did stay on emerged as functional illiterates. Nevertheless, those who charge the commissioners with bias also agree that the complaints against the system were substantial. Matthew Arnold, the staunchest supporter of Kay Shuttleworth's methods and objectives, agreed that the system had many flaws and needed administrative alterations.[2]

The majority report of the commission suggested a compromise moderate enough to win Arnold's general approval. It endorsed the existing system while proposing some modifications. One recommendation was that a local grant be made out of county rates to supplement the grants handed out by the central government. These local grants were to be tied to the number of children in a particular school who passed tests in simple reading, writing, and arithmetic, set and administered by county examiners. The commissioners believed that decentralization would make it possible to cut back the large staff of the Education Department and ease the drain on the Treasury; at the same time the government could continue to aid the hard-pressed clergymen who had frequently to dip into their own pockets to pay the deficits for their schools. The majority report recommended the 'payment by results' principle. By using it the state could, supposedly, force teachers to bring all or most of their pupils up to a minimum standard and discourage them from teaching only precocious students and esoteric subjects.[3]

Once the Newcastle Commission had made its report, Palmerston and his ministers had to decide how to react to it. They knew they could not step without trespassing on powerful interests; they knew the opposition would talk loudly about bureaucratic waste but use their powerful clerical lobby to make things difficult for the government. On the other hand, the ministers responsible for foreign and military affairs were pressing hard for economies in the civil establishment so that England could ready herself for a possible conflict with France. The Committee of the Privy Council, attended by Granville as lord president, Lowe, in his capacity as vice-president, along with the chancellor of the exchequer and the first lord of the admiralty, held a series of meetings. They listened to Lowe's prediction that the government would not be able to pass a single clause of an educational reform bill and concluded that the best tactic would be to circumvent Parliament and proceed by means of a departmental minute. They instructed Lowe to go ahead with its preparation. Using this expedient, the experts could put together a comprehensive revision of the educational code without harassment from politicians and lobbyists. The government would then have time to observe the reaction and 'see how the cat really jumps in Parliament on the subject.' That decision having been made, the committee was delighted to turn the responsibility for framing policy over to the vice-president.[4]

Lowe had no intention of simply translating the Newcastle Commission report into a new code. His Australian experience had convinced him that only the central government was sufficiently capable and detached to set uniform standards and maintain them. The struggle between the state and the church would be difficult enough, he thought, without introducing into it a host of amateurish and self-interested county authorities. Therefore he called in Henry Cole from the Department of Science and Art and Ralph Lingen, Kay Shuttleworth's successor as secretary to the committee, and asked them to draft a different plan. They agreed with their chief that it would be a mistake to put one more patch on a patchwork system. So, without bothering to consult the inspectors in the field, they set to work.[5]

With the advice of the Committee on Education but acting on his authority as vice-president, Lowe adopted Lingen's draft and issued it as a departmental minute on the day the queen prorogued Parliament in the summer of 1861. The provisions of the Revised Code were deliberately unconciliatory. The most important features were these: payment was to be made according to the number of children who had attended a school for a prescribed number of days during the school year; on examination day, inspectors were to group pupils according to age, not level of attainment, and quiz each child individually on his ability to read, write from dictation, and do sums; failure on any one of these three 'Rs' would cause the school to lose a third of the capitulation grant which the pupil had earned by his attendance. Other deductions would be made if the inspectors reported a school to be deficient in teachers holding certificates from teacher training colleges or deficient in equipment and facilities. On the premise that teachers would not need elaborate training to be able to ready their charges for simple examinations, subsidies to teacher training colleges were to be cut back and the number and amount of Queen's scholarships, open to pupil teachers, reduced.[6]

Few would have disagreed with Lowe's comment in *The Times* that the scheme was 'exceedingly ingenious.' Where the Newcastle Commission had left loose edges or recommended some light pruning, the minute tidied up and cut into the wood. Performance was to be the test, and no excuses. Trust to the 'passions of the human mind,' Lowe counselled; enlist the hope of reward and the fear of penalty and then see how quickly difficulties are overcome. 'Hitherto we have been living under a system of bounties and protection; now we propose to have a little free trade.'[7]

Tactically it might have been wiser not to boast about ingenuity or to invoke the spirit of free trade. Few of the features of the minute were new. The 'payment by results' principle had been suggested by Henry Cole who had been applying it for a number of years in his subsidies to teachers of science and art in the schools. Under Kay Shuttle-worth the Education Department had directed inspectors to hold examinations in reading, writing, and arithmetic, and to withhold funds from schools where the results were unsatisfactory. It was true that in fact most of the inspectors had ignored this directive and that no school had suffered because of a poor showing; nevertheless, Lowe could have claimed that the practice of setting examinations on prescribed subjects was, like Payment by Results, an established practice and that he was merely tightening accepted procedures. Instead he made a point of calling attention to the innovations. These innovations, although not fundamental, were significant. Not only did the new code force inspectors to · abide by the examination requirements but the first version of the code directed them to examine the children individually instead of following the older practice of putting questions to groups of children. This meant that the inspector would have to decide whether to give the school all, part, or none of the grant which the child had earned by his attendance, depending on that child's performance on examination day. Lowe's intention here was to concentrate authority, to apply to the school system the stimulus of free trade, and to simplify the enormously complicated clerical work at the Privy Council office. He was proud of these 'improvements' and said far too much about them.[8]

Though the changes made by the first Revised Code were less spectacular than its sponsor claimed, they were enough to send alarm signals to rectories throughout the land. Those involved with the assisted schools found much to complain about: inspectors would be hard-pressed to find time to examine individually all the children in their extensive circuits; school managers would not be able to predict with certainty what their school's income would be for any given year; certified teachers would lose their autonomy and some of their status by being placed under the thumb of their headmasters. Various though the interests of the inspectors, managers, and certified teachers were, they could all find common cause against the Revised Code. Their numbers were considerable – over twenty thousand; they were articulate, well led, and had access to Nonconformist radicals in the Liberal party and to the many strong Anglicans among the Tories. Lowe and Lingen, on the other hand, would have almost no committed people on their side. They would be abused by the opposition without and subverted by their own servants. Even had the two men been temperamentally inclined to make an attempt to win over their inspectors (and neither were), they would not have succeeded. Many of the inspectors were themselves clerics; their appointments had been jointly approved by the government and the societies whose schools they served. Consequently, their loyalties, at best, were divided. Even under the Conservatives their influence on policy-making had been curbed. Lowe cut it off entirely when he came to the office. When asked in the House if he thought he could trust his own inspectors, he replied, 'Certainly not.' Because he was convinced that conciliation would not work (and Lowe was always easily convinced of that), he resolved to be bold and provocative. He would carry the fight to the bishops; he would expose for all who had eyes to see the fact that the prelates and their henchmen 'have become a smooth organization for extortion.' Compromise on details he knew to be hopeless since the real issue was one of principle: should the churches or the state be the senior partner in the joint responsibility for educating the children of the poor? He dared not openly admit that his reform was, among other things, aimed at winning a victory for the state, so he couched his appeal to Parliament and to the public in terms of free trade and efficiency. In doing so he exposed himself to the charge that he was a narrow-minded Gradgrind, capable only of treating children as though they were so many little commodities.[9]

Clerical school managers and their supporters did not take seriously Lowe's protests that he was a friend of religion. A stream of sermons and pamphlets pointed out that religion was not one of the three 'Rs.' By withdrawing subsidy the government was indicating that it did not care what children read so long as they could read – a most distressing symptom of the age. The secularists, they pronounced, were intent on undermining religious faith under the guise of educational reform.

The old system did have defenders who were interested not merely in the effect of the changes on religion but also in their effect on the quality of the education offered in the schools and on the teachers and pupil teachers. Kay Shuttleworth and Matthew Arnold both entered into the pamphlet war with reasoned arguments. The Revised Code, they claimed, totally ignored the fact that every school operated in a different social surrounding; what might be good for one would certainly be bad for another. Schools in prosperous regions might profit from Payment by Results since they drew from a disciplined and civilized clientele. But in impoverished or remote areas, where children needed to be rescued from barbarism, taught rudimentary manners, and shown, quite literally, how to stand upright, it would not be possible or desirable to cram their minds with information in order to pass a government examination. The result would be that the schools most in need of state subsidy would be the last to get it. To apply free trade logic to such a situation was, both critics argued, perverse. As Arnold put it, 'a lame man walks ill and to make him walk better, you break his crutches.'[10]

All of the thousands of letters, pamphlets, and petitions of protest spoke of the callous indifference of the Education Department to the morale of teachers and pupil teachers and to the ignorance of the code's framers about actual conditions. Lingen and Lowe would require that all grant earners be present on the dread examination day regardless of the effect of harvests, festivals, epidemics, foul weather, or ill-tempered parents – conditions outside the control of the school managers. The insistence that children be grouped by age rather than by level of attainment was, the protesters insisted, another example of bureaucratic blindness. Had Lowe and his secretary bothered to consult their own inspectors they would know that in the urban slums constant migration and the breakdown of family discipline made nonsense out of the assumption that age and ability to read, write, and do sums had any relation to each other.[11]

Politicians could not ignore these criticisms and these flashes of 'clerical lightening.' Members of Parliament protested about the tactic of waiting until the last day of the 1861 session to release the minute. Lord Granville tried to calm them by explaining that the new way of making grants would not go into effect until the following year, after Parliament had reassembled and been given a chance to suggest alterations. This did not mollify W.E. Forster, a radical MP and a member of the Committee of the British and Foreign Society, or Lord Robert Cecil, a spokesman for the National Society. Both men complained to Palmerston that the clauses affecting pupil teachers and training colleges would apply immediately. The prime minister then intervened and ordered a complete suspension of the minute. When, during the recess, the outcries of the anti-code lobbyists greatly increased in volume, he wanted to shelve the matter indefinitely but was met by stiff resistance from Granville, who complained that the morale of his office would be badly shaken, and by Gladstone, who praised the Privy Council for its attempts to reduce expenditures. The result was the inevitable compromise. When Parliament came to debate the suspended minute in the spring of 1862, it was presented with a Revised Code, again revised. Schools would be allowed to retain some of their capitulation grants, no matter how badly their children performed on examination day, infants under six would be excused from examination, and, much to Lowe's disgust, children would not be grouped for examination purposes according to age but according to whatever level of accomplishment their teachers thought proper. No child, however, could earn a grant for a school if presented more than once in the same standard. All of these modifications were in answer to some of the more reasonable objections raised by the critics. None of these critics were satisfied, but the Conservative leaders saw that nothing more could be extracted from the government and decided to let the measure go through without strenuous opposition.[12]

Lowe did not take kindly to these compromises. The Whigs, he felt, had once again put him in an exposed position and then, when the 'interested and therefore implacable opposition' put on the pressure, had failed to back him up. He had come to regard the first Revised Code, now so shamefully tampered with, as a thing of beauty. He could not denounce the compromises or strike back with all his power against the clerical 'nest of privilege' in the House of Commons so, as usual, he turned to *The Times*.[13]

Leader after leader thundered out fulminations against the clerical conspiracy to defraud the nation. School managers might well shed tears at losing their comfortable sinecures, he wrote; they now had to face the prospect of losing their cosy patronage and of being compelled to hire teachers who could teach. The Revised Code would force them to require that students did their lessons; it would provide school managers with incentives to do the job cheaply and well. Teachers were reminded that they had the least justification of anyone in the land to make calls upon the public purse; they were 'not young ladies and gentlemen, but poor children trained for a life of labour.' They had been raised from poverty by public subsidy and scholarship to positions of 'affluence and comfort.' Perhaps they had become so 'over-trained and over-educated,' so spoiled by 'sickly refinement' that they could not bear the tedious chore of drilling their charges in the fundamentals. If that were so, then it was high time they be exposed to bracing drafts of competition. If descending to the world of reality lowered teachers 'to the level of their work,' then so be it. It was obvious, Lowe wrote, that environment affects learning processes, but it was also obvious that progress comes from responses to challenges. The fault of the environmentalists was that they would avoid challenge and indulge in sentimental drivel about such 'impalpable essences' as the 'moral atmosphere,' the 'tone,' or the 'mental condition' of a school. These fine phrases were meant to cover slackness in providing the skills working people desperately required. School managers who talked about moral atmosphere were usually on the look-out for loopholes they could use to cheat parents. That was why the decision to drop the provision for grouping by age was so pernicious; now headmasters would put as many as they could into the lowest standards where the children would pass and earn a full grant for the school. These and other comments and predictions he served up in a dozen leading articles. Through all of them ran the refrain: men are by nature grasping and educators are no exception. Subsidy and efficiency are forever in conflict. Relaxation of centralized control will always mean that costs will swell and work will be scamped. Unless care be taken, Englishmen may well see the day when 'the expense of Education is ranked next to the great services among the demands which the taxpayer has to pay.'[14]

These *Times* articles do not make edifying reading. Many of those who have made the history of Victorian education a specialty have regretted that fate gave England an education minister with so narrow and dogmatic an outlook. They lament with Matthew Arnold that the ark of English education did not have a 'wiser carpenter than Mr. Lowe.' A study of elementary education, published in 1931, says that it was 'little less than a tragedy' that a man like Lowe presided over the Education Department at so crucial a period. More charitable historians have since blamed the times rather than Lowe but have not, on the whole, sharply disagreed with Arnold's claim that the Revised Code was 'the heaviest blow dealt at civilization and social improvement in my time.'[15]

Those who share Arnold's indignation point to the unfortunate effects of the code, effects which lasted throughout the mid-Victorian period. Teachers experienced little or no loss of income although their real wages tended to remain stationary during a generally prosperous period. The code was not the only or probably the most important cause; an over-supply relative to demand restrained the advancement of wages in the decade after 1862. It was the status and self-respect of the teachers that, over the short term, suffered most. There is evidence that teachers responded to the discipline of the new code by paying more attention to fundamentals; this was a gain, but not a pure gain. The boredom of having to drill and be drilled made teachers impatient and pupils restless and this led to an increase in the application of punishment. It has been argued that the teachers' training colleges were as much to blame as the code for the failure to make the teaching of fundamentals more interesting, and yet it is not entirely fair to hold the training colleges responsible for poor performance when they were suffering the effects of official stinginess. There is no doubt that the inspectors as well as the teachers found their work less rewarding than previously. Under the old regime the inspectors had thought of themselves as advisers and counsellors, but when they were forced to spend most of their time giving examinations, they came, inevitably, to be regarded as inquisitors. They were in the unenviable position of standing between the central office, always pressing for higher standards of performance from the schools, and the teachers and school managers who had an economic interest in keeping standards low. Many of the inspectors retaliated by filling their reports not merely with complaints about their own difficulties but with evidence to show that the curriculum was becoming less humane. They privately charged that Lowe had sacrificed quality to quantity, not because of necessity but because he had a narrow vision of the responsibilities of the state.[16]

Lowe tried to anticipate that charge by claiming that a minimalist position had been forced upon him by the need to work within a faulty system. But he had also said in the House of Commons that his code, whatever its inadequacies, would bring about some improvements: 'if it is not cheap it shall be efficient: if it is not efficient it shall be cheap.' This crisp, insensitive, slogan remained in people's memories far longer

than his more generous statements of principle. As we have seen on
several occasions already, his impulse to put ideas into graphic language
made him a good journalist and, if not a bad politician, at least a frequently misunderstood one. His position on education for the poor is a
conspicuous example. Those who disapproved of his actions charged
him with seeking to restrict social mobility by deliberately impoverish-
ing the quality of education offered to children of the working class.

The previous chapter has argued that his views on education for all
classes were not, in the context of the times, reactionary. His actions,
public statements, and private correspondence relating to the Revised
Code support that contention. On many occasions and as early as 1858,
before he became vice-president, he stated plainly that he believed the
system of state subsidy to voluntary societies was wrong in principle
and could not be made into an adequate means of providing the kind
and amount of education which modern society required. In Parliament
in June 1858, and in *The Times* in November 1859, he attacked the
complacency of the ruling classes, especially their self-satisfied belief
that the 'march of intelligence' would somehow enlighten the nation.
He said that he could see no grounds for such optimism. It was true
that most people were becoming literate, but reading did not seem to
lead the urban poor to observe the most simple laws of sanitation.
Workmen now had accessible to them the works of the classical economists; despite this, unions were growing in strength and strikes were becoming more frequent and violent. Friendly societies had been in existence for a century, and yet confidence men could easily dupe artisans
into joining fraudulent mutual benefit societies. Following closely the
argument of Book Five of *The Wealth of Nations*, he cautioned against
the easy assumption that material progress and popular enlightenment
would advance hand in hand. On the contrary, specialization of function tended to turn workers into 'drones.' Effective education, not mere
literacy, was needed to counteract this tendency. It was distressing,
therefore, that England, the most advanced industrial society in the
world, had to make do with a voluntary system barely adequate to combat illiteracy. He asked the members of Parliament who supported the
status quo to reflect on the fact that England had experimented for
twenty years with Kay Shuttleworth's compromise system and had ex-
pended millions on it with a pathetically meagre return. Public education was, he stated, significantly behind that offered in America, much
of Western Europe, and all of the English-speaking colonies. No nation
would be inclined to look to England for a model of how to run a
rational system of public instruction. He asserted that every intelligent
statesman in the country knew that what he said was true but lacked
the courage to admit it. Humbug decreed that England should have to
live with a faulty system. Volunteerism had been a 'gross mistake,' he

said in 1870. It had forced the government to follow where it should have led. 'No person,' he claimed on that occasion, 'could have been a more consistent opponent of the voluntary system than I have been.'[17]

He was just as forthright about what he wished the system to be. Freed from the voluntary system, the state could establish local educational districts, set a local rate, provide central inspection to insure uniform standards, and give aid from the national treasury to areas of extreme rural and urban poverty. He did not favour free tuition or compulsory attendance; he thought such measures would ignore economic realities and weaken moral fibre. Nevertheless, the state could provide incentives; it could, for example, open the lower echelons of the civil service to elementary school graduates. By doing that, working class parents could be shown in ways they would immediately understand that it was in their long-run interest to sacrifice the income from their children's labour.[18]

These and other ideas he elaborated to Lord Brougham whose advice he solicited during the Revised Code controversy. Probably he was hoping that Brougham would assure the non-sectarians that the new code was only intended as an expedient. How, on such a question as this, he asked Brougham, could a politician be expected to act strictly according to the dictates of reason? Humbug was England's curse but it was a power in the land. How could a minister in a department of government which was expected to administer, not innovate, presume to declare a revolution simply because he understood it to be necessary? Lowe assured Lord Brougham that he was prepared to do his duty as a practical man of affairs even though he found no joy in it.[19]

Cole and Lingen convinced him that the payment-by-results principle, if strictly enforced, might be the way to work within the faulty system and extract the maximum of benefit from it. Clerical school managers and their allies among the inspectorate would protest and drag their feet, but the state must not be deterred by that. It must do all that it could within the confines of possibility. It must make the first step of bringing the schools up to a national minimum. It must make sure that everyone had the basic educational tools required for self-help. Lowe pointed out that cheap or free libraries, mechanics institutes, evening and extension classes, were already available in many places. By punishing laxness in the teaching of the three 'Rs,' the state could prepare individuals to educate themselves. Lowe agreed with the Newcastle commissioners that the rudiments were not being taught. He had hired National School children to read to him only to discover that they could not manage words of more than three syllables. If that bad record could be improved, if ambitious youths could be brought to the point where they could understand *The Wealth of Nations*, Blackstone's *Commentaries*, Cassell's *Education*, and Arnot's *Physics*, then they would have what they needed to advance a rung up the social ladder or make better use of the station into which God had called them.[20]

Quaint though this reading list may seem, it does show that he expected the three 'Rs' to be taken to a high level of attainment. It also shows that he believed the methods of instruction should emphasize understanding and not mere reading facility. One of the charges against the Revised Code is that it increased the use of drill methods. Whether it did or not (and in all likelihood it did not), it is beyond dispute that its sponsor was an outspoken enemy of rote learning. He tried with some success to get more lively and stimulating textbooks adopted. One of his major failings was his faith that economic incentives would induce teachers and training colleges to experiment with more imaginative ways of teaching the fundamentals. In this he was mistaken, but his error was one of optimism and not, as was so often the case with him, one of pessimism.[21]

The emphasis the Revised Code put on standardized examinations is not an indication that its framers wanted to impoverish the curriculum. Lowe kept answering his critics by saying that the state's first responsibility, given the restraints imposed upon it by partnership with voluntary societies, was to see that the schools, whatever else they did, taught up to a minimum. The three 'Rs' were, he insisted, a minimum, not a maximum. There was nothing in the code to prevent the teaching of history, literature, religion, or other subjects that are not simply skills and therefore cannot be measured by standardized, objective testing. If teachers were sincere in their claims to professionalism and idealism, then they would not be deterred by the fact that humane studies earned no government subsidy. Since Lowe did not believe the protestors were sincere, this line of argument has something disingenuous about it. He was making a debater's point in a particularly bitter controversy. That is not to suggest that he rejoiced at reports that school managers were restricting their offerings, but he could hardly have been surprised or entirely displeased to see his premises vindicated. If humbug were the great evil, then he could reflect that his code was already having a good effect. What caused him great anger was the discovery that when he departed from the Education Department, his successors began to bribe school managers into broadening their curricula by extending the examination and subsidy formula to inappropriate subjects. He thought this witless and lazy. Payment by results had never been intended to be so misused, he told a Tory vice-president. He continued to worry about this breakdown in his system during the rest of his public life. His first speech after he had gone to the House of Lords in 1880 was about the stupidity of 'cramming phrases and catchwords into children who do not understand them.'[22]

Lowe valued quality as much as he did quantity. He did not wish to give priority to quantity but felt constrained to do so by a faulty system that had to be accepted as a fact of life. Consistently he tried to make the structure of elementary education as commodious as those constraints permitted. One of the reasons why the first minute appealed to him was because he thought it offered a way to reach large numbers of completely neglected children in poor and remote regions. School managers under the old system had no hope of applying successfully for a grant unless they employed a satisfactory number of teachers with certificates from teacher training colleges. Lowe concluded that if he could find a way to relax these requirements without seriously debasing standards and to spread education more evenly without greatly inflating costs, then he could work a real improvement. Grouping children by age for examination was, he believed, the best means to that end. Any other procedure would permit school managers to hire cheap, poorly trained, teachers and avoid the consequences by presenting their children, no matter how old they were, in the lowest standards. But if that could be prevented, then schools in poor regions would be forced by economic necessity to find able, if unpolished, schoolmasters – or more likely, schoolmistresses. Young women who specialized in the relatively simple skills would not be frustrated by having to teach them. The central government would not have to provide two or three years of expensive education in a training college to so many and could divert money into aiding those children and schools most in need. Lowe knew that grouping by age would work hardships, especially during the transition period, but thought the gains worth the losses. Therefore he was greatly perturbed when the cabinet ordered him to delete this feature of the first Revised Code.[23]

As soon as grouping by age was dropped, Lowe surprised the certified teachers and the staffs of the training colleges by becoming their champion. His change of position was as logical as it was disconcerting. If school managers were to be permitted to indulge in fraud, then certification would be the only means left to protect the public. Thus when his employer, John Walter, presented a motion to the House that fifteen hundred schools be given grants even though they lacked certified teachers, Lowe stoutly opposed it. Certification was a monopoly, he agreed, but so was all licensing. Adam Smith, he reminded the House, believed an ocean voyager should not be allowed to decide whether or not he preferred a captain who could navigate. Children no less than travellers needed protection if there was grave danger to their safety and to the safety of others. And with the revision of his Revised Code, there was, he asserted, grave danger. Having denied the parents protection, it was up to the government to do everything possible to provide the youth of the nation with teachers who had a professional pride in their work. Teachers, he said, are the agents of civilization in many small communities; in every school they are the agents of light. Expanding on this theme Lowe struck a lyrical note which must have sounded strange to the ears of his listeners: 'A school, like a church, is militant, continually fighting with innumerable foes – ignorance, vice, and crime – which encompass it on every side. It may be compared with a luminous circle, but its energies, though strained to the utmost, are often unable to make any impression upon the black mass around. Its work is never done; it is always beginning, never ending. Every child born in the world recruits the powers of ignorance, and you require all the inducements and stimulants that can possibly be applied in order to continue, with any hope of even partial success, what must be called a perpetual warfare.'[24]

Matthew Arnold found it 'impossible to repress a smile' when he observed a *Times* writer lecturing *The Times*'s proprietor on the civilizing mission of the school militant. He found it amusing that Walter had embarrassed Lowe by presenting him with a 'practical, immediate *reductio ad absurdum*' of the premises on which the Revised Code rested. Many others must have considered Lowe a hypocrite. Only months before he had warned that if schoolmasters thought they could get away with it, they would invent cunning schemes to cheat the government and the parents. They would construct ramshackle, ill-ventilated, badly-drained schoolhouses and, if not prodded and policed, would make their schools into sanctuaries where they could indulge in leisurely pursuits, unsuited to their station in life. It must be granted that the shift of tone was dramatic and, as always, exaggerated. It is also easy to understand why people who did not share Lowe's trust in the power of regulatory devices could not believe that shift to be in any way sincere. And yet Lowe was not aware of any contradiction in believing that schoolmasters were weak vessels, open to temptation, and, at the same time, warriors battling to hold back the encircling gloom. He believed it was the artificial restraint or direction of laws and administration which deflected human instinct away from selfish barbarism towards civilization.[25]

On balance, Lowe's virtues as an educational reformer were more substantial than his shortcomings. Unlike most liberal politicians of the period, he believed mass education to be of the first importance. He saw that there was no chance to give England an educational system adequate to its needs so long as the state was the prisoner of the voluntary system. He was undoubtedly correct in assuming that there was no way that the state could escape from that trap while religious passions and rivalries were intense and directly tied to politics. His Revised Code was an attempt, and not an inconsequential one, to make the best of a situation he knew to be bad.

One of the reasons why Lowe's enemies were so irate and vindictive was that they suspected him of trying to place a Trojan horse outside the walls of the Anglican establishment. Lord Robert Cecil was sure of it when he learned through informants within the Education Department that Lingen was bribing headmasters in National Society schools to adopt 'conscience clauses' in return for building grants. Conscience clauses were arrangements used in Irish schools allowing clergy from all denominations to enter schools to instruct children according to their own faiths. Lingen's action was clear proof, Cecil charged, that the vice-president was 'insidiously and clandestinely' attempting to undermine the voluntary system. Lowe admitted approving the action but tried to claim that the motives were purely economic: he wanted Anglican schools to serve Roman Catholics and Nonconformists in places where it would be impractical to build separate and competing facilities. Cecil and the bishops were sure that this was not the only reason. They complained that Lowe intended to use his conscience clauses to make religious instruction a subsidiary rather than a primary activity of the schools. Lowe came close to admitting the charge on a number of occasions. In 1870, at a prize day ceremony at the Mechanics Institute in Halifax, he told his predominantly Nonconformist audience that the Revised Code had tended 'very forcibly to the secularization of education' because it gave no grants for religious instruction. Matthew Arnold noted after reading the speech: 'of course his great ambition was to go further.'[26]

Arnold was, of course, correct; but how far did Lowe wish to go? So long as he was a responsible minister he had to claim he had no intention of laying irreverent hands on the voluntary system, however opposed he might be to it in principle. In 1867, however, he dropped that pretence. Carried away with his own prophetic oratory on the occasion of the passing of Disraeli's household suffrage bill, he warned the politicians who had allowed this constitutional change to go through with so little opposition that, even though they did not seem to be aware of it, an era of 'permanent stability and mutual confidence' was coming to an end, and the 'perpetual whirl of change' was about to begin. In the past voluntarism had, after a fashion, done good service; now its inefficiencies could no longer be tolerated and must be replaced by a national, rate-supported system of the widest possible scope. 'I believe,' he told the House, 'it will be absolutely necessary that you should prevail on our future masters to learn their letters.' Posterity credited him with the more arresting phrase: 'We must educate our masters.' Obviously he did not intend quite that. The following year, late in 1868, he told an audience at the University of London that if the ruling classes persisted in enfranchising ignorance, they would be giving 'an exhibition of rashness and folly which any intelligent American would treat with the most absolute scorn.' He claimed that every informed observer of the United States understood that in that country education was the only 'antidote' to democracy's evil effects. But when he came to recommending specific antidotes on this occasion it was obvious that some of his boldness had passed. He proposed to keep the voluntary schools intact while forcing on them a conscience clause and then 'filling the gaps' by compelling local bodies to build rate-maintained, nonsectarian schools in places where voluntary societies did not reach. By 1868 he had been forced to concede that 1867 had not really changed the atmosphere and that exhortation was not going to bring about a comprehensive change in popular education.[27]

The responsibility that came with a return to office later in 1868 caused him to moderate his rhetoric; it also gave him another opportunity to move elementary education a step further in the direction he wanted it to go. In 1869 he responded to a cabinet circular sent by Gladstone asking for advice. His suggestions were adopted by W.E. Forster, the vice-president of the committee, in his draft of an educational reform bill. Lowe sent in a 'filling in gaps' plan similar to the one he recommended in his London University speech. Forster and the cabinet agreed that this plan should become the working draft. Therefore the famous Forster Act of 1870 was partly Lowe's creation. It borrowed his recommendation that the government make a survey of the educational provisions or lack of provisions in each parish, publish its findings, and wait for the voluntary societies to re-establish new schools in parishes where the report showed provisions to be inadequate. If voluntary societies failed to respond within a reasonable period, the government was to direct the local authorities to elect a school board, build a school, and support it with rates. Naturally these board schools were to be nonsectarian. Lowe was pleased that these provisions were accepted but alarmed at another provision which gave the voluntary schools support from the rates. He predicted that Nonconformists would make the most strenuous objections to being assessed for the support of Anglican schools even if those schools did have conscience clauses. When the rest of the cabinet refused to act on this warning, Lowe feared that his secular-minded constituents at London University would demand an explanation from him. He wrote to Gladstone that if that happened, he would have no recourse but to resign, a threat the prime minister affected not to hear and adroitly deflected.[28]

Because he did not get his way on this point and because a new storm of sectarian passion did sweep the country, Lowe never claimed any part in the authorship of the 1870 act. Still, he did hail it as the first acknowledgment by the government of its duty to educate its citizens. Ironically his own provision that the voluntary societies be given time to fill in gaps brought about a flurry of activity. The National Society in particular built many new schools and thus considerably expanded the amount of denominational education available. In this curious way Lowe made a contribution to the sectarian system he despised, but he received no thanks from the Anglican forces within the Conservative party – and, of course, deserved none.[29]

Those forces had been able to do no more than blunt the full effect of the Revised Code in 1862, but they did manage to get revenge against its author two years later. Lord Robert Cecil had no trouble in finding faults in the administration of the code; many inspectors and civil servants within the Education Department were happy to bring him whatever damaging information he required. The department staff was large and chaotically housed and organized. Lingen had inherited this chaos from Kay Shuttleworth and had tried, with total contempt for tact, to tighten the reins. Complaints began to reach Tory ears from the moment Palmerston's government took over in 1859. Lowe, as the responsible political official, had to answer questions about reports of authoritarian behaviour. In 1861 he was asked to comment on why he allowed his inspectors' reports to be censored before they were tabled in Parliament. Lowe answered that it had long been government policy to return any report which contained objectionable or irrelevant material to its author, accompanied by a reminder about the rules inspectors were to observe in making their reports. He denied that the offensive passages were underlined. This had been the practice during the previous administration, but he had ordered it dropped. By his order inspectors were given the discretion of making whatever amendments they thought appropriate, and if they did not make the necessary amendments, their entire report was suppressed. He said that any speculative opinion was subject to this self-correction, not just opinion which senior officials disliked, and that the object was not to suppress damaging information but to instill in the department some badly-needed discipline. When similar accusations were made after the code was adopted, Lowe asked the House to consider what would happen if inspectors were allowed to form 'an Aulic Council,' free to criticize any regulation that caused more work or inconvenience. Civil servants were not responsible to Parliament and therefore could not be allowed to criticize publicly the policies of their responsible superiors.[30]

Had tempers been calm this statement of the obvious would have been acceptable. The practice of censorship had begun under Adderley during the previous administration and Lowe's order to cease the underlining of offending passages could be taken as a liberalizing step. Tempers were, however, never calm where Lowe was concerned. In April 1864 Lord Robert Cecil returned to the charge that Lowe had 'mutilated' those reports which showed his precious code was not working. Although the despotic Lingen was most likely Cecil's target, he moved a vote of censure against the responsible minister, the vice-president, for having used authority with arrogant 'ferocity' and for having deprived Parliament of information. John Walter, still smarting at having been defeated over his attempt to amend the code, seconded the motion, a particularly damaging move, since Walter was a Liberal and owned a pro-Palmerstonian newspaper. He, at least, made an attempt to keep the censure on the level of procedure and principle; Cecil, on the other hand, adopted a sneering tone. Palmerston, in describing the incident to the queen, remarked that Cecil had been unusually cruel: 'he never loses an opportunity of saying or doing an unhandsome thing.'[31]

Lowe replied to Cecil's angry charges in an even, contemptuous voice that reminded a listener in the press box of the hiss of a snake. Yes, he allowed criticisms of the code so long as they were constructive. No, his department did not mark offensive passages for deletion. But while he was talking, Cecil was circulating from hand to hand a report with underlined passages. The denial and the contradictory evidence reached the eyes and ears of the lightly attended House almost simultaneously. Lowe, who could not see what was happening, was disconcerted by the hum and laughter moving along the benches. When he had got up to speak, many on the government side, including most of the front bench, expecting a prolonged debate, had gone off to get their dinners. Thus when Lowe sat down he discovered that he had only Sir George Grey on hand to speak for him. Grey made his few laboured remarks and slowly ground to a halt. Cecil, seeing the opportunity, called a snap vote. Cardwell, Palmerston, and Gladstone managed to get back in time to get into the government lobby, but they could not find many colleagues to bring along with them and the motion of censure passed, a hundred and one to ninety-three, with a dozen Liberals voting with the majority. When the teller read the count, the House exploded with shouts and laughter.[32]

Six days later Lowe rose to announce his resignation from the vice-presidency. He complained of the ungentlemanly conduct of his opponents. He claimed that if he had been aware of what had been in the report that circulated, unseen by him, while he spoke, he could have made a perfectly satisfactory explanation. It was the habit of his secretaries to mark passages in order to bring them to Lingen's attention. If Lingen, after consultation with his superiors, made an unfavourable judgment, the report would go back to the inspector unmarked. Lowe said that he had not been aware of this procedure, since reports were always read to him to save the strain on his eyes. He had learned about the practice eventually and had immediately ordered it stopped. The report the House had seen had been marked before his restraining order and had been sent to Lord Granville. By mistake it had gone directly from the lord president's office to the inspector with the markings intact.[33]

A Select Committee chose to accept this rather laboured explanation, and the House then withdrew the censure motion. But by the time they did so Lowe was a private member. He told the House that the findings of the commission and the action of the House, though personally gratifying, had no bearing on the issue which had caused him to retire from office. After all, he had merely been vice-president of the committee, a junior minister, and thus not the responsible official. His resignation, he said, was not on constitutional grounds but on a point of personal honour; his integrity had been questioned, the House had given him the lie.[34]

But if he took the censure to be personal, not official, then why resign from office and not also resign his seat in Parliament? Was he responsible for the policy of the Committee on Education or was he not? In 1865 a parliamentary committee tried to find the answer and got conflicting opinions. Lowe said that the committee as a body was responsible; Lord Granville said the committee was mainly advisory; H.A. Bruce, Lowe's successor, thought that technically the responsibility rested nowhere, but that the vice-president did, in fact, make the important policy decisions. Lowe must have known Bruce was right; his unwillingness to admit that this was so shows that he was unsettled by his humiliation and desperately seeking excuses. When confident and sure of his course, he was always eager to seize the initiative but when forced on the defensive by some error, he had the disconcerting habit of denying personal responsibility.[35]

Lowe was a poor loser. The spectacle of Lowe humbled did not inspire pity in the hearts of his enemies. Cecil and Disraeli went through the ritual of expressing regret at the loss to the nation of a man of great talent, but they used the occasion to rub salt into open wounds. Cecil wished Lowe had been frank from the beginning about the confusions in his office and not tried to claim spotless virtue. He hoped this unfortunate incident had taught a lesson which all leaders needed to learn: that loyalty from subordinates must be earned, not simply commanded. Had the vice-president put some restraint on Lingen's rough-shod way of dealing with inspectors, had he, in particular, forbidden Lingen to drive one of the Roman Catholic inspectors out of his job, then civil servants would have been less ready to run to the opposition with departmental secrets. Disraeli followed this up with more instruction on the art of leadership. He thought it a matter of regret that this brilliant public servant seemed not to inspire loyalty from his colleagues. He wondered why it was that the Liberal front bench had in this, 'as in many other instances,' withheld the support that a junior minister normally has a right to expect from his superiors.[36]

These backhand thrusts were well aimed. Lowe had assumed, probably he had been led to assume, that if he were only patient he would get a cabinet post as soon as a vacancy occurred. In 1861 Sidney Herbert, worn out by his labours at the War Office, resigned. Cornewall Lewis took his place and there was a minor cabinet reshuffle. Lowe waited to be called but heard nothing. Then in 1863 Lewis died and again Lowe waited expectantly. But the opening went to Lord de Grey, a man Lowe thought inferior to himself in everything except nobility of birth. At a considerable cost to his pride he went to Cambridge House to plead his cause before Palmerston in person, but, as Delane told Granville, did not 'derive much consolation from his interview.' Granville did what he could but with no better success; the de Grey appointment was already settled, Palmerston said, and if any new post opened up, Clarendon had first call on it. When this was conveyed to Lowe, he told Delane that his patience was at an end and that he planned to resign. Granville was hesitant about speaking directly for fear of compromising the government, but in a long letter to Delane passed on the advice that nothing could be gained by quarrelling with 'the most good humoured Statesman in existence.' Their mutual friend could, Granville acknowledged, 'become a thorn of the first quality for the Government – and thereby get the reputation of a superior Horsman.' That, Granville thought, would be a pathetic way to end a career: Edward Horsman was a Liberal politician who had resigned a junior post to become an independent and rather tiresome parliamentary gadfly. Granville suggested that Delane intercede. Delane got in touch with Gladstone and Sir Charles Wood. They all wrote warm, flattering letters, containing carefully-worded reminders that Palmerston was not immortal. Lowe responded to this unaccustomed attention. He admitted that he was 'a good deal shaken by the extraordinary demonstration which they have made towards me and which commits them in every possible way to consult my interests at the first opportunity.' But this glimmer of optimism quickly faded. Two weeks before Cecil's censure motion Clarendon got the chancellorship of the Duchy of Lancaster and a seat in cabinet. This, Lowe told Cole, was the last straw. With two of his ancient enemies, Russell and Clarendon, guarding the gates he did not see how he could ever get through them. He restrained himself in public but fired off a leading article about how Clarendon was a man who thirsted after office, any office.[37]

Close upon this disappointment came the censure. Apparently all of the cabinet members thought Lowe had made a mess of things. They called him on the carpet and lectured him. Lowe told Cole that he had been 'pitched into like a criminal.' Each in their turn, Cole reported, 'told him it was for his own good' when, in fact, 'he knew it was for theirs.' This ordeal, on top of three years of expectation and disappointment, was more than he could bear. He announced to the government his intention to resign. Palmerston was surprised when told the news.

He said that though he could sympathize with Lowe's indignation over Cecil's tactic, he thought resignation unnecessary and a bit silly.[38]

There were some compensations in this 'ugly business.' John Walter sent an apology for having acted hastily and letters of consolation came from a variety of Whig notables. This soothed his pride. He wrote to Delane that he was glad to be rid of his impossible position and that he would never go back again except as a cabinet minister. He asked Delane if he had seen the latest parody in *The Owl* about his resignation – he thought it rather good:

> To vote contents his natural desire.
> He draws no stipend,
> But he eats no mire.[39]

12

In the Cave of Adullam

Lowe's political prospects did not appear to be bright in the spring of 1864. He had done hard and dangerous work for the Whigs and had received no rewards. When Palmerston needed the support of *The Times* in 1855, Lowe had been moved upward; but now, a decade later, the prime minister was too secure to be influenced by such considerations. He was generally popular in the country; his government seemed impregnable to attack, both from the opposition and from his own radical left; and he had made his treaty arrangements with Delane. It was true that the eighty-year old statesman could not, despite appearances to the contrary, live for ever, and that the political arrangements and balances he had constructed would not long survive him. As Lowe pointed out in a leading article, a shifting of alliances was likely to take place as soon as Palmerston was gone and then the 'new men,' most of whom had grown old and tired with waiting, would at last have a chance. But Lowe could not have expected any immediate benefits for himself in a change of leadership. If Russell and Gladstone succeeded, they would be likely to reintroduce the parliamentary reform issue, a move which would make the party an inhospitable place for Lowe. Perhaps the result of a move to the left would produce a new coalition of moderate men, dedicated to Palmerstonian principles, and in that case Lowe and the 'new men' would get their promotions. Speculations along these lines were not uncommon in the circle around Lord Lansdowne, the son of Lowe's old patron, but they were speculations which rested on many variables. It was certain that the immediate future offered Lowe no way out of the political limbo.[1]

The freedom to do and say what he pleased was a compensation. Lowe knew that he was secure at Calne so long as his noble patron did not need the seat for one of his own. There were leading articles to write about the iniquities of Lincoln and his armies, tricks to play on public school headmasters, speeches to make about the folly of defending Canada. He took up once again the subject of criminal law reform and wrote an article on the subject for the *Edinburgh Review* in which he exposed the 'mass of confusion' inherited from the dark ages and repeated some of his old arguments about the inutility of public executions. These projects and trips to Paris and Germany relieved the monotony of the dull parliamentary session of 1864. And then, early in 1865, his attention began to focus on the question of franchise reform, the issue that was beginning, even before Lord Palmerston died, to trouble the Liberal equilibrium.[2]

After his 1860 reform bill expired, unmourned, Lord John Russell had decided to wait, with what John Bright felt to be indecent patience, for signs that a 'popular breeze' had sprung up. 'Rest and be thankful,' Russell had advised an after-dinner audience at Blairgowrie. Many middle class people had taken a rest from class militancy in the prosperous mid-century years – to such an extent that Gladstone had cause to complain in his private correspondence about a spirit of selfish conservatism which he believed to be spreading through the kingdom in the early sixties. He particularly regretted that this spirit was producing a 'real though far from universal reaction' against the extension of the franchise. Bright discovered that this complacency had spread to many members of the working class. His efforts to arouse interest in the subject by a series of public rallies in the Black Country had not produced an enthusiastic response. But if there was little interest in agitation there was progress in organization of the radical working class and middle class leadership. A group of businessmen and professional men in Manchester formed a Reform Union in 1864 to work for a household suffrage and not long afterwards some trade unionists put together a Reform League, with manhood suffrage as their objective. Contacts between the two encouraged Bright to think that it might be possible to mend the rift between middle class and working class radicalism which had weakened the progressive cause since Chartist days. In the mid-sixties news of the improving fortunes of the Union armies in the American Civil War and Garibaldi's heroic campaigns in Sicily and southern Italy gave many Englishmen the sense that popular breezes had begun to blow elsewhere and might soon reach their island as well. By 1865 those breezes were strong enough to quicken the political instincts of Henry Brand, the Liberal Whip. He asked Palmerston, during the July elections of that year, if the cabinet had 'ventured to look the future in the face?' Palmerston made a noncommittal answer; he refused to make parliamentary reform an election issue but was careful not to cut off the possibility that some move might be made later in the year. Even earlier, in September 1864, Lowe had picked up rumours that some of the ministers were thinking of opening up the subject again. He gave warning that this might be true to the readers of *The Times*, and in doing so made a contribution to the resurrection of the subject from four years of neglect.[3]

These stirrings alerted a group of Whigs, many of them friends of Lord Lansdowne, to the possibility that Russell might soon try to introduce one of his 'half-way' measures. If he were allowed to do so, they believed, it would then be impossible to avert a slow drift into democracy. Some members of this group, most notably Lord Grey, the former colonial secretary and Lowe's old antagonist, believed that a fundamental, 'organic' change in the constitution needed to be made before popular agitation had a chance to build up. Grey had been worried about a possible drift into democracy ever since Russell had reintroduced the subject of reform into parliamentary debate in the 1850s. In an essay called *Parliamentary Government*, first published in 1858 and revised and reissued in 1864, he had argued that piecemeal amendments to the 1832 settlement would in time lead to universal suffrage. He recognized that it would be impossible to meet the rising ambitions of the working people unless concessions were made but urged that those concessions come all at once and be accompanied by carefully contrived safeguards, so that the great mass of citizens might have a voice in the constitution but not have a voice so powerful that it would drown out every other. His plan was to make a drastic extension of the franchise and, in the same comprehensive measure, provide for cumulative voting schemes, life memberships in the House of Lords, indirect election procedures, and other mechanical devices designed to preserve the ascendency of the minority and protect the nation against the evils of democracy.[4]

Grey's essay went virtually unread when it first appeared, but in 1859 he summarized some of his arguments in a public letter of protest against the methods that his own party was using to defeat Disraeli's reform bill of that year. Repeated and protracted discussion of the subject, he wrote, might create the atmosphere of instability and class hostility which the bills were supposedly designed to avert. He called on moderate men of all parties to take the subject out of party contention and to accept Disraeli's measure as a vehicle on which a comprehensive constitutional change might be grafted.[5]

Because it came from a leading Whig this criticism of Russell's tactics produced a lively discussion and gained several recruits to Grey's cause from within the Liberal party. One of them was Edward Horsman, a man who prided himself on his reputation as an independent-minded member. Another was Lord Elcho, later the Earl of Wemyss, a former Peelite, an arm-chair general, and Britain's most enthusiastic Volunteer,

a man who worried throughout his long public life about the encroachments of socialism and unionism and consequently was open to suggestions about how the drift, which he perceived everywhere, could be
stopped. Horsman and Elcho spoke out in the House of Commons
against Russell in 1859 and openly opposed (in conspiracy with several
dozen dissident Liberals) the reform bill sponsored by their own party
in 1860. Since Russell withdrew his bill, no confrontation took place,
and during the next four years the subject nearly disappeared from parliamentary notice. Then in 1864, perceiving the subtle indications of
renewed interest, Elcho, Horsman, and Grey sought out their former
confederates and canvassed among their Whig connexions. The dissident
group they collected met first at Elcho's house and then later accepted
the hospitality of Lord Lansdowne. Since Lowe was an active subversive in 1860 and since he sat for Lansdowne's borough of Calne, it
seems more than probable that he took part in these strategy meetings
from an early date. He had no use for Grey's 'organic' schemes, colonial
or domestic, but he had decided to oppose the government should it
make a move in the direction of reform and was aware that he needed
some base for his operations.[6]

Lowe's public commitment to the anti-reform cause came in May
1865 when Edward Baines, son of the editor of the *Leeds Mercury*, introduced a private member's bill asking for the reduction of the borough franchise from the existing ten pounds to six pounds. He had
introduced the same bill the previous year with one spectacular result:
during the debate Gladstone had made his electrifying statement that
'every man who is not presumably incapacitated by some consideration
of personal unfitness or of political danger, is morally entitled to come
within the pale of the constitution.' When Palmerston sent him a sharp
remonstrance, Gladstone gave an intricate explanation to show that he
had meant nothing revolutionary, but no one made much of an effort
to puzzle out his reasoning. Radicals rejoiced, while loyal Palmerstonians expressed in the strongest language their shock. Lowe gave the
chancellor of the exchequer a sound thrashing in *The Times* for having,
with his nonsense about the 'Divine Right of multitudes,' laid the
groundwork for a 'sweeping and levelling democracy.' In the past, Lowe
continued, everyone had assumed that Gladstone shared the liberal
vision. 'We had dreamt of an England made up of a society rising by distinct and well-marked gradations from its base to its summit, each part
discharging its destined functions without envy and without discontent,
with absolute personal freedom, under an equal law, divided between
thinkers and workers, between owners and producers of wealth, with all
that inequality between man and man which is the result of unrestricted
freedom.' But now, Lowe thought, Gladstone must have concluded that
this dream of freedom within a stratified society was really slavery;

future biographers, he hoped, would pass lightly over this unfortunate episode in the life of a distinguished statesman.[7]

This opinion Lowe expressed under the cover of anonymity, but when Baines brought in his 1865 bill, Lowe decided to make his first statement in the House of Commons on the subject. The speech he made on this occasion produced a great impression because, despite the fact that the question had been debated at great length for fifteen years, few members had ever heard their own convictions so articulately and comprehensively expressed. Most of them seem to have been aware that Lowe had made a bold and perhaps foolhardy gesture in stating, in such uncompromising terms, his opposition to any concession at a time when it seemed likely that Palmerston and Russell or possibly Derby and Disraeli were weighing the political advantages of some moderate alterations. Lowe had deliberately allowed himself no room for equivocation. 'It is no use putting my hand to the plough and looking back,' he wrote to an old Nottingham friend. 'I have adopted the inductive method for what seemed to me good reasons. The first principle is to start unprejudiced, and abandon yourself wholly to the teaching of experience.' In abandoning himself wholly to the dictates of inductive logic Lowe was to enhance his reputation as a political philosopher but not as a practical politician.[8]

The speech on Baines's bill in 1865 and the more celebrated speeches of the following year demonstrated how effectively the utilitarian-liberal hypothesis could be used to challenge the presuppositions of many of the Liberal reformers. Lowe's method was to make a list of those presuppositions, his 'chart of fallacies,' and then dismantle them, one by one. The following brief summary of his chart and his comments on it will give an idea of his general approach during the entire reform debate which lasted from 1865 to 1867.

The first item on his chart was the metaphysical fallacy. Gladstone had been the victim of this delusion in 1864. In speaking about *a priori* rights the Liberal minister had introduced a political theory which had 'formed the terror and ridicule of that grotesque tragedy, the French Revolution.' Bentham and others had long ago exploded the natural rights argument, therefore it was unnecessary to explore its philosophical weaknesses. To grasp its inanity, members of Parliament need only to reflect that if voting were a right natural to all men, then no human being, Aborigine or Hottentot, could justly be turned away from the polls.[9]

The second, or sentimental fallacy had a much greater appeal to Englishmen because it rested on a well-intentioned desire to elevate the working class and to reward it for good behaviour. John Stuart Mill was the leading sentimentalist. He believed that good will between classes was the greatest good. No doubt it was a worthy end, but it was not the immediate end of government. The art of legislation was a 'practical matter of business and statecraft,' the object being good government. And the legislator must be aware that the majority of poor people have a natural tendency to prefer short-run advantages, to their own and society's detriment. This they do, not because they are depraved but because their range of experience is limited. Thus, speculations about moral feelings and subjective motives are irrelevant. Constitutional changes, conceived as rewards, were not only wrongly conceived but ineffective in producing the desired result. American and Australian experience demonstrated that the average working man cares little for the gift of the franchise. When in those places he does bother to 'pick his ballot up out of the gutter,' he often uses it to elect men who favour high tariffs, promote tax exemptions for the majority, water currency, and put restraints on free enterprise. With the existing ten-pound franchise it was already possible for the working man who did value the privilege of voting to earn that privilege by practicing self denial. Under the present system, by foregoing the odd pint, he could spend a few more pounds on his rent and qualify; and by being required to earn his reward the workman would at the same time receive a lesson in responsibility. Thus in the long run the moral life of the nation would be improved, not through paternalism, but through the exercise of self help.[10]

Lowe emphasized that his pragmatic position was not, as some critics charged, an overly simplified, vulgar form of utilitarianism. He said he was not ignorant of the fact that Bentham had included feelings in his calculations about quantities of happiness. Doubtless it was true that subjective feelings had to be reckoned when working the felicific calculus. Should it ever become obvious that failure to grant concessions to some popular passion or some irrational aspiration might provoke profound civil strife, then wise statesmen, guided by the 'inductive' method, would do whatever was necessary to avert that strife. But even in allowing foolish or misguided legislation to pass, they would be guided by rational calculations of what would best promote good government. If, for example, reformers could demonstrate that failure to extend the franchise would produce class conflict or even class bitterness, then rational men would have to consider ways of diminishing these feelings. But rational men would look for hard evidence and would not be impressed by arguments from abstract moral hypotheses. They would also look for demonstrations that constitutional changes would, in fact, promote the general welfare. No sane proposer of reform had so far offered up evidence that the majority of the unenfranchised were disgruntled or even much interested in the question. Until that evidence was produced, the sentimentalists need not be seriously considered.[11]

The argument from necessity, Lowe maintained, applied only to a country threatened by dangerous unrest. And England was at rest, more so than she had ever been in her long history. Bright and the representatives of the various leagues and unions had discovered this when they had attempted to stump the country and stir up agitation. The country had greeted their tub-thumping with a collective yawn. Fallacious indeed were those who counselled a healthy body to take medicine; more foolish still were those who, in time of difficulty, advised suicide as a first, rather than a last, resort.[12]

The third and final fallacy – the fatalistic argument – came about not through a failure to apply tough-minded reason but through a failure of nerve. Fatalists were people who had been mezmerized by historical determinism. Even de Tocqueville had fallen victim to this 'coward's argument'; determinism was 'at once the foundation and the blemish' of his otherwise monumental work. Faint heartedness was no argument: 'If this Democracy be a good thing, let us clasp it to our bosoms; if not, there is, I am sure, spirit and feeling enough in this country to prevent us from allowing ourselves to be overawed by any vague presage of this kind, in the belief that the matter has been already decided upon by the fates and destinies in some dark tribunal in which they sit together to regulate the future of nations. The destiny of every Englishman is in his own heart ...'[13]

Having thus disposed of the arguments put forward by Gladstone and Mill, to his own satisfaction at least, Lowe then tried to show how a bill which proposed to enfranchise only the working class élite could endanger the 'balance of interests' and open the door to democracy. He contended that in some of the industrial cities the four-pound reduction Baines proposed would give the artisan class a preponderance, since it would combine with the petty bourgeoisie in a 'sort of chemical affinity.' This 'swamping' argument was, he acknowledged, tiresomely familiar to the members who had listened to past debates on the subject. They would recall that Russell, Mill, and, to a certain extent, even Bright had tried to answer it by making two points: (1) that the skilled workers would not behave as a class, and (2) that 'fancy franchises' could insure that the workers had a chance to realize their legitimate aspirations without endangering the ascendency of the wealthy and educated. By 'fancy franchises' he meant devices, such as plural voting, artful boundary drawing, literacy tests, which reformers relied on to protect the ruling classes from the effects of democracy.

Anyone who put trust in either of these propositions, Lowe asserted, was being either naïve or dishonest. America and Australia offered illustrations of how easily and inevitably these fancy franchises could be swept aside once the trend towards democracy had been allowed to

run. In England the process would be even quicker because, for historical reasons, English working men had developed a sense of solidarity
and had a longer experience of co-operative association in unions and
friendly societies than any other working class in the world. In the
human as well as in the natural order, Lowe thought, 'aggregation and
crystallization are strong just in proportion as the molecules are minute.' Who then could honestly doubt that people, schooled by strikes,
would permanently remain ignorant of their united power? 'You cannot treat them like pigs or cattle, or like Curran's fleas, "which, if they
had been unanimous, would have pulled him out of bed."' The answer
he thought obvious: inventors of artificial contrivances were simply in-
dulging in wish-fulfilment of simple-minded trust. 'I can fancy no employment more worthy of the philosopher and statesman than the
invention of safeguards against democracy but I can fancy no employment less worthy of either statesman or philosopher than counselling us
to give a loose rein to democracy in order that we may see whether we
can get back what we have given in another way.'[14]

He finished the speech by stating his liberal faith in progress through
a gradual amelioration of the troubles of mankind and his belief that
true progress can be promoted by 'pure and clear intelligence alone.'
Because he was a liberal he maintained that he was bound to stand fast
against any force which would prevent the application of that productive intelligence.[15]

The *Pall Mall Gazette* thought it heard echoes of Kidderminster brickbats in the speech. Bright's *Daily News* reported that two-thirds of the
Liberal MPs were 'in ecstacies.' Lord Lansdowne said that reading the
account in *The Times* had soothed his gout. Matthew Arnold read
extracts in the *Telegraph* and rejoiced that 'vulgar Liberals' would now
have to make 'a more searching treatment of the whole question of Reform,' and perhaps learn, in the process, some new platitudes. Congratulations poured in from many quarters. Those who had laughed
loudest at the quip about Curran's fleas and had applauded most enthusiastically his hits at Gladstone and Mill were the same people who had
most enjoyed his debacle over the censorship of the inspectors' reports.
This was balm to his hurt sensibilities. At the same time he was aware
that he would have to pay a price for the compliments he received.
After so detailed an explanation of why any concession would be fatal
to good government, he could not, without publicly eating his words,
support any kind of Liberal bill, no matter how moderate. Indeed he
would be a liability to any ministry wishing to preserve flexibility on
the issue. But he was in too fractious a mood to worry about counting
the costs. The Whigs had abandoned him; he would make them regret it
by saying out loud what most of them believed but dared not say. If
they continued to reject him, he would be no worse off than he was at

present. If they decided to make amends and send him an offer, then that would be a sign that the leadership had decided to shelve their reform plans, and that would not only be a personal triumph but a service to the country. There was always the chance that at some date in the future it might be possible, as Lord Grey hoped and predicted, to put together a fusion party of moderate men opposed to democracy and in that case his determination to put his hand to the plough and not look back would be remembered to his advantage.[16]

In that month of May 1865, with election talk already in the air, Lord Elcho, after consulting Lord Grey, wrote to Russell, suggesting that a Royal Commission might be the safest way to dispose of the reform issue. He also wrote to Disraeli, asking him to support the commission plan because it would 'cut the ground from under agitation' while the election was under way. He was afraid that candidates might be pushed by their constituents into making pro-reform pledges. Disraeli passed the suggestion on to Derby who vetoed it because he feared that the Tory party might be bound to accept whatever a commission recommended. Elcho's intentions were clear; he wanted a commission not only as a delaying tactic but as a possible nucleus around which 'moderate' Liberals and 'advanced' Conservatives could gather should Bright and his followers force Palmerston and Russell to put together one of their piecemeal constitutional bills. To keep this from happening his group was ready to form a subversive alliance with the opposition. 'I am most anxious in all this to act as far as possible in accordance with your views,' Elcho had written in a postscript to one of his communications with Disraeli. Thus, more than two months before Palmerston led his party to an election victory in July, Derby and Disraeli knew that there was a bomb planted in the ranks of their opponents, already assembled and fused.[17]

Three months after the election Palmerston died. 'Who will replace him?' Lowe asked in leading articles. Happily, the country need not fear another experience with Lord Russell, for he was too old, disliked by the Irish, notorious for 'creating zealous and eager opponents,' and totally oblivious to the opinions of his colleagues and the public. Gladstone was a stronger contender, Lowe thought, but 'deficient in tact and temper,' and, since he was a favourite of the radicals, too much distrusted by the majority of the party. Only Lord Granville, Lowe and *The Times* advised, had the ability to attract friends and conciliate enemies.[18]

Delane and Lowe hoped that these articles would influence events, and they did, the Duke of Somerset believed, contribute importantly to the difficulties the Liberal leaders experienced in putting their new ministry together. But protests from *The Times* did not prevent Russell from assuming the leadership. Everyone suspected that Lowe had written the articles, therefore their main effect was to rekindle bad feeling between the prime minister and himself at a time when Russell was considering whom to invite into the cabinet. A powerful group, Gladstone, Granville, Wood, Alderley, Stanley, spoke to Russell about Lowe's destructive capabilities and about the advantages of retaining friendly relations with Delane. Russell did not respond, so, in his absence, the members already picked for the cabinet asked Granville to sound Lowe out on reform. If Granville could bring back assurances that Lowe would not make trouble for them on that issuc, then Russell's most valid objection might be removed. And in spite of his bold talk about never looking back Lowe did, it seems, risk a quick glance. He told Delane that he would not take the Duchy of Lancaster even if offered by a better government than this one; but that if Russell were to do the unexpected and give him 'some enormous bribe,' he might be persuaded to consider it. The Colonial Office would probably have been big enough, and Sir George Grey thought he might have had it but for that 'unlucky speech.' In any event, Granville had no grand bribes to offer. Lowe told him that he had thought of some concessions which he might be willing to make on parliamentary reform but that he saw no point in going over them since it was plain that Russell was looking for any excuse to pass him by. He wrote to Delane after the interview: 'Lord John doesn't want to have me and invents the best reasons he can find for his decision which is really activated by private animosity which I have very well deserved.' Besides, he added, the ministry would not last and there was 'no honour to be gained by joining it.' He was, he said, content to wait. 'If they go in for Reform they are ruined if they don't they give me much higher position than mere office could give.'[19]

Lowe was, of course, correct about Russell's animosity. The prime minister knew that he needed to mend fences now that the Palmerstonian truce had ended but stuck at the prospect of associating with a man who could indulge in such hatred on the leader page of *The Times* – a hatred 'so strong that every other consid^n is sacrificed in order to indulge it.' During the negotiations in forming the ministry in November, Russell wrote in the notes he prepared for drafting his letter to the queen: 'Another and I hope final attempt was made by Lord Granville in favour of Lowe for the Cabinet – he and Cardwell are Lowe's strongest supporters. The abject fear of the Times is most despicable.' Should Delane's agents ever set foot in the cabinet, he told Sir Charles Wood, 'he would walk out of it.' He made no difficulties about the other members of the Elcho group. He considered Horsman for the Duchy of Lancaster but found that the cabinet did not want him. He offered Elcho's friend, Sir William Gregory, an Admiralty lordship, but got a polite refusal. He tried to bring in Lord Stanley, the man many of the dissidents looked to as a possible 'third party leader' (Lowe had given him a puff

in *The Times* by saying that he had a logical mind, full of information
'derived from Bentham's political arithmetic'), but Stanley, on advice
from Disraeli, reluctantly backed away. Thus the members of Elcho's
group stayed firm, not because they were cohesive but because Russell
was unwilling to make the necessary effort to bribe or seduce them into
conformity. As most of his cabinet colleagues were aware, this would
mean that a reform bill would almost certainly bring on a revolt led by
men who, except for Lowe, were not in themselves particularly formidable but who had the backing of powerful Whig families. These Liberal
rebels were determined to prevent what they considered to be an imminent danger of a radical take-over of the Liberal party, even if that act
of rebellion meant wrecking, at least temporarily, their own party.
Lowe was certainly ready for the test. In December 1865 he wrote to
his brother giving advice about what needed to be done with sick cattle
and added: 'meanwhile I will try to turn out the government which if
not victory is revenge.'[20]

Knowing the odds against him, Russell nevertheless announced his
intention of bringing in a parliamentary reform bill during the next session. Why he moved with such unnecessary haste aroused and arouses
much speculation. Prudence must have told him to accept Elcho's suggestion and put the question into the hands of a bipartisan commission.
That would have pleased the cabinet, including even Gladstone, whose
first priority was cutting back on expenditures. Russell listened to the
words of caution, hesitated, and then gave the order to go ahead with a
bill. Those observers who interpret the events of 1866 and 1867 as responses to the need to balance and adjust tensions 'between and within
and across' parties point to the fact that the Liberal leadership had to
make peace with the radicals in the party and to respond to pressures
from the Reform League and Reform Union. More specifically, there is
some evidence to suggest that Russell decided to move immediately in
order to 'neutralize' W.E. Forster, who had been offered a Colonial
Office undersecretaryship as a gesture towards the Nonconformist radicals and who had made his acceptance conditional on the government
proceeding immediately with a reform bill. Those who favour this
explanation acknowledge that Russell's reaction to Forster's threat of
refusal was out of proportion to the damage that refusal could have
done. Delay until 1867 would not have sent the radicals scurrying into
the Tory party and it would have prevented the defection of the Whig-
Palmerston faction which was meeting at Lord Lansdowne's house. It
is possible, as one commentator has suggested, that Russell had got
caught up in his own tricky manoeuvrings and had 'slightly lost his grip
on affairs.' Or perhaps he was, as many thought at the time 'an old man
in a hurry,' an autocratic individual whose ego had become so involved
with the issue of constitutional reform that he could not listen to the

promptings of common sense. No one who observed his behaviour in office could deny that he was partial to sudden and unilateral actions; colleagues in previous ministries had frequently been annoyed by his sometimes maddeningly arbitrary actions. On the other hand, he was not, even as an old man, easily addled. His native obstinacy had not prevented him from seriously considering delaying tactics in November 1865. If he had been guided in his timing by purely tactical considerations he would surely have delayed and taken the slight risk of a radical revolt instead of going ahead and deliberately accepting the certainty of a revolt on his right. It would seem, therefore, not only charitable but reasonable to conclude that among the many reasons why Russell set Gladstone to work on a reform measure in December 1865 was a conviction that delay might lead to agitation on a large scale and that an atmosphere of tension would not allow the passage of a moderate bill, best suited to what he thought to be the country's best interests.[21]

Lowe's behaviour also seems to have been a compound of factional tactics, personal interests, and sincere convictions. During the first round of debate on reform in 1866, Bright congratulated Horsman on having recruited Lowe into his Cave of Adullam where 'he may call about him everyone that was in distress and everyone that was discontented.' Discontented and inclined to sulk, Lowe certainly was. But none of his enemies, except perhaps Russell, ever questioned the sincerity or the intensity of his anti-democratic sentiments. His remark about wanting revenge was not inconsistent with a genuine belief that the public interest would gain. He admitted that he was open to an 'enormous bribe' and was disappointed when none was offered him, but that was before the Russell government had committed itself to reform. If Delane is to be trusted, Lowe did have a bribe dangled in front of him in January 1866, when it was known that a Liberal bill was in the offing. Delane told Bernal Osborne that the India Office had been suggested for their mutual friend along with a promise of transference to the Home Office as soon as it became vacant. It is not clear how seriously this offer was made or by whom but it is certain that Lowe spurned the suggestions without hesitation. By January he had taken up his dwelling place in the Cave of Adullam and was not about to attach himself to a government so obviously and deservedly 'in extremis.'[22]

The signal for the beginning of the Adullamite rebellion was a debate not about parliamentary reform but about sick cows. First detected in June 1865, the 'Rinderpest' reached epidemic proportions by early summer – the first devastating cattle plague since the mid-eighteenth century. Farmers tried innoculations, totally without success. The Board of Trade issued regulations about compulsory slaughter and limitations on shipment but left the initiative for implementation to local authorities who, for the most part, did little or nothing. Dairymen, cattle raisers, railway managers, importers, denounced the Palmerston government both for its actions and its inaction; but neither the government ministers nor the bureaucracy were inclined to be hurried. Three months went by before the minister responsible asked for a Royal Commission to find out what the disease was and how it could be contained. Parliament granted the commission and named Lowe a member. He consulted with Simon and other medical authorities, determined that the only solution was to stop all movement of cattle, slaughter or quarantine imported animals, compel owners of exposed cattle to slaughter them – drastic actions which, he was convinced, only the central government had the authority to undertake. Knowing that the Board of Trade was far from eager to order rural landlords to massacre their herds, he tried to force its hand; he bullied the commission into adopting the stiff wording of a report which he drafted and into making it public in the near-record time of three months. By the time the report came out Russell was prime minister. As Lowe had expected, the new ministers stalled and then passed some emasculated legislation which did nothing to curb the epidemic. By the end of January, when Parliament opened, the monthly death toll had reached 120,000, and newspapers were writing about the prospects of a meat famine. With MPs from agricultural areas demanding action, Russell decided to suspend the agenda he had planned for the opening of the new Parliament in order to give precedence to a bill calling for compulsory slaughter but compensating the cattle-owners generously.[23]

The terms of the bill were far short of the drastic remedies the commission had recommended. This belated action did nothing to remove the impression of slackness caused by the previous inaction and the bill's compensation clauses seemed unfairly generous to those who thought the influence of the agriculturalists in Parliament was unfairly disproportionate. John Stuart Mill made a speech in which he objected to the policy of paying tax money collected in large part from the poor to the rich farmers and landlords who were already profiting from the high price of meat. He wanted the agriculturalists to take care of their own out of a fund raised by a special land or cattle tax. This proposal brought Lowe into action. He treated the front bench to a scathing resumé of their fumblings and their apparent inability to seize on a principle and then act decisively on it. After making that point against his own party, he turned his scorn on Mill, the Liberal MP for Westminster. Since most members of the House had mixed feelings about having a famous philosopher in their midst, they were relieved and pleased to observe a professional politician matching wits with Mill, challenging his reasoning about the conclusions of political economy, and, some thought, getting the better of the exchange. Lowe had expressed the opinion that the member for Westminster 'is, I am afraid, a little too clever for us in the House.' Tory squires who had become accustomed to disapprove automatically everything Lowe proposed were pleasantly surprised to hear him cautioning against an excess of cleverness and upholding the justice of handing out subsidies to cattle owners out of the public purse! Did the English squirearchy have, as the *Spectator* supposed, an unexpected new champion? This image of Lowe as the leader of the nation's bucolic hosts was meant to be amusing and to hint at the Whig-Adullamite conspiracy, news of which was now reaching informed journalists. It is doubtful that Gladstone (the majority leader in the Commons now that Russell had become a peer) was much amused by this performance. He could detect that Lowe's emphasis on the point that the government seemed to be unable first to decide on a clear principle about the government's responsibility for controlling an epidemic and then to act quickly and efficiently was meant for a larger target than the Rinderpest affair; it was obviously a prelude to the battle the Adullamites would conduct against the reform bill. Their line of criticism would be the folly of piecemeal tinkering and the failure of the reformers to establish a clear principle for their proposed constitutional changes.[24]

Everyone was aware that Lowe and some of the other Liberals who spoke against their government on the cattle plague bill were preparing the ground for a much more significant confrontation. During the days when the daily press was filling its columns with closely printed articles on what to do if one's cows seemed listless, the Adullamite plotters were holding strategy meetings, negotiating with Disraeli, and sounding out potential supporters. An important addition to their group was Earl Grosvenor, later the first Duke of Westminster. He had been first approached by Elcho and, after a long talk with Lord Grey about organic reform, had agreed to act as titular head of the cave. Elcho, who had a pompous style of speaking which did not go down well with the House, was glad to have a figure-head. Horsman was cranky, quaintly grandiloquent, and a lone operator; Lowe was able but idiosyncratic; Lansdowne and Grey were in the House of Lords and, like most of the other discontented Whig grandees, preferred to keep in the background and send nephews and younger sons into the front lines of the House of Commons. Grosvenor, however, had none of these drawbacks. He was dignified, faultlessly respectable, and known to be above partisanship. In all respects he was a model aristocrat: his stable was the finest in England; his art collection was unsurpassed; his philanthropic enterprises ranged from contributions to charities for providing drinking fountains and cattle troughs to chairmanship of a committee to feed starving Armenians. His obituary records that he could 'pass from a race course to take the chair at a missionary meeting without incurring the censure of the strictest.' Such a man would give the odd assortment of politicians, the many varieties and sub-species of Liberals within the Cave of Adullam, an appearance of high-mindedness. From the time he had entered the House of Commons in 1847, fresh from Oxford, he had tamely occupied a back bench and voted as the Liberal Whip directed. He voted for Russell's reform resolution in 1859 and for Baines's bill in 1864, although he changed his mind in 1865 and voted the other way. It is likely that his stiffening on the reform issue was related to his father's resentment over the support which John Stuart Mill received from the party in the family's Westminster preserve. And yet there is no reason to doubt that his concern about radical influence in the party was genuine. Grosvenor was by no means a profound political thinker but that, in many ways, was an advantage. His political innocence proved to be almost as valuable an asset to Elcho and Disraeli as his respectability.[25]

The plotters were now ready and confident. Three days before the reading of the queen's speech, Disraeli predicted that Gladstone would circumvent Bright and bring in a bill which the radicals would find distressingly moderate, but that, moderate or not, a faction in the Liberal party could be induced not only to vote against their government but to lead the attack. With their help Disraeli knew that he could bring down or humiliate the government. According to his calculations thirty-five Liberal defectors would be sufficient to do the work, and he commissioned Sir Stafford Northcote to go out and see if he could find them. If necessary, Lowe and Horsman could be promised cabinet posts. He would approach Horsman and Northcote could have a word with Lowe.[26]

Northcote arranged a dinner with a friend of Lowe's but with discouraging results. Lowe, it appeared, had 'contempt' but not 'dislike' for Disraeli – a rather fine distinction – but he had 'supreme contempt' for Horsman, his fellow conspirator. Lowe wanted Northcote to know that on all matters except the franchise he considered himself to be a radical. However, if 'moderates' could construct a broad-based coalition under a suitable leader – Stanley or Somerset would do – then he might be tempted. Northcote reported this to Disraeli, adding his opinion that neither prospect was sound. Lowe and Horsman would both frighten the strong Anglicans in the Tory party and would in all matters be unreliable. It would be far better, he thought, to concentrate attention on the 'old' Whigs.[27]

A brief skirmish, carried out by the Adullamite leaders on a motion by a radical back bencher, gave strength to Northcote's advice. James Clay moved to give a vote to every man able to read, write, and work the 'four rules.' Few, aside from the mover, took the proposal seriously, but Elcho decided that it would do no harm to make the point that

Clay had a principle for his bill and was not merely tinkering. Therefore he and some of the other disaffected Liberals spoke in favour of the bill although Lowe did not join them, being kept in reserve in case Gladstone took the bait and decided to speak. Gladstone wisely chose to ignore the proceedings, and the Adullamites made a poor showing. Lowe and Horsman had been gossiping freely about their strategy so that most of the members present at the debate knew that the speeches in support of Clay were not sincerely meant. Everyone agreed that the Adullamites had not been impressive, and Disraeli expressed dismay at the thought of making 'such empty fellows' into cabinet colleagues. He agreed with Northcote that it would be unwise to enter into a formal coalition with them and decided that the best strategy would be to use the cave to bring Russell down, discrediting Gladstone in the process, and then wait and see what new configurations might materialize. That way the Conservative party could keep itself free to take whatever position on reform seemed expedient after the event. Obviously it would not be necessary to offer the Adullamites any bribes; they were ready to go into battle at the first signal. Lowe had sent the encouraging word to Tory headquarters through Adderley that he could secure enough Liberal votes to defeat 'any bill that lowers the borough franchise by one sixpence.'[28]

This kind of assurance was extremely useful to Disraeli, who was having difficulties with Lord Derby. Never particularly ambitious for power, the Tory leader could not decide whether to make a bid for office and, if so, when to make it and what strategy to use. Early in March he called his party together and announced that they would wait to see what kind of a bill Gladstone produced before deciding what course to take. Given this indecision, assurances from Lowe and Elcho that they were prepared to assist in any wrecking action was an important factor in persuading Derby to oppose the bill and do so by concentrating on the failure of the Liberals to include with their franchise bill a plan for the redistribution of seats. Disraeli decided that Grosvenor should be the one to move an amendment asking for a 'whole' bill; then the Tory party could oppose a reform proposal in detail instead of opposing reform in principle and so preserve flexibility on the question. It would be convenient for them if the Adullamites did the talking about principles; they could be used as Janissaries in the front line of the assault and then disposed of, if need be, after they had fulfilled their assignment.

Thus the political generals on both sides had carefully worked out in advance their fields of fire, confident that they had anticipated what moves the other side would make. Gladstone and Russell, knowing that a bold step either to the right or left would encounter dangerous hazards, decided to be cautious. In introducing the bill on 12 March, Gladstone said that he was 'mindful that unhappily the limbo of abortive creations is peopled with skeletons of Reform Bills' and that he and the other architects of the Liberal measure had determined not to undergo yet another unfortunate miscarriage. Therefore what he asked for would be modest: a seven-pound rental franchise in the boroughs, enough to give 150,000 skilled artisans the vote – a substantial but hardly overwhelming number. These new voters he would balance off by giving a vote to middle class lodgers who paid ten pounds a year rent and to people with fifty pounds in a savings bank. In the counties he proposed to drop the occupation franchise from fifty to fourteen pounds, a figure sufficiently high to exclude farm labourers and sufficiently low to strengthen middle class interests. He thought that no one need be alarmed at a proposal which was even more moderate than Russell's circumspect 1860 bill. Half of the four hundred thousand additional voters would be farmers, small retailers, professional men, the rest would all be working men of impeccable respectability. Here was a chance to integrate the working class élite into the established order without endangering that order in the slightest. What he did not say, but hoped wavering Liberal moderates would understand without being told, was that 'respectable' working men, small traders, lodgers, professional men, and even many farmers would be likely to vote Liberal. Obviously this was meant to be a 'Palmerstonian' bill, drawn up to appease those who were nervous about the menace of radicalism and inclined to suspect that Bright had Gladstone in his pocket.[29]

The bill's framers knew that a weak point was the lack of provision for a redistribution of seats. This would allow opponents to claim that it was impossible to identify the 'safe' voters before knowing where and what the constituencies were to be. Another draw-back was that Bright had, unfortunately, publicly endorsed a 'single-barrelled' bill; moderates would, therefore, suspect that the radical features of the bill might be hidden in the redistribution scheme. On the other hand, the Liberal leadership knew that if they disclosed which seats would be menaced, they could expect that the members affected would hasten immediately into the Cave of Adullam. Besides, Gladstone was already overtaxed with his many responsibilities and had no time to unravel the snarls one could expect to find in any scheme to draw new borders of constituencies and shift representation. Knowing that they would be damned whichever course they chose, they took the easier one. The result was that Gladstone had to enter the struggle aware that he would have to defend a half-measure which was, as Horsman was to charge, 'ill-timed' and 'ill-conceived.' This helps to explain why the bill was, as Horsman also charged, 'ill-conducted and therefore ill-fated.'[30]

As everyone expected, Lowe fastened on the bill's lack of coherent principle for the general theme of his first great philippic of the session. The occasion was the first reading of the bill on 13 March 1866. The Prince of Wales, the Duke of Cambridge, and other luminaries were in the gallery, and the floor of the House was crowded and expectant when Lowe rose. Standing rigidly, he began nervously and then gained confidence when he sensed that his listeners were in a receptive mood. He said that he was not 'very particularly wedded to anything just because it exists'; he had 'no prejudice in favour of the existing state of things.' As an abstract proposition he was prepared to agree that a case could be made for any franchise, any arrangement of constituencies, any political system. But in the realm of action, experience and induction must be the test of institutions. Touching back to his argument of 1865, he asserted that practical politics did not deal with abstract justice but with expediency. Symmetry, equality, logical order – so essential to law – could safely be violated when constructing legislative and administrative machinery so long as the constitution which resulted proved to be efficient and liberal. Thus he had waited, he claimed, with open mind and good humour to hear what demonstrations the chancellor of the exchequer might offer to prove the existing Parliament defective and to show how a seven-pound franchise could correct the deficiencies in the administration of government. But all that he had heard was a discussion, made 'with the utmost sagacity and felicity,' about 'annual value,' and 'gross estimated rental,' about 'compound householders, tenants of flats, lodgers, and other abstruse personalities.' The only reference to principle which he had detected was the claim that the working class interests had no representation and should be given some, and this was a false principle, since it implied that the franchise was an end in itself. Not only was this a false principle but it rested on an error of fact. Statistics, gathered by the Poor Law Board and presented only days before the debate, showed that the working men already made up 26 per cent of the borough constituencies.[31]

Although Bright and others might rightly complain that the statisticians had applied extremely generous definitions of what constituted the working class, the disclosure by the Poor Law Board was bound to be embarrassing to the reformers. Even if the reformers were able to show that fewer than 26 per cent were workingmen, they would still be forced to admit that the 1832 system, without anyone being aware of it, had been adjusting itself, after a fashion, to accommodate the increasing wealth and power of the employed workers. Inflation, increasing real wages, high rents – the products of prosperity – had, it seemed, allowed what Lowe called 'a process of spontaneous enfranchisement' to work. Anti-reformers could plausibly claim that the constitution already contained a self-adjusting mechanism which worked to skim off

what Lowe's listeners considered to be the cream of the 'lower orders.'
It would be difficult now for Bright to assert without qualification that
one of the great interest groups in the nation was totally excluded from
the constitutional balance; nevertheless, reformers could make some use
out of the statistics. Mill, for example, could ask the Adullamites to explain why this secret block of workingmen, who apparently already had
sufficient strength to shake the institutions of liberal England to their
foundations, have 'so obstinately persisted in not doing it, that the hon.
Gentlemen are quite alarmed, and recoil in terror from the abyss into
which they have not fallen.' This was an excellent question but it did
not meet Lowe's contention that the existing system could provide for
workers as soon as they met middle class standards of steadiness, prudence, and sobriety. Moderate Liberals could see nothing wrong with
the claim that if 'spontaneous enfranchisement' was already going on,
then the burden of proof lay on the reformers. Gladstone, Lowe said,
was bound to do one of two things: show that a measure of democracy
was good in principle and of itself or show how an enlargement of this
26 per cent would achieve some useful object or correct some existing
malfunction. Talk about how moderate the proposed changes were was,
Lowe insisted, totally irrelevant. And instead of offering those proofs,
Gladstone had merely offered up unintelligible gibberish about compound householders and gentlemen lodgers.[32]

Matthew Arnold thought Lowe's line of reasoning was what could be
expected of a philistine, interested only in machinery and not in the
purpose which machinery was supposed to serve. He ridiculed Lowe for
claiming that the existing parliamentary instrument was as close to perfection as civilization was ever likely to achieve. But Arnold either had
not paid close attention or did not wish accuracy to stand in the way of
ridicule. Lowe stated on this and many other occasions that all was not
well with the instruments of government; that Parliament had increased
its power since 1832 to the point where it threatened seriously to impede the executive in the performance of its complex tasks. Lowe complained that matters which formerly had been left to the discretion of
ministers were being delegated to a host of committees, authorities, and
commissions. Here was a failing in the existing system but a failing
which he believed any movement towards democracy would accentu-
ate. He praised the American founding fathers for having the foresight
to protect the executive arm of government from legislative harassment.
The American constitution had provided for a separation of powers, a
protection England would not have were her legislators to become delegates of a mass electorate. And strong as those safeguards were in
America, they did not seem to be strong enough to protect Lincoln's
successor, President Johnson, from the revengeful passions of the post-
Civil War Republican Congress.[33]

In this first speech in 1866, Lowe concentrated on the long-term consideration which he thought Gladstone had ignored in his desire to lull the House with good news about how men from the lower middle classes would be brought in to balance off the new workingmen voters. The former member for Kidderminster had memories of how the publicans and their hangers-on had behaved and refused to be comforted by the assurance that this shopkeeper class would have greater influence. It was when he came to consider them that he used the unfortunate phrases which were to be remembered for a generation and which were to be hurled back at him so often in the months ahead: 'Let any gentleman consider – I have had such unhappy experiences, and many of us have – let any gentleman consider the constituencies he has had the honour to be concerned with. If you want venality, if you want ignorance, if you want drunkenness, and the facility for being intimidated; or if, on the other hand, you want impulsive, unreflecting, and violent people, where do you look for them in the constituencies? Do you go to the top or the bottom?'[34]

After that he moved into his peroration. It began with a quotation from Virgil about the Trojan horse, a passage from which Gladstone had adorned his message of reassurance. Lowe showed how Virgil's words could be used in an opposite sense: as a warning not to accept innocent-looking gifts. This came off well and there was great laughter. Laughter turned to cheers when, addressing Gladstone directly, he granted that history might prove the optimistic version to be well chosen: 'But, Sir, it may be otherwise; and all I can say is, that if my right honourable friend does succeed in carrying this measure through Parliament, when the passions and interests of the day are gone by, I do not envy him his retrospect. I covet not a single leaf of the laurels that may encircle his brow. I do not envy him his triumph.' Then concluding with a line taken from one of his Australian speeches: 'His be the glory of carrying it; mine of having, to the utmost of my poor ability, resisted it.'[35]

According to one report, Disraeli turned his head away when the cheering started and knitted his brow. Brilliant though the performance had been, the Tory leader could see that Lowe had, once again, overargued his case. Everyone present, including Gladstone, appreciated the skill with which he had applied utilitarianism as a criticism of this patchwork bill. Many Liberals secretly rejoiced to observe Mill being lectured about the dangers of *a priori* reasoning and Gladstone being corrected about the meaning of a quotation from classical literature. So long as Lowe had used an empirical approach to show democracy to be inexpedient for Britain, he was sure of a friendly hearing. But almost no other Liberals, indeed almost no Adullamites, were prepared to apply empirical arguments to show that the constitution of 1832 had to remain forever inviolable. Moncton Milnes, who described himself as a 'Palmersto-nian,' recalled that he had been totally wrapt in admiration while the speech was underway, but that afterwards his neighbour on the bench had remarked, 'This goes against 1831, not 1866.' Milnes said that he replied, 'It is against 1688, and is all for a wise despotism.'[36]

Milnes had lost the thread of the argument. Although Lowe had not been prepared to say that wise despotism was either evil or good *per se*, he was prepared to reject it for England since it had produced not good government but James II. Milnes's neighbour was closer to the point. He saw that the Reform Act of 1832 had been, or was seen to be in 1866, a concession, if only a partial one, to the spirit of justice – justice for part of the middle class. Had the decision to impose one uniform franchise qualification on the counties and another on the boroughs not been a concession to the principle of equality? Was it expedient in a country with England's traditions to deny that considerations of justice and equal treatment were relevant? If so, was it expedient to say so publicly and explicitly? Denunciations of the 'Rights of Man,' 'mere numbers,' Saint Simon, strikes, and corruption were familiar and acceptable; a declaration that morality and justice need not be considered was another thing entirely.[37]

Reaction to the way Lowe had used his 'inductive' method was mild compared to the cry of outrage which greeted the words 'venality,' 'ignorance,' and 'drunkenness' – directed, or so it seemed, at the unenfranchised. It is difficult to think of another remark more maladroit in all of Victorian political history. Matthew Arnold predicted that people would understand that Lowe was partially deranged by 'apprehensions for his Philistine or middle class Parliament,' and that they would not take his insults 'seriously to heart.' But people did take the insults seriously. As Lowe himself said some time after his March speech, 'no man in the world has been subjected to more abuse than I have been during the last month.' The *Manchester Guardian* wrote that the public seemed to be taking a morbid interest in the 'habits of life and forms of speech' of the member for Calne as if he were a 'leper, a great criminal, or an utter and avowed unbeliever.' Naturally, working class and middle class radicals made as much as they could of the opportunity Lowe had handed them and worked to sustain the feelings of outrage. To give three cheers for Gladstone and three groans for Lowe became the accepted way to bring reform rallies to a close. Let the words of Lord Lansdowne's MP be 'printed upon cards, and ... hung up in every factory, workshop, and clubhouse,' Bright urged an audience in Birmingham. 'Let us arouse the spirit of the people against these slanderers of a great and noble nation.'[38]

Lowe was indignant at what he considered to be a deliberate distortion of what he had meant and said. When sixty formerly tame Liberal

electors at Calne published a letter of remonstrance against their representative, he cut short a visit to Paris so that he could reply to this 'insurrection among my constituents.' He pointed out that if the good
people of Calne would take the trouble to read his words in context,
they would immediately see that he had not been talking about unenfranchised artisans when he made his reference to 'venality'; a great
many of these artisans were, he agreed, prudent, self-reliant, citizens.
He claimed that the object of his remarks had been that notorious
group of venal, lower middle class voters who, as everyone knew, existed
in a great many boroughs. And had his constituents followed instructions and re-read the passage they would have been forced to concede
that he was at least technically correct. But radicals had no wish to give
the passage a cool and impartial reading. Immediately after the publication of Lowe's letter, Joseph Guedalla of the Reform League publicly
charged Lowe with slander against the working class and demanded a
retraction. He got a snappish public reply. To individuals who deliberately incite their followers, through virulent abuse, to take vengeance,
Lowe wrote, 'I have no courtesies to interchange.' Pride in martyrdom
sustained him now as it had in the past, as this passage from a letter to
his brother, Henry, shows: 'I am like Caesar in one respect, at least I receive warning to take care of my life, and not to walk alone, and always
to go to the House in a cab. I am, I am happy to say, constitutionally
indifferent to such things, and really think that perhaps the best use I
could put my head to, would be to have it broken in so good a cause.
As President Johnson says, the blood of the martyrs is the seed of the
Church.'[39]

But this time his head escaped injury. The worst of the many verbal
wounds he received were inflicted by Gladstone, who, in a speech at
Liverpool, quoted the, by now, famous question: 'Where do you look
for them?' But he edited out the words that followed: 'in the constituencies.' As soon as Lowe noticed this he dashed off a letter to *The
Times*, complaining about the deliberate unfairness of this treatment,
and he insisted in the letter and on the floor of the House of Commons
that the venal ones he had referred to were the old 'freeman' class: publicans, petty tradesmen, people who offered their votes for sale, and
who corrupted the unenfranchised with drink and violent talk. His
point had been, he insisted, that Gladstone's so-called 'moderate' bill
would give this element an opportunity to exercise their corrupting influence more systematically.[40]

The difficulty with this explanation was that immediately following
the remarks about venality he had gone on to ridicule those people who
were ready to admit that beer-house and lodging-house keepers made
up the dregs of the constituencies, and yet persisted in arguing that it
would only be necessary to take one step down the social ladder to dis-

cover a virtuous artisan class. This sentimental belief in the existence of
a 'virtuous stratum' just underneath the corrupt and venal reminded
him, Lowe had said in his speech, of the ancient superstition which held
that just on the other side of the North Wind lay the land of the Hyper-
borians, 'where the climate was always warm and the people happy.'
How then, Gladstone quite properly inquired, could Lowe, following
the point of that image, claim to have been entirely misunderstood?
There was no answer. Lowe might have asserted his belief that all men,
high as well as low, were poor creatures who were kept sober and virtuous, and that only intermittently, by cultivation, education, the benefits
of leisure, and the restraint of law. But to explain away the Hyperbo-
rians with a statement of that kind would have convinced nobody and
possibly only sunk him in deeper. His joy in vigorous, striking language
and imagery, a thing he so much admired in Icelandic poetry, had
trapped him once again. He chose to believe that it was his honesty
which had betrayed him. He was sure, he told Moncton Milnes at a dinner party, 'that candour was the original sin.'[41]

As we have seen on numerous other occasions, Lowe was intensely
class conscious – like a great many mid-Victorians who had been born
just outside the circle of aristocratic privilege. But he was not, as his
enemies described him, a pathological hater of the poor. In fact, he considered himself, with justification, to be a crusader against injuries done
to the poor by callous manufacturers, educational profiteers, indifferent
judges and lawyers. What lay behind his bluntness in speaking about
class issues was not any extraordinary fund of ill-will, but a conviction
that working people, about whom he had only the scantiest direct
knowledge, were as class conscious as he was. In his mind the working
class was already as homogeneous a group as any other in society and in
the process of becoming more uniform in its social and political objectives. He was not interested in making distinctions between the élite
group of skilled operatives, the 'respectable poor,' and the impoverished
'residuum.' He was aware that these and other distinctions existed
within the class but he thought the distinctions far less important than
the sense of solidarity shared, he believed, by everyone beneath the
middle class.

He tried, for example, to defend himself against charges of class hostility by dredging up a speech Bright had made in Rochdale. In this
speech the supposed 'friend of the people' had mentioned the intemperance and profligacy of the 'excessively poor.' These low creatures, Bright
had said, were incapable of voting consistently with their consciences,
'if they have any.' This, Lowe claimed, was far more unfeeling than any
sentiments he had ever expressed; he could not see why his condemna-
tion of a whole class was any more slanderous than this uncharitable
statement. What Bright had automatically assumed was that his audience

of employed artisans would make a distinction between themselves and the 'residuum' and would not feel themselves to have been slandered by remarks directed at the dislocated and often unemployable bottom strata of the poor. In refusing to make this qualitative distinction Lowe was disassociating himself from a convention. It was a comforting discovery for the relatively well-off members of all classes that prosperity had developed what has recently come to be called the 'labour aristocracy' – that portion of the working population which had absorbed the socially approved goals of hard work, self-sacrifice, sobriety, and 'good taste.' It had been a comfort to the owning classes to discover that the 'progress of civilization' was working its way through a portion of the urban working class. Most gentlemen understood that one way to insure the continuation of this process of co-option was to insist, in the press and in public utterances, that it had already successfully done its work. Parliamentarians customarily used highly ritualized and sentimental language when referring to the 'respectable' class of workingmen. Both Gladstone and Russell believed that class conflict would diminish with the spread of 'intelligence,' and they believed in the self-fulfilling power of optimistic prophecy. They also assumed that the responsible, literate élite of the workers would act to contain the dangerous, explosive element beneath them. The bill the Liberal leaders had prepared was designed to further this process of accommodation of the working class élite into the bourgeois-liberal society and therefore designed to prevent, not advance, the spread of democracy. Lowe's great sin in March was that he refused to play the game. He would not indulge in 'humbug' about the virtues of the humble. 'There is,' he said in April, 'considerable risk that the basis of our institutions may be complimented away.' Hardly any of those who cheered him in March agreed that this was a danger. Most believed that the risk lay in the other direction. 'If I heard one or two more such speeches,' muttered one Conservative listener, 'I think I should have voted with the government.'[42]

Although Lowe's impressive speech did more to impede than to advance his cause, the Adullamites gained strength during the second reading of the bill. In April Grosvenor moved his resolution censuring the government for having failed to submit a redistribution plan along with their franchise reform. Gladstone tried to head off defeat by promising to lay on the table a redistribution bill after the second reading of the franchise bill had successfully passed. To many Liberals it seemed pigheaded to stake the fate of the government on the Grosvenor motion and to delay making public the vital information Grosvenor was calling for while at the same time tacitly acknowledging the merit of the Adullamite case. Brand assured Russell that much of the worry felt by influential members of their party about the 'single-barrel' tactic was perfectly 'bona fide' and could easily be allayed by a gesture of good will.

Gladstone agreed but told Brand that there was another class of disaffected Liberals who were 'opposed in their hearts to Reform' and were using the Grosvenor issue because it was the most convenient weapon handy. This group did not want, he thought, to overthrow the government, only to delay or obstruct parliamentary reform. He believed that they could be brought into line if the government showed its determination not to yield to their dishonest tactics. Such, at any rate, was the reasoning he used on Brand; probably his and Russell's stubbornness was due, not primarily to calculation, but to the fact that they were both tired, in bad tempers, and full of indignation at the 'insidious character' of the opposition. Therefore they sought a showdown in mid-April.[43]

The quality of the speeches on Grosvenor's motion was high, due, many thought, to the standard Lowe had previously set. Members expected a major effort from him on this crucial occasion and were not disappointed. Even Gladstone was full of praise for the quality of the performance. This called for generosity, for Lowe had directed most of his sarcasm at the Liberal leader. Possibly Gladstone had a guilty conscience. He had made a speech at Liverpool in which he had pointed out that the new voters would be taxpayers and Christians, 'of our own flesh and blood,' and that it was therefore absurd to haggle about the precise number who might be admitted to the franchise. On reflection Gladstone may have admitted to himself that this was a specious argument. He may also have been sensitive to criticisms he was receiving about his having rehearsed before the public outside what should have been saved for the deliberation of Parliament. Lowe, as might be expected, made as much as he could out of these lapses of logic and what was then considered good parliamentary manners.

How unfortunate it was, Lowe said, that the chancellor of the exchequer first rehearsed his speech out of doors and then 'favoured us with a languid *rechauffe* ... and thus the baked meats of the Philharmonic Hall did coldly furnish forth the tables of the House of Commons.' Those baked meats, especially the talk about 'flesh and blood,' no cultured man could be expected to stand for a moment. The subject had possibilities; animals too had flesh on their bones and blood in their veins. Did Gladstone perhaps propose 'another "Beasts" Parliament,' patterned on the one in Reynard the Fox? But he would pass over the subject since Gladstone's rhetoric at Liverpool was undoubtedly intended to 'work on the minds of the people at large.'[44]

These and other references to Gladstone's supposed addiction to the applause of the multitude opened the speech. It was Adullamite-Disraelian strategy to suggest that Gladstone had strong inclinations towards demagogy. Although resentment at the 'Gladstonian Captivity' was modified by respect and admiration, back-bench Liberals were highly susceptible to suggestions that their leader in the Commons was on the path towards becoming a Brightian democrat.

Lowe planted that barb and then turned to deal with Mill. The philosopher's speeches had disappointed the House during his first year as an MP. What he had said had made good sense but his delivery had been punctured by embarrassing pauses, some of them lasting as long as a minute. But on the second night of the debate on Grosvenor's resolution, he responded impressively to Lowe's challenge to present specific complaints against the existing system and to give practical demonstrations of how the gift of the franchise to the urban workers might improve the government of the country. Mill offered a list of evils which plagued the nation: 'the curse of ignorance, the curse of pauperism, the curse of disease, the curse of a whole population born and nurtured in crime.' These were specific evils which the government of the country since 1832 had not been able to combat with any degree of success. If, he maintained, Parliament could hear in its lower chamber the voices of the people who had experienced the 'miseries of an old and crowded society,' it might be moved to act and the zeal of its members might be stimulated. Lowe, he gallantly conceded, was one of the few who did not need such stimulation; on the contrary, as minister in charge of education he had initiated changes useful to the working class even though they had been indifferent to the benefits (Mill was not being ironic) he had attempted to confer on them. Mill said that he made his criticism of Parliament in a general sense. Alert though some parliamentarians might be, Parliament was, on the whole, both ignorant and apathetic on the subject of poverty and needed awakening and enlightening.[45]

In answer Lowe tried to argue that the point about poverty supported his case, not Mill's. Granted that a democratic Parliament would not be apathetic on the subject, was this not at the heart of the problem? The poor did understand what it was to be hungry but they did not understand, and probably did not wish to understand, the laws of supply and demand. They had no 'horror of a paternal and interfering Government.' They would certainly insist that taxpayers build them houses to live in, insist that the weak be given the same wages as the strong, and insist, in the name of liberty, equality, and fraternity, that society cease to be liberal and become 'Communist.' He stressed that he was not simply engaging in frightened speculation; examples from the daily press abounded. Operative stonemasons and tailoring unions were at the moment or had recently been demanding the closed shop, elimination of piecework and overtime work, elimination of sub-contracting, chasing (the speed-up), and other restraints on the ability of free and enterprising labour to improve itself by the exercise of unusual effort. If further proof were required, members of Parliament had only to look abroad. 'America out-protects protection,' and Canadians have raised up tariff barriers against the people who pay to protect them. Look, he suggested, at the democratic government of the Australian colony of Victoria; there the governor and his protectionist ministry are acting out a low comedy in their campaign to force tariffs through a stubborn Supreme Court and upper chamber.[46]

Most of Lowe's listeners, of course, shared his premises and fears and thought he had given a satisfactory answer to Mill's charges, but when he proceeded to his own anti-reform arguments, they were less impressed with his logic. Once again he emphasized that it would be foolish to imagine that artificial safeguards or ingrained habits of deference would be more than a temporary protection. Give the hungry a taste of 'equality' and the 'Religion of Humanity' and they will be sure to want and get more. The movement towards democracy, once started, is, he proclaimed, irreversible and in the iron grip of a universal law. At this point some of his listeners may have remembered that the man who was making these alarming proclamations had only recently denounced, with great vehemence, the 'coward's argument' of determinism. His critics were aware that his class analysis, so explicitly stated in all of his speeches, contained still other contradictions. On the one hand he predicted that the working masses, disciplined and made class conscious by the common experience of strikes and protest agitation, would eventually secure the governmental instruments and enabling powers to achieve their socialist objectives and would quickly shove aside any 'intermediate institutions' which the upper classes might erect in their path. But then, almost in the same breath, he was maintaining that any considerable enlargement of the franchise or of the size of the electoral districts would make it impossible for any but the rich, and especially those rich with large amounts of movable wealth, to contest a riding. The results would be dreadful. Plutocrats would either buy votes to get themselves elected or back demagogues skilled at inflaming the honest, innocent, but ignorant feelings of the common man with enthusiasm for nationalistic wars and imperialist adventuring. Which was the greater danger, the working class's militant purposiveness or its innocence and pliability?[47]

In May, during his third major speech, Lowe seemed to fear plutocracy rather than socialism. He described the 'frightful expenses' of contesting South Lancashire (£17,000) and the North Riding of Yorkshire (£27,000), and then asked if anyone thought increases in the numbers of constituencies of that size would send more aristocrats, gentlemen, professional men, and individuals of modest means but sterling talent to Westminster. He thought not. Such a trend would be 'favourable to a plutocracy working on democracy.' And if any should doubt his contention that the masses were limitlessly gullible, let them cast their memories back to the days of the war in the Crimea, let them recollect how easy it had been then to delude the 'half educated and unreflective!' Do not forget, he cautioned, that only a decade ago 'we actually got up an enthusiasm on behalf of that most abominable and decrepit despotism – the Turkish empire.'[48]

Fault-finders might well ask him how a recital of the inanities of the mid-1850s proved the unsuitability of either democracy, plutocracy, or 'plutocracy working on democracy.' Nevertheless, taken one by one, his warnings about the consequences of creating a mass electorate were not only plausible but prescient; it was when they were taken together that they caused difficulties. Were the workingmen becoming increasingly conscious of their class interests and thus increasingly difficult to put off with artificial safeguards and increasingly difficult to restrain with old-fashioned sentiments? Or were they developing not a consciousness but a kind of semi-literate semi-consciousness which made them fair game for anyone skilled at bamboozling them with facile arguments and emotional appeals to their instincts? And if the second, what kinds of people would be likely to do the manipulating – the plutocrat with his fat purse, the tub-thumper with his ranting about glory and empire, or the socialist with his slanders against free enterprise capitalism? The answer seemed to depend on which anxieties Lowe wished to arouse at a given moment. If he wanted to reach the back-bench squirarchy, he called up the spector of a Parliament made up of 'hard-faced men who looked as though they had done well out of trade' (to paraphrase Stanley Baldwin's comment on the 1918 House of Commons). If it was the city men and the railway board chairmen he wanted to arouse, then he came down hard on the trade union dictators.

That the threat might come from a conspiracy between these disparate elements – the capitalist, the imperialist demagogue, and the union organizer – was a possibility which he did hint at in his speeches. Then in an article which he wrote for the *Quarterly Review* in 1867, called 'Trades Unions,' he briefly returned again to this conspiracy theory. Most of the article is a fire-breathing assault on trade unionism: its autocratic nature, its class militancy, its ignorance of the 'laws of nature,' its violence. For the most part it is remarkable only for the comprehensiveness with which it sums up the fears of the mid-Victorian establishment. But in a comment about the history of the movement in America he did directly state that on the question of protection, if only on that, there was a distinct possibility that labour and capital might form an alliance and combine their various kinds of power over the democratic electorate to shake the great edifice of emancipated trade and emancipated labour. Unfortunately he simply stated the possibility of this formidable conspiracy against the community at large without much elaboration; no doubt it would have been impolitic for him to have said more. There is no doubt, however, that he held that conspiracy theory. It was partly because he anticipated the possibility that these seemingly antithetical interest groups might combine that he wished so fervently to construct a meritocracy to administer the affairs of the nation impartially.[49]

Most of Lowe's listeners, including many of his critical ones, were too enthralled by the excitement of the moment during the debate on the Grosvenor motion in April to be inclined to pick holes in his reasoning. What the *Daily News* afterwards called 'his soaring flights of heroic cynicism' repeatedly brought the Conservative and some of the Liberal MPs to their feet, wildly cheering – most exuberantly when he made this opulent ending and then dropped suddenly to his seat:

> Surely the heroic work of so many centuries, the matchless achievements of so many wise heads and strong hands, deserve a nobler consummation than to be sacrificed at the shrine of revolutionary passion, or the maudlin enthusiasm of humanity? But, if we do fall, we shall fall deservedly. Uncoerced by any external force, not borne down by any internal calamity, but in the full plethora of our wealth and the surfeit of our too exuberant prosperity, with our own rash and inconsiderate hands, we are about to pluck down on our own heads the venerable temple of our liberty and our glory. History may tell of other acts as signally disastrous, but none more wanton, none more disgraceful.[50]

Contrary to custom, no member attempted to address the House for several minutes afterwards. The old Earl of Shaftesbury doubted 'whether a speech better adapted to place, persons and circumstances was ever delivered in any country or any age.' Shaftesbury was an enemy of franchise reform and inclined to be biased. George Brodrick, an eccentric academic who wrote an intelligent dissection of Lowe's use of Benthamism, was a friend of reform and had perspective, and yet he too was nearly carried away with admiration. He thought Lowe's speeches in 1866 were 'the most brilliant and argumentative series of Parliamentary orations delivered in that decade of political history.' Lord Stanley and Speaker Denison wrote eulogistic notes to Georgiana. But the comment which Lowe treasured most in later years appeared in the thoughtful, independent, *Pall Mall Gazette*, and it was about the style rather than the content of his oratory. It referred to his easy but not colloquial way of speaking and found it 'essentially *sui generis*.' His best things seem impromptu, as though they had dropped from him by accident; 'he gives the impression of being always in earnest and sometimes angry, and he uses fewer words in proportion to his matter than any living man of distinction in Parliament.'[51]

It is possible that some MPs were moved by his eloquence and logic to cross into the opposition lobby on 27 April, but their number could not have been large. Brand predicted that Grosvenor's resolution would fail by fifteen. The actual margin for the government was only five; thirty-three who called themselves Liberals had voted for Grosvenor. When the results were announced, 'such a scene ensued,' wrote *The Times*, 'of waving hats and handkerchiefs and loud cheering as has probably seldom been witnessed on any Division in the House of Commons.' Prominent among the shouting, waving throng was Lowe, 'flushed, triumphant, and avenged.'[52]

Afterwards, according to Lord Carnarvon, the Carlton Club looked 'much like a hive of bees upset and ready to swarm.' But, as it turned out, the swarming had to be delayed for a few months yet. The Liberal government had been hurt and humiliated and still it had managed to survive. Between April and June Gladstone disclosed the terms of his seat redistribution plan and thus made the bill 'whole'; the working class leaders recognized more urgently the need for concerted action with the middle class radicals; people in large numbers began to agitate with mounting spirit; and, finally, the opposition had to adopt cruder, more obviously obstructive, tactics. Pleasant though the vote had been for Disraeli, it had not quite fulfilled his expectations. It would be harder now for his party to play the watchful but positive critic.[53]

This was manifest in the next wrecking action undertaken by the Adullamites and their allies. William Hayter, a newly elected Liberal member from Wells, submitted a resolution saying that Gladstone's scheme for grouping together a number of small boroughs was 'neither convenient nor equitable.' Wells was one of the boroughs to be grouped. Unlike the Grosvenor motion, this one could not be defended on disinterested grounds. To support it, dissident Liberals would need to come out directly against their party without any protective cover of conscience. In addition, a financial crisis, caused by the failure of a prominent investment house, Overend and Gurney, made some of the more conservative Liberals think twice about toppling their government, especially since this crisis happened when Prussia and Austria were threatening to go to war with each other. Some of these cautious men left the cave, never to return; others, including Grosvenor himself, began to hesitate. Lowe railed against the 'cowards and waverers.' He wrote to Mrs Billyard that he found people to be 'just as mean and just as hard to keep up to the mark here as in Australia ...' He worked himself into a near frenzy over the government's continued demonstration in the seats' bill that it was totally denuded of principle. The need to act from principle was, therefore, the main topic of his third major speech on 31 May.[54]

This effort lacked the elegance of those that preceded it and added little that was new to the discussion. It did have its dramatic moments, particularly the part about how any error made in reconstructing the

constitution would be 'absolutely irretrievable': 'We are about to surrender certain good for more than doubtful change; we are about to
barter maxims and traditions that have never failed, for theories and
doctrines that never have succeeded. Democracy you may have at any
time. Night and day the gate is open that leads to that bare and level
plain, where every ant's nest is a mountain and every thistle a forest
tree.' If rulers of nations must commit patricide, he concluded, give the
House, 'at any rate, time to gather its robes about it and to fall with de-
cency and deliberation.' Then to a silent, much moved House, he para-
phrased Isabella's plea for her brother Claudio in *Measure for Measure*:
'Tomorrow! Oh that's sudden! Spare it! Spare it! It ought not so to
die.'[55]

Shouts and cheers came from the Tory benches, but no amount of
melodrama could make the Hayter motion acceptable on the other side
of the House, especially when Grosvenor announced his intention, on
this occasion, to vote with the government. Hayter tried to withdraw,
but the Speaker, owing to a procedural confusion, forced a division. As
some Conservatives fled the chamber, other MPs tried to enter. In the
scramble, Lowe was bruised; his cause suffered a certain amount of injury also. The cave, remarked Bernal-Osborne, 'has shrunk to a Grotto.'
Lord Elcho was rueful but more hopeful: 'Our David has left our Cave
and made friends with Saul, for a night at any rate.'[56]

It was not until mid-June that the Conservatives and Adullamites
found a successful formula for defeating the bill. Russell's cabinet, after
much wrangling, had decided to base the borough qualification on an
assessment of rents; Lord Dunkellin, for the Adullamites, submitted an
amendment proposing to base it instead on the rates. Only by an effort
of will could most back benchers begin to understand the argument
that followed, and few were disposed at this stage to summon the effort. Probably only a few of those who spoke on the issue (some with a
fair degree of passion) had more than a vague notion about the complexities involved. Gladstone, as might be expected, mastered and
relished them. He lectured the House, in his inimitable way, about the
niceties and variations of compounding practices – arrangements by
which poorer renters agreed to have their rates deducted out of their
rental payments by the landlord and paid by him to the parish. Since
compounding practices differed markedly from place to place, a franchise based on them would, as Gladstone tried to explain, create absurd
anomalies. But Conservatives had no objection, in theory, to anomalies;
besides, their object was to bring the government down. Some Liberals,
however, mostly though not exclusively the Adullamites and their Whig
backers, believed that they had discovered that long-sought-after principle which might allow change without beginning an erosion of the
established order. It was their contention that while a rental franchise

might be whittled away, a rate-paying franchise might hold firm. Their reasoning was that those who took the trouble and, in some cases, accepted the additional expense of paying their rates in person, testified in doing so to their willingness and ability to accept public responsibility. They argued that if the nation were to accept the principle that demonstrated responsibility rather than some mythical 'right' entitled a man to vote, then it might be possible to make a generous reform without beginning that downhill slide to the 'bare and level plain' of democracy. 'The rate-book is the sheet anchor of a sterling franchise,' stated the Adullamite newspaper, the *Day*, several months after the 1866 debate ended. There is no reason to doubt that many who took this line, particularly those who shared Lord Grey's desire to make a positive counter-move to democracy, sincerely believed that they had at last found a way. Others, of course, were looking for any 'principle' which would allow them to vote against the bill without branding themselves as enemies of reform, for by June it was obvious that many MPs would have to undergo some severe questioning from their aroused constituents. Thus Lowe, who did not believe that 'rating' was a principle, and Elcho, who did, were able to fill the cave again and pass the Dunkellin amendment by eleven votes. After a week of hectic discussion and scurrying about, during which time many Adullamites testified to their loyalty to the party if not to the bill, Russell and Gladstone decided to resign and on the night of 28 June went to Windsor to inform the queen. Gladstone noted afterwards in his diary: 'A crowd and great enthusiasm in the Palace Yard on departure.' The popular breeze was picking up force.[57]

Lowe received a different reception from the crowd. On his way home from a late evening sitting during the resignation crisis, a large gathering of what his friends described as riff-raff, and his enemies as a band of honest working men, gathered around him, jeering, heckling, and pushing. A fellow MP, passing in his carriage, offered assistance. Lowe, who had borne the ordeal cheerfully, paused as he mounted the carriage step to give the demonstrators an ironical salute, but while attempting to do so, managed to drop his gloves in his face.

He had won a round in the battle against parliamentary reform and the victory was sweet. With Russell out of the way his own political future seemed more promising. 'I have reached a position I never expected in my wildest dreams to attain,' he wrote to his correspondent in Sydney. His speeches that spring had made him into a national figure - an object of awe in the House of Commons and in the combination rooms of Cambridge and Oxford, but also an object of hatred in the country at large.[58]

13

The Cassandra of Calne

On the night the House of Commons divided on the third reading of the Reform bill of 1867, Viscount Cranborne remarked: 'I think that when the historian of the future comes to review what has passed in the last fifteen years he will say that a more remarkable exhibition has never been witnessed on the part of public men.' Cranborne spoke of the many unexpected twists the reform issue had taken since Russell first reintroduced the issue into Parliament. This last episode, he thought, was the most remarkable of all. He recalled how in 1866 Derby and Disraeli had frequently called together the Tory and Adullamite anti-democrats and exhorted them to remain firm and true in the cause. True they had remained. They had defeated the bill, forced the Liberals from office, and brought the protectors of the constitution to power. What 'strange and mysterious marvels' had then occurred! They were that night on the verge of passing into law a measure more extensive than any politician would have dared to contemplate a scant year before. And instead of registering shock, supposedly responsible and moderate men were ready to applaud Disraeli's 'policy of legerdemain.' Cranborne then spoke of his grave forebodings about the future of English politics.[1]

In the House of Lords a week later the Duke of Argyll also searched history to find an explanation. He rejected the notion that treachery had caused the surprising reversals. He thought the interesting question was: what circumstances had given the adventurers their opportunities? He believed he had found the answer in the breakdown of the two-party system in 1866. Because the Tory leaders had available to them a Liberal cave, they had been able to conceal their designs. The Adullamites looked for a principle; the Tories looked for power. As a result of this situation debates took place and divisions were called on issues which almost everyone knew to be other than what appeared on the surface. No division had been *bona fide*. According to Argyll, Tories became accustomed to talk about 'principle' even though, as good Tories, they did not believe in principle. That tactic worked over the short run; the Adullamites who really were searching for principles were deceived and the Russell ministry was destroyed. But then this tactic doubled back on the Tory leaders. To keep the third party on their side, they claimed to have found a principle, the 'principle' of a rating suffrage, for their own reform bill. Once committed to that principle, the Conservatives found themselves 'hustled from one conclusion to another till the Bill has been so changed that it is virtually no longer the same measure.' The Conservative government, Argyll said, was the victim of its own policy of expediency, but expediency was itself the product of an unstable three-party system.[2]

Argyll thought it ironical that Lowe, the man of principle, had been the agent of expediency. How was it, Argyll asked, that a man of such insight and grasp of political philosophy had not understood that third parties lead to anarchy and that anarchy always gives advantages to radicals? Why had he needed to wait for the events of the past few weeks to prove that familiar truism? Argyll expressed mild impatience that Lowe should now be quivering with indignation at Disraeli's trickery. The member for Calne speaks about the 'rage, and grief, and shame' with which he regards 'the present position of affairs; and,' said Argyll, 'well he may.' 'My Lords, it is a hard thing for a man of first-rate ability to find out that all his eloquence and all his exertions – perhaps I may say without offence, all his manœuvring – has ended in nothing else than this – the precipitation of those very changes which he was most anxious to avoid, and the proposal by his confederates, in what I think was a Parliamentary sin, of the very measure which he was endeavouring to resist.'[3]

Lowe tried to answer this charge ('nothing is more disagreeable to me than to be so charged') by posing as a hero who knowingly takes risks and exposes himself to 'brute force and treachery,' rather than turn coward or hypocrite. 'Was Athens to yield up everything after the battle of Chaeronea?' But had he been as brave and honest as he claimed to be, he would have conceded that Argyll's point was valid. He had risked everything on the success of a third party and when the gamble failed, complained of having been deceived and ill-used.[4]

When the Adullamite leaders heard of Russell's decision to resign and, without calling an election, ask the queen to appoint a new government, they believed that their hopes for a third or 'Fusion' party had an excellent chance of being realized. When Lowe wrote on 24 May 1866 that he might soon be attaining a position beyond his wildest dreams, he undoubtedly anticipated being asked to join in a coalition government headed by Granville, Clarendon, or Lord Stanley and supported by men who were determined to protect England from the trade unionists, the democrats, and the equalitarian sentimentalists. The cave leaders expected resistence from Derby and Disraeli but thought they could overcome it. There seemed to be a good chance that Derby might step down because of poor health. Ralph Earle, Disraeli's private secretary, had assured Elcho and Grosvenor that this was a strong probability. To help matters along Lowe met in the third week of June with Elcho, Horsman, and the other cave leaders and agreed to send word indirectly to the Conservative leader that they could not guarantee to support a purely Tory government but would willingly join a fusion government under a Whig leader. They recommended that Clarendon be the prime minister and that Stanley lead in the House of Commons – a suggestion which Disraeli, understandably, found 'preposterous.' Although Disraeli talked magnanimously about his desire to sacrifice his position if that would facilitate a fusion of moderate men, he seems to have worked with all his great skill in the opposite direction. 'Dizzy is all for pure Tories,' Lowe reported to Delane on 28 June.[5]

On that day the Conservative leaders met and endorsed a plan to form, or attempt to form, a coalition under Derby. If nothing came of that, they decided, they would try to put together a minority government. Accordingly, Derby interviewed Grosvenor and Lansdowne the following day, 29 June. The Adullamites caucused at ten o'clock that evening and sent Grosvenor back with their answer at midnight. Grosvenor brought the message that none of the prominent cave-men would serve under Derby but would agree to give unofficial support to a minority government. 'So much for Adullamite cooperation' was Derby's comment. He was annoyed but not deeply disappointed. Lowe and the anti-clerical Horsman would have been uncomfortable bedfellows in a predominantly Conservative administration.[6]

The Adullamites had made their bid and lost. Nevertheless, they could console themselves with the thought that if they could stay together, they would be in a position to hold the balance of power. Other possibilities for constructing a third party would, very likely, turn up. Lowe wrote to a friend that the times were not 'ripe for the Administration that I wish for, but they are tending towards it.' His major worry (and this was in July 1866) was that Disraeli might do some 'mischief' before the 'remedy' arrived. Should the Tories ever open up the reform question again, then all was lost, not only for his own ambitions but for the new Palmerstonian party he wanted to help create. By November most of his optimism had vanished. 'You are quite mistaken if you think I am going to be Prime Minister or any other Minister at all,' he told Mrs Billyard, who had written enthusiastically from Sydney on hearing the news of the July crisis. She must, he wrote, dismiss the notion of his leading in the Commons. 'I could not do it if I would, and would not do it if I could. It would ruin my eyes, and I, not being ambitious, know of nothing this world has to give that would compensate me for sitting ten hours a night from 4 p.m. to 2 a.m. listening to all sorts of nonsense and perpetually making speeches about what I don't understand.'[7]

It is possible that he actually believed what he said at that moment, for the strain of the last five months was beginning to have its effect. Also his domestic life was becoming almost intolerable. Georgiana was suffering from dropsy in her legs and apparently not keeping her suffering to herself. She had loyally struggled up the stairs to the Visitors' Gallery when the reform debates were on to watch each of Bobby's triumphs. Lowe appreciated this but was driven to despair by her constant chatter and complaints about her pains. Frequent trips to take the waters at Carlsbad did little good. By the end of 1866 Lowe had become so desperate that he was thinking of selling his Surrey estate so that he could escape the 'purgatory' of constant exposure to his wife. 'My motto used to be "my own house rather than any one's" now it is any one's rather than my own,' he wrote to Delane. He tried to arrange a separation; Georgiana threatened a public row. His protests about lack of ambition to the contrary, Lowe immediately backed away from a scandal that would be damaging to his future prospects. He was afraid that his wife's talent for producing and orchestrating a scene would be too generous a gift to his enemies. He wrote to Delane, whose own marriage had been unhappy: 'I must go on as I am unless I am prepared at this time for a public scandal and that without any specific fault to allege as you had. I dare say you think me a Coward but seeing my isolated position in politics my unpopularity with the lower orders the absence of any family connexion to support me and the very long time we have been together I shrink from such a step and prefer to bear the ills I have.'[8]

His solution was to go out alone in society as much as he could. His alliance with the Conservatives over the reform issue in 1866 had opened doors previously closed to him. Most of the personal letters that survive from this period were mailed from the Earl of Carnarvon's estate or from Hatfield House, the home of Robert Cecil, his former enemy but now one of his closest confederates. A favourite retreat was Cortachy Castle in Scotland, where he would spend weekends in the delightful company of Blanche, Countess of Airlie, a comparatively conventional member of Lord Stanley of Alderley's eccentric brood. There he would occasionally meet Blanche's brothers, Henry, a Mohammedan convert, and Algernon, who ended his life as a Roman Catholic bishop – 'two very middling specimens of humanity whom the sweet sister seems to regard with perfectly just and adequate measure of contempt.'[9]

Mary, Marchioness of Salisbury, was another witty, beautiful lady who comforted Lowe during his private tribulations and introduced him into the society of powerful Whig and Tory noblemen. She was the young wife of the old Marquis of Salisbury and therefore Cranborne's step-mother, although the two were the same age. Widowed in 1868, she married, soon after, the fifteenth Earl of Derby. She and Lowe met at Highclere one weekend and heard the news of Palmerston's death. They travelled back to London together on that occasion, talking 'without one moment's intermission from Newberry to Paddington.' After that she and Lowe became 'great friends.' With her he could let down his guard, disclose his anxieties, ask for and receive comfort and affection. One of his letters to her reads: 'I have had too much to do with the battles and struggles of life, and ... with the baseness and *meanness* of human nature to aspire to that kindness and gentleness which marks you out among all people I have ever seen.' On another occasion: 'My Genius is reborn before you, like that of Antony before Octavius.' From Paris: 'I wish I could look over your shoulder when you look in the glass ...' From Carlsbad Spa, about a popular French novel: 'There is something in it that strikes me. The man is in the position so many men are in with nothing left but of feeling of Truth and Honour.' He found it 'rather curious to see how such a subject is treated. He seems to have died of grief because he was parted from a woman whom he did not care for and united to one whom he adored. I don't think I should die of that even if a baby was thrown into the scale.' Responding to one of her letters, he writes: 'Tell me about the man like me. Is he an albino and short-sighted and very fond of you? If not how is he like me?'[10]

Other men adored Lady Salisbury but for Lowe the relationship had a special importance. She chided him affectionately for his tactlessness and lack of proportion, gave him advice about his relationship with important people, and applauded him when she felt he deserved it. It must have been profoundly satisfying to have been so regarded at a time when he was feeling particularly isolated and disliked. Not only did she give him emotional support but in many practical ways she strove to advance his interests. On the second anniversary of their first meeting he wrote to her: 'It was a happy visit to Highclere two years ago. How much I owe to our kind hosts and how much to you. How many happy hours, how much sympathy, how much valuable information!'[11]

Her intimacy with the Cecils and the Stanleys gave her many opportunities to aid her protegé. Undoubtedly it was she who turned the feud between Lowe and Lord Cranborne into a close, if temporary, alliance. She also managed the difficult task of persuading Lord Clarendon, another of her admirers, to mix socially with the man who had wounded him so savagely in *The Times*. The experience of being included in an aristocratic circle tended to warp Lowe's judgment in an unusual way:

it made him optimistic. He managed to convince himself that a new cave, far more influential than the old one, could quickly be formed should the Derby ministry succumb to Disraeli's wiles and make a move toward parliamentary reform.

Thus Lowe believed that affairs were moving in his direction in the summer and early autumn of 1866. He had scant respect for most of his old Adullamite associates; he knew that Disraeli was probably up to some kind of mischief; and he was aware that the increasing momentum of the reform demonstrations would tempt politicians into making some kind of move. But until the last moment he seems to have believed that a threat from himself and from his new Whig and Tory friends would head off a reform bill or at least postpone it for a year. If threats failed then it might be possible to approach Lord Stanley again and persuade him to lead a coalition supported by Lords Cranborne, Clarendon, and Carnarvon – all close friends or relatives of Lady Salisbury. He did not see, or did not wish to admit to himself, that the moment had passed for putting together coalitions to suit the convictions of a few powerful magnates. By the autumn of 1866 popular feelings had reached such a degree of intensity and organization that it could not have been ignored in any political strategy.

The debate still goes on about whether or not the Reform bill of 1867 was the product of that popular pressure. Two modern historians, whose answers to that question differ, agree that neither the class conflict nor the party conflict interpretations are sufficient in themselves. Royden Harrison thinks politicians 'surrendered to events'; F.B. Smith thinks that the Hyde Park Riot and subsequent demonstrations changed the nature of reform from an abstract question into a pressing issue that no government could safely have ignored. However, Smith does not think that Derby or Disraeli decided to go ahead with a reform bill because they were fearful or felt themselves to be coerced. Maurice Cowling goes a step further and claims that Derby decided that reform 'might be a good hare to start,' not simply because he wanted to make a concession to the agitators but also because he wanted to 'keep in step' with the hostility the agitations were producing among the upper classes.[12]

There seems to be general agreement that the agitations precipitated the events, although students of the events disagree about the motives of the actors and the forces and calculations that moved them once the drama began. It is usually conceded that Lowe's 'venality' speech was an important factor in that steady build-up of pressure and that Argyll had a point when he accused Lowe of having helped to bring about the opposite of what he intended. Although such a contention does not lend itself to convincing refutation, it does seem questionable. It is tempting but, perhaps, misleading to be impressed by fate's perversity. Had Lowe kept a gloomy silence in 1866, it is more than likely that the

Conservatives, aided by Liberal rebels, would have defeated Gladstone's bill, if not in the Commons, then in the Lords. Without Lowe's supposed insults to enliven them, workingmen would still have paraded and petitioned in increasing numbers after the bill's defeat. The men who led the demonstrations were organized and working before the 1866 debate began; they could have found a satisfactory, only slightly less provocative, *bête noir* in Lord Elcho. As it was Elcho received his share of abuse. Lowe was surprised that his own windows remained intact while those of Elcho and Disraeli were smashed. The events of 1866 and 1867 would have been less interesting if Lowe had not taken a prominent part in them and the debates would have been less intellectually probing, but the outcome would probably not have been different.[13]

Lowe's reaction to the agitations show how anti-reform politicians could be moved in several directions by these pressures. On the one hand he was sincerely convinced that the meetings and marches were producing a powerful conservative reaction. At the same time he came to agree that it would be dangerous to refuse to make any concessions to the supporters of the Reform League and the Reform Union. When the crowd scuffled with police, overturned railings, and occupied Hyde Park, he was greatly annoyed by the weak response of Derby's ministers. The home secretary, Spencer Walpole, had actually wept with gratitude when Edmund Beales, the leader of the demonstration, had offered a few conciliatory words. On hearing of this, Lowe could scarcely express his scorn: 'Marcellus might cry over the ruins of Syracuse, but rails and dwarf walls are hardly worth the tears of a secretary of State.' That was in July 1866. Between summer and early winter the rallies and processions got bigger, more frequent, and better disciplined. In September Lowe wrote to Delane and Lady Salisbury saying that he was sure the activities of the workingmen had aided the anti-reform cause since they had greatly increased the anxiety about Bright among respectable people. He thought this reaction would weaken Gladstone's already shaky position in the party. The party rank and file were coming to see that the masses wanted universal suffrage and would never settle for less – at least, not for long. Outside of England the excesses of democracy were, he believed, also beginning to produce their inevitable reaction. The United States seemed to be on the verge of a constitutional revolution. If Congress succeeded in impeaching President Johnson, then surely the ruling classes of Britain would stiffen. He thought he detected signs that the reform movement was deteriorating into 'the vulgar Chartist type'; if that were so, a show of force might disperse them as effectively as it had dispersed the Chartists on Kennington Common in 1848. 'The game is won,' he told Lady Salisbury, 'if we had only the courage to win it; just as Hamlet should have killed the king as soon as he was satisfied of his guilt.'[14]

Between October and the end of the year he abandoned his resolve to make a last-ditch stand. He was ready by December to admit that the reform movement could not be shattered merely by a show of middle and upper class resolution. He even worked out a reform proposal of his own. He wrote to Delane that he had a plan which should 'satisfy the only people really in earnest' and yet not start a 'glissade' down the icy slope of democracy. He would 'supplement' rather than change the existing system by giving all who paid income taxes a vote. If this were done, a workingman earning two pounds a week would qualify. Ambitious workers of the better sort could earn their vote; professional people who did not own property would also add a valuable element to the electorate. He did not back away from his contention that a revision of the rating or a rental franchise would begin the glissade. The ten-pound borough franchise should remain inviolate. But since the income tax franchise had a 'built-in limiting principle,' it could safely be superimposed. Obviously, Hamlet-like thoughts were beginning to enter his brain. The demonstrations had not frightened him into changing his position on democracy but they had convinced him that some kind of gesture needed to be made. The time had come to include popular feeling when reckoning the felicific calculus.[15]

The House of Commons learned in February 1867 that the Derby government had come to the same conclusion. Disraeli announced that he would reopen the reform question by presenting not a reform bill, but a series of resolutions. Lowe was displeased but not surprised by this manœuvre. He and the other prominent Liberals had expected Disraeli to come up with a plan, not to settle the reform issue, but to divide the Liberal party. They assumed, with justification, that he had designed a trap: he would hand Parliament some generalized objectives and then ask it to work out the details, knowing, of course, that it was over the details that his Liberal opponents would squabble. Reform had wrecked the Russell ministry in 1866; it might preserve Derby's minority ministry in 1867. If, as the agitations seemed to demonstrate, the country was no longer apathetic about the issue, then some kind of reform was inevitable. The Tory leaders recognized that their survival as a party might be in jeopardy should the Liberals be allowed, ever again, to make the cause of reform their exclusive property.

Had Disraeli been able to bait his reform proposals with a clause calling for household ratepayers' suffrage, this initial move might have had a chance of success. Both he and Derby had been inclined to try household suffrage. They knew the radicals would have been compelled to support such a suffrage. The Adullamites and Tory backbenchers would be frightened but might be reassured with promises of dual votes for those with wealth, education, and professional skills. Disraeli tried the idea on the cabinet, but when General Peel's eyes lighted up 'with insanity' at the mere mention of household suffrage, he withdrew that clause from the resolutions. The results were disastrous; no one could see any merit in the vague statements of principle that remained. Jeers went up from all sections of the House and most of the press. Disraeli then withdrew the resolutions and promised something more substantial. Having drifted for so long, the cabinet found it impossible to construct a new and necessarily complicated bill on short notice. Disraeli came forward again with his household suffrage, dual votes bill; the cabinet at first agreed, then when its right wing had time to digest its implications, divided into factions. Faced by a threatened rebellion, Disraeli abandoned his household suffrage plan for the second time and substituted an improvised bill which bore an embarrassing resemblance to Gladstone's ill-fated measure of the year before. This 'ten-minutes' bill lasted only a few days. It too had to be withdrawn in view of its hostile reception from all quarters. At this, Peel, Cranborne, and Carnarvon resigned and Disraeli was allowed at last to put through his household suffrage proposal. This final bill appeared in March. Four changes of plan in as many weeks![16]

While these alarums and excursions were going on, Gladstone and then Disraeli were making approaches to the Adullamites. A Liberal gathering at Gladstone's house on 26 February found all the former rebels there except for Lowe, who was already trying to separate himself from the cave. Grosvenor denounced the 'ten-minutes' bill on the familiar ground that it lacked a constitutional principle. He pledged Adullamite support for any bold measure which might provide a 'resting place.' When Disraeli was finally permitted to bring in his household bill, some of Grosvenor's colleagues were afraid that this might be carrying boldness too far. What would be the consequences if the fancy franchise were to be removed? If Disraeli's bill were shorn of its two-year residence clause, its dual votes, and its provision that the vote be given only to those householders who paid their rates in person, then household suffrage, 'pure and simple,' might be left standing in its shocking nakedness. Former cave-dwellers who respected Gladstone and supported his Commons leadership, but who had rebelled against his reform bill in 1866, quitted the cave in early March. Lowe and other Adullamites who distrusted Gladstone but distrusted Disraeli still more soon drifted back into the party fold.[17]

This left only a rump of some twenty-five, led by Elcho, Grosvenor, and the railway magnate, Samuel Laing. Not only were their numbers reduced but their independent position was threatened. At first they tried to act as mediators; they offered a compromise. They proposed to retain personal payment of rates as the 'principle' and to make compounding compulsory for all householders occupying premises rated under five pounds. Their hope was that Gladstone would be forced by the moderates to agree, since his own expressed desire for a five-pound rating bill would, in effect, be realized. Grosvenor and Elcho hoped that then the Liberal party would be reunited and the radicals contained – all through the wise leadership of the cave. They had reason to believe that Russell would be open to this compromise; Disraeli had let it be known that he was, in general, sympathetic. But this optimism was dashed when Gladstone firmly refused to make concessions to the 'timid men' who had thrown him 'overboard' in 1866.[18]

When Gladstone challenged the government by moving his own five-pound proposal, the Adullamites had to decide which side to back. They chose to support Disraeli. In their minds a Tory defeat would be a triumph for Bright. Also they sincerely believed that household suffrage was a 'principle.' Therefore they joined with a group of radicals who thought Gladstone's amendment too moderate. These two incongruous factions met in the Commons Tea Room and agreed to vote against Gladstone's motion. On 12 April they filed into the government lobby and gave Disraeli a vital majority. Later the Adullamites made it possible for Disraeli to survive another similar challenge from Gladstone in the committee stage. Once those crises were safely passed, Disraeli promptly lost interest in Adullamite principles. Grosvenor eventually withdrew his five-pound, compounding proposal since he now had no one beyond his own small band who would support it. Then, as the Liberal leaders had feared, Disraeli allowed many of the 'safeguards' to fall, with the result that backbenchers awoke to find they had allowed through a household suffrage bill, if not 'pure and simple,' at least closer to it than most of them would have wished or thought possible in March. By the time the government supporters made that discovery, most of them had managed to convince themselves that shooting Niagara might be an exhilerating if not altogether safe sport. But Lowe, who had watched the proceedings with the deepest dread, was sure that Parliament had been hoodwinked into making a revolution, the consequences of which most of its members had not yet begun to contemplate. He retired to Carlsbad to take the waters and brood on Cicero's lamentations over the fall of the Roman constitution.[19]

At no time had he even considered supporting the Adullamites in their search for a 'resting place.' When Grosvenor gave a dinner in February for what Clarendon called 'the Squadrone Volante,' Lowe agreed to attend. If the purpose of the meeting was, as some reports suggested, to win Lowe over, it was not a success. He told his former confederates that no gentleman who valued his honour could propose a five-pound franchise after having campaigned against a more moderate measure only a year before. Contemptuous though he still was of Gladstone's leadership, he nevertheless decided that he had to make a rapprochement. Lord Stanley, the man he had looked to as a third party standard bearer, had decided to 'go fishing for a policy' and had hooked onto Disraeli's disreputable resolutions; Cranborne had been true but had not been able to gather a large Tory cave around him. Therefore Lowe had no alternative but to seek reinstatement as a loyal Liberal and to work from inside to stiffen Gladstone in resisting Disraeli and the followers of Bright.[20]

Of course Lowe was absurdly wrong in his belief that Gladstone was a potential democrat and putty in Bright's hands. In October 1866 Gladstone had complained to Brand about Bright's demagogery and the devisive effect it might have on the party. The Liberal leader did not need Lowe to warn him that Bright and his followers might desert to the Tories if they thought they could profit from doing so, nor did he need reminding that Disraeli had deliberately given his bill a 'double aspect' – that he had designed it to comfort the right while tempting the left. Immediately after the announcement of the 18 April bill, Cranborne paid a call on Gladstone and found him 'in a state of anxiety, approaching to despair'; he was sure, he told Cranborne, that a household suffrage, entirely 'unguarded,' would be the eventual result. In his own anxiety Lowe did not stop to consider that the man who had once talked about the 'natural right' of all men to vote might be as apprehensive as he was. Therefore he sent letters urging that some kind of blocking action be taken before the Tory bill reached a second reading. If not nipped in the bud, he warned, momentum might carry the bill into committee; once there, radical pressures combined with fear of dissolution would work into Disraeli's mischievous hands. He exhorted Gladstone not to be misled by the dual vote and the other safeguards; they would prove to be totally impractical and would immediately be shoved aside. The rank and file, he feared, would not see the trap, therefore it was necessary to assert discipline, to 'enforce obedience' on any who questioned the authority of the party leadership. Gladstone's thoughts on receiving such advice from the former 'idol of the Cave' are not known but can be imagined.[21]

In time Lowe came to recognize that he had misjudged Gladstone. Ten years after the Reform bill of 1867 had passed into law, Lowe wrote to him saying, 'In almost all subjects except the franchise I agree with you more than, I think, with anyone else.' He wrote this in the midst of a prolonged journalistic fencing match with the Liberal leader about the advisability of extending the franchise to farm labourers. But what these articles in the *Fortnightly* and the *Nineteenth Century* show is how close, not how far apart, the two men were in many of their basic assumptions about constitutional questions. Between 1867 and 1877 Gladstone had moved closer to Bright's position on the suffrage while Lowe had remained firm in his opposition. At the same time they agreed that the goal of government was the happiness and contentment of the people and that utility was the only practical test of happiness. They both assumed that a leisured and specially educated élite would know how to promote the general welfare and that the great majority of poor and uneducated people, for all their good intentions, would not. Therefore they assumed that it was essential that this élite be given a large degree of discretion in exercising the power delegated to it. They both believed democracy to be a threat to that discretion. They agreed that politics was the key to social change; they also agreed that political mechanisms must be carefully balanced and adjusted to protect the public interest against the constant tendency of vested interests (usually in league with the Conservative party) to undermine free trade, individual liberty, and the institutions of industrial capitalism. Gladstone conceded to Lowe, in this public exchange in 1877, that Disraeli's Reform Act had lowered the tone of Parliament, had given advantages to plutocrats, had made it harder for young and independent spirits to find seats in Parliament, and had, generally, made the vital task of legislation and administration more difficult.[22]

Gladstone took Lowe to task, not for being an élitist, but for being blind to 'the great currents of conviction, sympathy and will' running through the lower part of the social pyramid. He thought Lowe valued intelligence too highly and neglected the quality of moral fitness. The Lancashire cotton workers, he argued, had shown a moral heroism and sureness of judgment during the American Civil War that educated men might well have emulated. He also pointed to the good sense and restraint the enfranchised urban labourers had demonstrated in the decade since 1867. While wealth, education, and culture made it possible for men to understand complicated issues, history did not show, he thought, that the wealthy, educated, and cultured were less selfish than ordinary people or less prone to abuse power. On the contrary, the poor had proven to be more trustworthy than the other segments of society whenever events presented clear moral choices. Therefore, he concluded, the élite must shape, guide, and modify the propelling force from beneath but never lose sight of where that great moral force was coming from or put unreasonable barriers in its path. He criticized Lowe for failing to perceive this force and for eternally conjuring up monsters out of the social depths. Gladstone thought this was a common fault among men who seldom had contact with the classes beneath them; Lowe, he charged, had less direct experience with working men than any other prominent statesman. To make matters worse, Gladstone wrote, Lowe's personality leads him to treat every subject immoderately: 'Whatever subject he touches, his first object is, like Ajax, to drag it into the light; into such a light as Tennyson would call a fierce light. Those who do not agree with him say that it is a light like the lights of Rembrandt, which leave much of the picture in deep shadow ...'[23]

In his rebuttal Lowe claimed his own position was the truly liberal one and that Gladstone's faith in moral forces emanating from below was essentially conservative. Precisely how, he asked, are the élite, if tainted by wealth and privilege, to go about shaping and guiding these 'imputed virtues?' If the poor are unselfish because relatively powerless, how will giving them power save them from the 'voice of the Tempter?' Gladstone, he pointed out, counted on the conservative superstition about 'deference' to explain why the poor, once they had the franchise, would be content to delegate their power to a privileged élite. To do so he would need to assume that the English working man, and especially the rural labourer, had a deep love of inequality. All things being equal, Gladstone had claimed, Englishmen 'love a lord.' To prove his point, he had mentioned the fact that a great many of the newly enfranchised had helped bring the Conservatives to power in 1874. Are we being invited then, Lowe asked, to give the poor equality 'because they hate it?' If they do hate equality now, can they be counted on always to behave so irrationally? To make an idol of deference is 'perverse'; to worship the 'goddess of inequality' is the 'meanest and silliest of all superstitions.' It was the Tories, not the Liberals, who were supposed to put their trust in ignorance. Social order, Lowe maintained, is not self-regulating but is the result of difficult and painstaking political construction. It followed that the work must be left to carefully selected agents. Gladstone, he implied, gave lip-service to this liberal premise but failed to remain logically consistent to it.[24]

Lowe was, as he claimed, the more consistent liberal; whether he was a better prophet depends on what point in the nineteenth or twentieth centuries one chooses to measure degrees of class hostility. But none of the differences separating the two men caused them to disagree about the potential dangers contained in the bill Disraeli presented to Parliament in April 1867. They were horrified at Disraeli's lack of reverence for political structures, his willingness to tamper with the delicate constitutional mechanisms, his disgraceful casualness about doing his homework. Though Gladstone did not fear the masses, he did not want them to influence the drawing up of budgets or to dictate tax laws. He wanted to move slowly on franchise reform, to extend power to the workingmen at the same rate that they were assimilating themselves into middle class culture. He agreed with Lowe that Disraeli's bill could be turned into a radical jump forward and that an acceleration might damage the steady progress of assimilation. But once the chipping away of the safeguards began and once it became obvious that wrecking tactics would not work, the differences in position between Gladstone and Lowe became immediately apparent. Gladstone believed in safeguards but held that they must be 'intelligible and not fantastic.' He could see that dual votes and the insistence on excluding the compound householder were not only unworkable but obviously discriminatory. He believed that isolation of classes and hostility between classes was far more dangerous to the liberal state than was democracy. Worried as he was about the possible consequences of making a leap in the dark, he was more worried about the consequences of dividing the nation. Therefore, for these and for more mundane party reasons, he worked, both directly and indirectly, to speed the dismantling of Disraeli's safeguards.

Lowe watched these proceedings with dismay. He wrote to Delane after the bill passed, 'I am furious with Gladstone after having done all he can to prevent Household Suffrage he now says it is a subject of congratulations.' While the bill was making its tortuous way through Parliament Lowe conducted a rear-guard battle from the floor of the House, but in spite of the great reputation he had gained in 1866 few paid serious attention to his speeches. Observers conceded that his reasoning was as sharp, his wit as keen, and his eloquence almost as soaring as in the previous campaign, but they noted that this time few were eager to applaud. The Adullamite organ, The Day, regretted that Lowe had chosen to throw away his great reputation by adopting a 'miserable attitude of negative spitefulness.' Even The Times, turning as usual with the weather-vane, reprimanded him for his pessimism and called him 'the Cassandra of Calne.' When Prosper Merimée read Lowe's last, bitter speech on 15 June he wrote to Panizzi from Paris that much as he admired the form – 'a model of Parliamentary style' – he had to admit that the content bore a 'slight resemblance to the Lamentations of Jeremiah.'[25]

Not all of Lowe's activities were negative. A few days before making his final gloomy speech, he tried to get the House of Commons to adopt a cumulative voting scheme. He proposed to give every voter in boroughs or counties with more than two members and having more than one seat vacant a number of votes equal to the number of seats vacant. The idea was that the voter could distribute or concentrate his votes in any way he chose. He admitted that this was a weak palliative, similar to the ones he had been denouncing for the past three years. If, however, his scheme allowed the 'intelligence in a community to combine,' even for a short while, then it might perform a limited service. Turning to Disraeli, who had reminded him of his tirades against safeguards, Lowe said that he acknowledged his inconsistency but added that this was better than 'political nihilism.' Bright then teased him by turning a figure from one of Lowe's 1866 speeches. 'Why,' Bright asked, 'if a man abstracted a snowball from an avalanche, would that prevent the danger or destruction that was impending?' Lowe could only reply, lamely, 'Is that any reason why we should not do as we can?' Mill and Fawcett voted for the amendment which lost by a large margin. A similar measure, sponsored by Lord Cairnes and Lord Russell, did, however, become law. By 1867, therefore, Lowe concluded that nothing he could propose had much chance of being considered seriously.[26]

The battle lost and the session over, Lowe set out for Germany to recuperate. He found the food bad and the atmosphere heavy; nothing there could dispel his dark brooding about Disraeli's 'treachery,' his 'sordid motives.' By this time mutual animosity had passed far beyond the conventions of parliamentary behaviour. Before leaving for Germany, Lowe had made a personal attack on the Tory leader for having so irresponsibly and unpatriotically untied the bag which holds the winds of 'change, alteration, innovation, and revolution.' Disraeli's reply was in kind. The House, he said, was continually being surprised by the 'spontaneous aversions' of the member for Calne and by the virtuosity of his 'rhetorical crescendo.' On this occasion, he said, they had to endure a 'series of the most doleful vaticinations that were ever listened to.' So heavily laced were they with erudite references – 'all about the battles of Chaeronea and of Hastings' – that, Disraeli said, he was reminded 'of the production of some inspired schoolboy.' After that exchange, no civilities again passed between them. When, in November 1876, Disraeli's beloved Mary Anne died, Lowe tried Lady Salisbury's patience by saying that Gladstone had shown 'his usual vulgarity and want of taste in alluding to Mrs. Dizzy in the House.'[27]

If Lowe ever blamed himself for having contributed to the advancement of democracy in Britain, he kept it to himself. Argyll's warning about the consequences of the breakdown of party discipline Lowe passed on to Gladstone in 1867, without noticing the irony. Lowe assured himself and his friends that his lonely sacrifice had been worth the insults that had been its reward. He was, he said, resigned to obscurity. He wrote to his brother that 'the pig-sticking interests' in Calne (Calne was and is a producer of sausages) had turned against him and, if the University of London 'don't take pity on me, I am very likely to go by the board.' When the university did take pity, Bright suggested he appear there in sackcloth and ashes. He had chosen not to do so, Lowe told his new constituents, only because, 'Gentlemen, I am no ascetic ...' Politics, led by Disraeli and Gladstone ('what a poor creature Gladstone is ...'), had, he decided, few attractions left for him. As he wrote to Lady Salisbury, 'Hin ist hin – verloren ist verloren.'[28]

14

The Exchequer:
The Good Years

Throughout the remainder of Derby's term of office and the ten months of the succeeding Disraeli ministry, Lowe sustained his mood of *schadenfreude*. Nothing at home or abroad, it seemed, would ever be right again. For the sake of Georgiana's health, he suffered through more trips to German spas. The meat in Carlsbad would 'disgust a cannibal'; Weisbaden concentrated 'in a small place everything that is odious to me, heat, gambling, glare, ugliness, monotony, and bad company.' The English papers he received were full of depressing news: the Tories were actually going to send an expedition into the forlorn wastes of Abyssinia to die of sunstroke simply because King Theordore had unceremoniously tossed one of Her Majesty's envoys into prison! 'Who could suppose that Pakington was fated to make war on Prester John?' Lowe wrote to Lady Salisbury in 1867. He was haunted, he told her, by the 'strongest presages of disaster.' Delane received similar cries of anguish: 'One does not like to be unpatriotic or always predicting evil,' and yet 'I have the strongest opinion that we are sending our army to destruction ...' Several bristling letters went off to *The Times* saying that it was criminal lunacy to intrude into 'miserable quarrels of barbarous and ferocious sectaries.' On his return home he repeated his predictions of disaster to the House of Commons and concluded with a fervent wish: 'Oh that we could only learn to mind our business!' As he had expected, the ministry, under the direction of its evil genius, was embarking on the course of imperial adventuring – a natural extension of its domestic adventuring. The prospect weighed heavily on his mind. Bishop Wilberforce complained after a weekend at Hatfield House that he had been forced to endure two solid days of listening to Lowe's diatribes against Disraeli; 'it was enough to make the flesh creep to hear his prognostications for the future of England.'[1]

And then, in 1868, when prospects seemed desolate, fortune took a dramatic turn for the better. Gladstone discovered an issue, the disestablishment of the Irish church. With it he would restore unity to his party. Once the opposition reunited, the Conservative government could only postpone its eventual dissolution. Disraeli would not be rushed; finally, in July, he asked the queen to prorogue Parliament and called for a general election in the autumn. Gladstone was confident of victory; he was sure that Tory extravagance would be a vote-winning cry and that disestablishment would bring the Nonconformists back to their natural loyalty to the Liberal party. Lowe was equally confident that the time had come for the humiliation of the Tories and 'their Mahomet.' They would be forced to pay for ignoring an elementary rule: 'if you are obliged to spend more in one direction you should retrench in another.' Lowe thought that no one understood this rule better than he did or was more steadfast in following it. He wrote to Lady Salisbury in September: 'I wish they would make me Chancellor of the Exchequer. I think I possess the faculty for saying No as well as anyone, and in that and not in super finance lies the real secret of financial prosperity.'[2]

When Gladstone formed his first ministry in December 1868, Lowe, to the surprise of nearly everyone, got his wish. It is possible that he had been encouraged in his hopes for the Exchequer; certainly he did expect to be asked to serve in the cabinet in some capacity. During the summer he informed Delane that he wished to break his long relationship with *The Times*, an indication that he was counting on receiving an invitation from Gladstone and wanted to be sure that Russell and other leading Whigs did not again make objections to his connexion with journalism. Also during that summer he agreed to be chairman of the board of a company to lay a second cable across the Atlantic. He explained to Lady Salisbury that he had no objection to earning an 'honest penny'; after all, had he not demonstrated in the past his willingness to 'renounce thousands?' 'Besides,' he said, 'I think it is just as well a little to extend the sphere of influence.' To Mrs Billyard he wrote that he was confident the autumn elections would produce a Liberal sweep and when that happened he would get something important, 'my sins in 1866 not withstanding.'[3]

His expectation had been aroused and then dashed so often in the past ten years that he was almost unable to believe in his good fortune when the invitation actually came. Lord Clarendon arranged for Lady Salisbury to tell him. This is her diary account of the interview:

Mr. Lowe came at 5. Sir H. Bulwer was with me. I could not talk. Mr. Lowe had no communication from Mr. Gladstone. He was all eagerness. I asked him to come back after dinner. He came and I told him he was to be Chancellor of

the Exchequer. He had no idea of it. He promised to write next day and fulfilled it when he accepted office. I had known all his troubles during the last
2 years and a half – had encouraged him in his honest truth speaking, had told
him his day would come; he had never believed it and thought it curious I
should have been the person to give him the news.[4]

He tried unsuccessfully to conceal his delight behind conventional expressions of humility. 'Dear Henry,' he wrote to his brother, 'I am Chancellor of the Exchequer with everything to learn.' To Mrs Billyard he
wrote the same day: 'I am almost angry with myself for not being more
pleased. One gets these things but gets them too late.' More spontaneous
was a remark he made to Henry Cole whom he met while walking to a
railway station: 'I am like a young Lear with my troubles before me.'[5]
    Reaction to the announcement was, as might be expected, mixed.
Lord Russell made no attempt to hide his anger. Walter Bagehot predicted good budgets but wondered if the new financial minister might
not prove too clever by half. Edward Ellice, the son of Lowe's old
friend, predicted that the new chancellor would be 'the real brains of
the cabinet.' As in the past, the permanent secretaries in the bureaucracy hailed the promotion of a kindred spirit; Sir Rivers Wilson, at the
Treasury, said it was a 'fortunate inspiration.' But whether pleased or
displeased, people tended to find Gladstone's choice of the arch-rebel
of 1866 curious, even eccentric. Some years after the ministry had
ended, Lord Acton asked Gladstone directly how he had come to fix on
Lowe. Gladstone replied that he had been greatly taken by a review of a
published collection of his budget speeches which Lowe had written for
Acton's journal, *The Home and Foreign Review*.[6]
    Gladstone was not being playful when he said this, nor is it likely
that he intended to flatter Acton by testifying to the influence of *The
Home and Foreign Review*. Gladstone was neither playful nor prone to
flattery. However, he was undoubtedly being selective when he searched
his memory. He had been one of Palmerston's ministers who had
strongly approved of the Revised Code and had tried to get Palmerston
to act more generously towards its author. Also, Gladstone had experienced directly Lowe's talent for being 'effectively disagreeable.' This
thought that the Liberal party owed a debt and had been severely punished for not paying it must also have been in Gladstone's mind in 1868.
Mention of the review article was probably his way of explaining that
he had been looking for a man who would be fierce and unflinching in
carrying through to completion the Peelite financial tradition. Reading
Lowe's emphatic statements about the heroic mission of economy probably confirmed his opinion that the reviewer was such a man.[7]
    Apart from its possible effect on politics, the review is worth some
attention in itself. It would make a valuable study for anyone who

wants to experience the full force of the mid-Victorian liberal passion
for retrenchment. Lowe began by saying that Gladstone had accomplished one of the great quiet revolutions of the modern age, a transformation of the economy and therefore of the nature of society. He had
found it restricted, protectionist, and monopolistic and had made it
free, expanding, and open to enterprise. Lowe examined the critical
moments in that revolutionary history, noted the mistakes and minor
regressions, and praised the triumphant budgets. In the second part, the
part that undoubtedly impressed Gladstone, he moved from praise of
past victories for free trade to a discussion of the task lying ahead. The
revolution, Lowe said, had been accomplished in the sense that all informed men gave lip-service to its principles and all future chancellors
of the exchequer would be forced to adhere to its premises; but the
revolution had not been completed.

An example of work still to be done, Lowe wrote, was the revision of
the tax laws on charities. At present, charitable bequests were not taxed.
What the charitable giver evaded, Lowe said, the taxpayer was forced to
make up; thus remission perpetuated an irrational system. But this was
only one of many finishing touches still needing to be made. The real
work for finance ministers in the years ahead, Lowe stated, would be to
ward off the continually present threat of a counter-revolutionary tendency – the self-generating pressure within the administration that caused
expenditures to grow. Bureaucrats and their political chiefs would, because they were human beings, constantly be on the look-out for ways
to divert more resources. It was a fact of life that lavish spending would
be popular and prudent saving would not. As the expense of government grew, so would the expectations of the general public. Parliament
could be counted on to talk piously about the virtues of economy but
practice extravagance. Only one impediment stood in the path of these
counter-revolutionary tendencies and that was the chancellor of the exchequer. He had the thankless task of defending 'the pockets of the
people against the attacks of their representatives.' Thus no office,
Lowe wrote, was more lonely, none more vexatious, none more vital to
the continued advancement of prosperity and domestic and international peace.[8]

Gladstone passionately concurred. He knew from having watched
Lowe's career that he was not the sort of person who would shirk the
weary service of 'saving money which no one wants to save' and 'pre-
venting extravagance which no one wants to prevent.' Gladstone did
not believe he needed a brilliant economist or a financial innovator; he
agreed with Lowe that all of the groundwork had already been laid.
What he believed he did need was an ally in the cabinet who would be
ruthless in saying 'No.' Lowe seemed fashioned by an inscrutable providence to be that ally.

As soon as the new chancellor of the exchequer took up his post, the prime minister sent him a list of guide lines. These Gladstone called 'remnants,' things he had failed in the past to get through cabinets or Parliaments. Taxes on charities were there, along with suggestions for the removal of tea licences and various conveyance duties, and small duties remaining on corn. Also listed was a proposal to reduce the income tax by stages as it ceased to be needed for facilitating the reduction of indirect taxes. Above all, Lowe was to keep tight-reins on the other departments of government. Cabinet colleagues who tried to appeal against acts carried out 'in defence of the public' would, Gladstone promised, get stony reception. 'All those on whose toes you will necessarily have trodden will look out with a preter-human sharpness for the joints in your own armour,' Gladstone concluded – advice which the recipient, at the time, must have found a trifle redundant. Lowe thought his past performance showed that he needed no such encouragement. At the University of London, where he went to give thanks for being re-elected after acceptance of office, he said that he hoped his supporters would make allowances if in the period ahead he made himself 'emphatically disagreeable to everyone all around.' They should expect, he said, to watch him endure more criticism and dislike than any of the other ministers. This was bound to happen since he would come closest to 'that most susceptible part of an Englishman's person, the pocket of his trousers.'[9]

When he took office late in 1868, retrenchment and disestablishment seem to have been the total of Gladstone's legislative programme. In 1874, after this remarkably productive ministry had ended, George Brodrick had a long interview with the Liberal leader in connexion with a projected history of the previous five years. He had expected Gladstone to say that he had begun his regime with a well mapped plan of reform, accumulated out of the arrears left behind by the relatively inactive Palmerston and Derby administrations. He was surprised to learn that this was not the case. Gladstone said that beyond reforming the Irish church he had no definite programme of reform but had simply 'utilized his surplus of Parliamentary energy for the Irish Land Bill, the Education Bill, and other legislative matters.' Gladstone certainly did not make this revelation apologetically; he subscribed to the still generally accepted convention that ministers existed not primarily to put through legislation but to carry on the queen's government. It should be remembered too that for old-fashioned liberals, retrenchment was nearly a complete programme of reform. Gladstone did not feel obliged to draw up a carefully articulated legislative agenda because he assumed that a general policy of economy in government would, as a matter of course, lead to certain specific actions. The prime minister would expect his ministers to run their departments efficiently. That would mean that the wasteful military services would be reorganized, the bureau-cracy would be rationalized, a non-aggressive foreign policy would be adopted, and the colonies would be induced to accept a greater respon-sibility for their own defence and administration. He believed his func-tion was to insist on economy and efficiency and support whatever initiatives this pressure produced. To men like Gladstone and Lowe re-trenchment was an active social policy, not an excuse for lacking one. Gladstone, at least, knew what the rookeries of St Giles looked and smelled like; he was not indifferent to the conditions of poverty in which almost a third of his countrymen lived.

Had he believed unemployment to have been a problem that govern-ment could solve by passing legislation, he would not have been inhi-bited by his prejudice in favour of individual initiative. Like most mid-Victorians of all political descriptions, he was a *laissez fairist* in general but not in particular. He was a passionate economizer because he had a social conscience; Lowe was a zealous economizer because he was a rationalist. Though profoundly different in their natures, both men were inspired by the thought that the less the government spent the more private enterprise could spend for labour and machinery. If Glad-stonian retrenchment was unpopular, it was not because most people questioned the assumptions behind it but because the economizers ap-peared to be cold-hearted, miserly, and unpatriotic. Lowe's pledge to 'save money by small economies and by avoiding inconsiderate risks' seemed sound to everyone who was touched by the self-help ethic. But, of course, no one found such statements inspiring or heart-warming; they were aggressively designed not to be. Gladstone and Lowe were ready, indeed eager, to accept the unpopularity this policy of 'small economies' was bound to provoke. That does not mean that they ig-nored or were unconcerned by the effects of that unpopularity on the fortunes of their party; such matters were soberly discussed and calcu-lated. But always such discussions were infused with self-satisfaction at the thought that every expression of outrage from a special interest group gave evidence that the liberal mission was progressing satisfac-torily.[10]

At no time did Gladstone caution his chancellor about the conse-quences of excessive frugality. On the contrary, he complained that Lowe was insufficiently vigilant. In 1873 Gladstone told Granville that Lowe had proven 'wretchedly deficient' in his ability to control the in-flation of estimates from the government departments and had shown a deplorable tendency to wilt whenever one of his attempts to stop reck-less spending touched off a public outcry. Thus Lowe, who gained an unenviable reputation for meanness, was regularly being chastized by his chief for prodigality. Seldom, however, was he criticized for the nar-rowness of his social and economic goals.[11]

Enemies as well as friends were ready to give him credit for the extra-ordinary energy with which he went about his duties. The moment he arrived at the Treasury he served notice that the slackness of the last two-and-a-half years was at an end. Edward Hamilton, the permanent secretary, wrote to a friend that his new head had been 'throwing himself into Treasury work with an energy which I have not seen in any of his predecessors.' In retrospect Lowe agreed that his labours had been 'super-human.' He had been, he claimed, the first chancellor of the exchequer to supervise directly the day-to-day business of the Treasury instead of turning over routine administration to the financial secretary – precisely the cause of so many of Lowe's troubles, Gladstone observed. Lowe said that he knew in advance that such dedication to minutiae would 'bring the press of the whole country against me.' He also knew that dedication of this kind would rile his cabinet colleagues. He would have to receive deputations of greedy citizens and incur their wrath; he would have to face members of Parliament in person and remind them of their public responsibilities. He was aware, he said, that the only applause he would get for his zeal would be from his own conscience – nowhere else – but that would be sufficient reward. Knowing that he lacked the genius for finance of a Peel or a Gladstone, he could, nevertheless, demonstrate what he had learned from studying Latin grammar: that 'economy was a great revenue.'[12]

It is hardly surprising that the financial secretary, the political official normally responsible for the details of administration, would not appreciate this interpretation of the chancellor's duties, implying, as it did, that his subordinates were either incapable or redundant. In view of the possibilities for bad feeling, it is unfortunate, to say the least, that Gladstone decided to give the post of financial secretary to Acton Smee Ayrton, the man Lowe had so often quarrelled with over compulsory vaccinations. The chancellor of the exchequer was not unique in disliking Ayrton; the member for the Tower Hamlets inspired hatred whenever he opened his mouth. When Queen Victoria heard that Gladstone wanted to bring him into the government, she objected strongly on the grounds that he was an arrogant boor who had made public remarks about her supposed dereliction of duty during her widowhood. Gladstone was too generous in his view of human nature and, at the same time, too stern in his belief in self discipline to be sensitive about the possible consequences of friction between personalities. He believed that public men should subordinate such pettiness, as, no doubt, they should. His response to the cries of distress from Queen Victoria and from Lowe was to agree that Ayrton was 'not exactly a sweetmeat' but to point out that he had made a great reputation in the House of Commons as a relentless watchdog over the public purse. Eventually, even Gladstone came to recognize that Ayrton's alleged virtues did not com-

pensate for his personal abrasiveness. Lowe made no attempt to work
with Ayrton (no one was ever successful in doing that); instead he side-
tracked all business around what had traditionally been the most bur-
densome junior ministerial posts in the government. One result was that
the financial secretary was of little use to the government or the Commons on question day. This situation was embarrassing for Ayrton, who
tried to cover up by making sarcastic replies. Ayrton-baiting became a
favourite blood sport for opposition MPs. After several ugly incidents,
Gladstone agreed to move him to the Board of Works, where he continued his open feud with Lowe, brought the queen to the verge of apo-
plexy, and spread despair among all the enemies of ugliness and philistinism. A.H. Layard, whom Ayrton displaced, warned 'men of taste' to
expect the worst from this vulgar, low-minded 'beast' and the other
pennypinching barbarians.[13]

Men of taste did have reason to fear the advent of 'Lowe, Ayrton and
Co.' From our vantage point in time the interminable bickering over
royal sewers, the charges and retreats in the architectural 'battle of the
styles,' the quarrels over monuments for dead heroes, over the Embankment, over Epping Forest, seem quaintly amusing, yet they contributed
in no small way to the rapid public disillusionment with one of the
most productive ministries of the century. Lowe was often blamed and,
to some extent, deserved to be. His temper, if sweeter than Ayrton's,
was not sweet. Yet examination of these incidents discloses that Lowe
was frequently the conciliator and the voice of common sense.

Three curious examples illustrate this point. The first has to do with
the grave matter of how best to remodel the sanitary arrangements of
Windsor Castle. The difficulty was this: in an attempt to reduce the
stench that flushed by Westminster Palace, legislators made some feeble
attempts to control the dumping of raw sewage into the Thames. Windsor Castle was an offender, so specialists at the Board of Works devised
a way to connect the castle drains and those of the Frogmore estates
with the conduits of the town. The queen objected to the mixing of
common with noble sludge, but Ayrton, persuaded that his engineers
had found the cheapest solution, refused to reconsider. Prince Christian
appealed to the Treasury and got a promise that engineers would construct facilities for giving the royal drainage special treatment on an
island in the river. Letters flowed back and forth between the Treasury
and the Board of Works but Ayrton was not receptive to advice. Finally
Lowe appealed to the prime minister himself who, with some difficulty,
managed to sooth the queen's disposition and save Lowe's honour by
writing, in his 'best manner,' to the minister of works, ordering him to
co-operate. 'I have achieved the drainage of Windsor and I die happy,'
Lowe remarked on his retirement from office.[14]

Another incident, which threw the two antagonists into a 'fit of violent economy' and provoked a well-publicised row, was over plans for the construction of the new Law Courts. The commission had been awarded to George Edmund Street. He complained that the proposed site on the north side of the Strand was too cramped for the neo-gothic palace he had designed. Ayrton would not listen and Lowe decided to take the matter out of his hands. Lowe knew that architects tended to be contemptuous of economy. He had complained to the queen during an after-dinner conversation about the 'lavish and extravagant decoration' of many of the new public buildings and had scolded Street for being prone to extravagance. Nevertheless Lowe was not entirely insensitive to Street's desire to create a monument to the majesty of the law. He tried to secure a location on the Embankment where there would be more space and the land would be cheaper. It was only when that plan failed that he ordered construction to begin along Chancery Lane. When the walls started to go up, jurisdiction passed from the Treasury to the Board of Works and then Street learned the true meaning of philistinism. Ayrton resented Treasury interference and made no secret of his anger. He haggled over the details of nearly every turret and every cornice, making it obvious that he considered architects and artists to be mere tradesmen who needed to be watched with a sharp eye if they were to be kept honest.[15]

Another example of Lowe's willingness to intervene to protect an artist from the Works commissioner's hammer-fisted economizing involved a monument for the Duke of Wellington. An earlier government had commissioned the sculptor, Alfred Stevens, to carve an equestrian statue of the hero of Waterloo for St Pauls. Twelve years went by and Stevens had still not put the duke and his horse on top of the marble tomb, although he had managed to spend most of the money appropriated by Parliament. Ayrton, snorting that this was what came from neglecting the principle of competition, took possession of the statue, put a hoarding around it, and circulated tenders inviting artists to bid on the work remaining. Steven's friends appealed to Lowe. Accompanied by a retinue, the chancellor of the exchequer visited the barricaded studio and subsequently fired off several blasts through his subordinates in the Treasury (by late 1870 the two officials had ceased to communicate directly) at the Board of Works. Thanks to Lowe, Steven's work of art, now with horse and rider, rests among the other dismal nineteenth-century sarcophagi in the cathedral.[16]

These examples do not prove that Lowe was a generous official or that his public image bore no relation to reality. The Treasury's involvement in disputes over a new Science School at South Kensington, over a museum on Bethnal Green, over the purchase of the Castellani jewellery for the British Museum, or over a proposal that the state make a contribution to the search for Livingstone, showed that Lowe's reputation for parsimony was not entirely a Tory fiction. When Epping Forest came up for sale, conservationists proposed that the central government buy it and make it a public woodland. Prodded by Gladstone, the chancellor of the exchequer refused, saying that since Londoners would be using the space, London should put up the money. As always, he explained his case all too well and managed, in the process, to convey the impression that he suspected the Metropolitan Board of Works of wanting to force widows in Cumberland to pay for the Sunday leisure of city-dwellers. Then, while the London press was still simmering over Epping, Lowe demanded that the Metropolitan Board of Works pay a high market price for two-and-a-half acres of Embankment land intended for a park. Once again, he was not content simply to do quietly what Gladstone expected of him but insisted on reading sermons on self-reliance to the inhabitants of the metropolis. Thus, as the years went by, an ever-increasing number of officials, art lovers, and ordinary citizens came to agree with W.E. Forster that the chancellor of the exchequer was making economy 'stink in the nostrils.'[17]

In these incidents as in the others, it was Gladstone who had demanded an uncompromising stand. No one, however, forced Lowe to be rude. From the moment Lowe came to the Treasury, the department gained a reputation for tactlessness and discourtesy. That bad reputation grew worse when Lowe brought Ralph Lingen over from the Privy Council to become his permanent secretary. As we have already seen, no two men in government were more capable of inspiring fear and resentment. They both were convinced that a fierce exterior was the best protector of the public purse. Appropriately, Lowe chose a cold, wet day in a small Scottish seaport to explain that his job called for great 'determination' of character, not a trait 'in which the amiable qualities of life shine remarkably.' Acting with that determination, he informed old friends, Delane included, that they must not expect privileged information or special favours. Also, he made no attempt to sugar-coat any unpleasant news he might have to communicate to the House of Commons; questioners got curt answers if, as often happened, the chancellor of the exchequer found their points to be silly. Delegations he treated with his best donnish manner. Rivers Wilson, Lowe's private secretary, recalled how smoothly Disraeli handled visitors and how abrasively Lowe performed the task. Delegations emerged from an interview with Disraeli, confused perhaps, but smiling; they usually emerged from a session with Lowe in a 'stamping rage.' Wilson described the technique. Lowe would courteously receive the men as they filed into his office. He would listen intently, never interrupting, to the presentation. When everyone had said his piece, he would then, with clinical precision, summarize and then dissect the arguments he had heard, always with formal courtesy. He would show no anger and speak in a quiet voice. Then, having exposed the faults in logic or hypothesis, he would terminate the interview, leaving the frustrated and often red-faced delegates to find their way out. On one occasion a party of brewers, led by the Liberal MP Michael Bass, came to object to the practice of taxing beer by the barrel. Lowe listened silently, as usual, and began his reply by asking Bass if he had not paid a visit the previous year and made the same complaint. Bass agreed that he had. Lowe then quoted from memory the statistics on the number of barrels the Bass brewery had produced that year. How many barrels did the Bass Company now pay the tax on, he asked. He was told the figure, a considerable increase. 'I congratulate you on the great expansion of your business,' Lowe said, and motioned towards the door.[18]

In almost all the public speeches he made as chancellor of the exchequer Lowe brought up the subject of his reputation for fierceness and claimed that it was evidence that he and his government were doing their duty. At Glasgow in 1872 he regretted that people had forgotten that tax revenue was really private money, appropriated for public ends. Individuals might have the right to be as careless as they wished with their loose change and to appear open-handed and jolly; the appropriators, however, would be morally derelict if they acted in that way. That, he said, was a statement that even the most ignorant man would immediately understand and agree with, and yet he had been condemned from 'year's end to year's end' for having promptly dismissed mendicants who came to him with small and seemingly innocent requests. 'Some people are said to have the art which one great man is reported to have had, who when people came to ask favours of him, "kicked them down stairs with so charming a grace that he seemed to be handing them up." Unhappily, that talent has been entirely denied to me. I say nothing about the former part, but the latter is totally wanting.'[19]

Cabinet colleagues often felt these sharp kicks. As soon as Cardwell took his seat at the War Office he was bombarded with advice on how to conduct his detailed affairs. In the first week he received a set of nine 'sound principles,' ranging from the general, 'never to employ a soldier for work a civilian can do,' to the specific, 'give [Henry] Vivian [whom Lowe thought incompetent] a private secretary always.' Granville, at the Colonial Office, got similar messages. He was asked to explain why his office had thirty-seven employees during the Crimean War, 'when we meddled in the affairs of so many communities,' and now, after the meddling had presumably stopped, it had fifty-three. 'Is not this rather too bad?' Could the Colonial Office not return 'to something like the Patriarchal Simplicity of 1853?'[20]

Granville and Cardwell were old friends and inclined to smile and take this meddling in stride – not so the Foreign Secretary, Lord Clarendon, who, notwithstanding Lady Salisbury's diplomacy, could not forget past grievances. He complained to Gladstone that the communications from the Treasury were worse than the insults that arrived from Ayrton – if such a thing were possible. On this occasion Clarendon had been sent a cluster of briskly worded notes asking him to explain why the diplomatic staff in Japan could not be reduced, why the consulates in Ragusa, Elsinore, and Buffalo should not be closed down, and why the Anglican chaplains, stationed in Chinese ports, should not be brought home. Would the prime minister please tell Lowe, Clarendon requested, 'that because he holds the purse strings he is not to pull all the other strings.' Gladstone tried to soothe him by pointing out that the Treasury's job was necessarily vexatious and that Lowe was carrying out orders. The prime minister agreed that this did not excuse tactlessness and said that he had spoken with Lowe about it on several occasions – with scant effect. Disregard for the feelings of others was, Gladstone feared, a character trait that would simply have to be endured, since it appeared to be due 'to a blank in his very extraordinary mental condition. Unhappily the matter does not improve. He goes and does it again.'[21]

The Conservative press and the opposition leaders were not slow to capitalize on the resentments thus aroused. They held up Lowe and Ayrton as prime examples of how liberalism, by its narrowness, could turn virtue into vice. The Gladstonians, in their frantic attempts to save pennies had, as usual, confused means with ends. National greatness could not be measured, as Lowe seemed to think, in pounds and shillings. Gladstone had come to power on a pledge to give the country sound finance, Disraeli said, but all the public seems to hear from his finance minister is 'the mere rattle of the dry bones of political economy.' As the years passed the electorate became increasingly responsive to this line of argument. The enthusiastic reception given to a burlesque, written by W.S. Gilbert, gives an idea of how firmly this image of cheese-paring fanaticism had taken root.[22]

The Happy Land opened at the Court Theatre in March 1873. Three mortals, got up to look like Gladstone, Ayrton, and Lowe, ascend to cloudland and instruct the fairies on how to manage their aerial estate. A packed audience roared its approval on the first night when the trio danced on to the stage, singing:

> GLADSTONE: We are three statesmen old and tried,
>   I know what I'm about.
> LOWE: And I all figures – fact deride
>   All precedents I scout.

AYRTON: And I love rows here, I love rows there
Here a row, there a row,
Everywhere a row!

The three earthlings then look around them and Ayrton exclaims: 'What an awful place! What taste in Art!' And Lowe: 'What lavish expenditure! Oh lor! Statues to public benefactors!' Then Ayrton again: 'Solid marble temple! Here's a waste. Put marble to such purposes as these! What's to become of brick and stucco I should like to know?'[23]

Customers flocked to the box office but the lord chamberlain ordered the directors to change the costumes and make-up of the impersonators. After that, the fun was lost and the play soon closed. *The Times* editorialized that satire of this sort bred a 'vulgar contempt for authority,' but admitted that the audience had appeared to be vastly pleased at the sight of the prime minister, the chancellor of the exchequer, and the commissioner of the Board of Public Works dancing the *can can* and talking grave nonsense.[24]

In 1873 unpopularity of this kind worried the Liberal leaders and caused them to wonder about the wisdom of hanging on to power much longer. But in the first two years of the ministry Lowe was able to enjoy jokes about his reputation. On a blistering day in June 1870 he went to Oxford to accept an honorary degree. When the chancellor of the University introduced him as 'frugalissimus,' he was delighted and joined in the shout of laughter. He could afford to do so; until 1871 he had every reason to consider his term in office a gratifying success. He had written to a friend in April 1869: '*Me voila donc lancé dans la carrière de finance* – in which many of my kind friends confidently predicted that I should break down. My office is not "the most important under the Crown," but it is as high as I have ever wished to climb, and I am what seldom happens to anyone, content. Summer has begun all of a sudden.'[25]

When he wrote this he was basking in the approval that greeted his first budget. It had been a virtuoso performance. Those who came to the House of Commons on 8 April 1869 expected to hear cheerless news. There were empty seats, here and there, on the floor and in the gallery. Artfully, Lowe began by darkening the mood. Except for an occasional quip, he stumbled along, pausing to puzzle out with his pocket magnifying glass figures written on the back of an old menu. He begged the indulgence of his audience for the 'difficulties and disqualifications peculiar to myself.' Then he made a lugubrious joke about the 'sheer ill-luck' that so few wealthy men had been carried away in the previous tax year: 'though Death has been busier than usual, he has avoided striking at those whose death would enrich the Revenue.' (There was a certain amount of restrained amusement at this point.) It was unkind of fate, he continued, to play such a trick, since the Treasury needed all the help it could get. The revenue 'shows not the slightest symptoms of elasticity.' It was, he said, more 'like the flaxen thread which the spinner draws out than the band which rushes back from which it has been dragged.'[26]

This was the premise behind the 1869 budget and it was a false premise. He was wrong to think the economy inelastic, although perhaps he should be forgiven for making a mistake of this kind early in 1869. The slump of 1866 had ended by then and for the next three years England experienced a boom which brought a flood of riches into the Treasury. Even Death helped to make the revenue elastic in the cold winter of 1869. At the time of the budget speech in April 1869 there was, however, an immediate shortage of funds. The Tories had sent General Napier, at the head of a colourful expeditionary force of Sikhs and elephants, into Abyssinia where he had, in Disraeli's fine phrase, 'planted the standard of St. George on the mountains of Rasselas.' Contrary to Lowe's predictions, no soldier died of sun-stroke or, indeed, of any other unnatural causes. Nevertheless the adventure had been costly in money if not in lives. Ward Hunt, the chancellor of the exchequer in 1868, had to ask Parliament for a supplementary grant and had to carry over a million and a half pounds of the war debt to 1869, a debt Lowe would have to settle. To make things more difficult for his successor, Hunt had overestimated the revenue for the 1867 tax year and had compensated for this by increasing the income tax. This action limited Lowe's area of manœuvrability; two income tax increases in as many years would be extremely unpopular. Adding still another unwanted inheritance from Hunt was a bill for the purchase by the nation of the chaotic, private telegraph system. Disraeli's ministers had arranged the transaction but had not paid for it. Advocates of the purchase predicted that, over the long run, the telegraph would more than pay its way, but no one expected it to do so in the initial period when capital costs would be extremely high. Therefore Lowe had the task of finding an extra four and a half million pounds to cover liabilities he had neither incurred nor approved of. For one dreary hour he told his troubles to the House.[27]

Then, when he came to the point where everyone expected to hear him announce the new taxes, he paused and smiled. With an actor's sense of timing, he quietly, undramatically unfolded his proposals for turning gloom into sunshine. Customarily, the income tax year ran from April to April, half the money payable in October, a quarter in January, and the last quarter at the end of the tax year. Lowe announced that instead he would collect the whole of the forthcoming tax in one January instalment, thus bringing in five quarters of revenue in 1869. This would give a surplus of £3,400,000. 1869 would borrow a quarter from 1870; 1870 would borrow from 1871 ... 'How this question will be settled when the world comes to an end,' he said, 'I am at a loss to know.' At this point the audience came to life. By a device Winston Churchill once described as 'anticipatory plagiarism,' Lowe had saved the day.[28]

Ward Hunt (who 'tried to look uninterested and failed') observed that all the chancellor of the exchequer had to do, after working that magic, was to wave his 'fairy wand' and deal out benefits right and left. A penny could come off the income tax; the duty on fire insurance ('a tax on providence') could be allowed to disappear. London cab and omnibus drivers would no longer be compelled to pay horse and carriage duties and might as a consequence, Lowe hoped, improve their notoriously sour dispositions. Repeal of license duties on tea, coffee, and cocoa would allow the British housewife to spread a cheaper breakfast table. And there was more. As blessing piled on blessing, the bemused listeners almost forgot to applaud. Lowe knew from the buzzing that came from the rows across the aisle that he had passed his first examination as a cabinet minister with first-class marks. He wrote to Lady Salisbury (now Lady Derby), 'I have had the greatest ovation I ever had in my life for the last two days, mixed up with just as much envy on the part of the Old Whigs as was necessary to give piquancy to the entertainment.'[29]

The press joined in the cheering. *The Times* reported that the chancellor of the exchequer 'led his hearers through a Lenton season of penitence, and then burst upon them in a sort of Easter festival of abundance.' This had been, a leading article said, 'the most ingenious Budget of the present century.' *The Economist* worried that 'catastrophic' tax collection might have a bad effect on the money market. It also disapproved of Lowe's quip that the 'money market must look after itself,' and his irreverent observation that the 'money market is composed of men of great ability, whose wits are sharpened to a preternatural keenness,' and therefore need no special protection. Those minor objections aside, the journal conceded that it had been 'one of the most remarkable in an age of remarkable Budgets.'[30]

The revenues collected after April 1869 exceeded the estimate by more than a million and a quarter pounds. In addition to that, savings brought about by reforms of the military establishment helped put the balance three and a half millions in the black, the largest surplus any chancellor of the exchequer had ever had at his disposal. Therefore it was not necessary to perform any sleights-of-hand in 1870; there was only the pleasant duty of deciding on what further reductions to make. The income tax, Lowe decided, should come down again, this time to four pennies on the pound. Soapmakers were to be freed of duties, partly because soap, even in 1870, had become a difficult commodity to define accurately. Englishmen were to be allowed to sweeten their untaxed tea with cheaper sugar. Hand gun owners were about the only people who were to be made to pay more. As a schoolboy, Lowe recalled, he had read the boast of an ancient historian 'that the Athenians were the first of the Greeks who laid aside their weapons and went unarmed among each other.' Technology, Lowe thought, was in danger of 'reversing the process' by giving the criminal or the Irish terrorist the ability to hold 'six men's lives in their power.' Higher license fees might slow the trend. Such asides as these enlivened slightly what was otherwise agreed to be a gratifying dull speech. Prosperity had come near to making almost popular a man seemingly 'imbued with a morbid horror of popularity.' Lowe replied to congratulations by saying that the credit was due, not to him, but to the lush prosperity which Gladstonian policies had made possible: 'The secret of all this success is the simplest in all the world – it is nothing on earth but economy.'[31]

It was a summer landscape that Lowe surveyed in the spring of 1870, but there was one dark cloud on the horizon – the determination of Gladstone to give Irish tenants protection against rack-renting landlords. With the possible exception of the Irish secretary, Chichester Fortesque, cabinet members were reluctant to enter again into the mists and bogs of Irish affairs, particularly since 'tenant right' brought into question the rights of property owners to do what they wished with their own. Most of the ministers were immersed in departmental reorganizations or planning new reform and were impatient at being distracted from them. Gladstone was not greatly worried by this resistance; it was not likely that there could be a cabinet revolt when government morale was so high. He knew that Argyll, Clarendon, Cardwell, and possibly Hartington would need delicate handling but he had no doubts about being able to bring them around. Lowe would be the one difficult case. Granville must be sent to handle him and to try to prevent him from organizing the cabinet waverers.[32]

The reason why difficulties were expected from Lowe was that he had, on numerous occasions in the past, made his views on Irish affairs only too explicit. In Parliament and in an article for the *Quarterly Review* in 1868, he had stated that the problems of Ireland lay in Ireland herself, in the tenacity of her historical memories, in the contentious, intemperate sensitivity of the Celtic race, and in a climate which prohibits any large-scale agricultural and pastoral diversification. It followed, therefore, that reforms generated in England or, as he put it, 'measures of clap-trap liberality,' would be entirely off the mark. He refused to admit that England had contributed in any fundamental way to Ireland's unhappy state – quite the reverse, 'Dives had taken Lazarus into partnership.' Thus he believed Gladstone's obsession with doing justice for Ireland was merely an example of the great man's 'passion for self-humiliation.'[33]

In his *Quarterly Review* article he had included disestablishment of the Irish church among the reforms which would do more harm than good. Bad as the Irish church was, he had written, it was one of the few institutions standing between the Irish people and 'complete barbarism.' Ridding Ireland of that injustice would not quell discontent among Catholics since discontent was the result of poverty and the 'peculiarities of the Irish character.' Fortunately for Lowe, the article was anonymous, otherwise he would have found it more difficult to get in step when Gladstone demonstrated that disestablishment was the best stick for beating Disraeli out of office. Once involved in that struggle, Lowe warmed to it and in April 1868 made one of the most scathing attacks delivered during the debate: 'You call it a missionary Church. If so, its mission is unfulfilled. As a missionary Church it has failed utterly. Like some exotic brought from a far country, with infinite pains and useless trouble, it is kept alive with difficulty and expense in an ungrateful climate and ungenial soil. The curse of barrenness is upon it; it has no leaves; it bears no blossoms; it yields no fruit. "Cut it down; why cumbereth it the ground?"' He could not reverse his position so easily on land reform; his pronouncements on that had not been anonymous. Also, he felt he could reverse himself on the church question, since that would not mean any sacrifice of principle; tenant right, however, could not be conceded in good conscience.[34]

When the question had come up for formal debate in 1866 and again in 1868, Lowe had invoked the doctrines of political economy to uphold the sanctity of private contracts. On both of those occasions his speeches had been criticized by no less an authority than John Stuart Mill. The philosopher had argued for pragmatism against the politician's insistence on orthodoxy. Political economy, Mill said, was a theory which must not be made into an indefeasible set of rules which must be applied without regard to place, time, or circumstance. Mill granted that his opponent was right, in the abstract, to claim that contractual relationships between capitalist farmers and hired labourers, based on rents and wages, were more rational and productive than the old, pre-capitalist, direct relationships between lord and peasant. He would even grant Lowe's point that what Ireland needed in the long run were fewer small holders, more large-scale dairy farming, and a more diversified economy. But what Lowe had overlooked, Mill maintained, were the facts that great numbers of desperate, land-hungry, peasant-minded Irishmen happened to be inhabiting the place and that the atmosphere of stability, trust, and confidence which allowed the capitalist-contractual system to work in the Three Kingdoms obviously did not exist across the Irish Sea and would not exist in the immediate future. Pea-

sant farming could not work without security of tenure, Mill said. To
answer, as Lowe had done, that peasant farming was obsolete and that
weakening of contract relationships prevented the modernization of
Irish agriculture was to prefer dogma to realism. 'Political economy has
a great many enemies,' Mill said in 1866, 'but its worst enemies are
some of its friends, and I do not know that it has a more dangerous
enemy than my right hon. Friend. It is such modes of argument as he is
in the habit of employing that have made political economy so thoroughly unpopular with a large and not the least philanthropic portion
of the people of England.'[35]

After this memorable exchange, repeated in 1868, Lowe had to resist
when Gladstone submitted an outline of his Irish Land bill to the cabinet in October 1869. His only hope of avoiding a collision between his
self-respect and his duty of loyalty as a minister was to force the prime
minister to postpone the measure or to get him to accept amendments.
As it stood the bill embodied everything that Lowe had called futile
and dangerous. It proposed to give compensation to tenants who had
been evicted, 'arbitrarily,' from their plots or who had been forced to
leave them by 'excessive' rent increases. Also, it provided that evicted
tenants should receive compensation for improvements they had made
to the land they had worked. To Gladstone, this proposal seemed
modest and conciliatory. The object was not to establish peasant pro-
prietorships but to provide relief for those who were injured by the
existing system. But Lowe was not impressed by this kind of moderation. On the contrary, this half-way measure contained all the evils of
Gladstone's moderate Reform bill of 1866: it weakened an existing
principle without substituting a new one and it did not cure or even
remedy the evils that it was designed to combat. The sanctity of private
contract Lowe thought essential to the development of a modern economy in Ireland; this sanctity the bill would violate. Furthermore, there
would be no compensations for the danger incurred. As Lowe explained
to Cardwell, Gladstone's plan would give compensation for injuries, but
compensations the land-hungry, ignorant, and distrustful tenant would
be most unlikely to claim. If he did claim them, the courts would not
be disposed to grant them. The courts were certain to be favourable to
the landowners and to interpret the words 'arbitrarily' and 'excessive'
(eventually amended by the Lords to the even more vague 'exorbitant')
in any ways they chose. And even if the poor tenant were by some mir-
acle to get adequate compensation, he would not be grateful; what he
wanted was security of tenure, not compensations for his insecurity.[36]

Experience with Gladstone's Irish Land Act shows that these objections were valid; they seemed so at the time to Cardwell, Granville, and
various other members of the cabinet. Gladstone, however, would not
be deflected. He understood that a gesture of good will was needed and

that any amendment which met Lowe's objections would have little chance of succeeding in Parliament or anywhere else. Therefore he tried not to discuss the matter directly with his chancellor of the exchequer and he pretended not to hear when word came to him that Lowe was threatening to resign if made to choose between his convictions and his allegiances. Eventually this tactic forced Lowe to come forward with a proposal for an amendment, thus allowing Gladstone to become the critic. The suggestion Lowe came up with was this: leave the existing laws untouched but set up special Courts of Conscience ('a species of Judicial dictatorship' was how Lowe described them) charged with deciding disputes between tenant and landowner and doing so on the basis not of any fixed rules of procedure, but of equity. Gladstone thought the suggestion clever but totally impractical. He could not see how either landlord or tenant could be led to trust a group of 'third rate Irish lawyers,' sitting in one of Lowe's Conscience Courts. He dressed up his objections in diplomatic language and sent them in a long letter to Granville with instructions that it be shown to Lowe. He also accepted Granville's advice to co-opt the recalcitrant cabinet minister by placing him on the committee responsible for drafting the bill. This tactic worked. Lowe grumbled to Lady Derby, Cardwell, and Lord Granville about the terrible risk the country would be asked to run, and then submitted. Granville was not surprised at the surrender. From the beginning he had assured Gladstone that Lowe would, if handled carefully, prove willing to 'stretch his conscience.'[37]

In this decision to surrender, Lowe's ego and his commitment to causes are so thoroughly mixed that it is impossible to isolate the various elements. He was intensely ambitious but believed himself more ready than most men to sacrifice himself for a higher cause. He thought of himself as a man of integrity, alone in a greedy, irrational world, condemned by his superior intelligence and education to persevere in doing what was right when others were bending to expediency. He seems to have believed that it was his own special fate to be continually faced with the dilemma of having to choose whether to stretch his conscience on one issue in order to accommodate another or whether to stand fast on his principles regardless of consequences. He expected to be misunderstood whatever choice he made and was intensely proud of his ability to stand up to abuse and ridicule. Because he had this kind of self-image, he did not indulge in introspection. He seldom bothered to examine his own motives and therefore left few clues behind about the inner workings of his mind.

Granville, who admired Lowe's character, never took the threat of resignation seriously. He knew his friend was too engrossed in his office to give it up unless deliberately provoked. While the cabinet was arguing about Ireland late in 1869 and in the first two months of 1870, information was coming into the Treasury which confirmed predictions of a huge revenue surplus. The chancellor of the exchequer who drew up the next budget or two would, it seemed, have an opportunity to put the finishing touches on the great edifice of free trade and go down in history as the man who finished the work Peel had begun. Lowe was conscious that resignation would give that opportunity to someone who might not know so well how to take advantage of it. In addition to that, resignation would almost certainly end all chances for putting through a reform of the civil service. Gladstone may not have wished to communicate directly with his finance minister about tenant rights but he had been responsive to Lowe's appeal for aid in putting through this reform. Lowe knew that to get the principle of competitive examinations accepted and implemented he would need constantly to appeal for support to the prime minister. To get that reform through Lowe was willing to eat a few words about the sanctity of private property.

And he did get it through. The reconstruction of the civil service procedures was by far his greatest achievement as chancellor of the exchequer. Oddly enough, he did not take much pride in this accomplishment; he was always more conscious of the compromises he was forced to make than of the innovations he carried through. Yet without his persistence, the old system would, most likely, have lasted another decade, perhaps longer. The creation of a professional civil service in the early seventies coincided with the abolition of purchase in the army and the ending of religious tests in the universities. The creation by these means of new opportunities for the sons of the upper middle class brought about in the mid-Victorian period what Noel Annan has called the 'Glorious Revolution' of the intellectual aristocracy. By integrating this university educated, intellectual élite with the civil service, Lowe created a 'safeguard' against equalitarianism. It was to prove far more durable than any fancy franchise or constitutional barrier. In that sense the reform was a more fitting memorial to Lowe's career than he recognized.[38]

Enthusiasm for administrative reform was a phenomenon of the 1850s, a consequence of the confusion of parties after 1846 and of the disillusionment over the conduct of the Crimean War. The movement had produced some results: the opening of the Indian civil service to first-class university graduates and the establishment of a Civil Service Commission to screen out the obviously unqualified among the nominated candidates. The commission administered an examination and gave certificates to those who passed it. In theory at least, department chiefs would then make their appointments from among the certified. In practice, the department heads often ignored certification or subverted the process by deliberately pitting their favourites against known incompetents, sometimes called 'Hayter's Idiots' after a Whig whip who frequently used this device. The reforms associated with the names of Northcote and Trevelyan were significant, but they did not prevent the various departments from going their own ways, working out their own procedures, continuing to provide patronage for the use of party whips, and continuing to give refuge to the less fortunate or less promising connexions of the ruling class.[39]

Although these abuses continued in the 1860s, fewer people seemed to think their reform to be a burning issue. By 1868 Gladstone had pronounced in favour of open competition but had not made the cause into anything like a crusade. Lowe was, of course, passionately committed but he could not expect much support. Among his allies in the Gladstone ministry he could count on Granville, Cardwell, and the prime minister; he could also count on the hostility of Bright, Bruce, and Clarendon. Outside official circles there were some journalists, MPs, and radical reformers who still complained about the growing costs of the civil establishment or about the delays and inanities of the 'Circumlocution Office,' but few of these people were particularly interested in competitive examinations.[40]

Undeterred by apathy or hostility, Lowe took the initiative in the autumn of 1869. He tried to open the question in a cabinet meeting but was snubbed. Then he wrote to Gladstone, asking for help: 'Something must be decided. We cannot keep matters in this discreditable state of abeyance.' Unless something were done, he continued, 'we are in danger of retrograding to the days of Hayter's idiot.' Gladstone agreed but warned about the difficulties of bringing their colleagues around. He suggested a compromise: allow departmental option, establish the machinery, and then let the ministers decide whether they would use it. Lowe hesitated but, on reflection, concluded that Gladstone's indirect method might provide more opportunities for the Treasury to exercise its influence than the direct method. He immediately decreed that the Treasury and its subordinate departments recruit new staff by means of competition. Then, with Lingen's help, he drew up an Order-in-Council which, when it became effective in June 1870, gave the Treasury control over all recruitment procedures.[41]

Clarendon, at the Foreign Office, and Bruce, at the Home Office, stubbornly held out against the Order-in-Council. They claimed that their departments dealt with confidential material; therefore the first requisite for their employees was not intellect, but character, a quality no test could measure. They were the only ones to refuse compliance; the other department heads, slightly bewildered by the fast footwork at the Treasury, agreed to go along. What they agreed to was this: the civil establishment would be divided into two classes, one for those involved in policy-making and the other for those doing routine work. The Civil

Service Commission would examine all aspirants. A candidate for the higher grade could select as many subjects as he wished from a list; each item on the list would be worth a given number of points; ratings would be calculated according to the number of points a candidate managed to accumulate. Lowe and Lingen did not leave the compilation of the lists to the commissioners but drew them up at the Treasury. They saw to it that the subjects offered in the higher grade list corresponded to the curriculum of the universities. They were not, of course, adverse to making a few improvements. They saw to it that the traditional subjects, classics and mathematics, received a proportionally high number of points but they also gave recognition to proficiency in the natural sciences, philosophy, modern languages, and modern literature. They assumed that this higher civil service would remain small in number and élite in character. They wanted pay to be sufficiently high to lure the most intelligent graduates away from university fellowships. This élite, Lowe said, should have 'the best education that England affords: the education of public schools and colleges and such things, which gives a sort of freemasonry among men which is not very easy to describe, but which everybody feels ...'[42]

Naturally, that freemasonry was to be exclusive as well as inclusive. Lowe and Lingen designed the examination for the lower, or assistant grade with class considerations in mind. Candidates for admission to this assistant grade would be able to choose from their list such subjects as book-keeping, indexing, copying, as well as geography, English history, and the three 'Rs.' Lowe testified before several parliamentary committees that it had been his intention to make the examinations correspond to what the elementary and technical schools were or should be offering. That way, he hoped that the sons of the lower middle class and some of the brighter working class boys might be encouraged to make full use of the educational opportunities open to them. If parents from the lower ranks of society could recognize that schooling opened the way to this new and relatively prestigious semi-professional occupation, then they might demand efficiency and modernization from the schools that catered for their needs. Perhaps the schools might then cease to value frills and teach practical knowledge; perhaps, in time, the English would come to value education as highly as the Scots did already. None of these objectives could, he thought, be attained if children of families with modest means were encouraged to think that someday, by hard work and self-sacrifice, they might graduate into the freemasonry of the élite. Then they would not value what was within their reach. That, among other reasons, was why, Lowe said, he arranged the provisions of his Order-in-Council so that there would be no movement from the lower to the higher grade.[43]

Members of several commissions inquiring into the civil service asked him how he could reconcile his liberal belief in the career open to talent with this prohibition. His answer was laboured and showed that he was aware of the difficulty of reconciling his belief in meritocracy with his desire to rest the bureaucracy on a class-bound educational structure. He agreed with his questioners that it was impossible to draw a clear line between routine work and intellectual work; he also agreed that it was possible that able young men in the lower grade might educate themselves in the subject matter of the higher grade examination and qualify, on the basis of competence and general education, for promotion. Abstract justice would decree, he admitted, that there be mobility within the system. But he saw no way to reconcile abstract justice with the facts of life. Justice would require that everyone start at the same low level and rise by demonstrated merit. Undoubtedly the young man with the first-class degree from Oxford would move up much more rapidly than even the brightest product of a middle class grammar school; but would that Oxford graduate be willing to enter into competition for routine work, even with the expectation of rapid advancement? Lowe thought not. Such a talented person would have other alternatives open to him and would take the one offering the highest pay, the highest status, and the most opportunity to exercise intelligence. A possible way out of this difficulty would be to retain the two grade system and start the university graduate in the higher, but allow those with an 'ordinary' education the chance to take the higher examinations and rise in grade. Unfortunately, this would create serious administrative problems. Department heads, being natural 'enemies of competition,' would constantly be on the watch for ways to evade it. They would have an interest in up-grading their staffs; they would be aware that every promotion would be an act of patronage – the higher the proportion of higher-level staff, the greater the prestige and power of the department head. This, Lowe thought, was the most obvious of the difficulties. More serious for the morale of the civil service would be the constant raising and disappointing of expectations. If the prospect of escape from routine work were constantly present, all but the most sluggish would quickly become discontented with their necessarily dull occupations and neglect them to find time to prepare themselves for entry into the higher grade. In some rare cases, Lowe granted, the lower grade civil servant might teach himself enough Latin, Greek, and mathematics to score well on the examination and qualify for promotion. But, Lowe maintained, promotion of this kind would be to no one's advantage. The meagre background of the self-taught person would be bound to show: 'perhaps he might not pronounce his "h's" or commit some similar solecism, which might be a most serious damage to a department in case of negotiations.' The administration of government would suffer 'if we allow everybody to rise up to everything,' and this was a far more important consideration than the suffering of a few individuals. 'The public service is not an educational body,' Lowe told the commissioners, 'but an executive body.'⁴⁴

It did not occur to any of Lowe's questioners to suggest that state scholarships be used to open the universities and public schools to the 'natural élite' of the nation. Many of the difficulties Lowe had mentioned would disappear if the brightest sons of the poorer classes could be systematically filtered out of the elementary stream and then be given a superior education, and taught to pronounce their 'h's' and master the nuances that bind together a freemasonry. Had such a revolutionary proposal been put to him, there is no doubt what his answer would have been. He had stated on many occasions that he believed a modern society, if it desired to keep up with the advances of knowledge and technology, must put the administration of the state into the hands of the best qualified among its citizens. He had repeatedly advocated that higher education be made cheaper and more accessible. He would have agreed that there was nothing sacred about the existing system of social stratification. He might have admitted that his own proposals for reform of the civil service were aimed at upsetting the old system of personal relationships and arrangements. But then he would have returned, as always, to his argument from practicality. A drastic reconstruction of the educational system would call for the creation of a huge bureaucratic structure and for the expenditure of large sums of public money. Even in the unlikely event that the privileged groups could be persuaded or tricked into agreeing to give up some of their class advantages, the creation of a powerful and expensive arm of the state would endanger free enterprise and individual freedom. He was in favour of an aristocracy of talent so long as its implementation did not conflict with the presuppositions of classical liberalism. Confined as he was within these suppositions, it never occurred to him that to co-opt the most intelligent from the working and lower-middle classes might be a way to ward off the equalitarian society he so despised.

If Lowe did not follow the logic of his premises as far as he might have done, he did progress along that path a considerable distance. He missed no opportunities to use the carefully contrived provisions of the Order-in-Council to impose his plan on the other departments and to increase Treasury control. According to those provisions, the Civil Service Commission needed to get the approval of the Treasury for any regulations it might make. Lowe and Lingen went further; they instructed the commission on what its regulations should be. They convinced Gladstone that the Treasury should co-ordinate the arrangements in the departments that chose to comply. Then they used that authority to make sure that uniform procedures were adopted. In several cases the department heads and their permanent secretaries objected to these initiatives or held out for special concessions. Often the Treasury did make concessions and compromises; and when bribery failed, Treasury officials indicated to department heads that their requests for increases in estimates would receive special scrutiny. These methods did not make friends but they did produce results. Lowe's old associate at the Board of Trade, Thomas Farrer, indignantly complained to an investigating committee that his own scheme for reforming the civil establishment of his department had been rudely ignored. He reported that the Treasury had sent him a peremptory instruction to put all of his copy work into the hands of a pool of '10d-an-hour writers.' At no time had he been consulted or the special problems of his office been considered. When questioned about this charge, Lowe said that his officials had not bothered to consult with Farrer because they knew he was trying to evade the intent of the Order-in-Council. The permanent secretary was not interested in reform, Lowe implied, but only interested in securing for his department an unnecessarily high proportion of higher-grade clerks; he wanted to make the Board of Trade 'like the Lacedemonian army, all officers and no men.' Farrer had been one of Lowe's admirers; until his temper had a chance to cool, he became an enemy. The Board of Trade did, however, eventually get into step.[45]

By 1873 Lowe's determination and Gladstone's tact had accomplished more than anyone would have thought possible when Lowe first raised the subject of civil service reform in 1869. The Treasury did not win all of the battles; some departments had to be bought off with salary and pension concessions which Lowe knew to be, in themselves, indefensible. Much to his chagrin, he was forced to defend these bribes before a Select Committee on Civil Service Expenditure. He tried to explain that he was forced to give the principle of competition priority over economy. Needless to say, this was not an admission that he enjoyed making. He also had to admit that he had been defeated by the Home Office and the Foreign Office. When Lowe was shifted from the Exchequer to the Home Office in 1873, he promptly applied the Order-in-Council there; but the Foreign Office failed to succumb. When Lord Clarendon died in 1870, he was succeeded by Lord Granville who had been a model of co-operation at the Colonial Office. But even Granville, hard pressed by Lowe, could not overcome the resistance of the Foreign Office to the idea of admitting people whose only qualifications were a university degree and intellectual competence. Granville reported that his subordinates had expressed to him their desire to 'preserve ourselves from adulteration,' and he had been afraid to 'throw the machine out of gear.'[46]

These failures were relatively trivial. Lowe, enthusiastically aided by Lingen, had managed to throw the machinery of most of the administration into a new gear. By helping to make the central government more efficient and less vulnerable to 'interests,' the chancellor of the exchequer had diminished the force of one of the traditional arguments against big government. He never conceded that point. In 1873 he was still proclaiming: 'Our business is to diminish not to increase the duties and responsibilities of government.' As Asa Briggs has commented, 'the logic was defective.'[47]

In 1870, at the end of two years in office, when the reputation of Gladstone's ministry was tarnished in places but still high and when the country was enjoying a bountiful prosperity, Lowe had reason to believe that success had come to him at last, and not, as he had feared, too late. In June he attended a ceremony at Oxford and received an ovation that went on, or so it seemed, for a quarter of an hour. 'There was just enough opposition to render the applause loud and energetic,' he reported to his Sydney correspondent. Then he added, 'we have had a very hard session, and have done a great deal of good work.' Some of his colleagues had not been able to stand the strain of these eventful years, but he had 'withstood the racket exceedingly well.' Unfortunately, this feeling of tired euphoria was not to last out the summer.[48]

15

The Exchequer:
The Unhappy Years

On the afternoon of 15 July 1870 a messenger handed Gladstone a note informing him that France had declared war on Prussia. From his seat on the Treasury bench the prime minister gravely wrote to an old friend, Michel Chavalier: 'I cannot describe to you the sensation of pain, almost of horror, which has thrilled through this country from end to end at the outbreak of hostilities, the commencement of the work of blood.' The work of blood was quickly done without England being able to affect the course of events. Seven weeks after the fighting started the main body of the French army surrendered to Bismarck's generals. In rapid succession moves were then made which changed or threatened to change the character of the European power system: the Communards of Paris proclaimed the republic; the king of Prussia became emperor of a united Germany; and the tsar sent a Russian fleet into the Black Sea, in defiance of the post-Crimean settlement. Gladstone discovered that he could do no more than secure some relatively minor concessions from the Germans and Russians. He and his ministers felt themselves to be the victims of circumstances – as no doubt they were. Nevertheless, many Englishmen held their government accountable for what appeared to be a national humiliation. To a considerable extent this dramatic shift in the power structure of Europe marked a turning-point in the fortunes of the Liberal ministry.

Catastrophic events abroad do not alone explain why the home government lost much of its popularity and energy in 1871; signs of decline were apparent before the Franco-Prussian War began. A period of reform generates a countervailing force. Nonconformists were furious at the prospect of paying rates in support of Anglican schools; labouring men were disgruntled over the slowness of the ministry in fulfilling its promises to give trades unions a secure legal status; admirals, generals, ordinance workers, and men employed on the docks were discomfited by the reorganization of the military services and systems of supply; and Irishmen were resentful that a government, pledged to do justice in their country, had imposed still another coercion bill. Gathorne Hardy paid Disraeli a visit more than a month before the French Council of Ministers decided to mobilize against Prussia and heard him predict that in two years' time Gladstone would be in serious trouble.[1]

The line of connexion between the war and Lowe's own serious troubles at the Exchequer is somewhat easier to trace. Sydney Buxton, a Liberal MP who specialized in financial policy, wrote that of all the many victims of Bismarck's war, Lowe was 'the strangest of all.' According to Buxton, the shock of the unexpected conflict and, more importantly, the pressure it put on the ministry to spend more for arms and soldiers, caused Lowe to misread the economic situation and therefore to miscalculate the economic condition of the country in 1871. One result of that miscalculation was a humiliating rebuff when he came to present his budget that year. Once put on the defensive, Lowe became irritable and careless in the administration of his office. Misfortune, both for himself and the ministry he served, followed from that carelessness.[2]

Buxton's interpretation, though obviously oversimplified, has considerable merit. Only initially was Lowe a victim of events. No English statesman expected the war to come as quickly as it did or to end as quickly. Any chancellor of the exchequer could be excused for acting cautiously until the war clouds lifted and trade conditions could be clearly seen. But Lowe was not merely prudent, he was pessimistic and insisted on remaining so when all signs pointed to optimism. His mistakes were due not to the circumstances but to his over-reaction to them. Once on the defensive, his self-confidence, so high in the spring of 1870, collapsed. We have remarked before on the fragility of his seemingly cast-iron ego. Gladstone once expressed his amazement that a man who was so formidable when attacking others was himself 'so helpless under attack that he was like a beetle on his back.' A civil servant, Edward Hamilton, who admired and liked Lowe, heard Gladstone remark on how curious it was that a man of such 'prodigious powers' could be so easily disconcerted by an unexpected reversal. Hamilton agreed; the criticism was 'quite true.' The unexpected reversal in Europe gave an unexpected blow to Lowe's plans to achieve another great victory for retrenchment in 1871. After that shock his optimism turned immediately into exaggerated gloom. He was sure, while the crisis lasted, that his reckless colleagues were intent on plunging England into war and economic ruin. He did calm down when the crisis passed but never recovered the confidence which the success of the first two budgets had given him.[3]

In November 1870 Disraeli commented that Lowe had been moving around in society trying to convert ladies to his 'only gospel, "Peace at any price."' This was accurate; Lowe could see no reason for paying the cost of involvement or rearmament. He was not impressed by Bismarck's disclosure, early in the conflict, that France had been thinking about incorporating Belgium. Lowe was greatly agitated when Gladstone signed a treaty pledging British intervention against the power who first violated the Belgian neutrality agreement. He snorted that this British obsession with the Lowlands no longer made sense. When Gladstone proposed to ask for a two million pound supplementary grant for the army, Lowe talked about resigning, though, after a night's reflection, he decided to hold his tongue. He told Cardwell that he drew back because 'the necessary explanation might very likely bring on a debate which in the present temper of men's minds might do mischief.' He said he was 'quite aware that I have no support to expect in the cause of peace.' He welcomed the Prussian offensive in August because it seemed to remove a potential cause of involvement. Did Cardwell not agree that since Belgium was no longer in danger, England would not now have to recruit more soldiers; could they not reconsider?[4]

The crushing nature of Prussia's victory in September and Bismarck's announcement that the new German empire would include Alsace and Lorraine shifted popular sentiment in England towards France. Lowe took this shift as further proof that democratic man was hopelessly fickle. Why should Britons concern themselves about the lost French provinces? Concern for self-determination was another form of Gladstonian sentimentalism; once war began, power must always decide the boundary settlements. Enmity towards Germany over this question would be idiotic: the balance of power may once have been a rational concern of England's; now it was an anachronism. Germany, Lowe announced in a public speech, had won because she was the more modern nation, because she had learned the value of science and popular education – 'look at the intelligence, the organization, the docility.' Pity for Louis Napoleon was more sentimental nonsense; his fall was a 'clearing of the moral atmosphere.' It did not matter that Bismarck happened to be ambitious on a continental scale and intensely anti-British; England was safe on her island, safer than she had ever been since 1815. All that was needed, he told Gladstone and Granville, was to keep the navy supreme. He thought it might be wise to institute drill in the schools; a four hundred thousand man militia would be more than sufficient for island defence and it would save the ruinous cost of a large professional army. He urged them, as liberals, to affirm that real strength, real greatness, had nothing to do with continental politics and everything to do with retrenchment, lower taxes, sound finance.[5]

But all his pleading seemed to be in vain. He wrote to Lady Derby in December 1870 that he was about to approve a huge military expenditure, produce an unpopular budget, and bear the burden for no good purpose, since he would need to raise taxes only to 'ward off imaginary dangers.' He wrote that he had hurt his wrist in a fall while skating with Lord Clanwilliam at Highclere; that, he admitted, had not lightened his general feeling of despair. However, since necessity had forced him to raise revenue, he meant to use his imagination. He would not take the easy way out and simply put a penny on the income tax; that would be like declaring a state of siege: 'any fool could do that.' 'What,' he asked Lady Derby, 'is your particular taste in the matter?' 'Don't say income tax ... I want something more recherché. My whole attention has been fixed on the taking off of taxes, and I never meant to put any on so I am caught unprepared.'[6]

Although he used the same flippant tone when speaking about his taxation plans in his 1871 budget speech, it would be a mistake to think that his approach to the subject was in any way frivolous. In fact he treated it with nearly as much reverence as Gladstone did. In one respect he differed with his great predecessor at the Exchequer: he did not believe the income tax to be an evil which must be tolerated only until the country was rid of that greater evil, protection. Instead Lowe believed the income tax to be 'an immense national resource.' Its unique merit, he thought, was that it expropriated money from people according to their ability to pay, or, as he preferred to put it, allowed the chancellor of the exchequer to 'distribute misery as fairly as he can.' Individuals should be spared as much pain as possible; appropriation was only justified if it could be shown to alleviate more pain than it inflicted. Thus he was not justified, he said, in raising taxes merely because some bureaucrat or politician was able to prove that an expenditure might, in some way, effect some benefit. Arctic researchers, he said, had discovered tiny creatures on the ocean floor capable of withstanding the pressure of three tons to the square inch. How? 'Because the pressure is equalized; and that should be the principle of taxation.' That being so, he would promise always to 'contrive to make everyone a little uneasy, so that life, if not enjoyable, should be at any rate tolerable.' To do that he would search for the right mixture of various kinds of taxes so that no part of the community would be relieved of pressure and no class forced to bear more than its share. His reluctance to rely on the income tax in 1871 was not due to any special prejudice against it or because, as he implied to Lady Derby, he found it boring, but because he believed he might be able to work out a fairer mix.[7]

The extra three million pounds for the army was not the only unusual expense to be provided for in the 1871 budget; there was also a large sum to pay the cost of ending the practice of purchasing commissions in the army. Lowe strongly approved of that second expenditure but regretted that it came to bear at such an awkward time. To meet these demands he decided to find a balance of direct and indirect taxes: a penny more on the income tax and a stamp tax on each box of matches sold. This match tax would, he knew, exert pressure most heavily on poor people who paid no income tax; that, he believed, was a merit, not a defect. To equalize that pressure, he would press on the rich by doubling the succession duties owed when the heir of the deceased was the next of kin.

The economist Stanley Jevons probably suggested to Lowe the idea of using the match tax. Jevons published a pamphlet not long after the budget of 1871 had made the tax notorious. In it he praised the tax's versatility. It was, he argued, cheap to collect and difficult to evade. Poor people could find relief by being frugal in their use of fire – an infinitesimal hardship. The export trade would not suffer, since there would be no taxes on matches sent abroad. A small reduction in domestic consumption might cause a few of the young match dippers and match-box makers to lose their livelihood, but since they did their work at home and had little fixed capital invested, they could move to other and healthier jobs at a small loss to themselves.[8]

Lowe must have seen a draft of this pamphlet before it was published because he followed its arguments closely in his budget speech. Unfortunately he chose to enliven his presentation with some light-hearted embellishments. He explained to the Commons that the match stamp would be embossed with a Latin pun: *Ex luce lucellum*. He did not bother to translate. Later Bernal Osborne explained to the 'successful capitalists whom I see around me' that the words meant 'From light, a little gain.' The House always found Osborne amusing and were ready to forgive him anything; they were not similarly disposed towards Lowe. After his joke about the stamp, the chancellor of the exchequer proceeded, in the same bantering tone, to confess that he had made inquiries into this 'combustible affair,' had discovered that the Americans were experimenting with this kind of taxation, and had decided to borrow this invention from the United States to show his 'humble admiration for her finance.' Most of the audience took that remark sourly. One Tory listener said that he counted eighteen jokes. He added that he found the merrymaking tiresome and wished that the finance minister, now that he had 'played his pranks and run his rigs,' might now return to his sober self.[9]

A 'combustible affair' it did, indeed, turn out to be! Londoners associated phospherous-tipped, or 'Lucifer,' matches with scenes of the most pitiful misery. Dangerously manufactured by sweated labour, the Lucifers were boxed by East-end waifs in slum garrets and sold usually by young girls, who fixed their wares on sticks and held them up to the windows of slow-moving omnibuses. A great many of the passengers who bought these matches did so out of charity; it was an economical way to make peace with their consciences. Therefore, in the metropolis, matches were symbols as well as necessities. It is hardly surprising that Lowe failed to consider these associations; it does seem peculiar, however, that no one cautioned him about the danger of offending romantic sensibilities. His colleagues might have been hesitant about raising such a point and risking Lowe's scorn. In any case, they had little chance to react since they did not learn about the budget's provisions until a few days before they were to be presented to the Commons. Lord Kimberley, Granville's replacement at the Colonial Office, noted ruefully, after the event, that the cabinet did not have time for a careful scrutiny because Gladstone had always kept his budgets back from Palmerston as long as possible and that this procedure had unfortunately become customary. Gladstone did see Lowe's budget nine days before it was presented to Parliament. He thought the match tax would create no serious difficulty; however he did suggest that Lowe have a talk about it with George Glyn, the chief whip, and see what the feelings of the House might be. Lowe apparently ignored that advice. If special interest groups complained about the treatment they were about to get, then so much the worse for them.[10]

Lowe soon learned that there were times when it did not pay to ignore the voices of private interests. When the managers of the Bryant and May Match Company read the account of the 1871 budget in *The Times*, they immediately rushed off a crackling letter to that newspaper, saying that they would have to close their doors if the match tax went through since consumers would turn to inferior and cheaper foreign products if prices went up. The consequence, they said, would be ruinous for the 'many thousands' in the East end of the city who depended on the trade for their daily bread. Children would starve and young women come to an even more wretched end, in order that the cynical chancellor of the exchequer might have his joke and 'pay the tribute of his admiration of American finance.' The opposition in Parliament immediately took up this theme. On 24 April, the second night of the debate, Disraeli wondered aloud at the coldness of heart that could lead a man to tax warmth itself and permit him to find amusement in the plight of young girls forced into the streets in search of bread. His reference to the streets was apposite. While he was speaking, young girls and boys were gathered in the streets around the Palace of Westminster. Earlier that afternoon the young employees of Bryant and May, led, it was reported, by Mr May himself and surrounded by assorted hangers-on, began to march from St Paul's Churchyard and Ludgate Hill towards the Embankment. With bands playing and banners flying, the procession surrounded the Houses of Parliament, and some of the demonstrators, while waiting for Lowe's carriage to pull up, scuffled with the police cordon. Gladstone arrived and got through easily, although there was much jeering. However the police advised Lowe not to take the same chances and spirited him into the Commons by way of the underground station. It was shortly after that experience that he had to listen to his bitterest enemy charge him with 'making war on women and children.'[11]

The cabinet met the next morning and agreed that the match tax would have to go. The outcry in the press about the match girls and rumours of a backbench revolt convinced them that humiliation for Lowe was better than defeat for the government. No Liberal could contemplate without horror the prospect of going to the people on the issue of this budget. The queen, herself, had been stirred by the pitiful spectacle, staged by the Bryant and May Company, and had written 'strongly' about her concern for all the little children who would be made homeless and destitute. Gladstone and his ministers were aware of the hypocrisy behind much of this sentimentalism but did not dare to hand Disraeli a heaven-sent chance to expound on the heartlessness of Gladstonian economy. The result was that on the following evening, 25 April, Lowe rose from his seat and curtly announced his intention to withdraw the budget and submit a revised one.[12]

The laughter that greeted that admission of defeat must have remained fresh in Lowe's memory for the rest of his days. The humiliation he endured that evening marked the point where he ceased to be an asset to his party and became a liability. Up to that point, his unpopularity had been tempered with respect and fear. Afterwards much of the respect and fear were gone. Had it been a clean defeat for his policies as a finance minister, he might have been able to accept it philosophically, but he did not even have that comfort. What was so galling about the furore over the match tax was the knowledge that the opposition had been able to use that one, relatively minor feature to mask their real motives. With good reason Lowe believed that the landowners who spoke so feelingly about the poor match girls were really worried about the future of their rich estates.

Had the match tax been the real issue, Lowe might have done some quick juggling, substituted another household commodity, and saved his experiment in 'balanced taxation.' The cabinet understood, however, that Liberal representatives from agricultural constituencies were more concerned with the side of the scale that affected the rich than with the side that affected the poor. Thus if the government were to survive, the entire budget would have to be revised and all innovations scrapped, even though this meant a repudiation of what Lowe had proclaimed to be an important instalment of liberal reform – his contribution to a rejuvination of a flagging ministry.

Soon after Christmas in 1870 Lowe wrote to Gladstone about the need to work up some new programmes which would strike the public imagination and convince the country that 'our cards are not yet played out.' Some of the proposals he then came up with were moderately radical, aimed at satisfying those who believed that the laws were maintaining the special privileges enjoyed by the owners of land. He recommended, for example, that the government act to change the intestacy laws so that real property and personal property would be treated the same. He offered to draft a bill along these lines. He also offered to put together legislation to make land transfers easier. A few days later he wrote to the prime minister again about a scheme for increasing the use of paper currency. He described the scheme as a 'striking' measure which would be sure to divert attention from the 'sombre' economic prospects for the year ahead. These proposals Gladstone received without enthusiasm. He tactfully answered that all of them were excellent but that they were likely to cause controversy and ought, for the moment, to be kept in reserve.[13]

Controversy, however, could not have worried the prime minister unduly, for he gave Lowe permission to include several sensitive items in his budget. One of them would touch landowners in a tender spot: their ability to pass on estates, relatively untrammelled, to the eldest child. It had been the practice to tax estates, on a graduated scale, starting at 1 per cent if the eldest child was the beneficiary and increasing as the relationship of the heir became more remote. Lowe proposed to double the rate for the next of kin and decrease the slope of the scale for the others. Landed gentlemen could not be expected to like the sound of this sort of thing. But, true to his theory of balance, Lowe also saw to it that commercial magnates should have cause for concern about the government's long-term objectives. He proposed to calculate the rate of income tax on a percentage basis rather than on so many pennies on the pound. Percentages, Lowe explained, would give the Treasury exactly what it thought it needed, while the addition or subtraction of a penny might bring in too little or too much. Monied men were not comforted by this explanation; they suspected that the chancellor had ulterior motives. If the nation needed an extra penny to meet an emergency, then well and good; but it would not do to give the bureaucrats at the Treasury a cunning device which they might use to juggle the figures every time they got into some kind of a scrape. Those who spoke against this proposal warned against the consequences of giving the chancellor of the exchequer convenient ways to escape from the consequences of bad planning and extravagance. If he were allowed such liberty, the country might soon wake up to find that income tax had become a permanent thing – not a prospect any prudent man could view with equanimity.[14]

Taken at face value these features of the 1871 budget do not appear to be sufficiently important or extreme to have provoked such strong feelings. One reason why so many MPs did not take them at face value was that Lowe went out of his way to arouse their suspicions. His proposal to increase the tax on estates passing to the next of kin did not, after all, threaten to divide and scatter the great landholdings of the aristocracy and squirarchy. Lowe mentioned how modest the change was but then went on to deliver a brief, entirely gratuitous, lecture on the irrationality of making distinctions in succession duties based on degrees of relationships. Some of his listeners must have remembered that he had questioned the value of primogeniture in a speech on a private members bill in 1859, and on that occasion had remarked that the law seemed always to be tipped unfairly to benefit the landed interests. In 1871 he certainly made no secret of his wish to treat younger children the same as the eldest. If that principle were allowed, what might follow in the future? Would the chancellor of the exchequer also like to destroy entail and strict marriage settlements – the economic basis of aristocracy?[15]

Not content with the alarm he raised over succession duties, Lowe served notice in his budget speech that he was prepared for the moment to tolerate the special tax exemptions which agriculturalists had traditionally enjoyed. But he could not resist adding the opinion that exemptions on work horses and farm wagons, like tax-free donations to collegiate funds, were inequities which could not forever be tolerated in a modern society. Speaking entirely for himself, he said, he could see no reason why certain segments of the community should be taxed differently from others or why all taxes should not be calculated purely on the basis of the ability of the citizen to pay. At the moment that principle was being violated 'in the most flagrant manner.' The public was deprived 'of a great deal of money for the benefit of a particular class.'[16]

Disraeli quickly took advantage of his opportunity to gather together the various hostilities and suspicions the budget aroused. Country representatives from both sides of the House could expect to hear from the farmers if they did not protest. Whig as well as Tory magnates were appalled at the notion that the chancellor of the exchequer could see no distinction between a bequest of land and a gift to 'supply petticoats to the widows of Evangelical negroes.' According to the rumours that were circulating about, a Whig cave was forming and would oppose the budget unless it were completely revised. Sacrifice of the match tax would not have been enough to appease them. Lord Halifax informed the queen that the succession duty would also have to be thrown out if there were to be peace. This threat had immediate effect. On 27 April Gladstone announced, with regret, that his government had decided to abandon their attempt to implement the principle of 'balanced taxation' and would instead meet the expected deficit by raising the income tax by two pennies. This was an almost unprecedented reversal for an English finance minister; it was also a damaging set-back for a ministry which had prided itself on superior financial acumen.[17]

Subsequent events showed that Lowe need not have raised any new taxes in 1871. Prosperity continued unchecked into 1873 and brought in revenues sufficient to cover all the extraordinary costs. By the third quarter of the 1871 tax year it was obvious that Lowe could have paid for rearmament and the cost of abolishing purchase of commission and still had enough to lower taxes. In his pessimistic mood he had misread the indicators. This, rather than a taste for recherché taxation or a tendency to over-explain, was his most serious shortcoming as finance minister. This is not merely a retrospective judgment; many contemporary experts advised him that signs were optimistic and that the anticipated post-war dislocation of trade was not going to take place. Not all advice tended this way. The highly respected *Economist* approved of his cautious approach. But a great many experts, especially City men, pointed to the buoyant trend and claimed that anyone who failed to see how it was running was either timid or blind.[18]

Lowe did not ignore this advice. He admitted in his 1871 budget speech that the economy had been showing great vitality, in spite of the 'stupendous happenings' across the Channel. He would not, however, invite 'a day of retribution' by acting as though that vitality would continue. When budget time came around in 1872, however, he had to admit that prosperity showed no signs of diminishing. Once again revenues had exceeded estimates. But still he was wary; the pattern could not continue. Nevertheless, it did continue through the year 1873. That spring the surplus reached nearly six million, the greatest embarrassment of riches Lowe was to experience as chancellor of the exchequer. He used these riches to reduce the income tax to three pennies and gave relief to the poorest taxpayers by increasing their abatement. He also was able to make a significant reduction in the National Debt. At this point he almost seemed to be optimistic about the future. In 1874 the downturn he had been waiting for finally appeared, but by that time he was no longer at the Treasury.[19]

It was his 'ludicrous lugubriousness' and his 'absolute obstinacy,' his opponents said, that made him so cautious. Bagehot, who tried to be fair, thought his misjudgment resulted from his bad eyesight – a handicap which forced him to rely on the timid advice of his civil servants (an excuse even Lowe, at one point, fell back upon). Several of the Conservatives assigned to shadow the Exchequer had a different explanation: they charged that Lowe and Gladstone suffered not from an excess of caution but from an excess of craft. One of them, James Wilson, suspected that the chancellor of the exchequer and his chief were afraid to admit that times would continue to be good for fear that this would invite raids on the Treasury and bring on an orgy of extravagance. Wilson said that for this reason neither man wanted to budget for a large reduction in the national debt, preferring to accumulate supposedly unexpected surpluses which they would then use to retire the debt. There may have been something to this charge. As followers of Ricardo, Lowe and Gladstone believed that the removal of burdens on industry should take precedence over the reduction of the debt. They may have decided that expressions of pessimism would help them to maintain that order of precedence. In 1875 Lowe advised Sir Stafford Northcote, the Conservative finance minister, that he should first accumulate a surplus, wait until he had got another, and then set about debt reduction. This does not indicate that Lowe believed debt reduction to be unimportant; even in the dark days following the recall of his 1871 'harum-scarum' budget, he was able to summon eloquence for the cause of debt reduction and move the press, including the *Economist*, to rapturous praise. But he did not want that worthy cause to interfere with free trade. Therefore craft may have been behind the cautious budgets of 1872 and 1873; in 1871, however, lugubriousness does seem to have brought about the damaging miscalculation.[20]

How damaging it was is not easy to estimate. Soon after the 1871 budget fiasco, a traditionally Liberal constituency in Surrey returned a Conservative in a by-election. Henry Fawcett thought that defeat indicated a revolt of the taxpayers against the mismanagement of the budget. Lowe disagreed; what the vote really showed, he told Granville, was that 'the nouveaux riches' wanted to appear 'genteel' when they moved out of the metropolis into the suburbs and believed voting Tory would help. Probably both men were right; the suburban movement was a strong current working against the Liberal party in Southern England, but specific actions and mistakes hastened the erosion.[21]

One of the most unpopular actions taken by the government in the later part of the regime was the settlement of the *Alabama* claims. Gladstone decided in 1871 that it was time the British government made amends for having allowed the Clyde-built Confederate raider, the *Alabama*, to sail from an English port during the American Civil War. As usual, the prime minister's reasons for wanting to remove that source of bad feeling combined idealism and calculating realism. He thought America's sense of grievance was grossly inflated but not entirely unjustified; England, therefore, could set an example for the international community by offering to rectify the injustice. But even if the Americans had no case at all, there would be strategic advantages in making a settlement. Since the growth of a German hegemony on the continent, Britain had found herself isolated; therefore the potential threat of American naval retaliation had to be seriously reckoned with. He was aware that a settlement sufficiently generous to pave the way for good relations with the United States would be costly to England in pride as well as money. He was prepared to accept unpopularity for the sake of international morality and national security.

John Delane thought the future of the ministry rested on that one issue in 1872: so long as the 'Alabama business' remained unsettled, the Liberals were safe; but if the dispute were resolved, then 'swift and just destruction will overwhelm them.' Some of the cabinet were of the same opinion and all were aware of the danger. And yet, divided as they were about how to deal with the spread-eagle Americans, they argued and decided their policy on grounds of principle and national security and not on party interest.[22]

The problem they had to solve was this: if they consented to arbitration, they would be acknowledging that they were bound to a retroactive legal principle. It might be in England's interest to establish that a neutral is legally responsible for knowingly allowing a privateer to be constructed in her shipyards and permitting it to slip into belligerent hands. However, it was difficult to accept responsibility for breaking a law that did not exist at the time of the offence. To accept such responsibility would seem to all the world like truckling. Lowe and Cardwell thought it would be wrong to recognize such an absurd principle; George Goschen, now at the Admiralty, talked about 'dishonour.' Granville, on the other hand, thought legalistic niceties were less important than the realities of power. He sent a warning to de Grey, the chief British negotiator in Washington: 'Lowe, low all over, objecting to the Commission, to concession, and to obtaining any settlement for the future.' But Lowe did not stick to his initial, legalistic position. When Granville put the case for realism to him, Lowe found he had to agree. He had, after all, been holding forth for many years on the future might of America and the need for Britain to come to terms with that fact. Once having accepted the argument that it was best to appease the Americans, regardless of the sacrifice of logic, pride, and treasure, Lowe became one of the most vigorous proponents in the cabinet for making a quick settlement.[23]

The crisis in the negotiations came when the British negotiators discovered, in December 1871, that the Americans intended to submit claims for indirect damages to the arbitration commission. The American argument was that the *Alabama* had disrupted the blockade placed by the North on the South and, by doing so, had delayed the ending of the war; therefore they contended that Britain should foot the bill for the entire cost of the latter stages of the conflict. The American emissaries did not enjoy their assignment; they knew this claim to be preposterous, and yet they knew they had to mollify the firebrands in the Senate and the violently anti-British secretary of state, Charles Sumner. For these reasons they felt compelled to embellish their case with insulting language, including a blast against Gladstone for having made supposedly pro-Southern statements during the early phase of the war. When he heard of the indirect claims and of the charges laid against himself, Gladstone was furious and inclined to be stubborn. At first Lowe agreed with him that Britain should immediately withdraw from arbitration. Then Granville and others pointed out that the American negotiators were as eager as their British counterparts to find a way out of the impasse. Lowe was persuaded. He went to Gladstone and tried to soothe him – an unusual reversal of roles. Never before had Lowe acted as cabinet peace-maker. At a crucial moment, when the prime minister was in bed with bronchitis, the chancellor of the exchequer called the cabinet together in his offices and persuaded the ministers that it would be best to tone down the language of their counter-case. He urged them to submerge their outraged feelings and, when assaulted with 'coarse and virulent invective,' to turn the other cheek. He wrote to Gladstone that the vital consideration was to remove the danger of provoking a ruinous conflict with the United States; to do so, they must not 'stand on trifles.' He promised: 'I shall put as much water in the wine as I can.' Henry Adams, the leading American diplomat, assisted by watering the wine on his side of the table and arranging in advance that the arbitrators would rule against the indirect claims. Lowe assisted Gladstone in getting their colleague into line behind this compromise and the settlement was made. When Granville heard the terms, he wrote to Lowe: 'The Award which I take it is about 3 millions and a half sterling, is pretty much what I expected. It would have been a great reflection on our policy if after having made so many admissions and overcome so many obstacles in order to put ourselves in the position of paying a good round sum we had not succeeded.'[24]

Lowe also appreciated the irony that England could only gain her objective by being forced to pay a good round sum. He did not worry about finding the money. In fact he took pleasure in announcing, in 1873, that unexpected receipts from a spirit excise had given the Treasury a windfall out of which the *Alabama* claims could easily be met, and he congratulated the British tippler for having risen to the challenge. This provoked one MP to remark that the chancellor of the exchequer seemed to believe that 'the habitual drunkard is the sheet anchor of the British Constitution.' Once again Lowe was making enemies for the government by joking about things that should be treated with mournful solemnity. And once again he was unable to suppress his impulse to explain in forceful language what might best have been left unsaid. Shortly after the unwelcome news of the *Alabama* award became public, he gave a widely publicized speech in Glasgow. He said that the press had dwelt far too much on the legalities. Everyone knew England was blameless; that was not the point. He explained that it had been the object of the government not to gain some kind of victory but to 'lay a permanent basis of good will and mutual kindness between the two nations speaking the same language.' That object had been attained. It would be foolish, after that, to inquire closely into the law of nations, 'which after all is no law at all,' but merely something the arbitrators had dreamed up. That being so, Lowe said, Chief Justice Cockburn, the British member of the arbitration board, should not have gone on about procedures and precedents; he should have stopped his grumbling and paid up.[25]

Gladstone and some of his ministers were deeply pained when they read the news from Glasgow. Lowe had given Cockburn, whose protests the general public had heartily approved, a rude slap. Even worse, the chancellor of the exchequer had implied that the high-minded sacrifice that the government made in taking the issue to arbitration had, in fact, been only an episode in the game of power politics. On top of that he had denied that international law existed or could ever exist. In saying this he was robbing Gladstone's ministers of one justification for their actions. Naturally, they remonstrated with him. Lowe then tried to explain and got himself in deeper. In his 1873 budget speech he tried to make it clear that he approved of the use of arbitration to settle disputes even though he was not impressed by the legal arguments used to cloak the practice. The point might well have been left alone, especially since he made it in a singularly injudicious way. When he came to the item in the budget for payment of the award to the Americans, he said that he hoped government ministers would be asked to make similar payments in the future. His startled listeners shouted 'Oh! Oh!' He then hastened to say that he had meant to endorse arbitration as a way to settle disputes and hoped it would frequently be employed in the future. But it was the 'Oh! Oh's,' and not the explanation, that were heard by the public at large. People who read the speech and the indignant editorial comments on it concluded that Disraeli's charges were indeed true: that Gladstone and his chancellor of the exchequer were actually proud to have humiliated the national pride and to have reduced England to the status of a second-rate power.[26]

Partly because of the *Alabama* settlement and the bad taste it left behind, the reputation of the Gladstone government reached a low ebb by the summer of 1873. A pamphlet put out by the Conservative Association gave a succinct summary of the 'scrapes and humiliations' the country had endured during the 'wasted session' just completed. Leading the list was the 'odious' award to the Americans. Then there was the

Irish Universities bill ('too clever by half'), which had failed in the House of Commons on 12 March and toppled the government. Resignation had not ended the misery. Disraeli had refused to form a minority government; therefore Gladstone and his dispirited group, the 'exhausted volcanoes,' had filed back into the cabinet room. From that time onwards nothing had gone right for them. Of the many calamities they then had to endure, the worst was the revelation that the Treasury had been guilty of scandalous mismanagement – and this in an administration so self-righteous about their financial rectitude! The only good Gladstone had done the nation, the Conservative pamphleteers said, was to demote the obnoxious and careless Lowe to the Home Office, 'where his courtesies' are likely to 'delight the country magistrates and borough corporations,' as much as they had delighted the Civil Service and, several years earlier, the clergy and the school managers.[27]

The scandals referred to in the pamphlet deserve attention not only because they had an important effect on party history but because they show in a particularly graphic way the limitations and contradictions of the 'old liberal' conception of the function of government. All the emphasis should not, of course, be put on these limitations. A lasting accomplishment of Gladstonian policy, in which Lowe figured in a supporting role, was the establishment of rational principles of Treasury control over the departments of the central government. In 1866 Gladstone put through the Exchequer and Audit Act, empowering a single officer, the comptroller and auditor general, to receive the daily accounts, to authorize the issue of money, to examine the books of the departments, and to make sure that they were spending their appropriations in ways and for things Parliament had intended. This official was to report his findings to a standing Public Accounts Committee for the information of the Treasury and interested MPs. The comptroller could also inquire into any activity that appeared to be wasteful, unnecessary, or suspicious. In 1868 this act was stiffened by a Treasury minute, making it mandatory for departments to get Treasury permission before they made increases in salary scales or pension arrangements. Before these and other Gladstonian reforms, Treasury control had, like the Austrian empire, been a despotism tempered by inefficiency; now Treasury officials could use uniform procedures to check the tendency of the various branches of the bureaucracy to become jealous, semi-autonomous feudal principalities.[28]

Impressive though this reform was, it had serious defects. The Treasury developed under Gladstone and Lowe into a professional, responsible, informed supervisor of the entire administration, but it was not allowed to grow beyond that into a co-operative agent for planning and co-ordinating government work. One reason for this failure was technical. Unless a minister asked for an increase in his expenditure, the Treassury lacked the formal authority to take part in the policy planning of the other departments, although it could do so in the revenue offices – the Customs, the Mint, and the Post Office – directly under Treasury supervision. But more important than technical difficulties were the reservations in the minds of the Gladstonian officials about the growth and exercise of centralized authority.

Some of the politicians who took an interest in administrative matters were puzzled by what seemed a curious reluctance to pursue the rationalization process to a logical conclusion and make the Treasury not only an efficient watchdog but also a more positive supervisory arm of government. They got several select committees appointed and summoned Lowe to appear and explain why it was that the Treasury seemed to be incapable of holding down salaries, pensions, and wasteful expenditures in the other departments. Lowe protested that the Treasury had severe restraints on its powers. He said that his officials had been 'accused of many things which really proceed rather from their weakness than from their will.' Asked if it were then a 'popular delusion' that the Treasury could exercise direct control over the expenditures, Lowe replied that it might not be popular but it certainly was a delusion. He thought the Treasury could not govern and should not; responsibility for policy must remain with the ministers and ultimately with the cabinet. Any active interference by the Treasury in the policy-making of other departments would weaken the responsibility and accountability of the department heads. He could as chancellor of the exchequer, he agreed, 'grumble and remonstrate'; he could try to use moral suasion when he found departments behaving in an authorized but wasteful manner. That the tendency towards waste and self-aggrandizement was constantly at work, he had no doubt. But he insisted that ministers must not be deprived of their autonomy, because, without autonomy, there was no responsibility. If a minister did not do his job properly it was vital that the prime minister and the Parliament know where to point their fingers.[29]

Implicit in this attitude and central to the dilemma facing the Victorian Treasury was, of course, the conviction that the growth of government detracted from economic productivity and weakened individual initiative and self-discipline. All of Gladstone's ministers tried to respond to directives ordering them to prune establishments; they did make important economies; but still they were acutely aware that the cost of the civil establishment continued to rise. Lowe never tired of sounding the alarm. At Glasgow in 1872 he made the dangers of bureaucratic expansion the central theme of a major speech. He said that public power must control private greed – the difficulty was that all the agencies of that public power were as greedy as the individuals and companies they supervised. 'I, knowing Government pretty well,' he said, 'have the most profound distrust of Government; and you and the rest of the community, knowing mercantile and manufacturing concerns much better than I do, seem to have an equally profound distrust of them.' He made it clear that it was the function of the Treasury, alone amid all this greed, to balance those distrusts and set them off against each other.[30]

Lowe profoundly agreed with one distinguished Gladstonian Treasury official who believed that 'a great part of the good we do in the world might perhaps be properly measured by the evil we prevent.' As we have seen, Lowe thought that the best way to prevent evil was to warn evil-doers that they were being watched by a stern policeman who could not be diverted by sweet talk. With considerable satisfaction, he answered a gentle reprimand from Granville by writing, 'I am tolerably pachydermatous and not in the least disposed to contend that the letters of the Treasury are models of style and courtesy.' Obviously, he did not think it part of his duty to be co-operative and positive. And yet the history of the growth of the central administration shows that much of that steady expansion was carried out by people who shared, to some degree at least, Lowe's negativism. Lowe himself is a good example. He was more than willing to exceed the formal powers given to the Treasury when he saw a chance to supersede the Civil Service Commission and put through his civil service reform. Had he been challenged on this he might have answered that he had decided to exceed his authority so that in the future he would have less need to assert it, but that rationalization could be used for almost any action.[31]

Two serious errors of judgment and administration, exposed almost simultaneously in the spring of 1873, show both sides of the paradox at work – the positive innovator, impatient of procedures, and the negative legalist, insisting on the strict limitations rightly imposed upon his office. The first of these scandals involved the telegraph which Disraeli's government had purchased for the nation. At the time of purchase five large companies and a host of smaller ones, each with its own scale of rates and transmission systems, offered the public a limited and expensive service. Complaints brought a Royal Commission investigation in 1865. The commissioners recommended that the government buy the telegraphs and give their management to the Post Office. A bill to that effect became law in 1868. Prominent in the investigation, the drawing up of the legislation for the purchase, and then in the implementation of the transfer was a civil servant named Frank Scudamore. He was a curious, Dickensian figure: short body and huge head, framed by a great circle of flowing silver hair. He was genial, whimsical (he wrote a book on the art of insomnia), and was single-mindedly devoted to his work at the Post Office. The press never mentioned him without the prefix 'indefatigable.' Because the Post Office was a revenue department, it came under the indirect control of the Treasury; therefore when Lowe became chancellor of the exchequer he inherited the problem of expediting the purchase and also inherited Scudamore, the master expeditor. Formally, Scudamore was answerable to the Post Master General, but since that office was as much a political plum as a working ministry, Scudamore had become accustomed to carrying out his tasks in almost total freedom from interference from his titular superiors. Lowe approved of the arrangement. He recognized in this intelligent, zealous public servant one of those indispensable men who need to be protected from Bumbledom and political harassment. He gave him the task of drafting the legislation providing for the establishment of a state monopoly over the telegraph, a bill which the chancellor of the exchequer, after some ritual expressions of disapproval for the principle of state-owned enterprises, managed to guide successfully through the House. Most parliamentarians were willing to overlook this departure from free enterprise orthodoxy partly because private ownership and competition was so obviously wasteful and inefficient and partly because they had been assured that the service would bring in large revenues and compensate the Post Office for its losses in handling the mails. Therefore Parliament quickly approved legislation authorizing the floating of a loan to cover the large initial costs of capital construction. Scarcely bothering to consult William Monsell, whom Gladstone had made postmaster general in 1870 as a good-will gesture to Irish Roman Catholics, Lowe told Scudamore to proceed with construction and organization of a national system. Scudamore responded with vigour. In 1872 he reported to Gladstone that he had managed to treble the number of stations, cheapen and standardize the rates, and increase the yearly transmission of messages from the pre-nationalization six million to the present sixteen million. Gladstone was impressed and so was Lowe. The feat performed by this exemplary public servant seemed to confirm the rule that when faced with a challenge that cannot be met by application of routine procedures, the best thing to do is to find an energetic, incorruptible, proconsul who knows his business and give him his head. Monsell made no objection to this arrangement. Whenever he or his officials went to the Treasury with the smallest request, they had to run a gauntlet of objections, lectures, and questions; but Scudamore seemed to get anything he wanted from the chancellor of the exchequer almost without asking. The arrangement seemed to be working to everyone's advantage, so why bother with the niceties of procedure and jurisdiction?[32]

In 1871 Scudamore notified the Treasury that, in the frantic press of business, he had overspent the capital appropriation by £171,775, had, as an emergency measure, made up the missing sum out of Post Office revenues and 'other balances,' and would therefore need a new appropriation to cover this deficit and to carry on expansion into 1872. According to routine, this communication should have gone through the hands of the financial secretary of the treasury, William Baxter, but Lowe did not like Baxter, thought he was lazy, overly fond of taking long vacations, and addicted to nit-picking, and had arranged for business which demanded quick action to be short-circuited around him. Scudamore could not possibly do his complicated work if ensnarled in the kind of red-tape Baxter cherished. Therefore Lowe received the communication directly and, without consulting anyone, saw to it that Scudamore got his appropriation. No questions were asked about the mysterious 'other balances.' Lowe did raise his eyebrows slightly, however, when he received a similar plea in 1872. This time the over-spending had reached the considerable sum of £400,000. Lowe got his secretary to write, asking for a detailed accounting. Three such letters went out from the Treasury, but Scudamore was 'busy' and neglected to answer. Lowe was also busy; he was, among other things, trying to extricate himself from a most embarrassing mix-up with the Post Office over a mail contract and did not notice the strange silence from Scudamore.[33]

On 21 March 1873 opposition members startled the chancellor of the exchequer with the disclosure that the 'other balances' were in fact receipts from deposits made by workingmen into the Post Office Savings Bank. It was generally assumed that the Post Office turned these deposits over immediately to the Consolidated Fund where they would begin earning interest. However, Scudamore had written the procedural rules governing the Savings Bank and had written them in language sufficiently vague to give him room to manipulate. These rules the Treasury had approved without bothering to consult the indifferent Monsell. Thus Scudamore had been able to hold back, without detection, the enormous sum of £656,000. He used the money to pay the often unpredictable bills for expanding the telegraph lines. Caught unprepared by this disclosure, all Lowe could do was to promise an investigation.[34]

A Royal Commission heard evidence and reported that alarming irregularities had been committed by Scudamore and allowed by Lowe. They were charitable towards the civil servant who had not profited in any personal way, but they offered no excuses for the behaviour of the Treasury. As *The Times* editorialized, Scudamore, of all the guilty parties, had come off the best, for his indiscretions had been the products of zeal, not of negligence. Sir Stafford Northcote, a Tory financial expert in the House of Commons, said that Scudamore's action reminded him of Nelson putting his blind eye to the telescope at Copenhagen. Most of the harsh words were reserved for Lowe and Monsell. Only the *Economist* attempted to offer words of comfort. It said it was natural for Scudamore's superiors to have trusted him, since what he had done had been inspired by that totally unpredictable factor, an 'outbreak of pure devotion.'[35]

Late in July 1873 a Conservative MP, Assheton Cross, gave notice of a censure motion against everyone involved. Gladstone and most of his cabinet feared the motion would succeed. They told Lowe that if the censure motion went through, only Monsell would have to resign. Lowe disagreed; he would go also. This stand forced the government to take evasive action. It had a motion brought in which included the substance of Cross's charges but used milder language. The government amendment passed, aided, Gladstone thought, by the hot weather which wilted energy for inter-party conflict. This action saved the ministry from an immediate crisis but it did not save Lowe's reputation.[36]

This was not the only reason that June and July 1873 were nightmarish months for him. On top of the telegraph scandal there came in those months the only slightly less embarrassing affair of the Zanzibar Mail Contract. Indeed, the two incidents had a similar pattern.

The background can be quickly sketched in. In the late 1860s David Livingstone was reported to have disappeared into the darkness of East Africa. The newspapers closely followed the various proposals for rescue and stimulated a considerable interest in his fate. One of Lowe's more unpopular acts in 1872 had been to refuse government aid to an expedition proposing to find the missionary explorer. Interest in Livingstone led to interest in what Livingstone called 'the running sore of Africa,' the slave trade which continued to flourish on the Eastern side of the Continent. When reports disclosed that the sultan of Zanzibar, ruler of a territory understood to be within the British sphere of influence, was facilitating the movement and sale of slaves, the government was deluged with petitions and demands for intervention. A parliamentary committee recommended vigorous action, whereupon Granville, the colonial secretary, pressed Gladstone to do something. Lowe seconded Granville, not, of course, because he had any philanthropic inclinations but because he was afraid that the public 'mania,' if not appeased, might lead to a movement for naval expansion. The prospect of spending money on ships to patrol the unhealthy and uncolonized coastline of East Africa was decidedly unattractive. Therefore he worked out a plan for inducing the sultan to co-operate in suppressing the trade. Britain should suggest to the tractable sultan that if he put a stop to the movement of slaves through his kingdom, a regular mail service would be established to link Zanzibar with Aden and with the Cape Colony. Lowe pointed out that the cost of such a service should be relatively small, especially if the Foreign Office were to induce Portugal and the Cape Colony to contribute something.[37]

The cabinet accepted this plan. They instructed the Post Office to make a contract with a suitable carrier and to pay the cost of the service out of its estimates, subject to approval by the Treasury. The postmaster general protested on the grounds that the object of this expensive, subsidized service was political, had little to do with improving mail service, and would bring in only a tiny amount of revenue. This objection Lowe impatiently brushed aside; if they waited for Monsell to appreciate the value of the plan, the government would soon find itself policing every barbaric place in the world! Lowe decided that the only thing to do was to take the business into his own office and get it done quickly and efficiently. At first Gladstone was wary about this procedure. He preferred to go a bit more slowly and to submit the matter to Parliament in the usual way and to ask for a separate vote of money. But he gave in when Lowe pointed out that Sir Bartle Frere was about to begin his negotiations with the sultan and needed to be empowered immediately to offer the bargain.[38]

Only one snag now remained, and that was the financial secretary, William Baxter. Lowe knew that Baxter, whose relatives were wealthy flax-spinners in Scotland and engaged in extensive international trade, had always taken a special interest in transportation contracts. He was on record as strongly disapproving long contracts and subsidies to steamship companies on the grounds that such arrangements prevented competition and slowed communications. Lowe had, in the past, made similar statements. In this instance, however, he was impatient with those who would apply theoretical propositions to a special case. He tried to talk Gladstone into shifting Baxter, 'a perfect cypher,' out of the way, but Gladstone refused to act on such general charges. Lowe decided that since the obstacle could not be removed, it would be ignored.[39]

While discussions about Baxter and about the mail service plan were still unresolved, Lowe decided that he would expedite matters by making exploratory inquiries into the cost of a steamship contract. He directed a Post Office secretary to make tentative probes. Officials of the Union Steamship Company, whose vessels already carried the mail from England to the Cape, indicated that they would extend their service to Zanzibar in return for a seven-year contract and an annual payment of £29,000. Shortly afterwards the Indian postal director wrote to say that the British India Steam Navigation Company, with whom he did business, would sail monthly from Aden to Zanzibar and then on to the Cape for £27,365, providing that it could have a ten-year contract. Lowe informed the Colonial Office and the Foreign Office of these offers and asked for their aid in persuading the Cape Colony and European governments to help with the costs. While this was going on, the Union Company applied for an extension of its contract for service along the west coast of Africa. This request, unlike the others, happened to cross Baxter's desk. He sent a long memorandum protesting against long contracts of any kind, but Lowe tossed it away. The Union Company representatives then heard about the rival offer for the Zanzibar run, approached the British India Company, and got it to agree to a joint proposal. The Union Company informed Lowe that if its west coast subsidy were extended, it would take the mails on from the Cape to Zanzibar for a mere £5000; for an additional £10,000 the British India Company would connect the sultan's kingdom with Aden. This seemed like an excellent bargain to the Treasury; a naval squadron would cost twice that amount to maintain. It was at this advanced stage in the negotiations that Lowe received formal authorization to act.[40]

On instructions from the Teasury, the Post Office closed the contract on the joint offer, and the two companies ordered new ships and quickly began service on the respective legs of their runs. This they did at a certain risk, for by an act passed in 1869 no contract was binding until the Treasury had tabled a minute explaining the terms and Parliament had given its approval. The Treasury, however, had assured the companies that there was no need to wait. As Lowe explained later, he was confident that the House would respond to the 'great ferment in the public mind' and approve the minute without difficulty. That confidence proved to be mistaken. Neither Lowe nor his subordinates had bothered to inquire if any other company was interested in making the run from England to the Cape. And there was such a company. A fleet of ships owned by a Mr Donald Currie had been making the run for a number of years, had been making it faster than the Union Company, and had been carrying freight and mails cheaper, without subsidy. When Currie learned that the Union Company contract had been renewed, he got friends to write letters to *The Times* and arranged for some lively demonstrations in Cape Town. Before news of these demonstrations reached England, the Treasury finally got around to preparing the necessary minute but neglected (Lowe said it was an oversight) to indicate that the Union Company had agreed to take a loss on the run from Cape Town to Zanzibar because it had been promised a renewal of its lucrative west coast of Africa run. Currie's efforts made that minute irrelevant. As soon as the Cape Town protest reached Lord Kimberley at the Colonial Office, he made it clear to the cabinet that the Union Company contract must not be finally approved. Lowe had to agree (a trifle belatedly the colonial secretary thought) that 'it is not worth getting into squabbles with the colonists.'[41]

Dropping the contract faced Lowe with a predicament. He could hardly expect the Union Company now to take a loss on the Cape to Zanzibar journey. So, to save the government's honour, and to get himself out of a corner, he revived the Union Company's original £29,000 estimate, talked them into shaving off £3000, and went to Parliament for approval in June 1873.[42]

The debate of 9 June was a near disaster. A colonial newspaper disclosed that the British India Company had made a low offer to connect Zanzibar with the outside world. Armed with this information, several Liberal backbenchers asked Lowe to explain his actions to the House. It was immediately obvious to everyone that the chancellor of the exchequer had completely forgotten about the original, unofficial tender the British India Company had made. Had a quick vote been taken, it would have gone against him. With Gladstone's help, he found a parliamentary device to postpone the debate for ten days. When he eventually rose to make his explanation he had to do so over the noise of almost constant hooting. In the opinion of many of those present, he might have got out of his difficulty had he pleaded human error and expressed his remorse, but, true to form, instead of offering apologies he tried to brazen it out. He hinted that the reason he had taken so many procedural short cuts was that he had felt the need to frustrate the many venal parliamentary lobbyists who had private interests in the contracts. After that, it is hardly surprising that his enemies showed him no mercy. They joined in a blistering recital of his misdeeds: his failure to show in the minute that the contracts were tied, his failure to submit the service to open tender, his failure to inform the financial secretary and the postmaster general, his willingness to grant long and unnecessary subsidies, his negligence or disingenuousness about the British India Company's offer, and so on. A solid core of Liberals then voted for a commission of inquiry – an ordeal that would prolong Lowe's miseries and subject him to further indignities. That satisfying work done, the House then agreed to accept the Union Company contract for the Cape to Zanzibar run, but only when the Treasury, after much anxious negotiation, got the directors to shave off another £6000 and after Lowe had sent out new regulations to tighten the procedures he had ignored.[43]

Hardly a week went by in the late spring and early summer of 1873 without some distressing disclosure or some complaint. Bad as the facts were, Lowe made them worse. When cornered he put the blame on Monsell, or negligent clerks, or the laxness of the National Debt Commission. Asked why he had ignored Baxter, he first denied that he had and then said that he saw no need to consult with a man who had prejudged the case. Asked why he had not forced Scudamore to produce the capital accounts, he answered that the Treasury did not have the power to exercise strict surveillance over other departments and should not have that power. His inquisitors wanted to know if the Treasury was powerless to interfere with the Post Office, a revenue department; did it really lack the authority to see that its receipts were paid into the Consolidated Fund? Lowe had to admit that in that case he had, perhaps, been 'too loath to interfere,' but even there, the Treasury must keep its distance. Certainly, the Treasury should not, as a commissioner suggested, attach any of its officials to another department in an advisory capacity; they might, Lowe thought, develop divided loyalties. What an 'extraordinary misconception of authority,' thought *The Times*. 'Misconception' was, under the circumstances, quite a charitable word. It is difficult to escape the conclusion that Lowe missed opportunities to make the Treasury a better co-ordinating agency in the administration not merely because he was suspicious and negative about the role of government but also because he needed an excuse for his blunders.[44]

But why did those blunders occur? Part of the answer lies, of course, in Lowe's personality: his tactlessness, his impatience with routine, his inability to suffer fools. On the other hand Gladstone was to blame for insisting on surrounding him, not perhaps with fools, but with men whom even the most good-humoured would have found difficult to work with. Because of his bad eyesight, Lowe was unusually dependent on his subordinates. If those subordinates happened to be urbane men who understood him and appreciated his style, he was generous with his trust – too generous, in some cases, as we have seen. Rivers Wilson and Edward Hamilton, who acted at various times as his private secretaries, were deeply distressed when the scandals broke over Lowe's head. They thought he had been 'cruelly misunderstood.' They thought he was being held accountable for the arrogance and disloyalty of men who had taken advantage of his handicap. Gladstone could not have been entirely oblivious to this problem and yet he had insisted over Lowe's vociferous protest on sending Ayrton and Baxter to the Treasury. He seems to have done so because he did not trust his chancellor of the exchequer to remain entirely steadfast in the religion of economy and wanted to bolster him by placing two zealots outside his door.[45]

In the case of Ayrton, Gladstone had, eventually, to admit that devotion to the cause of economy was not an adequate compensation for an inability to co-operate. In the last months of the ministry, when the government was reeling under a flurry of heavy blows, the works commissioner went out of his way to create petty scenes in the House. One of those scenes brought the prime minister thundering down on him. A Conservative member had asked Ayrton why he proposed to spend £8500 for an extension to the Thames Embankment, a sum the questioner thought excessive. Ayrton replied that he had no idea why so high a figure was in his estimates. His office had wanted only a small extension made to the Embankment in order to provide the Palace of Westminster with a bit more space. Lowe, Ayrton said, had intervened and changed the estimate – with what object, 'I do not in the smallest degree know.' He then added that if the House really wanted to learn about that item, it would have to ask the minister who prepared it. At that, Gladstone rose and sternly reminded Ayrton that it was the duty of the Treasury to take the initiative at certain times but that such action did not remove responsibility from the minister in charge. Collective responsibility, Gladstone assured the House, did still apply in his government. Ward Hunt then remarked that hon. members had just witnessed the most curious of many curious episodes which had occurred that session. Was it true, he asked, that the chancellor of the exchequer and the first commissioner of public works were not on speaking terms? At this, there was a shout of laughter.[46]

Hunt's question was pertinent. An administration which had not developed well-understood routines for co-ordinating its policies needed to depend to a large extent on personal trust and good-humoured relationships. Paradoxically, Lowe made an important contribution, through his civil service reform and through the organizational minute he issued in the wake of the scandals, to the formation of a rationalized administration where 'ordinary decencies' were made easy by the existence of generally understood mechanisms. But to create these mechanisms, Lowe needed to be able to work within the system of personal relationships. It was, for example, vital at a time when accounting procedures had not been fully worked out that the chancellor of the exchequer be on good terms with the auditor. Had Sir William Dunbar been well disposed towards Lowe he might have been able to prevent many of the Treasury's mistakes. But the two men could not abide one another and were on what amounted to a war footing at the beginning of the disastrous 1873 session. Because Lowe was unable, perhaps incapable, of working out ways of preserving the civilities with men like Dunbar, Baxter, and Ayrton, he impeded the rationalizing process which he also helped to further. Contradictions can be found in the life of any public man, but seldom do they so completely define an entire career.[47]

By the end of July 1873 Gladstone could see that he would have to make changes in the government but wanted to wait until interest in the scandals had a chance to wear down. A letter from Baxter on 2 August convinced him that the reorganization could not be postponed. The letter threatened another noisy, internecine row. Baxter, it seemed, was still annoyed about the Zanzibar affair. The final contract with the Union Steamship Company would, Baxter wrote, be presented the next day. He complained that once again the Treasury officials had not consulted with him but had put the contract on his desk with the comment that the chancellor of the exchequer expected him to sign it. He had obeyed under protest and wanted to submit his resignation. Gladstone hurriedly asked for an explanation. Lowe denied using strong-arm tactics; he also presented evidence that Treasury officials had tried on many occasions to find and consult Baxter but had each time discovered that he was off somewhere on one of his frequent pleasure jaunts. Gladstone knew that the facts of the case were unimportant; what mattered was that another blow-up was imminent. He appealed to Baxter to delay announcing his resignation until it could be accepted as part of a major change in the ministry. Baxter agreed and Gladstone set about re-structuring his government.[48]

Monsell, of course, would have to vacate the Post Office and retire from the ministry. Gladstone had been thinking for some time about shifting Ayrton into that post but changed his mind after the scene in the House over the Embankment. He had to agree with the queen that he must not be given anything that might bring him into contact with people. The only sinecure the prime minister could think of that answered this description was a vacant judge advocate generalship; so the mulish Ayrton was sent there with instructions never under any circumstances to communicate directly with the queen. Georgiana thought her husband's two enemies, Baxter and Ayrton, got off much too easily. Had Gladstone not shown 'the spirit of a mouse,' he would have sent those dreadful men packing and kept 'Robin' at the Ex-chequer.[49]

Her Robin knew that was impossible. When he believed he had got the Zanzibar affair finally settled, he wrote to Gladstone that he felt he could not go on being the focal point of bitterness and animosity. He had, he knew, become an embarrassment to the ministry. Gladstone agreed but looked for a way to let him down easily. With Granville's ad-vice he worked out an arrangement whereby Bruce would go to the House of Lords as a reward for vacating his home secretaryship and turning it over to Lowe. The prime minister would himself take over the Exchequer. Gladstone was aware that the queen would object to retaining Lowe; she had made no secret of her disgust over the scandals at the Treasury. Gladstone admitted to her that his wayward colleague had an 'ability almost amounting to genius for getting himself into "scrapes,"' but added that he could do as much harm out of office as in, that he had always proved to be docile enough at times of crucial decision for the government, and that he had, all things considered, done much good service. He could not, Gladstone wrote, abandon such an eminent colleague at such a difficult time in his career. He promised to send a warning, making it clear that 'if he persists in treating the rest of mankind as fools and knaves,' his official life would come to an abrupt end. Accordingly, the prime minister sent the penitent Lowe a 'stiff note' – stiff, but softened by a characteristic humanity.[50]

Gladstone began by confessing that he had always found politicians a particularly difficult species of mankind to comprehend. Nevertheless he would proceed boldly with his lecture, mindful that he was not clever at interpreting human behaviour.

I think the clearness, power and promptitude of yr. intellect are in one respect a difficulty and a danger to you. You see everything in a burning, almost a scorching light. The case reminds me of an incident some years back. Sir D. Brewster asked me to sit for my photograph, in a black frost, and a half-mist in Edinburgh. I objected about the light. He said, 'this is the best light. It is all diffused, not concentrated.' Is not your light too much concentrated? Does not its intensity darken the surroundings? By the surroundings I mean the relations of this thing not only to other things, but to persons, as our profession obliges us constantly to deal with persons. In every question flesh and blood are strong and real if extraneous elements, and we cannot safely omit them from our thoughts.

Gladstone continued by agreeing that anyone who goes to the Exchequer and tries to do his duty there has to stand up to abuse from all quarters. Then, 'taking another scrap of paper for the purpose,' the prime minister continued with the 'faultfinding': 'I note then two things about you. Outstripping others in the race, you reach the goal or conclusion, before them, and being there, you assume that they are there also. This is unpopular. You are unpopular the very day with a poor devil, whom you have appraised that he has lost his seat; and you have not told him *how*. Again and lastly, I think you do not get up all things, but allow yourself a choice, as if politics were a flower garden, and we might choose among the beds: and as Ld. Palmerston did, who read the F.O. and War papers, and let the others rust and rot. This I think is particularly true, I don't say of your reading, but of your mental processes.'[51]

Lowe's reply began meekly: 'I am very much obliged to you for your kind aid in self knowledge of which old as I am I fear I stand greatly in need. I will do my best to mend but am not sanguine I shall succeed. However the age that makes the difficulty succeeding makes the failure less important.' That said, and without transition, Lowe then launched into a detailed and cock-sure disquisition on the reasons why Gladstone (the 'poor devil,' who had been advised that he had lost his seat) was legally bound to submit himself for re-election to the voters of Greenwich because he had added the Exchequer office to his duties. On receiving this Gladstone was half annoyed (he was certain to lose at Greenwich) and half amused; the reply was such a perfect example of what the lecture had been aimed at correcting! He showed the exchange of letters to Granville and commented that Lowe had first told him that there would be no difficulty about the seat since, being prime minister, he was already a Treasury lord. Now, only days later, he had 'rushed into' the opposite opinion. Obviously, Gladstone thought, the point about the dangers of too prompt an intellect had not taken.[52]

Lowe did try to behave himself at the Home Office, not entirely successfully. At first he was greatly relieved to be there. He had expected to be sacked and now he was saved. Friends noted that he seemed almost jubilant and was loud in his praise of Gladstone's generosity. That mood dampened considerably when he went to Osborne House and felt the queen's disapproval. After that he became irritable and began to justify himself. 'His self-delusions about his own faults and merits are extraordinary,' wrote Granville. Since business was slack at the Home Office during the period between parliamentary sessions, he began to be bored. Fortunately, as one of the civil servants remarked, he was not there long enough to do any great damage. He did manage, however, to give the Irish a 'good kick' by stubbornly refusing Gladstone's request that he be merciful to some prisoners who had committed acts of political sabotage. He also displeased Gladstone by going to Sheffield and telling a gathering there how splendidly he had performed at the Treasury. In fact, he said, all of the cabinet had behaved heroically. Even if they were to be defeated in the next election, they would be able to 'carry into private life the applause of our own consciences.' Gladstone did not like the smugness or the suggestion that the next election would send them all into private political life. The prime minister wrote to Granville: 'Lowe's speech at Sheffield is really too bad, and free as I believe it is from evil intention, it illustrates the incurable solecism of his extraordinary mind.'[53]

Gladstone, at any rate, was not in a defeatist mood. He was preparing a budget designed to give the Liberal party new life and victory at the polls. His budget would accomplish the great feat of abolishing entirely the income tax! To make that possible some additional cuts would need to be made in the army and navy estimates. His colleagues, however, were not greatly impressed. The departments affected put up a stiff resistance. The prime minister was too tired to take part in any more cabinet skirmishes. His considerable self-control had been strained by the difficulties of the past year. He was troubled about the question of his Greenwich seat, and was undergoing personal pressures, so, without consulting anyone, he suddenly announced on 24 January 1874 that he intended to ask the queen to dissolve Parliament and call for a general election.

Gladstone counted on the 'prestige of great promises' to win the voters, but they proved to be indifferent to the splendours of tax reform. The election, everyone agreed, was extremely dull. One of its livelier features was an exchange of insults between Lowe and Disraeli. At Newport Pagnall the Tory leader congratulated himself on his own 'characteristic magnanimity,' his 'prescience,' and his 'eye to the main chance' – qualities which had moved him in 1867 to find a seat for his old enemy at the University of London; for by doing so, he had made certain 'that no Cabinet, even if it be brought into power by an overwhelming majority, can long endure and flourish, if he be a member of it.' Lowe saved his own best barbs for Disraeli. He referred in an address to his constituents to the Tory leader's statement that the country had been plagued over the past five years by 'incessant and harassing legislation.' This was obscurantism of the purest form, Lowe said. A man who could say that must prefer 'custom to law' and must wish to 'stereotype every abuse, and substitute the blind guesses of barbarians for the clear and well-considered conclusions of a civilized age.'[54]

The Conservatives won a forty-eight seat majority, a victory that had little to do with income taxes, torrents of gin and beer, or scandals in the Post Office, but much to do with superior organization and with the movement of the better-off among the middle classes to the suburbs. Lowe was far from despondent about the defeat. He had survived without having to contest his seat and was glad of a chance to exchange the faded glories of office for the chance to restore his reputation and position in the party. Meeting his Conservative friend, Gathorne Hardy, he offered congratulations, said he was glad to have the Irish Home Rulers snuffed out, and not at all displeased that some of his 'extreme friends, who want to pull down everything,' would now be kept in their places. In high spirits he thanked his university backers for having returned him and for having given him a 'certificate of character.' They, at any rate, could apparently see that what the press was fond of calling 'scandals' had in fact been only mistakes. A dispassionate examination of those mistakes would disclose, he said, that 'probably nobody was guilty.' Apparently he had entirely forgiven himself for past sins. It was a perverse fate that had punished him for his great accomplishments. For a friend he wrote this jingle:

> Twelve millions of Taxes I struck off,
> Left behind me six million of gains;
> Of Debt forty million I shook off,
> And got well abused for my pains.[55]

An anonymous rhymer sent him a less flattering appraisal:

> Here lie the bones of Robert Lowe;
> Where he's gone I do not know;
> If to the realms of peace and love,
> Farewell to happiness above;
> If to a place of lower level,
> I can't congratulate the Devil.

Gleefully Lowe translated these lines into Greek and Latin and sent them to his friends, accompanied by Latin and Italian renditions Gladstone had made.[56]

The most sober and balanced appraisal of Lowe's performance as chancellor of the exchequer came from Walter Bagehot. He did not consign Lowe either to the upper or to the lower regions. The now deposed finance minister, Bagehot wrote, had done much that was good for the economy, much that was good for the nation. He did little that was blameworthy, although he was often blamed. 'Mr. Lowe,' Bagehot wrote, 'is a great man, but he is also a great irritant.' He has that natural disadvantage of most intellectuals in politics: 'he has not learnt, and we fear cannot learn, the decorum of commonplace.'[57]

16

At War with 'Beaconsfieldism'

Gladstone said that the Liberal defeat in 1874 was the greatest act of 'public disappropriation' that any government or any political leader had received in living memory. He avoided the House during most of the remainder of the 1874 session, resigned his leadership soon after the session ended, and at the age of sixty-five entertained thought of the grave. He was sure that the Tories would, as they had before, misman-age the finances of the nation and lead it into reckless adventures abroad. They would pander to the baser instinct of the masses and, at the same time, introduce class legislation.

Lowe shared Gladstone's apprehensions but not his mood. Defeat had released the former chancellor of the exchequer from real burdens; opposition had always been his natural environment. Immediately he shook off all self doubts and recovered his relish for life and struggle in liberal causes. With a Hebrew bible in his pocket, he made an excursion to Norway where he climbed, rowed, and hiked, amazing a young niece who accompanied him with his appetite for food, scenery, and Norse literature. Home again, he received an Indian civil servant named Cot-terell Tupp, who complained that the government of Bengal was cir-cumventing the India Act of 1873 by staffing posts in the bureaucracy with military officers. Would the champion of the competitive system use his influence with *The Times*? Lowe assured him that he had no in-fluence whatsoever with that newspaper: it had treated him during the last two years with 'marked animosity.' Nevertheless he promised to do what he could to harass the guilty officials if Tupp would supply him with the facts. Two or three times a week throughout 1874 and 1875 he met with Tupp to plot strategy. Lowe wrote a long letter to *The Times*, made public speeches, raised the question in Parliament, and button-holed responsible officials with a dedication and grasp of the details of Indian politics which overwhelmed the grateful Tupp. Eventually the government took some half-hearted remedial action.[1]

This experience confirmed his view (hardly in need of confirming) that the government of Lord Beaconsfield would take no initiative to see that justice was done but that it could be made to perform its duty, provided those in opposition were prepared to make ministers 'wince.' Lowe, in contrast to Gladstone, was more than prepared.[2]

Of course this pessimistic estimate of Tory capacity for rational action proved to be greatly exaggerated. Even by the standards of the reform administration they had displaced, the Conservatives compiled an impressive record. No other ministry in the century passed so much constructive social legislation. Between 1874 and 1876 the labour unions were relieved of the most serious restraints on their rights to strike and picket, reforming borough councils were empowered to condemn slum property and to authorize private builders to construct low-cost housing, and women and children in the factories received significant protection from some of the grosser forms of exploitation. This record does not prove, however, that Gladstone and Lowe were entirely mistaken in their conviction that Conservatives could only be kept honest and alert by constant harassment. The social legislation which R.A. Cross and W.H. Smith sponsored were the products, as one modern historian has put it, of a 'confused and nervous empiricism.' The election had clearly indicated that wealthy, middle class suburbanites in Lancashire and the southern counties were moving over into the Conservative party. Had the author of *Sybil* and his ministers wanted to make a bid for the newly enfranchised workers by implementing 'Tory Democracy' (and evidence suggests that the desire was not keen), they would have risked alienating the men of 'substance' who were voting Tory in ever growing numbers. As a result, Conservative ministers, including Cross, tried to find a minimalist position on social reform – sufficient remedy to still the most urgent demands of labour but not so much that the new recruits to the party would be alarmed. While they tried to find this delicate balance they had to listen to demands from the opposition that the concessions to the poor be real and lasting. In a number of important cases Lowe was the spokesman for that radical opposition.[3]

Lowe found all his collaborators in this work objectionable, on personal or ideological grounds. He thought W.E. Forster a bumbler and a boor. He liked Sir Charles Dilke but repudiated his 'new liberalism' and had once tried to 'crush' him for having preached republicanism. A.J. Mundella, the wealthy hosiery manufacturer and friend of trade unionism, he could not tolerate. Walking one day in Hyde Park, Lowe refused to acknowledge the salute of the king of Belgium. When Leopold asked him to explain the snub, he apologized with the remark, 'I thought you were Mundella.' Another associate in the fight to protect the rights of workingmen, the Positivist leader, Frederic Harrison, Lowe respected personally but also feared. To him, Harrison was an example of the sort of person who was bound to come forward in a democratic age to feed the hungry but indiscriminating intellectual appetite of the awakening masses. Furthermore, Harrison believed that the history of mankind contained material for a scientific theory of morality, and that made him one of those misguided and slightly ludicrous 'apostles of a new Religion of Humanity.'[4]

Sentimentality and woolly-minded idealism was, Lowe noted with distress, gaining favour among the younger generation. They had learned from the economists Stanley Jevons and Alfred Marshall and from the Oxford philosopher T.H. Green to doubt Ricardian economics and hedonistic psychology – the underpinnings of free-trade liberalism. The new liberals professed to believe that men were capable of changing their basic natures and were in the process of evolving from creatures ruled by their animal instincts into altruistic beings who were becoming progressively more responsive to the moral dimensions of life. This advancement of intellect and technological civilization had, they believed, removed, or was in the process of removing, the need to goad people into productive labour; work was ceasing to be a painful necessity and becoming a creative activity. If this were true, then the penalties and rewards of a competitive economy might be moderated and regulated by the state without destroying incentives. The state could remedy the inevitable inequities caused by free enterprise capitalism; it could become a positive agency for enlisting the moral sensibilities of a working class which was becoming, through education and the broadening effects of mobility, more disciplined in its habits and respectable in its behaviour. With participation, a sense of personal identity would grow and with it a more enlightened interpretation of the meaning of liberty. As this process matured, the state would cease to be regarded as a gathering of separate egoisms and be accepted as a moral entity.[5]

The new liberals claimed that in the more humane and other-regarding culture that was evolving, trade unions would, like all institutions, change their characters and functions. They held there was evidence that this change had already occurred: in the larger unions, workers were being encouraged to save and to invest; arbitration procedures, on the pattern of those which Mundella had introduced into the hosiery and glove industry, promised to change the atmosphere of industrial bargaining. Thus the institutions developed by the working classes must no longer be looked upon as threats to liberal, capitalist society. They concluded, therefore, that it was now time to repeal those laws which had been fashioned deliberately to restrict or punish trades unions and to adopt a positive approach which would support and hasten this encouraging movement towards class reconciliation and the formation of a common culture.

Lowe rejected these arguments, but not out of hand and not without consideration and appreciation of their merits. He agreed that there was a progressive tendency in history, that the masses of men were becoming more rational, and that their concepts of self-interest were widening to include moral and ethical considerations. He stated his belief on many occasions that there was a march of civilization and mind which must improve the habits of the poor as it had already improved the habits of the aristocracy. The process that had caused the nobleman to lose some of his joy in battle and drink must gradually extend down the social ladder. He was also aware, as we have seen, that the extension of the franchise and the effects of the constantly quickening pace of technological change called for some alterations in the relationship between the state and society. He was even willing to concede that with the development of the science of statistics an inductive, sociological approach to public policy might some day replace or supplement the deductive and admittedly two-dimensional approach of political economy.

But if not a pessimist, neither was he an optimist. He thought it extremely unlikely that in the foreseeable future sociologists would be able to derive 'comprehensive generalizations' out of the 'shreds and fragments' which history has presented to us, 'mutilated, unvouched, and unauthenticated.' Perhaps the time would come when men would find a solution to this problem of finding objective evidence and be able to predict human behaviour more accurately than the classical economists, with their crude premises, had been able to do. Then, but only then, would it be wise to abandon the teachings of Adam Smith. The assumption that human beings were moved by the desire for personal gain obviously did not explain everything about behaviour. It was little help to us in foretelling how men would act in matters of politics, religion, or morals. History had demonstrated that in periods of stress or religious enthusiasm actions were controlled by a bewildering complexity of motives; but where economic behaviour was concerned, it would be wise to heed the deductive logic of the political economists and acknowledge the 'absolute supremacy of the desire of wealth and aversion from labour on which the whole science is based.' A man in love or in danger could be expected to behave in ways both strange and unaccountable, 'but once place a man's ear within the ring of pounds, shillings, and pence, and his conduct can be counted on to the greatest nicety.' If sentimental souls found that conclusion rigid and cold-hearted they should be reminded that politicians, acting by this logic, had removed the 'absurd system of bounties and drawbacks' which had retarded progress and borne so heavily on the poor. He would, Lowe wrote in 1878, prefer these achievements of the old liberalism 'to the shadowy and unrealized anticipations of the future.'[6]

He also refused to admit that a belief in evolutionary progress justified a fundamental change in liberal attitudes towards the proper relationship between the individual and the state. On the contrary. He pointed out that evidence that habits were improving was the best argument possible for excluding the state from the private affairs of individuals. He thought Joseph Chamberlain and the other 'gas and water socialists' correct in their contentions that crime was the product of the degrading conditions of the urban slums but wrong in proposing to curb vice through municipal regulation. When, for example, Chamberlain proposed to decrease the temptation of drink by closing down half the public houses in Birmingham, Lowe rushed into print with a warning that such action would infringe liberty without achieving its benevolent object. The new breed of 'progressive' liberals seemed to be in danger of forgetting, in their impatience to hurry the march of civilization, that evil habits lay outside the range of government control. Those who fashion laws aimed at eliminating drunkenness, over-population, and improvidence ignore the fact that violence, lust, and greed cannot be removed from human nature simply by removing temptations and corrupting influences from the environment. The steady improvement of habits, evidence of which Lowe was willing to concede, did not, he insisted, imply that men were losing their capacity for evil although they did indicate that men were developing their capacities to think ahead and exercise self-restraint.[7]

This combination of scepticism and optimism is also apparent in his attitude towards the working class in the later seventies. He agreed with Dilke, Mundella, and Harrison that the poor no longer constituted a separate nation within the community but had been to a large extent absorbed into a common industrial society. The revolutionary rhetoric of Chartist days seemed to have been forgotten and, for the moment, the politically active element within the working class appeared to be willing to work within the constitutional framework. He also agreed that the advance of education would tend to bring many workingmen to the realization that the interests of employers and employees were not opposed. At the same time he worried about those who drew complacent conclusions from these optimistic signs. The process of assimilation would be slow and never complete. If a sudden downturn in the economy occurred, demagogues might easily persuade the literate but still naïve masses to rebel against the inequalities inevitable in a capitalist society. Then the improvement in discipline and the advance of self-respect amongst the labouring poor might prove not a boon to the liberal society but a great menace. The progress of civilization might then make men more calculating and effective in pursuit of class objectives. After all, had the progress that had been achieved since 1832 not produced a growth in the influence of special interests? As the society became industrial and urban it became more complex and generated a host of new interests, each hostile to the general good and each warmly opposed and supported by particular groups, while the population as a whole looked on with indifference. The forces which were creating a more homogeneous culture were also creating a more pluralistic society. Provided that the economy was well managed and the legislation passed did not aggravate class feelings, this process might continue to break down classes into interest groups and tend to remove the threat of class war and socialism. But if sentimental liberalism and opportunistic conservatism were on the advance, as Lowe believed them to be, then there was danger that England would fail to pass through this transition period successfully.[8]

Because of these fears Lowe agreed to take the lead in the Commons in the early years of the Beaconsfield administration of the campaign to remove legal discrimination against unions and workingmen and worked harmoniously with men whose premises he deplored. It is clear that he did not take up this work simply for party or personal reasons. In 1873, while Gladstone was still prime minister and when Lowe had moved to the Home Office, a large number of workers gathered in Edinburgh to protest against the Criminal Law Amendment Act of 1871, a measure which had effectively prohibited picketing by making even the mildest forms of molesting subject to criminal action. The men were also protesting against the Master and Servant Act of 1867. According to that act an employee who quit his job without notice or left work unfinished could be fined or imprisoned as a criminal but an employer who broke a contract with one of his employees was subject only to a suit for damages in a civil action. When Lowe read about the demonstration he sent off a letter to Gladstone stating its importance and the need for the government to pay attention to the complaints. The Edinburgh meeting, he wrote, was a 'very serious event': it showed that the masses were 'just awakening to the consciousness of power.' He wanted the cabinet to consider ways to meet the rational objections the speakers in Edinburgh had made. Not to do so might be dangerous. The workingmen had made a logically irrefutable case that the two laws were aimed directly against only one element in the society, namely themselves. If unions were to be permanent features of the economic life of the nation, and unfortunately that seemed to be the case, then they must be encouraged to become responsible. That would never happen if class legislation goaded them into rebelliousness. If the double standard built into the Master and Servant Act is a good principle, he asked Gladstone, why restrict it to labour contracts? If a bad principle, why apply it to any contract?[9]

Gladstone agreed, but it was obvious that he was not really interested. He answered complacently that he had no objections to his Home Secretary looking thoroughly into the issues of law and principle. Indeed it might be useful. For his own part he had, he said, no fear of the labouring classes, 'were it only because the *adamantine clavi* are driven so hard into them, except the fear of being embarked against them in a bad cause.' That his government was already well embarked on a bad cause had not occurred to him before the disastrous election of 1874 and scarcely did so afterwards.[10]

As might be expected Lowe did look into the question thoroughly. In June 1875 Cross introduced his proposals to remove all breaches of contract from criminal action except in certain extreme cases and to change the conspiracy laws so that trade unions would not be penalized for acts which were not in themselves criminal. Lowe made several objections. One was to a provision which would imprison a man, in breach of contract, who refused to give security that he would return to his employer's service or who failed to pay instalments of the damages assessed against him. This, Lowe thought, was imprisonment for debt in a different guise. Also, he argued that if those employed in the vital gas and water industries ought still to be held liable to criminal charges (and he thought they should), then owners and managers of utilities should also be sent to jail if they let the lights go out or turned off the water. In general he warmly supported Cross. After hearing one of Lowe's speeches Disraeli told the queen that, now, the entire opposition would be forced to join in the chorus of commendation.[11]

But Lowe did not simply act in a supporting capacity. Cross had refused to meddle with the provision of the Criminal Law Amendment Act which affected picketing. The supporters of the trade unions, led by Lowe, pressed the government to be consistent in removing special legislation aimed at one class of society. So effective and persistent were they in the House and behind the scenes that in mid-July of 1875 the cabinet decided to give in and clear away the last obstacle to peaceful picketing.[12]

That accomplished, Lowe turned his attention during the next three years to other legal abuses. One was on a subject which had long interested him: the effects of the bankruptcy laws. In a *Fortnightly* article he asked, 'Have we abolished Imprisonment for debt?' His answer was, 'no.' Someone whose debts exceeded £30 could become a bankrupt, but the poor man whose paltry debts prevented him from joining this 'aristocracy of insolvency' could face forty days in jail without the court needing to discover whether or not the debtor had a large hungry family or a sick wife. If he had an income, then he must pay or languish in jail. Such a procedure might be a protection for the publican who extended credit to the indigent, but obviously that kind of easy credit was an inducement to improvidence and intemperance – the curses of the poor. It was remarkable, he observed, how often the law tended to 'protect the rich and powerful against the poor and the weak.' Bankruptcy was a case in point.[13]

Another abuse he sought to rectify was the dictum (which Lowe said judges fabricated out of thin air) that when an employee took a job he contracted for the risk that his fellow workmen might, through negligence, cause him injury. According to this reasoning, the worker had accepted the risk and, therefore, was not entitled to compensation. Gradually this concept of 'common employment' had been extended in the courts to cover managerial personnel to the extent that a mine or factory owner could evade liability. All he needed to do was to hire a salaried manager. Lowe thought this situation intolerable, partly because it went in the face of common sense and partly because it came about without the action or knowledge of Parliament. He demanded a select committee, took the chair, and tried to get his draft report adopted. It called for Parliament to declare that delegation of supervisory authority did not remove responsibility from the person in whom final authority rested even if the action which caused the injury was not authorized by the employer. The draft report had some pungent things to say about this being an example of how the rights of workers were being eroded away without their knowing it through the workings of legal ingenuity, exercised by judges on behalf of the wealthy. Conservatives on the committee defeated this draft eight to four. Alexander MacDonald, who had voted with Lowe, then brought in a private bill asking, substantially, for the same things. Lowe strongly supported MacDonald and was disgusted when the government's obstructive tactics buried the measure. He persisted in raising the issue whenever he could, even on the floor of the House of Lords, where he seldom spoke a word on any subject.[14]

There was no chance that his outspokenness about legal favouritism towards the rich would turn him into a popular figure. Various workingmen's associations sent appeals to him but they knew that his interest was in removing barriers to individual initiative, not in promoting collectivism. He wanted to diminish class hostilities by acts of reasonableness, not further the interests of trade unionism or redistribute the income in favour of the poor. Still, in the climate of the late 1870s this rigorous application of the doctrines of the old liberalism could seem progressive to the left and hazardous to the right.

Henry Lucy, who published a diary of his experiences in Parliament during this period, wrote, in the spring of 1875, that Lowe was proving to be the one member of the opposition who was capable of effective action. It puzzled Lucy that, despite his intelligence and effectiveness, no one believed Lowe could ever be the party leader. But before long,

Lucy discovered the answer. On the night of 21 February 1876 the House of Commons debated Disraeli's purchase of the Suez Canal shares. Lowe, Lucy noted, had swooped down on the many solecisms in the prime minister's explanation 'like a hawk on a sparrow,' but without pausing to register whether the sparrow was worth the swoop or what effect the attack would have on the House or public at large. Like the hawk, he had a 'microscopic view.' Instead of concentrating on the important questions of state policy and national security involved in this commitment in Egypt, he had selected out for special attention the £100,000 commission which Baron Rothschild would be paid for getting up the purchase price on short notice. And then, when the House began jeering, 'here was Lowe peering around the House in palpable astonishment,' wondering if, perhaps, he had upset an inkpot by mistake.[15]

This judgment, that Lowe lacked a sense of perspective, is a familiar one, but in this particular case does not do him full justice. When the Liberal leadership first learned of the purchase of the Kedive's shares, Lowe pronounced Disraeli's action a great coup. Lord Derby, who probably heard of that pronouncement, wanted to send Lowe to Egypt as the negotiating agent, a suggestion Disraeli firmly vetoed; he wanted a conciliator, not a man who 'throughout his life ... has quarrelled with everybody.' In any event, Lowe on reflection quickly changed his mind. If Disraeli were behind it then it must be fraudulent; besides, the move would have dangerous implications for future foreign policy. Most of Gladstone's former cabinet agreed but, in view of the great popularity of Disraeli's imaginative stroke, they decided not to come out directly against the purchase but, instead, be 'critically oracular.' They decided that the former chancellor of the exchequer should open up on the government after the speech from the throne, taking the familiar theme of Tory fiscal recklessness. The method, if not the fact of the purchase, was to be offered by way of illustration. Thus Lowe cannot be entirely blamed for having taken what most people thought was a niggling attitude. But having adopted what proved to be an unpopular tactic, he proceeded to make the worst possible job of it. Disraeli's spies gave warning that Lowe was to be 'awful – crushing, overwhelming: a great invective against a stock-jobbing Ministry.' Instead, Disraeli was pleased to note that the narrow, peevish speech distracted the House and the press from the more pertinent criticisms. The speech was badly received, especially in the royal household. But it was the beginning of a vitriolic and more far-reaching campaign by Lowe on Disraeli's 'forward policy,' on imperialism in general, and on the irrationalities, pretensions, and fripperies that go with empire.[16]

The theme of his anti-imperialism was the same as it had been in the sixties, only now it was full of foreboding that his earlier warnings about the excitability and bellicose propensities of democratic man were on the verge of becoming reality. He thought that Disraeli, with his day-dreams of glory, would direct the fickle attention of the public away from the increasingly serious economic questions and on to such *idola theatri* as the Suez venture had been, and he would do this in order to traffic on the weaknesses and passions of the newly enfranchised. What would begin in silly national vanity and 'ridiculous anxiety' over India would end in war; and war in the era of Bismarck meant democratic war: conscription, the military state, and the consequent loss of liberty. His utilitarian position did not allow him to claim that a moral foreign policy was always a good in itself. He conceded that plunder and tri-bute had served some material and psychological needs in the past, but he held that they had no positive value in the age of industrialism and international trade. His constant refrain from 1876 to the election of 1880 was that Disraeli's secretive, deceitful game of power politics was demonstrating that an advanced industrial nation could only lose by chasing after prestige and 'glittering exhibitions.' In the House, in jour-nals, in public speeches, in the letter page of *The Times*, he sounded the alarm so shrilly that Granville and even Gladstone worried at times whether he had not perhaps gone too far.[17]

The substance of his message in the later seventies, so often repeated, was as follows. When the Turks murdered Bulgarian civilians, Disraeli and Derby had refused to assume any responsibility. Then when the Euro-pean powers offered to settle the Balkan question by means of a com-mission, the prime minister had wrecked all hopes of concerted action. He had threatened Russia while concealing from Parliament Russia's conciliatory moves and had deliberately provoked Russia into sending her troops, unilaterally, into the Balkans. Having tricked the Russians, the other European powers, and his own people, he proceeded to trick the Turks who he had pledged to defend against a non-existent danger. He did this by making a secret deal with Russia, a deal which secured for Britain a worthless Cyprus and lasting Turkish animosity. But these enormities did not exhaust the duplicity of the Tory leader. Putting his secret treaty in his pocket, he went to Berlin pretending to negotiate fairly with the European powers. This evil deed accomplished, he con-gratulated himself for having brought back 'peace with honour,' waited until Parliament was recessed, and then made pointless war on the Afghans – jeopardizing Indian security which he was supposedly pro-tecting. On top of that he spent five million unauthorized pounds to help a reckless pro-consul wage war on the Zulus in order to capture a 'poor naked savage and thrust him into prison.' Beaconsfieldism, Lowe preached, was not even effective power politics; it was inspired by irra-tional calculations and conducted by methods so patently cynical that they defeated themselves. Ben Johnson, he told Lady Derby, had written a line which perfectly described the results of Tory Great-England-ism: 'We sit in utter darkness varied at intervals by cheats and delusions.'[18]

'If Russia is Lord Beaconsfield's "hobgoblin,"' wrote *The Times* at the height of the excitement over the Eastern Question, 'Lord Beaconsfield appears to be Mr. Lowe's.' It was true that, as in the case of his feud with Governor Gipps, Lowe had whipped himself into such a state of moral outrage that he could make no distinctions between the Devil and his works. All subtleties disappeared. Russia, he announced to a large gathering at Croyden, had become the leader of the moral world. With her England should join to liberate the oppressed people of the Balkans. Given his philosophical premises he could not advocate this course on grounds that England had any special duty to act as the guardian of the feelings of humanity – that would be Gladstonian sentimentalism. Therefore he tried by means of a dubious analogy – which greatly amused his audience – to show why England had a special responsibility in this particular case. If a man owns a vicious dog which he knows to be vicious and has the means to restrain him, then he is legally responsible if the beast bites someone. The Turk was that beast. That he was mean, destructive, devoted to idleness, wanton cruelty, and the 'grossest sensuality,' all of history has demonstrated. England became his owner when she established the policy of maintaining Turkish integrity and sticking to that policy after it was perfectly clear that the Turk was a poor watchdog to protect the rest of the world against a Russia which did not need watching in the first place. England had the means of restraining the beast's movements but instead was goading him on, or rather Disraeli was doing so, for, by the prime minister's own admission, the people and the government were utterly divided on this issue.[19]

Granville thought the speech clever but rash, and Gladstone thought it 'a misfortune not a crime.' Gladstone, who was passionately embarked on his crusade to drive the Pashas and Bimbashis, 'bag and baggage,' out of Europe, applauded the assault on the Tories but was appalled by the implications of Lowe's positive recommendations, and, in particular, by the last line of a letter to *The Times* which Lowe sent off in the wake of his Croyden speech. In that line he deplored the deprivation of the 'right of self-government, which we have, it would seem, wrung from powerful kings, but cannot wrest from Ministers, the creatures of our own creation.' This was treacherous ground. In his speech and in the letter he had stated that since the government and the people were totally at odds, since Disraeli had arrogantly chosen to ignore the popular will, since Parliament was not in session to debate and, hopefully, to repudiate that 'pest of Europe,' the 'balance of power,' the crown should call Parliament to an autumn sitting so that the voice of public opinion, expressed through elected representatives, could make itself felt. This was an extraordinary suggestion from one who had so frequently expressed fear about the influence of popular passion. It caused much raising of eyebrows. Obviously, his obsession with the hobgoblin of Beaconsfieldism had diminished his ability to square his liberalism with his reservations about democracy. Still, a certain ambivalence had always been there, even in 1867.[20]

His flirtation with jacobinism was short-lived, but his obsession with Disraeli's wickedness was not. It landed him in the last spectacular scrape of his political life, a public quarrel with the queen over her desire to be called the empress of India. That it was her desire and that her vanity was the moving force was fairly well known in leading circles, but it was a subject to be talked about with circumspection. Busy with his negotiations on the Eastern Question, Disraeli stalled her off, then in 1876 reluctantly agreed to sponsor the necessary legislation, knowing that he would have to invent some plausible reasons of state to use as arguments and knowing that the reception would be hostile. His reluctance and embarrassment probably explains why he neglected to give Hartington advance notice and why he refused to admit in the beginning that the title 'empress' was in fact the one he was seeking. His explanations were far-fetched and none more so than an argument from precedent, where he disclosed that a schoolgirl had found the queen described as empress of India in *Whitaker's Almanac*. Why should the House be made to listen to the 'lispings of the nursery?' Lowe asked in one of his many acid remarks during the debate.[21]

These and the other unfavourable reactions made by most Liberals and some Conservatives were seconded in much of the press. The proposed title sounded un-English; it smacked of Oriental despotism; it was probably meant as a gratuitous insult to the Russians. *The Times* reprinted observations made by a M. Lemoinne in the *Journal de Debate* to the effect that Disraeli had decided to play courtier to the royal fancy, despite the fact that he found the whole thing 'puerile' and a distinct embarrassment to his diplomacy. Thus, by a convenient device, the newspaper could get at the facts and at the same time disassociate itself from any direct criticism of the queen by affecting to be disapproving about foreign portrayers of malicious gossip.[22]

Lowe was aware of the conventions which surrounded the mention of royalty but in his indignation disregarded them. Twelve days before the title was proclaimed, he went up to Retford to speak on behalf of the Liberal candidate in a Nottingham by-election. He distressed the worthies on the platform by using the occasion for a diatribe, not this time against the title itself but against the way it had been shoved, by 'more than political pressure,' through Parliament. Bad though he found this action in itself he was more disturbed by 'the most painful appre-

hension that it is only the beginning of much evil,' evil which a courageous minister might have averted. This was running close to the line.
The following went clearly over it: 'The title of the Queen, I strongly
suspect, is not now brought forward for the first time. I violate no confidence because I have received none, but I am under a conviction that
at least two previous Ministers have entirely refused, although pressed
to do so, to have anything to do with a change. However, more pliant
persons have been found, and I have no doubt the thing will be done.'[23]

His flustered host tried to get reporters to suppress this passage, but
failed. Gladstone, whose devotion to the monarchy was profound and
ritualistic, read the account with the greatest pain and wrote a letter to
the *Observer*, flatly denying the implication that he had been one of the
ministers Lowe had referred to. He sent a draft to the queen with apologies for intruding her name into a public discussion. There is no reason to question his honesty or memory. In all likelihood Lowe had received his confidence from Granville, who had been approached on the
matter on several occasions by Ponsonby, the queen's private secretary.[24]

At that point nothing could be more irrelevant than the precise truth
of the charge and the denial. Disraeli saw that here was the chance to
stop all 'gossip about the Court, on any subject for a long time.' He saw
that his ancient enemy was at his mercy and must have known that, if
handled carefully, Lowe could be trusted to compound his own humiliation. The 'right occasion was,' as he reported to Ponsonby, 'rightly
seized.' Charles Lewis, an unpopular MP, called for a return of the oaths
taken by a privy councillor as a pretext for giving Lowe a dressing down
in Parliament. He used his most officious, police-court manner. His victim took the bait. Lowe snapped that he would not be put to the inqui-
sition in such an offensive way for remarks made outside the House at a
'convivial' meeting. If he were to answer for those words, he would jeopardize the freedom of speech and the integrity of Parliament – a defensive device he had used during his fracas with Alderman Macdermott, in
Sydney, thirty years earlier. On this occasion, as on the previous one,
the explanation was nearly as offensive as the act. When Disraeli rose to
speak, he sensed that the members on both sides of the House would be
gratified if Lowe were soundly punished, and the prime minister was
delighted to oblige. His voice quivering with emotion – so much so that
when he repeated the word, 'pliant, pliant,' he seemed almost to choke
– he delivered a memorable chastisement, ending with a fatal thrust: he
communicated to the House (over shouts of 'order, order!') that the
queen had personally denied Lowe's allegations.[25]

Under normal circumstances, this would have been an extremely dangerous procedure. It was indeed out of order for the prime minister to
have introduced the queen's name into a political discussion. Also, in

the heat of the moment, he had given the House the impression that Queen Victoria had never taken any initiative in the matter. It was fairly common knowledge that, in fact, she had. But there was no chance that he would be challenged or exposed, the ritual sacrifice of Lowe had made the subject taboo.[26]

Two days later, and two days too late, a chastened Lowe made a simple, forthright apology. Lord George Hamilton, who listened from the government side, wrote later that he felt sorry for him. He was not a man who knew how to bear up under that kind of pressure, but, thought Hamilton, 'for all his faults he was an intellectual of the first rank, a fearless fighter, who under his saturnine exterior had a kindly instinct, of which I had the benefit on several occasions.' Disraeli was not, at that moment at least, moved by a similar feeling of charity. He informed Lady Bradford: 'One of those occasions which rarely, and yet in a certain sense always, come to the vigilant, came to me, and I smashed that wretched Lowe.' And to Lady Chesterfield: 'He is in the mud, and there I leave him.'[27]

17

Into the Dark

After the disclosure of the Treasury scandals in 1873, the queen had placed Lowe in her outer ring of darkness, from which, after the Retford speech, he could never expect to emerge. Royal indignation deepened some months after Retford when Lowe spoke and wrote against a bill, dear to the queen's heart, to regulate, as she put it, 'the horrible, disgraceful and *unchristian* vivisection.' Lowe was particularly fond of animals and used to drive down to Caterham with his two dogs, Bow-wow and Elfin, on the back seat of the carriage, with a cat in between. However, it was essential that he support the surgeons at the University of London who had sustained him in his seat; besides, he found it absurd that the wording of the bill would penalize scientists who inflicted pain for the benefit of mankind but not touch people who caused agony to monkeys out of morbid curiosity or punish cooks who boiled lobsters alive for dinner. The queen did not appreciate the point. Nor could she be indifferent when her treasured prime minister came under such intemperate abuse during the crisis over Russia's invasion of the Turkish Balkans. She was pleased to see that the papers had begun to censure Lowe for the 'shameful vulgarity' and 'mere invective' of his foreign policy statements, and for his insinuations that the Tories were using the royal prerogative as a shield for their buccaneering. It consoled her to hear reports that Lowe was frequently becoming confused in his delivery. To make quite certain that her feelings be known, she made no secret of her resolution that if the Liberals should ever get back in she 'never could' accept Lowe or Dilke or, it went without saying, Ayrton – all men who had been personally offensive to her. When in 1880 that dreaded possibility did materialize and Gladstone came to discuss his new cabinet, she was relieved to find that he did not press the point. He gave in readily on Dilke and told her that Lowe had already been informed that he was too old to be considered. Ayrton's name, presumably, did not come up.[1]

The royal veto was a barrier which Gladstone could have removed had he stubbornly insisted. But there could be no reason why he should court unnecessary unpleasantness; he would soon need his reserves to push aside her objections to Chamberlain. Advanced age was a convenient excuse; it was also a recognition of fact. In 1879, in the middle of a speech on the war with the Zulus, Lowe's memory had suddenly broken down. His set speeches had always been written in advance and committed to memory. From his Australian days onward he had needed this crutch and never more so than in the increasingly noisy and raucous atmosphere of Parliament in the late seventies. He had experienced occasional lapses over the years but none so serious as this. He fumbled with his notes for several minutes in an attempt to recollect, while the House encouraged him with a cheer. And then abruptly he sat down. George Goschen, who had been absent, tried to be tactful when they met soon afterwards by saying, 'I hear that you suddenly fell ill yesterday in the House while you were speaking.' 'No, there was no illness,' Lowe said with a smile, 'it was only *Anno Domini*.' This did not mean that he entirely ceased to function in the House or that he stopped thinking of himself as one of the opposition leaders. He continued to speak, briefly and haltingly, until the end of the 1879 session and occasionally gave long and pungent public addresses. But it was obvious to everyone that he would no longer be a dangerous man to ignore. Also, his place would be needed if 'Chamberlain and Co' were to be accommodated and party unity preserved. If passed over, Chamberlain and Dilke could make serious trouble; Lowe could not. He knew that this was so and what that meant to his strategic position, but he was not quite seventy and still physically vigorous, so he clung to hope that past services would be remembered.[2]

In 1877, before Charles Trevelyan moved one of his many resolutions to extend household suffrage to counties, the opposition leaders met and decided to back it, with only Lowe and George Goschen in dissent. Afterwards, Harcourt overheard the old campaigner say to his recruit to the anti-democratic cause: 'Now look here, Goschen. I have a career behind me, but you have yours still to look forward to. Don't be a fool! We cannot permanently resist this movement. Go with the rest.' Goschen did not take this advice and eventually moved out of the party. As we have already seen, Lowe proceeded to carry on a running duel with Gladstone over the suffrage in the pages of the *Nineteenth Century* and the *Fortnightly*, although he did take special pains privately to make sure that the exchange did not produce a serious rift. When the subject came up again, in March 1879 – at a time when it was obvious that the Tory government was on its last legs, he spoke against a further exten-

sion of democracy but did so without his customary bite and rhetorical
flourish. His speech was brief and delivered with a quiet gravity which
surprised and moved the House and the packed gallery. Obviously he
wished to preserve his integrity without giving his party an excuse to
dump him.[3]

He behaved with the same, uncharacteristic circumspection during
the election campaign of 1880. To his University of London constituents he said that the Tories were to blame for sowing the dragon's teeth,
and that Gladstone, if mistaken in his desire to accommodate the
masses, was at least open and consistent about his objects. Lowe re-
viewed his objections to democracy and then confessed that he found
himself in a dilemma. He was, he said, 'a practical man.' He knew that if
he joined the Tories in their opposition to a county franchise bill they
would be sure to betray him once again. Therefore he must admit to being 'beaten in this matter.' He had said nothing about his decision to
surrender before the election because, 'I did not believe, knowing your
great kindness to me, that it would make any difference, and the old
Adam within me - pride - would not allow me to put it in anyone's
power to say that I had obtained your suffrage by any concessions
whatever ...'[4]

In saying that, he was making a plea not to be cast aside when the
new Liberal government took office. Northcote (now become Lord
Iddesleigh) wrote in his diary that he had heard from Disraeli about the
decision to sidetrack Lowe by making him a viscount. His conclusion
was harsh but accurate: 'Certainly his unblushing retraction of his objection to extending the County Franchise, followed by his *not* receiving
the reward of his apostasy, and crowned by his accepting a Peerage, is a
rather humiliating close to his political career. We shall have epigrams
from him, spoken as well as written, but his influence as a Statesman
has departed.'[5]

Accepting a viscountcy proved easier than getting it. Queen Victoria
made objections; a baronetcy would be 'ample,' more than that would
be 'objectionable.' Gladstone insisted. His former colleague was not a
'violently ambitious man,' but should not be insulted. He agreed that
'his mind, like his career, is peculiar.' And yet he was the oldest servant
of the crown, excepting himself, in the House of Commons, and during
those years had established two great measures: the Revised Code and
the reform of the civil service. He reminded her 'that in the year 1866
there was no person in the House of Commons who stood on the same
level as Mr. Lowe, with the single exception of Lord Beaconsfield.'
Even then it is possible that with all these blandishments (and the last
one must have come painfully), the queen might still have resisted had
Lord Beaconsfield not reminded her of Lowe's 'very abject apology' for
his Retford speech and advised her to 'forget and take no more notice

of it.' This action was impressively generous, in view of their mutual hatred, especially since Lowe had stooped to make a slur about Disraeli's Jewish background in a recent election speech.[6]

Thus on 25 May 1880 Robert Lowe became Viscount Sherbrooke. He explained his decision to his niece: he could still exercise some influence in the Lords and that was better than to withdraw from Parliament after putting the university to election expenses or to stay in the Commons and 'become a frondeur ... where I was once a leader.' While preparing for the ceremony he wrote to his brother, 'As Vespasian said when he was dying, I am beginning to become a god.' It was all very grand and expensive, he supposed, but, 'for myself, I feel very much as if I had got again into the company of the four neuter verbs of the Latin Grammar,

Vapulo – I am beaten.

Veneo – I am sold.

Exulo – I am banished.

Fio – I am done.'[7]

Gladstone tried to soften the blow by asking him to be the unpaid chief of the Civil Service Commission and got a tart refusal: if his faculties were so impaired that he could not have a place in the cabinet, then he was unfit for any other post. 'There was a time, I venture to think, when I was fit for better things. As that time has in your judgment passed by, you should I think seek for someone not so disqualified and pay him according to his deserts.' Gladstone was amused and continued to make friendly gestures. He invited him to dinner from time to time, offered him a first-class pension (politely declined), and a Grand Cross of the Bath (gratefully accepted, 'as coming from a hand from which I have received so many other kind and unlooked for favours'). These were compensations, but the bitter feelings of rejection died slowly. Approached again by Tupp with a grievance, he wrote, 'When I was in the House of Commons and could make myself disagreeable, I could do something. Now I am nothing, and no attention will be paid to me. Now I am like Giant Despair in Pilgrim's Progress, who could only grin at the people whom he once could have eaten.'[8]

For the first year or two he went regularly to the Lords but for the most part sat silently. A visit to the House of Commons shortly after his elevation led to a comic-pathetic scene. Seated in the gallery, he mechanically put on his hat as he had done for nearly thirty years. He blinked at the messenger who motioned to take it off, assuming that the man must be drunk. An Irish member, noticing the disturbance above, shouted 'Order!' His colleagues joined in, until the new peer grasped what the uproar was about, pulled off his hat, and, at the first opportunity, slipped out.[9]

Embarrassing though this scene was, it was at least a recognition that Lowe's name and presence still counted for something in the political world. The Irish MPs had reason to remember him. During the late seventies when Parnell and his supporters had seized on any opportunity to create disturbances in the House, Lowe had recommended draconic remedies. In a widely reported speech in 1877, he had urged that offenders against order have their right to speech suspended for the remainder of the session. He thought this would make no martyrs since no one would be likely to sympathize with a person who had been 'obliged to shut his mouth.' Then within the first two years after going to the House of Lords he wrote three journal articles on the subject. In them he developed the theme that the 'great degradation of the franchise,' which had at first been difficult to detect, was now becoming apparent. He thought that in the decade after 1867 the improvement of railway service and telegraph communications had brought the constituencies and their representatives closer together, gradually transforming the House of Commons into something like a city state in a decadent period. It took until the late seventies before the radical minority had worked out efficient techniques for disrupting parliamentary procedures, but they had finally learned from Tory duplicity and Parnell. American-style filibustering in a time of rapid, far-reaching publicity was now a formidable weapon which could turn 'asses into lions' and give Parnell and his Irishmen the veto which had long since been relinquished by the crown. Not entirely without satisfaction, he reminded his readers of his predictions during the reform debates that once Britain had caught the levelling disease, mild though the symptoms might be at first, there was no cure.[10]

He was, as always, prepared to suggest means of coping with this distemper. Strict closure rules would help and so would a streamlining of parliamentary procedures. First readings made sense in the days of parchment and the quill pen but not now. Third readings were also redundant, unless the Lords made substantial amendments. Why stick with 'true British tenacity' to these outmoded ways? Since the new methods of political warfare, as devastating as gunpowder had been to conventional warfare, were already being deployed, they must be met with new defences or the 'work of centuries will crumple into dust,' and if that happens, 'chaos is come again.'[11]

The endless bickering over the seating of Charles Bradlaugh seemed to him to be another vindication of his prophecies, an indication that intolerance was a probable consequence of giving power to the people. Bradlaugh, a freethinker, had been excluded because he would not say 'so help me God' when he took the oath required for admission to the House of Commons and then excluded again when he agreed to go through the motions. Lowe thought this exclusion deplorable and wrote off an article which called into question the whole process of oath taking. If an MP were required merely to swear allegiance to the sovereign, as some peacemakers had suggested, that would be absurdly superfluous. If the oath were broadened so that a man need only affirm his belief in some deity, then the 'worshipper of a star or stream' would take his seat while a philosopher 'who has lost his way in the mazes of deep thought and the shock of conflicting theories' would be turned away. No amount of unction can hold a man to his duty if he lacks a sense of duty. 'When Iago slandered away the life of Desdemona,' he asked, 'was the crime at all less because the lie was not accompanied by an oath?'[12]

These four articles, and others on bankruptcy and monetary policy, published in the *Nineteenth Century* between 1880 and 1882, have the same bite, wit, self-congratulation, exaggeration, and iconoclasm which make his unsigned articles in the *Atlas* during his Australian experience or in *The Times* during the fifties and sixties easy to identify. To us a century later they seem more relevant perhaps than they did to the comparatively few people who bothered to read them when they were written. But in the mid-eighties the almost continuous flow of journalistic opinion which had come from his pen for more than forty years came to a stop. In his mid-seventies he was rapidly losing his ability to concentrate or to see the world around him. Henry Bruce, by then Lord Aberdare, met him at the Athenaeum late in 1884 and was saddened to hear him confess that his head was no longer of much service. Bruce mentioned Lowe's collection of verses which had recently been published with the title *Poems of a Life*. These were for the most part the polemical lines he had turned out in Australia or that he had written to amuse his hostesses on country weekends. One reviewer aptly commented: 'One wants but little here by Lowe/Nor wants that little long.' But they had not been written with the higher criticism in mind, and their publication must have caused their author some embarrassment. He had no pretensions as a poet. 'Macaulay,' he once remarked, 'was not made for politics, and I was not made for literature.' He produced a copy from his pocket, gave it to Bruce, and explained that Georgiana had asked him to publish it so that she might see the volume before she died, but that she had gone into a coma just before it came from the press. Now, he said, he was alone and sad and old. Three months later Bruce saw his old friend again at the Athenaeum and this time congratulated him on his marriage to Caroline Sneyd. Bruce told his wife, 'He spoke simply about it, as of his only way of escaping utter helplessness.'[13]

Much as he depended on her total loyalty, he must often have wished for release from Georgiana's peculiarities and constant illnesses. Augustus Hare paid her a visit in the seventies and gave this sample of her amusing, obsessive chatter: 'I said to Mr. Lowe: "If you will go down-stairs with the cockatoo on your shoulder, it will fly away out of the window, and you'll lose him," but Mr. Lowe would do it, and you know he's so obstinate; and it was just as I said, and the cockatoo flew out of the staircase window and Mr. Lowe was in a fine way about him. There are a lot of boys watching for him now, and he'll come back someday, for everyone knows Mr. Lowe's cockatoo ... etc. etc. ...'[14]

Now, after nearly a half century together, she was gone, and Lowe made one more grasp at life. A cataract had grown over his one rela-tively good eye and the world which he had always seen dimly was al-most dark. He waited for the Jubilee service in 1887 and then travelled to Switzerland with his much younger wife, stopping off in Germany to consult a specialist about the feasibility of an operation. The cataract was removed but he did not regain his sight. The surgeon observed that he bore this with equanimity, as though he had submitted to please his wife and not in hope of improvement. He continued to ride his horse in Hyde Park – 'I am one of the standing dishes in rotten row,' he told his brother – and accompanied by an old servant to peddle on his Olympia tandem. Occasionally Caroline guided him through the crowds at cere-monial social gatherings, where he moved about seemingly without in-terest in what was going on about him. The couple made a last visit to the continent during the winter of 1888-9. In Rome Lowe sat for a sculptor. The American artist was struck with his 'great square lofty forehead and deep-set eyes.'

The beautifully executed marble bust now rests in a niche on an open porch of St Margaret's Church, directly across from the Parlia-ment buildings. On the porch wall is a Latin inscription, written by Lord Selborne, which reads in part:

> 'by the force of his genius,
> having attained the highest offices of the State,
> faithfully fulfilled them,
> and in the neighbouring Senate House
> of the British people
> always preferred the good of the country
> to the favour of party.'[15]

It is a pity that Lowe did not bother to write his own epitaph; it would have been less solemn and conventional. Nevertheless Selborne did manage to touch on the theme which gives Lowe's career its extra-ordinary consistency: his desire to open the offices of state to men of force and cultivated intellect and to make them the guardians of the general good in a society becoming increasingly complex and pluralistic.

Abbreviations

CO	Colonial Office
CP	Cardwell Papers, Public Record Office
DP	Delane Papers, Archives of *The Times*
EP	Ellice Papers, National Library of Scotland
GP	Gladstone Papers, British Museum
Gr.P	Granville Papers, Public Record Office
Hansard	*Parliamentary Debates*, 3rd series
Hist. Rec. of Aust.	Historical Records of Australia
HLRO	House of Lords Record Office
LP	Lowe Papers, National Record of Archives
ML	Mitchell Library, Sydney
PP	Parliamentary Papers
RA	Royal Archives, Windsor
SMH	*Sydney Morning Herald*
T	Treasury Papers

Notes

INTRODUCTION

1 James Bryce, *Studies in Contemporary Biography* (London 1903), 297-310
2 Asa Briggs, *Victorian People* (London 1954), 243-75; Ruth Knight, *Illiberal Liberal: Robert Lowe in New South Wales, 1842-1850* (Melbourne 1966). For reappraisals of the Revised Code of Education, see Christopher Duke, 'Robert Lowe – A Reappraisal,' *British Journal of Educational Studies*, XIV, 1965, 19-35, John Hurt, *Education in Evolution* (London 1971), 186-222, and D.W. Sylvester, *Robert Lowe and Education* (Cambridge 1974). In addition to Arthur P. Martin, *Life and Letters of the Right Honourable Robert Lowe, Viscount Sherbrooke*, 2 vols. (London 1892), there is a sketchy work by James Hogan, *Robert Lowe, Viscount Sherbrooke* (London 1893) which contains little additional information.
3 *The Times*, 10 Dec. 1858, 6
4 *Economist*, 14 Aug. 1869, 353-5

5 All these points are discussed more extensively and amusingly in Michael Young, *The Rise of the Meritocracy, 1870-2033* (London 1958).

CHAPTER 1

1 Robert Lowe, 'A Chapter of Autobiography' (1876), in Arthur P. Martin, *Life and Letters of the Right Honourable Robert Lowe, Viscount Sherbrooke* (London 1892), I, 5-7
2 Ibid., 7-10
3 Roundell Palmer, *Memorials*. Part I: *Family and Personal, 1766-1865* (London 1896), I, 104-6
4 Ibid.; Robert Blake, *Disraeli* (London 1966), 441; Lowe, 'Autobiography,' 10-12
5 Lowe, 'Autobiography,' 34
6 Lowe, 'The Importance of Energy in Life,' nd, LP, S
7 Martin, *Life*, I, 47-50; Adelaide Workley, *A History of Bingham* (Oxford 1954), 29, 53-4; Karl de Schweinitz, *England's Road to Social Security* (London 1943), 121-2

8 Lowe, 'Autobiography,' 14-16, 20-2; PP, 1952, vol. 22, 12-13; James Pycroft, *Oxford Memories* (London 1886), I, 160, 163

9 *The Times*, 14 June 1872, 5; Martin, *Life*, I, 88-90

10 John Mowbray, *Seventy Years at Westminster* (Edinburgh 1900), 33; Palmer, *Memorials*, I, 130-2

11 *The Times*, 11 March 1856, 9. An 'office diary' with lists of assignments for leading articles was not begun until January 1857. Benjamin Jowett, 'Lord Sherbrooke: A Personal Memoir' (1876), in Martin, *Life*, I, 482-3

12 Francis Doyle, *Reminiscences and Opinions* (London 1886), 115-16; Lowe, 'Autobiography,' 16-17

13 Ibid., 23-4

14 Ibid., 24-5; A.E. Gathorne-Hardy, ed., *Gathorne Hardy, First Earl of Cranbrooke: A Memoir* (London 1910), I, 29

15 Lowe, 'Autobiography,' 28; Asa Briggs, *Victorian People* (London 1954), 245

16 Lowe, 'Autobiography,' 28-30; Robert Lowe, 'Shall We Create a New University?' *Fortnightly Review*, XXI, 1877, 163; Hansard, 21 March 1866, vol. 182, cols. 696-9; 26 July 1877, vol. 235, cols. 1891-3; 31 May 1878, vol. 240, cols. 1045-8; 12 June 1876, vol. 229, col. 1746; 6 March 1873, vol. 214, cols. 1484-95; 26 April 1877, vol. 233, cols. 1981-2

17 Lowe to Gladstone, 21 Jan. 1854, GP, Add. MS 44301, ff 2-5, and 8 April 1854, ff6-8

18 PP, 1852, vol. 22, 72, 79; 1854, vol. 5, 296; Hansard, 29 June 1854, vol. 134, cols. 902-5

19 *The Times*, 22 Feb. 1877, 4; 26 Feb. 1877, 8; 27 Feb. 1877, 8

20 *Political Economy Club, Revised Report* (London 1876), 6-10; Adam Smith, *The Wealth of Nations* (London, Cannen ed. 1904), II, 249-60

21 Lowe, 'Autobiography,' 16-17; Lowe to R. Mitchell, 8 Aug. 1838, LP, A/3; *The Times*, 27 Sept. 1872, 6; R.T. Davidson and W. Benham, *Life of Archibald Cambell Tait* (London 1891), I, 68

22 Lowe, 'Autobiography,' 34-5

23 Martin, *Life*, I, 136, 139

24 SMH, 16 Sept. 1846

25 Lowe, 'Autobiography,' 36-7; Ruth Knight, *Illiberal Liberal: Robert Lowe in New South Wales, 1842-1850* (Melbourne 1966), 21-2

26 Lowe, 'Autobiography,' 37

CHAPTER 2

1 Georgiana Lowe to Mrs Sherbrooke, [?] Dec. 1842, LP, C/3; John Oldham and Alfred Stirling, *Victorian* (Melbourne 1934), 13-14; Lowe, 'Autobiography,' 38-40

2 Lowe, 'Autobiography,' 40-1

3 Henry Parkes, *An Emigrant's Home Letters* (Sydney 1896), 129-30; Georgiana Lowe to Mrs Sherbrooke, 28 May 1843, LP, C/16

4 Ruth Knight, *Illiberal Liberal: Robert Lowe in New South Wales, 1842-1850* (Melbourne 1966), 38-9

5 Ibid., 50-4

6 Georgiana Lowe to Mrs Sherbrooke, 8 Nov. 1843, LP, C/8; Georgiana Lowe to Agnes Lowe, 20 Nov. 1843, LP, C/9; Arthur P. Martin, *Life and Letters of the Right Honourable Robert Lowe, Viscount Sherbrooke* (London 1893), I, 187; Gipps to

Stanley, 10 Nov. 1843, *Hist. Rec. of Aust.* ser. I, vol. 23 (Sydney 1925), 613

7 Martin, *Life*, I, 193

8 A.C.V. Melbourne, *William Charles Wentworth* (Brisbane 1934), 57-9

9 Knight, *Lowe*, 26-7

10 T.H. Irving, 'The Idea of Responsible Government in New South Wales Before 1856,' *Historical Studies Australia and New Zealand*, XI, 1965, 192-205

11 Knight, *Lowe*, 27-8; Melbourne, *Wentworth*, 64-6

12 Georgiana Lowe to Mrs Sherbrooke, 8 Nov. 1843, LP, C/8

13 Knight, *Lowe*, 57-9; SMH, 7 Dec. 1843, 2

14 SMH, 2 March 1845, 2; 31 March 1845, 2; 26 April 1845, 2

15 Ibid., 31 May 1847, 2

16 Ibid., 15, 16, 21, 22 Dec. 1843; Lord Sherbrooke, 'What Shall We Do With Our Bankrupts?' *Nineteenth Century* (Aug. 1881), 315; Knight, *Lowe*, 60-1

17 SMH, 25 Jan. 1844

18 Colin Roderick, *John Knatchbull: From Quarterdeck to Gallows* (Sydney 1965), 137, 236

19 Ibid.

20 Georgiana Lowe to Mrs Sherbrooke, 28 Feb. 1844, LP, C/13

21 SMH, 25 Jan. 1844; 14 Feb. 1844, 2; *Zoist*, Oct. 1844, 313

22 *Atlas*, 15 Feb. 1845, 141; 22 Feb. 1845, 146

23 John D. Davis, *Phrenology, Fad and Science: A 19th Century American Crusade* (New Haven 1955), 3-6, 99; Robert K. Webb, *Harriet Martineau: A Radical Victorian* (London 1960), 253; J.F.C. Harrison, *Learning and Living* (Toronto 1961), 114-17. For

an example of a popular lecture see SMH, 25 May 1844, 2

24 SMH, 11, 24, 26 March 1845

25 *Atlas*, 29 March 1844, 2; 15 March 1845, 182

26 Ibid., 184; 17 Oct. 1846, 493; 8 March 1845, 171

27 Robert Lowe, *General Education Vindicated* (Sydney 1844), 3. This pamphlet contains the Report of the Select Committee and Lowe's speech on education at the School of Arts, 7 Sept. 1844. SMH, 9, 10 Oct. 1846; Knight, *Lowe*, 84, 87-90

28 [Robert Lowe] *The Articles Construed by Themselves* (Oxford 1841), 11-12; W.G. Ward, *A Few More Words in Support of No. 90 of the Tracts for the Times* (Oxford 1841); Robert Lowe, *Observations Suggested by 'A Few More Words' (by W.G. Ward) in Support of No. 90 (by J.H. Newman)* (Oxford 1841). See also Knight, *Lowe*, 18-20. Most treatises on the Oxford Movement ignore Lowe's contribution, although it does receive a brief, uncomplimentary mention in Richard W. Church, *The Oxford Movement: Twelve Years* (London 1891), 255.

29 *Atlas*, 10 May 1845, 276; 17 May 1845, 289; SMH, 10 Oct. 1846; Knight, *Lowe*, 152, 234-9

30 Knight, *Lowe*, 71-2, 85-7

31 *Atlas*, 14 Dec. 1844, 34

32 J.D. Lang Papers, ML, A 2222, vol. 2, 27-8; Knight, *Lowe*, 69-70; James Hogan, *Robert Lowe: Viscount Sherbrooke* (London 1893), 179-80; Martin, *Life*, I, 209-10

33 SMH, 4 July 1844, 3; 10 Oct. 1845, 3

34 Ibid., 4, 5 July 1844, 2; Knight, *Lowe*, 98-101

35 Knight, *Lowe*, 74-6; Martin, *Life*,

I, 220-1. James Macarthur sent the packet of letters about Broadhurst back unread. Macarthur to Lowe, 14 Aug. 1844, Macarthur Papers, ML, vol. 37, A 2933

36 J. Gordon Legge, ed., *A Selection of Supreme Court Cases in New South Wales from 1825 to 1862* (Sydney 1896), I, 236ff

37 Knight, *Lowe*, 103

CHAPTER 3

1 SMH, 21 Dec. 1843, 2; *Hist. Rec. of Aust.*, ser. I, vol. 23, 290ff; Misc. Manuscripts, ML, As 47/1

2 Ruth Knight, *Illiberal Liberal: Robert Lowe in New South Wales, 1842-1850* (Melbourne 1966), 58-86; *Hist. Rec. of Aust.*, ser. I, vol. 23 (Sydney 1925), 709

3 S.A. Donaldson to J.W. Donaldson, 18 June 1844, Donaldson Papers, ML, Ad 65/12; Georgiana Lowe to Mrs Sherbrooke, 15 Aug. 1844, LP, C/14b

4 *Atlas*, 25 Jan. 1845, 97; 1 Feb. 1845, 109; 8 Feb. 1845, 121; SMH, 28 Jan. 1846

5 Knight, *Lowe*, 74-8; SMH, 31 May 1847; Robert Lowe, *The Impending Crisis: An Address to the Colonists of New South Wales on the Proposed Land Orders* (Sydney 1847), 4

6 SMH, 20 March 1845, 2; Knight, *Lowe*, 126-30; *Atlas*, 6 June 1846, 265-6

7 Knight, *Lowe*, 227-8. The full text of the obituary can be found in James Hogan, *Robert Lowe: Viscount Sherbrooke* (London 1893), 196-209.

8 Georgiana Lowe to William Whitely, 20 July 1845, LP, C/15; *The Echo*, 22 May 1890, 2; SMH, 16 Nov. 1924; *Sunday Times* (Sydney), 1 Sept. 1907; *The Truth* (Sydney), 19 April 1925; Lovina Mundy to James Macarthur, 3 July 1854, Macarthur Papers, ML, A 2923, ff227-9

9 Hansard, 14 June 1855, vol. 138, cols. 1989-92

10 A.C.V. Melbourne, *William Charles Wentworth* (Brisbane 1934), 89-90

11 Lowe to R. Mitchell, 30 Nov. 1846, LP, C/19; Georgiana Lowe to Mrs Sherbrooke, 12 Sept. 1846, LP, C/17; *Atlas*, 9 Oct. 1847, 493

12 Lowe, *Impending Crisis*, 3-6; SMH, 21 June 1847, 14 June 1849; *Votes and Proceedings of the Legislative Council of New South Wales*, vol. 2, 513-20; SMH, 24 June 1847; *Atlas*, 9 Oct. 1847; Arthur P. Martin, *Life and Letters of the Right Honourable Robert Lowe, Viscount Sherbrooke* (London 1893), I, 347-55; Knight, *Lowe*, 171-5

13 John Ward, *Earl Grey and the Australian Colonies, 1846-1857* (Melbourne 1958), 19-23, 57-8; CO, 8 May 1857, 201/500, 289-94

14 [R. Lowe] *The Speech of Robert Lowe, Esq. Delivered at the Victoria Theatre on the 19th January, 1848* (Sydney 1848), 3; Ward, *Earl Grey*, 76-80; Knight, *Lowe*, 184-5

15 See for example Sir Alfred Stephen, Diary, Jan. 1850, ML, MSS 777/2, pts. 6-30.

16 SMH, 24 Jan. 1849; *The Times*, 31 July 1863, 6

17 Martin, *Life*, I, 358-60; Knight, *Lowe*, 194-205; G.W. Rusden, *History of Australia*, 2nd ed. (Melbourne 1897), II, 368

18 SMH, 1 Aug. 1848

19 Knight, *Lowe*, 207; Martin, *Life*, I,
371; Lowe to Parkes, 20 Jan. 1849,
Parkes Correspondence, ML, A 71,
ff15-17; SMH, 24 Jan. 1849

20 SMH, 10 Sept. 1849

21 Ward, *Earl Grey*, 200-1; *Atlas*, 17
Oct. 1846, 493; 10 Oct. 1846, 482

22 Knight, *Lowe*, 215; Angus MacKay
to Parkes, 15 March 1849, Parkes
Papers, ML, A 69, f132

23 Rusden, *History of Australia*, II,
473n; SMH, 19 June 1849

24 Martin, *Life*, I, 385-90

25 Ward, *Earl Grey*, 209-15; Hansard,
10 May 1853, vol. 127, col. 22; *The
Times*, 28 Aug. 1862, 8; 15 Dec.
1862, 8; 19 Dec. 1862, 8-9; 5 Dec.
1863, 8; 17 Dec. 1863, 8

26 SMH, 26 Sept. 1849

27 Ibid., 6, 11, 12, 13, 20 Oct. 1849;
Knight, *Lowe*, 246-8

28 Diary, Stephen Papers, ML, 777/2,
6-30; Harrison to Parkes, 22 Oct.
1875, Parkes Papers, ML, A 987,
f342

CHAPTER 4

 1 Bodelean MS, Top. oxon., c179,
f44; *The Times*, 26 Feb. 1851, 4

 2 Sir Gavin Duffy, *My Life in Two
Hemispheres* (London 1898), II,
109; Goldwin Smith, *Reminiscences*,
ed. A. Haultain (New York 1910),
312

 3 James Hogan, *Robert Lowe: Viscount Sherbrooke* (London 1893),
342-3; [W.C.M. Kent], *The Gladstone Government. Being Cabinet
Pictures by a Templar* (London
1869), 183; A.E. Helps, ed., *Correspondence of Arthur Helps* (London 1917), 329; *The Times*, 17
Sept. 1877, 7

 4 Parkes to Ellice, 9 Oct. 1855, EP,
MG 24, ser. A 2, vol. 30, f9861;
Delane to Dasent, 22 March 1856,
DP, 7/35; E.C.F. Collier, ed., *A Vic-
torian Diarist: Extracts from the
Journals of Mary, Lady Monkswell*
(London 1944), 24; Lowe to Henry
Lowe, 17 June 1835, LP, Box 1;
Percy Colson, ed., *Lord Goschen
and His Friends* (London 1946), 81

 5 G. Smith, *Reminiscences*, 310, 312;
Constance Brooks, *Antonio Panizzi*
(Manchester 1931), 146; Robert
Lowe, 'A Chapter of Autobiography,'
in Arthur P. Martin, *Life and Letters
of the Right Honourable Robert
Lowe, Viscount of Sherbrooke* (Lon-
don 1892), I, 43; Justin McCarthy,
Reminiscences (London 1871), I,
339-40; F.L. Mulhauser, *The Corre-
spondence of Arthur Hugh Clough*
(Oxford 1957), II, 592-3; Queen
Victoria, Diary, 7 Jan. and 6 March
1869, RA; *Notes and Queries*, Jan.–
June 1897, 304

 6 Ellice to Parkes, nd, Joseph Parkes
Papers, University College, London,
Box 1; Charles Dilke, Autobiographi-
cal Notes, 1878, Dilke Papers, BM,
Add. MS 43932, ff185-6; Delane to
Ellice, 30 Aug. 1861, EP, MG 24, ser.
A 2, vol. 40, ff13668-9; G. Smith,
Reminiscences, 312

 7 *The Times*, 23 March 1850, 5

 8 Parkes to Delane, 16 March 1852,
DP, interleaved binder marked
'Delane Papers, 1'

 9 *The Times*, 21 Sept. 1863, 6

10 Ibid., 12 Aug. 1865, 9

11 Edward Whitty, *St. Stephen's in the
Fifties* (London, 1906), 19; Philip
Bagenal, *Life of Ralph Bernal Osborne* (London 1884). *The Times*,
5 Jan. 1882, 11. For an example of

Osborne's artistry on the hustings, see *Manchester Guardian*, 6 Feb. 1867, 4.

12 *The Times*, 15 April 1863, 8

13 Ibid., 18 Nov. 1868, 6

14 H. Grote to Ellice, 29 July 1860, EP, MG 24, ser. A 2, vol. 39, f12924; *Proceedings of the Political Economy Club* (London 1921), IV, viii-xxi, 72-9; Walter Bagehot, *Biographical Studies* (London 1881), 352

15 Martin, *Life*, II, 1-3

16 R. Lowe, *Speech on the Australian Colonies Bill at a Meeting at the Rooms of the Society for the Reform of Colonial Government* (London 1850), 5-28

17 Parkes to Delane, 13 March 1852, DP, interleaved binder #1

18 William White, *The Inner Life of the House of Commons* (London 1897), I, 167; Hansard, 29 Nov. 1852, vol. 123, cols. 755-60; 7 Dec. 1852, vol. 123, cols. 1080-1

19 Henry Bruce, *Letters of the Rt. Hon. Henry Austin Bruce, Lord Aberdare of Duffryn* (Oxford 1902), I, 119; George Trevelyan, *The Life of John Bright* (London 1913)

20 Hansard, 13 Dec. 1852, vol. 123, cols. 1348-68; *The Times*, 14 Dec. 1852, 5

21 Hansard, 16 Dec. 1852, vol. 123, cols. 1660-1

22 Justin McCarthy, *History of Our Own Times* (London 1880), IV, 61; *Spectator*, 7 July 1866, 744; Henry Lucy, *Men and Manner in Parliament* (London 1874), 90-1; James Hogan, *Robert Lowe: Viscount Sherbrooke* (London 1893), 335-9; Robert Blake, *Disraeli* (London 1966), 344-5

23 Hansard, 2 May 1853, vol. 126, col. 966; Charles Parker, *Life and Letters of Sir James Graham 1792-1861* (London 1907), II, 205; Graham to Ellice, 2 April 1853, EP, MG 24, ser. A 2, vol. 26, ff8700-2

24 R.J. Moore, *Sir Charles Wood's Indian Policy* (Manchester 1966), 27-30; Sir William Lee Warner, *Life of the Marquis of Dalhousie* (London 1904), II, 219-23, 228

25 James B. Conacher, *The Aberdeen Coalition* (Cambridge 1968), 81-4

26 Lytton Strachey and Roger Fulford, eds., *Greville Memoirs* (London 1938), VI, 412-13; Lowe to Delane, 27 March 1853, DP, 5/14

27 Strachey and Fulford, eds., *Greville Memoirs*, VI, 413; Whitty, *St. Stephen's*, 208-10; Hansard, 23 June 1853, vol. 128, cols. 633-41; 11 July 1853, vol. 129, cols. 51-2; 15 Feb. 1858, vol. 148, cols. 1416-17; *The Times*, 4 June 1853, 6; 13 July 1853, 5

28 Hansard, 23 June 1853, vol. 128, cols. 640-1

29 *The Times*, 22 Feb. 1855, 12; Whitty, *St. Stephen's*, 244-5

30 Parker, *Graham*, II, 209; John Morley, *The Life of William Ewart Gladstone* (London 1903), I, 510. Jowett's clever work is disclosed in R.J. Moore, 'The Abolition of Patronage in the Indian Civil Service and the Closure of Haileybury College,' *Historical Journal*, VII, 1964, 246-57.

31 Moore, *Wood's Indian Policy*, 71-2; Eric Stokes, *The English Utilitarians and India* (Oxford 1959), 267; PP, 1856, vol. 25, 269

32 Hansard, 21 July 1853, vol. 129, col. 559; 25 July 1853, vol. 129, cols. 785-7

CHAPTER 5

1 *The Times*, 22 Feb. 1855, 12
2 Ibid.; Hansard, 23 Feb. 1855, vol. 136, cols. 1783-4
3 G.P. Gooch, *The Life of Lord Courtenay* (London 1920), 71; Alex Russell to Ellice, 11 Feb. 1855, EP, MG 24, ser. A 2, vol. 29, ff9706-8; Hansard, 25 May 1855, vol. 138, cols. 1222-3
4 Elcho to Grey, 28 Dec. 1880, Howick Papers, Durham; Delane to C.J. Bayley, 7 March 1854, DP, 5/72
5 [Stanley Morison], *History of The Times* (London 1935-52), II, 556. For candid appraisals of Delane, see W. O'Connor Morris, *Memories and Thoughts of a Life* (London 1900), 131-2, and Lord George Hamilton, *Parliamentary Reminiscences and Reflections* (London 1917), I, 24-9.
6 *History of The Times*, II, 166-73; memorandum by Granville, 25 Jan. 1855, Gr. P, PRO 30/29/18; Lytton Strachey and Roger Fulford, eds., *Greville Memoirs* (London 1938), VII, 115; *The Times*, 23 Feb. 1855, 6; 26 Feb. 1855, 8
7 Strachey and Fulford, eds., *Greville Memoirs*, VII; Millicent Fawcett, *Life of Sir William Molesworth* (London 1901), 334; *The Times*, 26 Feb. 1855, 8
8 Olive Anderson, *A Liberal State at War* (New York 1967), 33-69, 75-6
9 Olive Anderson, 'The Janus Face of Mid-Nineteenth Century English Radicalism: The Administrative Reform Association of 1855,' *Victorian Studies*, VIII, 1965, 232-42
10 *The Times*, 22 Feb. 1855, 12
11 G. Hogarth and M. Dickens, *The Letters of Charles Dickens* (London 1879-81), I, 392; G. Waterfield, *Layard of Nineveh* (London 1963), 265-8; Layard Papers, BM, Add. MS 39053, f6
12 *The Times*, 28 April 1855, 9; 13 June 1855, 8-9; 19 June 1855, 9
13 Ibid., 10 Aug. 1855, 6; 24 Aug. 1855, 6; *History of The Times*, II, 565; Goderich to Layard, 25 Aug. 1855, Layard Papers, Add. MS 38984, ff160-1
14 *History of The Times*, II, 264, 257
15 Strachey and Fulford, eds., *Greville Memoirs*, VII, 92; *History of The Times*, II, 260-70; John Prest, *Lord John Russell* (London 1972), 376
16 Arthur Dasent, *John Thadeus Delane* (London 1908), I, 224; Hansard, 30 April 1855, vol. 137, cols. 2022-7
17 Hansard, 25 May 1855, vol. 138, cols. 1213 passim; 25 May 1855, col. 1300
18 Layard to Gregory, 23 Feb. 1871, Layard Papers, Add. MS 38949, f86; M.E. Grant Duff, *Notes from a Diary 1889-1891* (London 1901), I, 102; Palmerston to Queen Victoria, 16 July 1855, RA, A 24/112
19 Nicholson to Cunningham, 12 Feb. 1851, Cunningham Papers, ML, A 3180; Stephen Roberts, *History of Australian Land Settlement*, 2nd ed. (Melbourne 1968), 218-22
20 *The Times*, 31 Oct. 1853, 6; Hansard, 10 May 1855, vol. 138, cols. 379-82; 17 May 1855, vol. 138, cols. 720-6; 14 June 1855, vol. 138, cols. 1989-2005; Wentworth to Macarthur, 15 July 1854, Macarthur Papers, ML, A 2923, ff236-7; Lowe to Parkes, 6 April 1853, Parkes Papers, ML, A 988, ff352-9; Nicholson to Macarthur,

21 April 1853, Macarthur Papers, A 2923, f153

21 Lowe to Stephen, 21 Oct. 1863, Correspondence of Sir Alfred Stephen, ML, ff203-6; Gavin Duffy, *My Life in Two Hemispheres* (London 1898), II, 264-5

22 *British Quarterly Review*, II, 1867, 200; Hansard, 26 April 1866, vol. 187, cols. 2156-63

23 Hansard, 16 April 1866, vol. 285, cols. 1367-9

24 SMH, 24 Jan. 1849; *The Elector: A Magazine of Politics and Literature* (Sydney 1848)

25 *The Times*, 10 Dec. 1858, 6; Alexander Barry to C. Nicholson, nd (probably the mid-1860s), Barry Papers, ML, Ab 69/4

26 A.E. Gathorne-Hardy, ed., *Gathorne Hardy, First Earl of Cranbrook: A Memoir* (London 1910), I, 128, 144; Hansard, 19 April 1865, vol. 182, col. 1673; 15 July 1867, vol. 188, col. 1613; Lowe to Henry Sherbrooke, 31 March 1860, LP, B/2; *The Times*, 4 Jan. 1860, 8; 1 March 1860, 8; 5 March 1860, 8; 21 April 1860, 9; 11 Sept. 1860, 6; 16 Feb. 1861, 8

27 *History of The Times*, II, 592; G.P. Gooch, *The Later Correspondence of Lord John Russell, 1840-1878* (London 1925), II, 213; Lowe to Macleay, nd (circa 1862), A. Macleay Papers, ML, Uncat. MS

CHAPTER 6

1 D.P. O'Brien, ed., *The Correspondence of Lord Overstone* (Cambridge 1971), II, 644-5

2 Lucy Brown, *The Board of Trade and the Free Trade Movement* (Oxford 1958), 21

3 Graham to Cardwell, 7 June 1857, CP, PRO 30/48/47; T.H. Farrer, ed., *Some Farrer Memorials* (London 1923), 67-8; Algernon West, *Contemporary Portraits* (London 1920), 81-4, 135-6

4 Hansard, 4 June 1857, vol. 145, col. 1162; Roger Prouty, *The Transformation of the Board of Trade, 1830-1855* (London 1957), 99-101

5 Arthur P. Martin, *Life and Letters of the Right Honourable Robert Lowe, Viscount Sherbrooke* (London 1892), II, 115

6 Hansard, 1 Feb. 1856, vol. 140, cols. 111-38. H.A. Shannon, in his 'The Coming of General Limited Liability,' *Economic History Review*, II, 1931, 267-91, notes that no debate followed Lowe's speech and adds, 'there could hardly be any after his speech, and the Bill passed easily.'

7 Henry Thring, *The Joint Stock Companies Act, 1856* (London 1856), 1-8; Hansard, 6 Feb. 1856, vol. 140, cols. 116-23

8 Ibid., cols. 129-31, 137-8

9 PP, 1854, vol. 27, 527-30; Charles Fairfield, *Baron Bramwell* (London 1898), 331

10 Farrer, *Memorials*, 92

11 John Clapham, *An Economic History of Modern Britain: Free Trade and Steel* (Cambridge 1932), 138-43; Hansard, 1 Feb. 1856, vol. 140, col. 138

12 Lord Denman to Granville, 14 Oct. 1855, and Lord Overstone to Granville, 1 April 1856, Gr.P, PRO 30/29/23 (pt 2). See testimony of Robert Slater, PP, 1854, vol. 27, 491.

13 Hansard, 6 Feb. 1856, vol. 140, cols. 111-38; Grey to Granville, 13 Aug. 1855, Gr.P, PRO 30/29/23, f2; *The*

Times, 2 Feb. 1856, 8; Russell to Granville, 7 Dec. 1855, Gr.P, PRO 30/29/18

14 Hansard, 26 July 1856, vol. 143, cols. 1439, 1477

15 Hansard, 4 Feb. 1856, vol. 140, cols. 160-77; Lowe to Palmerston, 3 Dec. 1855, Broadlands Papers (not indexed)

16 Edmond Fitzmaurice, *The Life of Granville George Leveson Gower, Second Earl Granville, KG, 1815-1891* (London 1905), I, 168; Martin, *Life,* II, 122

17 Hansard, 4 Feb. 1856, vol. 140, cols. 160-77, and 25 Feb. 1856, cols. 1332-8

18 Ibid., cols. 1353-4

19 Graham to Cardwell, 28 Feb. 1856, CP, PRO 30/48/47, f12; Hansard, 26 Feb. 1856, vol. 140, cols. 1353-4; Thomas Higginson, *English Statesmen* (New York 1875), 325; *The Times,* 26 Feb. 1856, 8-9; Martin, *Life,* II, 125

20 Hansard, 25 July 1856, vol. 143, cols. 1437-50

21 Graham to Cardwell, 28 Feb. 1856, CP, PRO 30/47, ff12-13

22 Parkes to Ellice, 30 Oct. 1856, EP, MG 24, ser. A 2, vol. 31, f10488; Parkes to Ellice, Jr, 15 Nov. 1856, ibid., f10507

23 *The Times,* 28 July 1856, 8

24 Ibid., 22 July 1868, 5; R. Lowe, 'The Past Session and the New Parliament,' *Edinburgh Review,* CV, 1857, 552-78

25 Lowe, 'The Past Session'; J.K. Laughton, ed., *Memoirs of the Life and Correspondence of Henry Reeve* (London 1898), I, 378

26 Lowe, 'The Past Session,' 552-8

27 Ibid., 559-62

28 Ibid., 576-7

29 Hansard, 4 June 1857, vol. 145, cols. 1137-8, 1161-73

30 PP, 1857-8, vol. 14, 620-4; confidential memo to the cabinet, 27 May 1872, Gr.P, PRO 30/29/66

31 Stanley to Canning, 18 April 1859, Canning Papers, India Office Library, no 6, letters from the Secretary of State, 1858-9, no 19

CHAPTER 7

1 Ellice to Rose, 15 July 1856, EP, MG 24, ser. A 2, vol. 31, ff10341-3

2 Arthur P. Martin, *Life and Letters of the Right Honourable Robert Lowe, Viscount Sherbrooke* (London 1892), II, 127-8

3 Ibid., 130; Lowe to Ellice, 13 Sept. 1856, EP, MG 24, ser. A 2, vol. 31, ff10397-8

4 EP, MG 24, ser. A 2, vol. 31, f10399; *Baltimore American,* 15 Sept. 1856

5 George Ticknor, *Life and Journals* (Boston 1876), II, 380

6 *New York Times,* 21 Aug. 1856, 1-2; *Toronto Globe,* 29 Aug. 1856, 2

7 Labouchere to Ellice, 27 Sept. 1856, EP, MG 24, ser. A 2, vol. 31, ff10421-3; Ellice to John Rose, 6 Oct. 1856, ibid., ff10452-3; Ellice to Labouchere, 10 Oct. 1856, Hudson's Bay Co Archives, Ottawa, A & V 2

8 Lowe to Ellice, 13 Sept. 1856, EP, MG 24, ser. A 2, vol. 31, f10398

9 Ibid., 21 Jan. 1859, vol. 36, f11993

10 Labouchere to Delane, 2 Aug. 1856, DP, 7/55

11 C.P. Stacey, *Canada and the British Army 1846-1871* (Toronto 1963), 97-101

12 Donald Kerr, 'Edmund Head, Robert Lowe, and Confederation,' *Canadian*

Historical Review, XX, 1939, 409-20;
Donald Kerr, *Sir Edmund Head*
(Toronto 1954), 150-71

13 Kerr, *Head*, 150-6
14 Joseph Pope, ed., *The Correspondence of Sir John A. Macdonald* (Toronto 1921), 133
15 Delane to Lowe, 12 June 1865, DP, 14/16; Lowe to Dasent, 13 June 1865, ibid.
16 Memo from Lowe to the Colonial Office on Wentworth's petition for federal union of Australia, 8 May 1857, CO, 201/500, ff289-94
17 Head to Lowe, 10 July 1858, DP, 9/49; *The Times*, 3 Sept. 1858, 6; 20 Sept. 1860, 8; 11 Aug. 1864, 8
18 John S. Galbraith, *The Hudson's Bay Company as an Imperial Factor* (Berkeley 1957), 331-40
19 Labouchere to Ellice, 27 Sept. 1856, EP, MG 24, ser. A 2, vol. 31, ff10421-3; Ellice to Labouchere, 30 Sept. 1856, ibid., ff10429-37
20 PP, 1857, vol. 15, 329-51; E.E. Rich, *The History of the Hudson's Bay Company 1670-1870* (London 1959), II, 773-5; Galbraith, *Hudson's Bay Co*, 341-3
21 *The Times*, 9 July 1858, 9; 10 July 1858, 8; 22 July 1858, 8; 4 Aug. 1858, 8; R. Lowe, 'The Hudson's Bay Territory,' *Edinburgh Review*, 109, 1859, 122-57
22 Ellice to Rose, 28 Dec. 1856, EP, MG 24, ser. A 2, vol. 32, f10570; Lowe to Ellice, 21 Jan. 1859, ibid., vol. 36, f11993
23 *The Times*, 26 Nov. 1858, 6; Martin, *Life*, II, 135, 137-8
24 Delane to Dasent, 31 Oct. 1856, DP, 7/77; 10 Sept. 1858, DP (not indexed); Parkes to Ellice, 29 Dec. 1856, EP, MG 24, ser. A 2, vol. 32, f10580

25 Lowe to Ellice, 26 Sept. 1861, EP, MG 24, ser. A 2, vol. 40, f13436; Lowe to Grey, 6 Dec. 1861, ibid., vol. 41, ff13607-9; Lowe to Ellice, 3 Feb. 1861, ibid., vol. 40, ff13262-4; 13 Sept. 1856, ibid., vol. 31, ff10398-9; *The Times*, 2 Dec. 1858, 6; 29 Nov. 1859, 8; 3 Nov. 1860, 6; 19 Aug. 1862, 8; 29 Sept. 1862, 6; 1 Oct. 1862, 8; 26 Jan. 1863, 8
26 *Edinburgh Review*, CIX, 1859, 122; *The Times*, 26 July 1858, 8
27 *The Times*, 26 July 1858
28 Ibid.; *Edinburgh Review*, CIX, 1859, 124-5, 141, 149-52
29 Stacey, *Canada and the British Army*, 123-8; Hansard, 23 March 1865, vol. 178, col. 150; PP, 1861, vol. 13, 312-22; *The Times*, 18 Oct. 1858, 6
30 *The Times*, 17 June 1861
31 Leslie Stephen, *The 'Times' on the American War* (London 1865), 5, 105-6
32 Delane to Dasent, 20 April 1865, DP, 14/10; *History of The Times*, II, 377-8
33 Walter to Delane, 29 Oct. 1866, DP, 24/21; Ephraim Adams, *Great Britain and the American Civil War* (New York 1958), II, 227-9
34 *The Times*, 7 Jan. 1861, 6; 12 March 1861, 6; 23 May 1861, 8; 25 Sept. 1861, 6; 7 Nov. 1861, 6; 19 Dec. 1861, 6
35 Ibid., 4 Dec. 1861, 8; Lowe to Ellice, 11 Dec. 1861, EP, MG 24, ser. A 2, vol. 41, ff13622-3; *The Times*, 13 Jan. 1862, 8; 20 Jan. 1862, 8
36 *The Times*, 1 Feb. 1862, 8; 5 Feb. 1862, 8; 30 May 1862, 8; 24 June 1862, 11; 31 July 1862, 10; 22 Aug. 1862, 6; 26 Jan. 1863, 8; 30 Jan. 1863, 6; 31 Oct. 1863, 8; 19 July 1864, 11

37 Ibid., 26 April 1862, 8; 15 Jan. 1863, 8
38 Ibid., 5 Aug. 1865, 8; 7 Nov. 1864, 6; 17 May 1864, 10
39 Ibid., 15 March 1865, 8
40 Ibid., 28 Nov. 1863, 8-9; 1 May 1865, 8
41 Martin, *Life*, II, 147
42 *The Times*, 21 Sept. 1863, 7; 12 March 1861, 9; 18 March 1861, 8; 4 July 1862, 9
43 Lowe to Ellice, 11 Dec. 1861, EP, MG 24, ser. A 2, vol. 41, f13624; *The Times*, 26 Feb. 1863, 10; 29 April 1863, 8-9; 18 June 1863, 10; 28 Sept. 1863, 6; 13 Sept. 1864, 8; 22 Nov. 1864, 6
44 Palmerston to Somerset, 26 May 1861, and Palmerston to Newcastle, 24 May 1861, Palmerston Papers, BM, Add. MS 48582, ff111-14; Palmerston to G.C. Lewis, 31 Dec. 1862, Broadlands Papers, GC/LE/249; Lucien Wolf, *Life of the First Marquis of Ripon* (London 1921), I, 200; Stacey, *Canada and the British Army*, 161-8
45 Hansard, 23 March 1865, vol. 178, cols. 148-54; 13 March 1865, vol. 177, cols. 1579-84. For samples of Lowe's sermons to Canadians on self-reliance, see *The Times*, 6 June 1862, 8; 21 June 1862, 11; 21 July 1862, 8; 29 Sept. 1862, 6; 26 Jan. 1862, 8; 29 June 1864, 10; 24 Oct. 1864, 6.
46 Hansard, 13 March 1865, vol. 177, cols. 1605-6, 1629; 23 March 1865, vol. 178, cols. 154-60, 171; Stacey, *Canada and the British Army*, 174
47 Hansard, 28 March 1867, vol. 186, cols. 757-62
48 E. Hamilton to Rogers, 22 May 1869, T 168/4, ff89, 168; David Farr, *The Colonial Office and Canada 1867-1887* (Toronto 1955), 68-9
49 Alfred Lyall, *Life of the Marquis of Dufferin and Ava* (London 1905), I, 286
50 Hansard, 13 March 1866, vol. 182, cols. 163-4
51 Parkes to Ellice, 29 Dec. 1856, EP, MG 24, ser. A 2, vol. 32, f10580

CHAPTER 8

1 Frances Gillespie, *Labor and Politics in England 1850-1867* (Durham, NC 1927), 110-30
2 *Victoria History of the Counties of England: Worcestershire* (London 1913), III (1), 165-6; John Burton, *A History of Kidderminster* (London 1890), 52, 183-4
3 *Worcestershire Chronicle*, 22 April 1857, 4; *Leeds Mercury*, 2 April 1857, 4
4 *The Times*, 31 March 1857, 9; Parkes to Delane, 13 March 1852, DP, interleaved binder marked 'Delane Papers' #1
5 See the leading article in *Berrow's Worcester Journal*, 10 March 1855, 3; *The Times*, 7 July 1852, 6; Delane to Dasent, 18 Aug. 1855, DP, 6/51; *Berrow's Worcester Journal*, 11 Aug. 1855, 8; 18 Aug. 1855, 6
6 *Worcestershire Chronicle*, 21 March 1855, 5; 15 Aug. 1855, 2; *Worcester Herald*, 5 Feb. 1857, 2
7 *Berrow's Worcester Journal*, 17 Jan. 1857; 4 April 1857, 4; *Worcester Herald*, 28 March 1857, 2
8 *Worcestershire Chronicle*, 17 Dec. 1856, 4; 22 April 1857, 2
9 *Leeds Mercury*, 24 March 1857, 4; Gillespie, *Labor and Politics*,

115-16; *The Times*, 28 March 1857, 8

10 *Berrow's Worcester Journal*, 14 March 1857, 5

11 *Worcestershire Chronicle*, 4 July 1855, 2; 15 Aug. 1855, 2

12 Ibid., 1 April 1857, 4; *Berrow's Worcester Journal*, 4 April 1857, 4; *Worcestershire Chronicle*, 1 April 1857, 4

13 *The Times*, 1 April 1857, 9

14 *Leeds Mercury*, 2 April 1857, 4; *The Times*, 31 March 1857, 9

15 *Worcestershire Chronicle*, 1 April 1857, 4; *Worcester Herald*, 4 April 1857, 2 (supplement); *The Times*, 30 March 1857, 12; 31 March 1857, 9

16 Queen Victoria to King Leopold, 31 March 1857, RA, Y 199

17 *Worcestershire Chronicle*, 15 April 1857, 2; 22 April 1857, 2; 15 July 1857, 3; 16 Dec. 1857, 4; 10 March 1858, 2; *Worcester Herald*, 25 July 1857, 2; *Worcester Journal*, 18 April 1857, 6; 25 July 1857, 3

18 Arthur P. Martin, *Life and Letters of the Right Honourable Robert Lowe, Viscount Sherbrooke* (London 1892), II, 172-3

19 *The Times*, 10 Dec. 1858, 6

20 *Worcestershire Chronicle*, 27 April 1859, 2

21 Hansard, 13 March 1866, vol. 182, col. 220; Martin, *Life*, II, 117

22 *Worcestershire Chronicle*, 4 May 1859, 3; Martin, *Life*, II, 177; Hansard, 13 March 1866, vol. 182, col. 220

23 *The Times*, 11 June 1859, 9

CHAPTER 9

1 *The Times*, 18 June 1859, 8; 22 June 1859, 8; Osbert Hewitt, *And Mr.*

Fortescue: A Selection from the Diaries from 1851 to 1867 of Chichester Fortescue (London 1958), 150; Lowe to Ellice, 26 Oct. 1860, EP, MG 24, ser. A 2, vol. 39, f13069; Lowe to Delane, 22 June 1861, DP, 10/99

2 Cole, 23 June 1859, Manuscript Diaries, Victoria and Albert Museum; Richard Redgrave, *A Memoir Compiled from his Diary*, ed. F.M. Redgrave (London 1891), 218-19

3 Sir John Simon, *English Sanitary Institutions* (London 1890), 275-8, 310-23; Arthur P. Martin, *Life and Letters of the Right Honourable Robert Lowe, Viscount Sherbrooke* (London 1892), II, 185-95; Royston Lambert, 'A Victorian National Health Service: State Vaccination 1855-71,' *Historical Journal*, V, 1962, 1-18

4 Lowe to Cole, 3 Dec. 1860, Cole Papers, Correspondence II, box 5; Lowe to Lewis, 28 Sept. 1859, Harpton Court Papers, Nat. Library of Wales, C/1983

5 *The Times*, 10 Dec. 1858, 6

6 Lambert, 'National Health Service,' 3-6; Hansard, 19 July 1859, vol. 155, cols. 14, 25

7 Ibid., cols. 13-25; Royston Lambert, *Sir John Simon* (London 1963), 277-9; Simon, *Sanitary Institutions*, 277

8 *The Times*, 4 Oct. 1865, 6; *British Medical Journal*, 7 Feb. 1874, 178

9 Hansard, 19 July 1859, vol. 155, col. 14; 10 July 1861, vol. 164, cols. 674-7

10 Martin, *Life*, II, 190

11 Lambert, 'National Health Service,' 99-100; Lambert, *Simon*, 391-3; Hansard, 14 June 1867, vol. 187, cols. 1883-5

12 Lambert, *Simon*, 414-17, 447-8, 450-3, 458-9, 513; Martin, *Life*, II, 193; *The Times*, 22 June 1877, 10

13 Winifred Burghclere, ed., *A Great Lady's Friendships: Letters to Mary, Marchioness of Salisbury Countess of Derby 1862-1890* (London 1933), 189; *The Times*, 25 May 1863, 8; Hansard, 17 June 1867, vol. 187, cols. 1996-8; *Lancet*, 15 Feb. 1868, I, 232; Lambert, *Simon*, 413-14; *Medical Mirror*, Jan. 1868

14 *The Times*, 18 Nov. 1868, 6

CHAPTER 10

1 Winifred Burghclere, ed., *A Great Lady's Friendships: Letters to Mary, Marchioness of Salisbury Countess of Derby 1862-1890* (London 1933), 149-50

2 *The Times*, 4 Nov. 1867, 8. The speech was published in an amended version as *Primary and Classical Education: An Address Delivered Before the Philosophical Institution of Edinburgh* (Edinburgh 1867).

3 *The Times*, 4 Nov. 1867, 8

4 Ibid.

5 Ibid., 24 Jan. 1868, 5. An amended version of his Liverpool speeches were published as *Middle Class and Primary Education: Two Speeches by the Rt. Hon. Robert Lowe, M.P.* (Liverpool 1868).

6 *The Times*, 24 Jan. 1868, 5

7 Ibid., 29 Oct. 1864, 5

8 Sir James Kay Shuttleworth, *Letter to Earl Granville on the Revised Code* (London 1861), 49-52. Lowe wrote a sneering rebuttal in his review of the *Letter* for *The Times*, 30 Nov. 1861, 7. *The Times*, 4 Nov. 1867, 8, and 24 Jan. 1868, 5; Lowe

to Simon, 31 Oct. 1863, LP, A/14

9 Lowe to Granville, 21 Oct. 1866, Gr. P, PRO 30/29/18; PP, 1865, vol. 28, 632-53

10 Matthew Arnold, *A French Eton*, in R.H. Super, ed., *Democratic Education* (Ann Arbor 1962), 295-6

11 Hansard, 20 July 1874, vol. 221, cols. 372-3; 7 July 1868, vol. 193, cols. 817-23; Burghclere, ed., *Great Lady's Friendships*, 168

12 *The Times*, 11 Jan. 1866, 8; 24 Jan. 1868, 6; 25 Jan. 1868, 8

13 Matthew Arnold, *Culture and Anarchy*, in R.H. Super, ed., *The Complete Prose Works of Matthew Arnold* (Ann Arbor 1965), V, 16-17, 107-9, 126-8

14 *The Times*, 24 Jan. 1868, 5

15 PP, 1865, vol. 27, 641-2; *The Times*, 24 Jan. 1868, 5; 4 Nov. 1867, 8; 29 Oct. 1864, 5

16 *The Times*, 29 Oct. 1864, 5

17 Ibid.

18 A.C. Weir, *Primary Education Considered in Relation to the State* (Edinburgh 1868), 5-14

19 *The Times*, 4 Nov. 1867, 8

20 Ibid.

21 Christopher Duke presents a strong case in support of this liberal reading of Lowe's remarks in 'Robert Lowe: A Reappraisal,' *British Journal of Educational Studies*, XIV, 1965, 30-3, as does D.W. Sylvester, *Robert Lowe and Education* (Cambridge 1974), 35-6

22 *The Times*, 29 Oct. 1864, 5

CHAPTER 11

1 Russell to Granville, 4 Jan. 1860, Gr. P. PRO 30/27/24

2 Asher Tropp, *The School Teachers* (London 1957), 63-77; Matthew Arnold, 'The Twice Revised Code,' *Fraser's Magazine* (March 1862), 360

3 PP, 1861, vol. 21 (Part 1), 157

4 Brand to Granville, 15 Jan. 1862, Gr. P, PRO 30/29/24; Granville to Palmerston, 31 Oct. 1861, Broadlands Papers, GC/GR/1889; PP, 1865, vol. 6, 55

5 Cole, MS Diaries, 9, 10, 17, 30 May 1860; Henry Cole, *The Duty of Government Towards Education, Science and Art* (London 1875), 8; Christopher Duke, 'Robert Lowe: A Reappraisal,' *British Journal of Educational Studies*, XIV, 1965, 27-8

6 PP, 1861, vol. 48, 369-84

7 *The Times*, 26 Sept. 1861, 6; Hansard, 11 July 1861, vol. 164, col. 736

8 Duke, 'Reappraisal,' 27; D.W. Sylvester, *Robert Lowe and Education* (Cambridge 1974), 49-57

9 John Hurt, *Education in Evolution* (London 1971), 43-4, 59-61, 192-3, 202; Hansard, 14 Aug. 1860, vol. 160, col. 1293; *The Times*, 25 March 1862, 9

10 Arnold's article, 'The Twice Revised Code,' was widely distributed and he followed it up with a long letter in the *Daily News*, 25 March 1862, on the 'Principle of Examination,' and an article in the *London Review*, 10 May 1862, called 'The Code Out of Danger' – all of these reprinted with explanatory notes in R.H. Super, ed., *Matthew Arnold: Democratic Education* (Ann Arbor 1962), 212-51, 347-64. Lowe wrote a sarcastic review of J. Kay Shuttleworth's *Letter to Earl Granville on the Revised Code* (London 1861) for *The Times*, 30 Nov. 1861, 7.

11 PP, 1862, vol. 41, contains a collection of memorials from critics of the Revised Code.

12 Granville to Palmerston, 11 Jan. 1862, Broadlands Papers, CG/GR/1894; Lowe to Granville, 14 Feb. 1862, Gr. P, PRO 30/29/18; *The Times*, 12 Feb. 1862, 9; Hansard, 17 Feb. 1862, vol. 165, col. 880

13 Lowe to Ellice, 30 Oct. 1861, EP, MG 24, ser. A 2, vol. 40, f13511; Lowe to Archbishop Tait, Tait Papers, Lambeth Palace Library, vol. 79, ff276-7

14 *The Times*, 26 Sept. 1861, 6; 28 Sept. 1861, 8; 2 Oct. 1861, 6; 5 Oct. 1861, 8; 28 Oct. 1861, 6; 13 Feb. 1861, 6-7; 3 March 1861, 8; 6 March 1861, 8; 8 March 1861, 9; 25 March 1861, 9; 5 May 1861, 8; 24 May 1862, 11

15 Arnold, 'The Code Out of Danger,' 251; Frank Smith, *History of Elementary Education 1760-1902* (London 1931), 254; Matthew Arnold, *The Works of Matthew Arnold* (London 1903-4), 13, 211

16 Mary Sturt, *The Education of the People* (London 1967), 260-94, makes a balanced but harsh judgment of the code and its authors; Hurt, *Education in Evolution*, 205-22, argues that the code was not a turning-point in English education and that its evil consequences have been exaggerated; Sylvester, *Lowe and Education*, 80-115, agrees with Hurt.

17 Hansard, 13 Feb. 1862, vol. 165, col. 229; 21 June 1858, vol. 151, cols. 147-50; *The Times*, 12 Nov. 1859, 8; Hansard, 15 March 1870, vol. 199, col. 2059

18 Hansard, 11 July 1861, vol. 164, col. 725; 13 Feb. 1862, vol. 165, cols. 197-8, 210; 27 March 1862, vol. 166, col. 225

19 Lowe to Brougham, 21 May 1862, Brougham Papers, University College, London

20 George Hamilton, *Parliamentary Reminiscences and Reflections* (London 1917), I, 157-8; *The Times*, 12 Nov. 1859, 8; 6 Dec. 1871, 3

21 Hurt, *Education in Evolution*, 205-6

22 Hamilton, *Reminiscences*, I, 158; Hansard, 13 Feb. 1862, vol. 165, col. 237; 5 May 1874, vol. 218, col. 1733; 31 May 1880, vol. 252, cols. 755-6

23 Lowe to Brougham, 9 and 21 May 1862, Brougham Papers

24 Hansard, 27 March 1862, vol. 166, col. 224; 5 May 1862, vol. 166, cols. 1239-43

25 Matthew Arnold, 'Mr. Walter and Schoolmasters' Certificates,' in Super, ed., *Democratic Education*, 258-61

26 PP, 1865, VI, 49-50, 53-4; Hansard, 8 March 1864, vol. 173, cols. 1659-82; PP, 1865, vol. 6, 49-50, 53-4; *The Times*, 6 Dec. 1871, 3; H. Lowry, K. Young, and W. Dunn, eds., *The Note-Books of Matthew Arnold* (Oxford 1952), 162; Sylvester, *Lowe and Education*, 58-9, thinks the 'Revised Code was above all an essay in the economics of education.'

27 Hansard, 15 July 1867, vol. 188, cols. 1540, 1549; *The Times*, 18 Nov. 1868, 6; Lowe to Parkes, 15 Aug. 1868, Parkes Papers, A 717, f31

28 Memorandum by Forster, 21 Oct. 1869, GP, Add. MS 44611, ff99-100; Lowe to Gladstone and Glad-stone to Lowe, 15 June 1870, ibid., Add. MS 44301, f148. For Lowe's statement in the House against rate-support for denominational schools see Hansard, 10 June 1870, vol. 219, cols. 1348-50; 7 July 1870, col. 1646; Sylvester, *Lowe and Education*, 116-43

29 Ibid., 15 March 1870, vol. 199, col. 2065

30 Lady Gwendolyn Cecil, *Life of the Marquis of Salisbury* (London 1921), I, 136; Hurt, *Education in Evolution*, 161-3; Hansard, 3 July 1861, vol. 164, col. 1834; PP, 1864, IX, 16-17; Hansard, 27 March 1863, vol. 170, cols. 22-4; 12 April 1864, vol. 174, cols. 908-9

31 Hansard, 12 April 1864, vol. 174, cols. 898-901; A.S. Bishop, *The Rise of a Central Authority for English Education* (Cambridge 1971), 67-77; G.E. Buckle, ed., *The Letters of Queen Victoria* (London 1926), 2nd ser., I, 171

32 Hansard, 12 April 1864, vol. 174, col. 912; William White, *The Inner Life of the House of Commons* (London 1897), II, 18-19

33 Hansard, 18 April 1864, vol. 174, cols. 1204-10; PP, 1864, vol. 9, 81; Granville to Palmerston, 26 May 1864, Broadlands Papers, GC/GR/ 1912

34 Hansard, 18 April 1864, vol. 174, cols. 1203-11; PP, 1864, vol. 9, 57

35 PP, 1865, vol. 6, 45-9; Hurt, *Education in Evolution*, 151-4; Bishop, *Central Authority*, 58-64

36 Hansard, 18 April 1864, vol. 174, cols. 1211-13, 1215-16; 13 May 1864, vol. 175, cols. 463-5; Sturt, *Education*, 257

37 Lowe to Delane, 22 June 1861, DP,

10/99; Delane to Granville, 20 April 1863, DP, 12/30; Granville to Delane, 21 April 1863, DP, 12/31; Delane to Lowe, 22 April 1863, DP, 12/33; Lowe to Delane, 22 April 1863, DP, 12/34; Cole, MS Diaries, 21 April 1864; *The Times*, 4 April 1864, 8

38 Cole, MS Diaries, 23 April 1864; Palmerston to Russell, 15 April 1864, PRO 30/22/15; Palmerston to Queen Victoria, 17 April 1864, RA, B 20/78

39 Arthur P. Martin, *Life and Letters of the Right Honourable Robert Lowe, Viscount Sherbrooke* (London 1892), II, 234; Lowe to Henry Sherbrooke, 20 April 1864, LP, B/4; Lowe to Delane, 16 April 1864, DP, 13/40 and 9 May 1864, DP, 13/45

CHAPTER 12

1 *The Times*, 3 Feb. 1864, 8

2 Lowe to Henry Sherbrooke, 22 July 1865, LP, B/5; R. Lowe, 'Criminal Law Reform,' *Edinburgh Review*, CXXI, 1865, 114-16, 131-5

3 Gladstone to Smith, 2 Aug. 1865, GP, Add. MS 44535; Brand to Palmerston, 29 July 1865, Broadlands MS, GC/BR/27; Palmerston to Brand, 3 Aug. 1865, ibid., GC/BR/32; Lowe to Cardwell, 11 Sept. 1864, CP, PRO 30/48/5/22; *The Times*, 5 Jan. 1865, 6; 23 Jan. 1865, 8; 18 Feb. 1865, 9; 20 Feb. 1865, 8; 24 April 1865, 8

4 Henry George Grey, *Parliamentary Government*, 2nd rev. ed. (London 1864), 185-282

5 *The Times*, 15 March 1859, 9; Elcho to Grey, 20 April 1860, Howick Papers, Durham

6 F.B. Smith, *The Making of the Second Reform Bill* (Cambridge 1966), 44

7 Hansard, 11 May 1864, vol. 175, col. 324; *The Times*, 31 May 1864, 8-9; 12 May 1864, 10; 31 May 1864, 11

8 Arthur P. Martin, *Life and Letters of the Right Honourable Robert Lowe, Viscount Sherbrooke* (London 1892), II, 239

9 Hansard, 3 May 1865, vol. 178, cols. 1424-5

10 Ibid., cols. 1425-7

11 Lowe's use of utilitarianism was questioned in G.C. Brodrick, *Essays on Reform* (London 1867), 5-15. Lowe answered in a review of the book in the *Quarterly Review*, July 1867, 246-50

12 Hansard, 3 May 1865, vol. 178, cols. 1427-8

13 Ibid., cols. 1426-7

14 Ibid., cols. 1432-6

15 Ibid., cols. 1439-40

16 *Pall Mall Gazette*, 8 May 1865, 4; *Daily News*, 4 May 1865, 2; Martin, *Life*, II, 265; Grey to Henry Taylor, 21 May 1864, Russell Papers, PRO 30/22/15

17 Elcho to Disraeli, 11 and 7 May 1865, Hughendon Papers, High Wycombe, B/XXI/E/120; Derby to Disraeli, (?) 1865, ibid., B/XX/5/340

18 *The Times*, 21 Oct. 1865, 8; 23 Oct. 1865, 6; 31 Oct. 1865, 8

19 D.P. O'Brien, ed., *The Correspondence of Lord Overton* (Cambridge 1971), III, 1093; Lord Torrington to Delane, 1 Nov. 1865, DP, 14/78; Abraham Hayward to Delane, 24 Oct. 1865, ibid., 14/71; Lowe to Delane, 30 Oct. 1865, ibid., 14/76; Grey to Brand, 1 Nov. 1865, Brand Papers, House of Lords Record Office, f47; Lowe to Delane, 14 Nov. 1865, DP, 14/92

20 Memorandum, 23 Oct. 1865, Russell Papers, PRO 30/22/15; memorandum, 13 Nov. 1865, Russell Papers, PRO 30/22/15; Wood to Brand, 24 Oct. 1865, Brand Papers, f41; Gladstone to Russell, 6 Dec. 1865, Russell Papers, PRO 30/22/15; Edmond Fitzmaurice, *Life of Lord Granville* (London 1905), I, 499-501; *The Times*, 15 Sept. 1865, 6; Arthur Buller to Russell, 24 Oct. 1865, Brand Papers, f43; Russell to Brand, 25 Oct. 1865, ibid., f44; Sir George Grey to Brand, 1 Nov. 1865, ibid., f47; William Gregory, *An Autobiography*, ed. Lady Gregory (London 1894), 240; Lowe to Henry Sherbrooke, 6 Dec. 1865, LP, B/9

21 Maurice Cowling, *1867: Disraeli, Gladstone and Revolution* (Cambridge 1967), 5, 85-6, 90-1; Smith, *Second Reform Bill*, 56-60, 252

22 The reference is to 1 Samuel 22 : 1-2. Hansard, 13 March 1866, vol. 182, col. 219; Delane to Osborne, 1 Feb. 1866, DP, 15/18; Martin, *Life*, II, 267-8

23 T. Wemyss Reid, *Memoirs and Correspondence of Lyon Playfair* (London 1900), 192-3, speaks of the 'indignation and contempt' which greeted the commission report. Philip Bagenal, *Life of Ralph Bernal Osborne* (London 1884), 224-5; Arvel Erickson, 'The Cattle Plague in England, 1865-7,' *Agricultural History*, XXXV, 1961, 94-103

24 Hansard, 16 Feb. 1866, vol. 181, cols. 609-21; *Spectator*, 17 Feb. 1866, 173; 24 Feb. 1866, 207-8

25 John Denison, *Notes from My Journal* (London 1899), 201-2; J. Winter, 'The Cave of Adullam and Parliamentary Reform,' *English Historical Review*, LXXXI, 1966, 48-51; *The Times*, 23 Dec. 1899, 6; Sir William Hardman, *The Hardman Papers* (London 1930), 148; Gervas Huxley, *Victorian Duke: The Life of Hugh Lupus Grosvenor, First Duke of Westminster* (London 1967), 82

26 Andrew Lang, *Life, Letters and Diaries of Sir Stafford Northcote* (Edinburgh 1890), I, 250

27 Ibid., 231-4

28 Smith, *Second Reform Bill*, 63; Hansard, 20 Feb. 1866, vol. 181, cols. 825-47; Lang, *Northcote*, I, 238; G.E. Buckle, *The Life of Benjamin Disraeli, Earl of Beaconsfield* (London 1916), IV, 428-9; *Manchester Guardian*, 10 March 1866, 2

29 Hansard, 12 March 1866, vol. 182, col. 58

30 *The Times*, 1 Feb. 1867, 10; Smith, *Second Reform Bill*, 59-69

31 William White, *The Inner Life of the House of Commons* (London 1897), II, 37-8; Hansard, 13 March 1866, vol. 182, cols. 142-7

32 Hansard, 13 April 1866, col. 1256; 13 March 1866, cols. 143-4

33 Matthew Arnold, *Culture and Anarchy*, in R.H. Super, ed., *The Complete Prose Works of Matthew Arnold* (Ann Arbor 1965), V, 108-9, 127-8; Hansard, 13 March 1866, vol. 182, cols. 156-60

34 Hansard, cols. 147-8

35 Ibid., cols. 163-4

36 *Daily News*, 10 April 1866, 3; T. Wemyss Reid, *Richard Monckton Milnes*, 2nd ed. (London 1890), II, 151

37 Gilbert Sproat, *Physical Politics of Mr. Lowe in 1867* (London 1867), 8,

criticizes the expediency of Lowe's use of expediency. *The Times*, 27 April 1866, 11; *Manchester Guardian*, 7 April 1866, 4; *Pall Mall Gazette*, 1 June 1866, 1-2; G.C. Brodrick, *Essays on Reform* (London 1867), 5, 25

38 Arnold, *Culture and Anarchy*, ed. Super, 151; Hansard, 12 April 1866, vol. 182, col. 1151; *Manchester Guardian*, 4 Jan. 1867; James Thorald Rogers, ed., *Speeches by John Bright* (London 1880), 377. See also Evan Jones, *The Life and Speeches of Joseph Cowan* (London 1886), 26-7

39 Martin, *Life*, II, 302; Lowe to Henry Sherbrooke, 8 April 1866, LP, B/14. Lowe printed the Calne and Guedalla letters and his replies in his *Speeches and Letters on Reform* (London 1867), 19-31

40 Hansard, 12 April 1866, vol. 182, cols. 1150-2; ibid., 26 April 1866, col. 2107

41 Ibid., 13 March 1866, col. 148; Reid, *Milnes*, II, 175

42 Lowe, *Speeches and Letters*, 16-17; Hansard, 26 April 1866, vol. 182, col. 2104; J. Denison, *Notes from My Journal* (London 1899), 192

43 Brand to Russell, 22 April 1866, Brand Papers, f71; memorandum from Gladstone, 22 April 1866, Brand Papers, f65; Russell to Queen Victoria, 3 May 1866, Russell Papers, PRO 30/22/16; Bertrand and Patricia Russell, *The Amberley Papers* (London 1937), I, 483

44 Hansard, 26 April 1866, vol. 182, cols. 2078-2118, 2090-2

45 Ibid., 13 April 1866, cols. 1258-63

46 Ibid., 26 April 1866, cols. 2099-2103, 2105-7

47 Ibid., cols. 2079, 2100-3, 2110-3

48 Ibid., 31 May 1866, vol. 183, col. 1629; 26 April 1866, vol. 182, col. 2105

49 *Quarterly Review*, Oct. 1867, 360-1. Abraham Hayward called these contradictions to Gladstone's attention: A. Hayward, *Correspondence of Abraham Hayward*, ed. H. Carlisle (London 1886), II, 138-9, and Gladstone made use of it: Hansard, 4 June 1866, vol. 183, cols. 1880-1.

50 Ibid., 26 April 1866, vol. 182, col. 2118

51 *The Times*, 27 April 1866, 6; Edwin Hodder, *The Life and Work of the Seventh Earl of Shaftesbury* (London 1886), III, 210; G.C. Brodrick, *Memories and Impressions* (London 1900), 222; Martin, *Life*, II, 291-2

52 *The Times*, 30 April 1866, 5; Joseph Irving, *Annals of Our Time, 1837-1871* (London 1871), 37

53 A.H. Hardinge, *The Life of ... Carnarvon* (London 1925), I, 279

54 Martin, *Life*, II, 294; Hansard, 31 May 1866, vol. 183, cols. 1625-60

55 Hansard, 31 May 1866, vol. 138, col. 1650

56 Ibid., 4 June 1866, cols. 1810-14, 1914; F.B. Smith, *Second Reform Bill*, 98-102

57 *The Day*, 25 March 1867, 6; Homersham Cox, *A History of the Reform Bills of 1866 and 1867* (London 1868), 76; A.S. Finlay and Lord E. Clinton to Gladstone, 21 June 1866, GP, Add. MS 44411, ff12-13, 48-9; John Morley, *The Life of William Ewart Gladstone* (London 1903), II, 211

58 *Manchester Guardian*, 27 June 1866, 4; Martin, *Life*, II, 294. As Cowling says, it would be interesting to know

what is omitted from Martin's 'rendering' of this letter: *1867*, 396 (note 6 for page 111).

CHAPTER 13

1 Hansard, 15 July 1867, vol. 188, cols. 1532-9

2 Ibid., 23 July 1867, cols. 1950-3

3 Ibid., col. 1950

4 Ibid., 15 July 1867, col. 1546

5 Maurice Cowling, *1867: Disraeli, Gladstone and Revolution* (Cambridge 1967), 110-11; F.B. Smith, *The Making of the Second Reform Bill* (Cambridge 1966), 122-3; Elcho to Disraeli, 21 June 1866, Hughenden Papers, B/xxi/E/120; Lowe to Delane, 28 June 1866, DP, 15/62

6 Memorandum, Derby to Disraeli, 30 June 1866, Hughenden Papers, B/xxi/E/120; Earl of Malmesbury, *Memoirs of an Ex-Minister* (London 1884), II, 357; G.E. Buckle, *The Life of Benjamin Disraeli, Earl of Beaconsfield* (London 1910-20), IV, 439-40

7 Arthur P. Martin, *Life and Letters of the Right Honourable Robert Lowe, Viscount Sherbrooke* (London 1898), II, 302, 307

8 Lowe to Delane, 12 Dec. 1866, DP, 15/164; ibid., 9 Dec. 1866, 15/161

9 Lowe to Delane, 19 Aug. 1866, DP, 15/124; Nancy Mitford, *The Stanleys of Alderley* (London 1968), 309

10 Winifred Burghclere, ed., *A Great Man's Friendship: Letters of the Duke of Wellington and Mary, Marchioness of Salisbury* (London 1927), 35-6; Lowe to Henry Sherbrooke, 7 Nov. 1865, LP, B/10; Winifred Burghclere, *A Great Lady's Friendships: Letters to Mary, Marchioness of Salisbury Countess of Derby 1862-1890* (London 1933), 82-3, 19, 126, 141, 191, 147-8

11 Burghclere, ed., *Great Lady's Friendships*, 148

12 Royden, Harrison, *Before the Socialists 1861-1881* (London 1965), 133-5; Smith, *Second Reform Bill*, 126-34; Cowling, *1867*, 253

13 Smith, *Second Reform Bill*, 14; Cowling, *1867*, 251; Martin, *Life*, II, 308

14 Burghclere, ed., *Great Lady's Friendships*, 80; Lowe to Delane, 29 Aug. 1866, DP, 15/124

15 Lowe to Delane, 22 and 26 Dec. 1866, DP 15/169

16 For detailed accounts of these complicated events, here crudely summarized, see Cowling, *1867*, 137-65, and Smith, *Second Reform Bill*, 134-64.

17 James Winter, 'The Cave of Adullam and Parliamentary Reform,' *English Historical Review*, XXXI, 1966, 45-9

18 Russell to Gladstone, 15 April 1867, GP, Add. MS 44293, ff257-8; Gladstone to Russell, 19 April 1867, ibid., f261

19 Cowling, *1867*, 202-16; Burghclere, ed., *Great Lady's Friendships*, 143

20 *Manchester Guardian*, 23 Feb. 1867, 4; John Denison, *Notes from My Journal* (London 1899), 202-3; Clarendon to Gladstone, 13 Feb. 1867, GP, Add. MS 44133

21 Gladstone to Brand, 30 Oct. 1866, Brand Papers, f111; Lowe to Gladstone, 21 March 1867, GP, Add. MS 44301, ff23-5; Gwendolyn Cecil, *Life of the Marquis of Salisbury* (London 1921), I, 244-5

22 Lowe to Gladstone, 17 Oct. 1877,

GP, Add. MS 44302; R. Lowe, 'A New Reform Bill,' *Fortnightly Review*, 1 Oct. 1877, 437-52; W. Gladstone, 'The County Franchise and Mr. Lowe Thereon,' *Nineteenth Century*, Nov. 1877, 537-60; R. Lowe, 'Mr. Gladstone on Manhood Suffrage,' *Fortnightly Review*, 1 Dec. 1877, 733-46; W. Gladstone, 'Last Words on the County Franchise,' *Nineteenth Century*, Jan. 1878, 196-208. George Potter wrote a commentary on this controversy, 'The Labourer and the Vote,' *Nineteenth Century*, Jan. 1878, 53-70

23 *Nineteenth Century*, Nov. 1877, 538-9

24 *Fortnightly*, 1 Dec. 1877, 736-45

25 Lowe to Delane, 9 Sept. 1867, DP, 16/100; *Day*, 2 April 1867, 4; *The Times*, 17 July 1867, 8; Louis Fagan, ed., *Letters of Prosper Merimée to Panizzi* (London 1881), II, 249

26 Hansard, 5 July 1867, vol. 188, cols. 1116, 1102-7

27 Ibid., 15 July 1867, cols. 1540, 1548, 1611-13; Burghclere, ed., *Great Lady's Friendships*, 103, 155

28 Martin, *Life*, II, 325; *The Times*, 18 Nov. 1868, 6; Burghclere, ed., *Great Lady's Friendships*, 126

CHAPTER 14

1 Winifred Burghclere, ed., *A Great Lady's Friendships: Letters to Mary, Marchioness of Salisbury Countess of Derby 1862-1890* (London 1933), 140, 142, 146; *The Times*, 16 Sept. 1867, 8; 25 Nov. 1867, 8-9; Hansard, 26 Nov. 1867, vol. 190, cols. 193-206; Reginald Wilberforce, *The Life of Samuel Wilberforce* (London 1882), III, 271

2 Burghclere, ed., *Great Lady's Friendships*, 197

3 Ibid., 195-6; Arthur P. Martin, *Life and Letters of the Right Honourable Robert Lowe, Viscount Sherbrooke* (London 1892), II, 357

4 Winifred Burghclere, ed., *A Great Man's Friendship: Letters of the Duke of Wellington and Mary, Marchioness of Salisbury* (London 1927), 36

5 Martin, *Life*, II, 358; memorandum by Cole, 6 Feb. 1869, Cole Correspondence, 2, Box 5

6 *Economist*, 12 Dec. 1868, 1409-10; W. McCullagh Torrens, *Twenty Years in Parliament* (London 1893), 94; Ellice to Delane, 10 Dec. 1868, DP, 17/97; Rivers Wilson, *Chapters From My Official Life* (London 1916), 38

7 R. Lowe, 'Mr. Gladstone's Financial Statements,' *The Home and Foreign Review*, Jan. 1864, 1-18

8 Ibid.

9 Gladstone to Lowe, 26 Dec. 1868, GP, Add. MS 44301, ff5-6; *The Times*, 22 Dec. 1868, 4

10 G.C. Brodrick, *Memories and Impressions* (London 1900), 240-1; *The Times*, 28 Jan. 1869, 7

11 Agatha Ramm, ed., *The Political Correspondence of Mr. Gladstone and Lord Granville 1868-1876* (London 1952), I, 407

12 Hamilton to Hennessey, 22 Jan. 1869, T 168/4, f56; *The Times*, 5 Sept. 1873, 3; Gladstone to Granville, 9 Sept. 1873, Gr. P, PRO 30/29/29A; Hansard, 8 March 1869, vol. 194, col. 852

13 H. Lucy, *Men and Manner in Parlia-*

ment (London 1874), 10-11; *The Times*, 9 March 1869, 9; George Hamilton, *Parliamentary Reminiscences and Reflections* (London 1917), I, 32-4; memoranda by Ayrton and Lowe, 2 Feb. 1869, T 186/4, f61; Hamilton to Gladstone, 6 July 1869, ibid., ff111-12; Philip Guedalla, *The Queen and Mr. Gladstone* (London 1933), I, 145-6; *Illustrated London News*, 7 Aug. 1869, 134; 3 July 1869, 10; Gladstone to Lowe, 3 Aug. 1869, GP, Add. MS 44537; Layard to Gregory, 2 Feb. 1870, Layard Papers, Add. MS 38984, f15; 23 April 1870, ibid., f34; 12 Sept. 1870, ibid., f63; 7 Dec. 1870, ibid., f71; 23 Feb. 1871, ibid., ff86-7; 13 June 1872, ibid., f108; Queen Victoria, Journal, 10 Nov. 1869, RA, f292; 11 Nov. 1869, ibid., f293

14 Arthur Ponsonby, *Henry Ponsonby* (London 1942), 179; Lowe to Gladstone, 24 July 1871, GP, Add. MS 44301, ff195-8; Ayrton to Gladstone, 2 Aug. 1871, ibid., f176; Lingen to Ayrton, 23 June 1871, T 26/6, ff191-3, and 24 June 1871, ibid., ff193-4; Gladstone to Ayrton, 10 Aug. 1871, GP, Add. MS 44540, ff84-5; Gladstone to Lowe, ibid., f85-6

15 Arthur Street, *Memoir of George Edmund Street, R.A.* (London 1888), 143-68; Queen Victoria, Journal, 6 March 1869, RA

16 Minute on the Wellington Monument, 27 March 1871, T 26/6, ff117-19; Lingen to Ayrton, 28 March 1871, ibid., ff111-12; Stansfeld to Ayrton, 17 Dec. 1870, ibid., ff17-18; Lingen to Ayrton, 29 May 1871, ibid., f174; Gladstone to

Lowe, 3 April 1871, ibid.; Wilson, *Official Life*, 283-5

17 Cole MS Diaries, 15, 16 March, 9 April, 1, 25, 26 June 1869, 8 Jan. 1870, 16 Jan., 10 Feb. 1871; Lowe to Cole, 16 March 1869, Cole Correspondence, 2, Box 5; Lowe to de Grey, 10 Jan. 1871, Ripon Papers, BM, Add. MS 43532; Hansard, 28 April 1871, vol. 205, cols. 1863-6; Leslie Stephen, *Life of Henry Fawcett* (London 1885), 312-21; Hansard, 8 July 1870, vol. 202, cols. 1760-6; Herbert Maxwell, *Life and Times of the Rt. Hon. William Henry Smith* (Edinburgh 1893), I, 204-5

18 *The Times*, 17 Sept. 1872, 6; Delane to Dasent, 25 Aug. 1869, DP, 18/58; Walter to Delane, 17 March 1869, DP, 24/53; Burghclere, ed., *Great Lady's Friendships*, 220-1; Wilson, *Official Life*, 31-2, 40-2

19 *The Times*, 27 Sept. 1872, 6

20 Lowe to Cardwell, 25 Dec. 1868, CP, PRO 30/48/22, f7; Lowe to Granville, 22 Dec. 1868, Gr. P, PRO 30/29/22A

21 Clarendon to Gladstone, 21 Sept. 1869, Bodleian MSS, Clar. dep. C 501, ff68-9; 21 Oct. 1869, ibid., f88; 17 Oct. 1869, ibid., f90; 23 Oct. 1869, ibid., f97; 29 Oct. 1869, ibid., ff100-1; Clarendon to Gladstone, 29 Oct. 1869, GP, Add. MS 44134, ff87-8; 27 Feb. 1870, ibid., f157-8; Gladstone to Clarendon, 28 Feb. 1870, ibid., f159

22 F. Latour Tomline [Gilbert] and Gilbert A'Beckett (A writer for *Punch* who may have collaborated), *The Happy Land* (London 1873)

23 Ibid., 13-14

24 *The Times*, 6 March 1873, 10; 8

March 1873, 11; 9 March 1873, 9;
10 March 1873, 9; 11 March 1873,
11; E.P. Lawrence, '"The Happy
Land": W.S. Gilbert as Political
Satirist,' *Victorian Studies*, XV,
1971, 161-4, 172-5
25 Martin, *Life*, II, 363
26 Hansard, 8 April 1869, vol. 195,
cols. 363-5, 373
27 Ibid., cols. 363-73
28 Ibid., cols. 379-85; 12 April 1869,
col. 629; B.E.V. Sabine, *A History
of the Income Tax* (London 1966),
169
29 William White, *The Inner Life of
the House of Commons* (London
1897), 148; Burghclere, ed., *Great
Lady's Friendships*, 223. Lowe probably borrowed ideas for the repeal
of taxes on insurance, locomotion,
and corn from R. Dudley Baxter,
*The Taxation of the United King-
dom* (London 1869), 11-162. He
acknowledged his debt ('I have
closely followed your advice, a fact
which out of kindness to you I conceal') in a letter to Baxter, printed
in Mary Baxter, *In Memorium: R.
Dudley Baxter* (London 1878), 69.
The best treatment of the budgets
of 1869 and 1870 is in Sydney Buxton, *Finance and Politics* (London
1888), II, 77-109.
30 *The Times*, 8 April 1869, 7; *Economist*, 10 April 1869, 409-12; 29 May
1869, 621-2; Hansard, 12 April
1869, vol. 195, col. 626. The five
quarter scheme did cause some confusion; Lowe tried to clear it up in
a letter to *The Times*, 12 June 1869,
12, and to the *Pall Mall Gazette*, reprinted in *The Times*, 24 Dec. 1869, 7.
31 Hansard, 11 April 1870, vol. 200,
cols. 1644, 1646

32 Ramm, ed., *Political Correspondence*, 58-61
33 R. Lowe, 'What Shall We Do For
Ireland?' *Quarterly Review*, CXXIV,
1868, 284-6; *The Times*, 25 March
1867, 8; 6 Nov. 1866, 6-7; Hansard,
27 Feb. 1865, vol. 177, cols. 766-75
34 Hansard, 2 April 1868, vol. 191, cols.
729-47
35 Ibid., 17 May 1866, vol. 183, cols.
1077-97; 12 March 1868, vol. 190,
cols. 1483-1502, 1516-26
36 Lowe to Granville, 1 Jan. 1870, GP,
Add. MS 44167, f2; Lowe to Cardwell, 18 Oct. 1869, CP, PRO 30/48/
22, f37; 24 Dec. 1869, ibid., ff51-2;
5 Jan. 1870, ibid., f61; Burghclere,
ed., *Great Lady's Friendships*, 231
37 Lowe, Cabinet memorandum, 11
Oct. 1869, GP, Add. MS 44301,
ff86-92; Gladstone to Lowe, 12 Oct.
1869, GP, Add. MS 44301, ff95-6;
Lowe to Granville, 16 May 1869,
Gr. P, PRO 30/29/66; 21 Dec. 1868,
23, 29 Dec. 1869, ibid.; Ramm, ed.,
Political Correspondence, I, 63-6,
79-85
38 Noel Annan, 'The Intellectual Aristocracy,' in J.H. Plumb, ed., *Studies in
Social History* (London 1955), 247;
D.W. Sylvester, *Robert Lowe and
Education* (Cambridge 1974), 36,
thinks that Lowe's civil service reforms 'sounded the death knoll of
the old class system.'
39 Maurice Wright, *Treasury Control of
the Civil Service 1854-1874* (Oxford
1969), 74-80
40 Ibid.
41 Lowe to Gladstone, 10 Nov. 1869, GP,
Add. MS 44501, f104; Gladstone to
Lowe, 22 Nov. 1869, ibid., ff106-7
42 Wright, *Treasury Control*, 98; PP,
1873, vol. 7, 672

43 PP, 1873, vol. 7, 665; *The Times*, 17 Sept. 1870, 5

44 PP, 1875, vol. 23, 159; PP, 1873, vol. 7, 672; Hansard, 9 April 1869, vol. 195, col. 488

45 PP, 1873, vol. 7, 605-8, 666-8; Farrer to Northcote, 25 July 1873, Iddesleigh Papers, BM, Add. MS 50039, ff74-7; Wright, *Treasury Control*, 81-95

46 PP, 1873, vol. 7, 420, 662-3; Lowe to Gladstone, 27 May 1873, GP, Add. MS 44302, ff125-6; Lowe to Granville, 5 Dec. 1870, Gr. P, PRO 30/29/66; Gladstone to Lowe, 5 and 6 Dec. 1870, ibid.; Granville to Lowe, 19 Jan. 1871, ibid.; Lord Hammond to Layard, 14 June 1870, Layard Papers, Add. MS 38954, f77

47 Asa Briggs, *Victorian People* (London 1954), 274

48 Martin, *Life*, II, 381

CHAPTER 15

1 A.E. Gathorne-Hardy, ed., *Gathorne Hardy, The First Earl of Cranbrooke: A Memoir* (London 1910), I, 296

2 Sydney Buxton, *Finance and Politics* (London 1888), 117-61

3 Georgina Battiscombe, *Mrs. Gladstone* (London 1956), 148; Hamilton, Diary, 7 Sept. 1880, Hamilton Papers, BM, Add. MS 48630

4 G.E. Buckle, *The Life of Benjamin Disraeli, Earl of Beaconsfield* (London 1910-20), V, 131; Lowe to Cardwell, 31 July 1870, CP, PRO 30/48/22, f97; Granville to Gladstone, 31 July 1870, GP, Add. MS 44167, f96

5 Winifred Burghclere, ed., *A Great Lady's Friendships: Letters to Mary, Marchioness of Salisbury Countess of Derby 1862-1890* (London 1933), 275-7, 289-90; *The Times*, 17 Sept. 1870, 5; Lowe to Cardwell, 19 Oct. 1870, CP, PRO 30/48/22, f103; ibid., ff58-9; 20 Dec. 1870, ibid., ff121-4; Lowe to Granville, 27 Oct. 1870, Gr. P, PRO 30/29/66; 1 Sept. 1870, ibid.; Lowe to Gladstone, 21 Dec. 1870, GP, Add. MS 44538; 3 Sept. 1870, Add. MS 44301, ff152-3

6 Burghclere, ed., *Friendships*, 292; Lowe to Gladstone, 20 Dec. 1870, GP, Add. MS 44301, ff64-7

7 Hansard, 11 April 1870, vol. 200, cols. 1638-9

8 W.S. Jevons, *The Match Tax: A Problem in Finance* (London 1871), 1-60

9 Hansard, 20 April 1871, vol. 205, cols. 1414-16

10 John Kimberley, *Journal of Events During the Gladstone Ministry*, ed. E. Drus (London 1958), 22; Gladstone to Lowe, 11 April 1871, GP, Add. MS 44539; A. Tilney Bassett, *Gladstone to his Wife* (London 1936), 186

11 *The Times*, 24 April 1871, 12; 25 April 1871, 10; Hansard, 24 April 1871, vol. 205, cols. 1652, 1632, 1622

12 Hansard, 25 April 1871, vol. 205, col. 1685; 27 April 1871, vol. 205, cols. 1774-7; Gladstone to Lowe, 24 April 1871, GP, Add. MS 44539; Queen Victoria, Journal, 25 April 1871, RA, ff102-3; ibid., 30 April 1871, f106

13 Lowe to Gladstone, 26 Dec. 1870, GP, Add. MS 44301, ff170-3; 30 March 1871, ibid., f187; 20 Nov. 1872, Add. MS 44619, ff107-8

14 Hansard, 20 April 1871, vol. 205, cols. 1412-14, 1416-18

15 Buxton, *Finance*, 122-5; Hansard, 22 March 1859, vol. 152, cols. 1143-4

16 Hansard, 20 April 1871, vol. 205, cols. 1409-10

17 Ibid., 27 April 1871, cols. 1780-3; 1 May 1871, col. 1951; Gathorne-Hardy, *Gathorne Hardy*, I, 298; Henry Fawcett, 'The Present Position of the Government,' *Fortnightly Review*, X, 1871, 548-50; Queen Victoria, Journal, 27 April 1871, RA, f104; Robert Wilson, *The Life and Times of Queen Victoria* (London 1887-8), II, 397-8

18 *Economist*, 22 April 1871, 465-7; 30 March 1872, 383; 12 April 1873, 433. See the letter from the railwayman, Samuel Laing, *The Times*, 1 May 1871, 12, and the speeches in Parliament, Hansard, 20 April 1871, vol. 205, cols. 1419-20, 1447, 1450; 24 April 1871, vol. 205, cols. 1623-4.

19 Hansard, 20 April 1871, cols. 1391-1400; 25 March 1872, vol. 210, cols. 618-19; 28 April 1873, vol. 215, cols. 1052-3

20 Ibid., 25 March 1872, vol. 210, cols. 612-13; 24 April 1873, vol. 215, col. 922; 9 May 1871, vol. 206, cols. 1452-67; 8 June 1875, vol. 224, col. 1544; *Economist*, 20 May 1871, 595; 10 June 1871, 682

21 *Fortnightly Review*, X, 1871, 550; Lowe to Granville, 30 Aug. 1871, Gr. P, PRO 30/29/66

22 Delane to Dasent, 16 Feb. 1872, DP, 20/62

23 Lucien Wolf, *Life of the First Marquis of Ripon* (London 1921), I, 246-7

24 Ibid., 256; Lowe to Granville, 30 Jan. 1872, and Granville to Lowe, 7 Sept. 1872, Gr. P, PRO 30/26/66;

Agatha Ramm, ed., *The Political Correspondence of Mr. Gladstone and Lord Grenville 1868-1876* (London 1952), I, 27-8, II, 312; Lowe to Gladstone, 6 April 1872, GP, Add. MS 44302, ff35-9; Lowe to Gladstone, 12 April 1872, ibid., f46; Arthur P. Martin, *Life and Letters of the Right Honourable Robert Lowe Viscount Sherbrooke* (London 1892), II, 411

25 Hansard, 7 April 1873, vol. 215, cols. 675-6; *The Times*, 27 Sept. 1872, 6

26 Ramm, *Political Correspondence*, II, 358; Lowe to Granville, 30 Oct. 1872, Gr. P, PRO 30/29/66; Hansard, 7 April 1873, vol. 215, cols. 663-4

27 *The Wasted Session of 1873* (London 1874), 4-15

28 Henry Roseveare, *The Treasury* (London 1969), 138-42; A.J.V. Durell, *Parliamentary Grants* (London 1917), 243-9

29 PP, 1873, vol. 7, 674-6, 668; ibid., 1875, vol. 23, 160

30 *The Times*, 27 Sept. 1872, 6

31 Hamilton to Stansfeld, 21 Oct. 1869, Hamilton Papers, T 168/4, f156; Lowe to Granville, 5 Nov. 1872, Gr. P, PRO 30/29/66

32 F.E. Baines, *Forty Years at the Post Office* (London 1895), I, 181-2, II, 3-24; J.C. Hemmeon, *History of the British Post Office* (Cambridge, Mass. 1912), 202-9; H.R. Meyer, *The British State Telegraphs* (New York 1907), 36-55, 74, 81; F. Scudamore, *The Day Dreams of a Sleepless Man* (London 1875); Buxton, *Finance*, 49-52; Herbert Maxwell, *Life and Times of the Rt. Hon. William Henry Smith* (Edinburgh 1893), I, 306-8; Scudamore to Glad-

stone, 24 July 1872, GP, Add. MS
44434, ff289-302; Gladstone to
Monsell, 1 March 1873, Add. MS
44542, ff93-4; Gladstone to Lowe,
25 March 1872, Add. MS 44541;
PP, 1873, vol. 7, 139, 217, 252. See
also the speech by Monsell, Hansard,
29 July 1873, vol. 217, cols. 1212-
14.

33 PP, 1873, vol. 7. The second report,
135-9, gives a summary of the affair.
Lowe's testimony is on 217-22, and
Scudamore's memorandum is on
252-5.

34 Hansard, 21 March 1873, vol. 214,
cols. 2056-9

35 *The Times*, 22 March 1863, 9; *Economist*, 26 July 1873, 899; Northcote to Chetwynd, 14 Sept. 1874,
Iddesleigh Papers, Add. MS 50052,
ff42-3

36 Gladstone to Queen Victoria, 27
July 1873, RA, A 46/46; Hansard,
29 July 1873, vol. 217, cols. 1189-
1229; memorandum by Granville,
(?) July 1873, GP, Add. MS 44641,
f173; Brand Diary, 29 July 1873,
Brand Papers

37 *The Times*, 15 July 1872, 9; Hansard, 12 Feb. 1872, vol. 209, cols.
209-10; memorandum by Lowe,
(?) Nov. 1871, GP, Add. MS 44617,
ff132-4; Granville to Gladstone, 16
Sept. 1872, GP, Add. MS 44169, f80;
Lowe to Gladstone, 29 Sept. 1872,
GP, Add. MS 44302, f65; Gladstone
to Granville, 17 April 1873, Gr. P,
PRO 30/29/62; PP, 1873, vol. 9,
359-60, 362, 278

38 Gladstone to Lowe, 26 Sept. 1872,
GP, Add. MS 44542, ff13-14; Lowe
to Gladstone, 28 Oct. 1872, GP,
Add. MS 44302, f80; memorandum
from Lowe, (?) 1872, GP, Add. MS

44302, f82; Gladstone to Lowe, 29
Oct. 1872, GP, Add. MS 44542, f30

39 PP, 1868-9, vol. 6, 331-2; *The Times*,
20 June 1873, 9; Hansard, 12 March
1869, vol. 194, cols. 1305-7; memorandum by Wilson to Gladstone, nd,
GP, Add. MS 44439, ff242-3; Lowe
to Gladstone, 12 Aug. 1872, GP,
Add. MS 44302, ff61-2; Gladstone
to Lowe, 22 Oct. 1872, GP, Add.
MS 44542; Cardwell to Gladstone,
22 Nov. 1871, GP, Add. MS 44119,
f285; Lord Wolverton to Gladstone,
10 Oct. 1873, GP, Add. MS 44348,
ff301-2

40 Lowe to Gladstone, 28 Oct. 1872,
GP, Add. MS 44302, f80; Gladstone
to Lowe, 29 Oct. 1872, GP, Add. MS
44542, f30

41 *The Times*, 28 Aug. 1872, 7; 31 Aug.
1872, 7; 17 Feb. 1873, 5; Kimberley,
Journal, ed. Drus, 39; Gladstone to
Lowe, 25 March 1873, GP, Add. MS
44542, f102; Lowe to Gladstone, 26
March 1873, GP, Add. MS 44302,
f119; W. Rathbone to Gladstone, 13
June 1873, GP, Add. MS 44439,
ff33-6; Holms to Gladstone, 13 June
1873, GP, Add. MS 44439, ff27-8

42 PP, 1873, vol. 9, 235-43. Lowe's
testimony is on pages 359-80.

43 Hansard, 9 June 1873, vol. 216, cols.
686, 711; 19 June 1873, cols. 1198-
1206; Lowe to Gladstone, 27 July
1873, GP, Add. MS 44302, f133;
Gladstone to Lowe, 28 July 1873,
GP, Add. MS 44542, f144

44 *The Times*, 30 July 1873, 9; PP,
1873, vol. 9; 363-4, 370, 372-3, 369;
PP, 1873, vol. 7, 218, 222-4; Hansard,
29 July 1873, vol. 217, cols. 1216-
17, 1221

45 Wilson to Hamilton, 12 Aug. 1873,
Hamilton Papers, Add. MS 48622

46 Hansard, 28 July 1873, vol. 217, cols. 1122-6; 30 July 1874, vol. 217, cols. 1259-70

47 Lowe to Gladstone, 26 Feb. 1873, GP, Add. MS 44302, ff113-14; S. Boys-Smith, 'The Relation Between the British Treasury and the Departments of the Central Government in the 19th Century' (unpublished MA thesis, University of British Columbia, 1967), 176-9

48 G. Buckle, ed., Letters of Queen Victoria (London 1926-8), II, 273; Baxter to Gladstone, 2 Aug. 1873, GP, Add. MS 44439, ff250-3; Gladstone to Baxter, 5 Aug. 1873, GP, Add. MS 44439, f256; Gladstone to Cardwell, 2 Aug. 1873, GP, Add. MS 44119, f112; Gladstone to Wolverton, 1 Nov. 1873, GP, Add. MS 44348, f313; Gladstone to Lowe, 4 Aug. 1873, GP, Add. MS 44302, ff141-2

49 Kimberley, Journal, 40-1; Gladstone to Queen Victoria, 27 July 1873, RA, 46/46; Gladstone to Ayrton, 6 Aug. 1873, GP, Add. MS 44439, f274; Charles Whibley, Lord John Manners (Edinburgh 1925), II, 163

50 Lowe to Gladstone, 4 Aug. 1873, GP, Add. MS 44302, ff137-8; Philip Guedalla, The Queen and Mr. Gladstone (London 1933), I, 372-3, 424-6

51 Gladstone to Lowe, 13 Aug. 1873, GP, Add. MS 44302, ff144-5

52 Lowe to Gladstone, 14 Aug. 1873, GP, Add. MS 44302, ff147-8; Gladstone to Granville, 14 Aug. 1873, GP, Add. MS 44542, f151

53 Ramm, ed., Political Correspondence, II, 390, 407; Liddell to Hamilton, 14 Sept. 1873, Hamilton Papers, Add. MS 48622; Lowe to Gladstone, 25 Nov. 1873, GP, Add. MS 44302, ff153-6; ibid., 29 Nov. 1873, ff157-60; ibid., 11 Dec. 1873, ff167-80; ibid., 3 Jan. 1874, f181; ibid., 17 Feb. 1874, ff186-7; Gladstone to Lowe, 4 Dec., 9 Dec. 1873, 1 Jan. 1874, GP, Add. MS 44543; The Times, 5 Sept. 1873, 3

54 The Times, 4 Feb. 1874, 5; Joseph Irving, Annals of Our Time, 1837-1871 (London 1871), 151

55 Gathorne-Hardy, ed., Gathorne Hardy, I, 336; The Times, 4 Feb. 1874; Martin, Life, II, 371

56 Martin, Life, 410-11

57 Economist, 16 Aug. 1873, 989-90

CHAPTER 16

1 Arthur P. Martin, Life and Letters of the Right Honourable Robert Lowe, Viscount Sherbrooke (London 1892), II, 400-1, 423-30; The Times, 19 May 1875, 8

2 Lowe to Tupp, 3 Dec. 1874, 17 May and 29 Aug. 1875, Bodleian MS, Eng. lett. d148

3 Paul Smith, Disraelian Conservatism and Social Reform (London 1967), 198-206

4 The Times, 6 Dec. 1871, 3; Lowe to Gladstone, 29 Nov. 1871, GP, Add. MS 44302, ff225-6; Gladstone to Lowe, 30 Nov. 1871, ibid., ff227-8; Hansard, 26 April 1866, vol. 182, col. 2078; Algernon West, Private Diaries of Sir Algernon West (New York 1922), 68

5 Gareth Jones, Outcast London (Oxford 1971), 1-10

6 R. Lowe, 'Recent Attacks on Political Economy,' 19th Century, IV, 1878, 858-68

7 R. Lowe, 'The Birmingham Plan for

Public-House Reform,' *Fortnightly Review*, XXI, 1877, 8-9; *The Times*, 16 Dec. 1872, 7

8 *The Times*, 16 Dec. 1872, 7

9 B.C. Roberts, *The Trades Union Congress* (London 1958), 88; W.H.G. Armytage, *A.J. Mundella* (London 1951), 145; Lowe to Gladstone, 29 Aug. 1873, GP, Add. MS 44302, ff151-2

10 Gladstone to Lowe, 3 Sept. 1873, GP, Add. MS 44542, f170

11 Hansard, 28 June 1875, vol. 225, cols. 658-64; G.E. Buckle, *The Life of Benjamin Disraeli, Earl of Beaconsfield* (London 1910-20), V, 372

12 P. Smith, *Conservatism*, 216-17; Hansard, 12 July 1875, vol. 225, cols. 1341-3, 1347

13 R. Lowe, 'Birmingham Plan,' 21, 1877, 307-16

14 PP, 1877, vol. 10, 558-63; Hansard, 10 April 1878, vol. 239, cols. 1066-7; 26 April 1880, vol. 256, cols. 68-9; Charles Fairfield, *Baron Bramwell* (London 1898), 335-8. Lowe wrote two public letters on the subject: *The Times*, 19 April 1878, 8; 17 Jan. 1880, 11.

15 H. Lucy, *A Diary of Two Parliaments* (London 1886), I, 71, 127-30

16 Buckle, *Disraeli*, V, 454, 458; Granville to Bright, 31 Dec. 1875, Bright Papers, Add. MS 43387, f104; Agatha Ramm, ed., *The Political Correspondence of Mr. Gladstone and Lord Granville 1868-1876* (London 1952), II, 475; Hansard, 21 Feb. 1876, vol. 227, cols. 566-72

17 R. Lowe, 'Imperialism,' *Fortnightly Review*, XXIV, 1878, 453-65

18 *The Times*, 14 Nov. 1876, 4; 15 Nov. 1876, 6; 5 Nov. 1879, 6; 25 March 1880, 7; R. Lowe, 'The Docility of

an Imperial Parliament,' *19th Century*, VII, 1880, 562-5; Burghclere, *Friendships*, 471

19 *The Times*, 14 Sept. 1876, 10

20 Ramm, *Political Correspondence of Mr. Gladstone and Lord Granville 1876-1886* (Oxford 1962), I, 8-9; *The Times*, 14 Sept. 1876, 10

21 L.A. Knight, 'The Royal Titles Act and India,' *Historical Journal*, XI, 1968, 488-9; Hansard, 23 March 1876, vol. 228, col. 515

22 *The Times*, 18 March 1876, 7; 28 March 1876, 5

23 Ibid., 20 April 1876, 4

24 Buckle, *Disraeli*, V, 477; L. Knight, 'Royal Titles,' 489; Gladstone to Ponsonby, 21 April 1876, RA, F 17/22, 23

25 Disraeli to Ponsonby, 3 May 1876, RA, F 17/41; H. Lucy, *Men and Manner in Parliament* (London 1874), 186; Hansard, 2 May 1876, vol. 228, cols. 2033-7

26 Ponsonby to Queen Victoria, 5 May 1876, RA, F 17/48

27 George Hamilton, *Parliamentary Reminiscences and Reflections* (London 1917), I, 105-6; Hansard, 2 May 1876, vol. 228, cols. 2023-7; 4 May 1876, vol. 229, cols. 52-3; Brand, Diary, 2, 3 May 1876, Brand, Papers, HLRO; Buckle, *Disraeli*, VI, 478-9

CHAPTER 17

1 Hansard, 9 Aug. 1876, vol. 231, cols. 915-19; A.H. Hardinge, *The Life of ... Carnarvon* (London 1925), II, 103-10; G.E. Buckle, ed., *The Letters of Queen Victoria* (London 1926-8), III, 48; Queen Victoria, Journal, 2 Aug. 1878, RA, ff48-9

2 Arthur P. Martin, *Life and Letters of the Right Honourable Robert Lowe, Viscount Sherbrooke* (London 1892), II, 447-8; Roy Jenkins, *Sir Charles Dilke*, rev. ed. (London 1965), 126

3 R.D. Elliot, *The Life of George Joachim Goschen, First Viscount Goschen, 1831-1907* (London 1911), I, 162-3; Martin, *Life*, II, 447-8; Hansard, 4 March 1879, vol. 244, cols. 209-14; H. Lucy, *A Diary of Two Parliaments* (London 1886), 467-9

4 *The Times*, 7 April 1880, 6

5 Iddesleigh, Diary, Iddesleigh Papers, Add. MS 50063 A, f326

6 Philip Guedalla, *The Queen and Mr. Gladstone* (London 1933), II, 91-2; memorandum by Queen Victoria, RA, C 34/65; Trevor Lloyd, *The General Election of 1880* (Oxford 1968), 106-7

7 Lowe to Henry Sherbrooke, 2 May 1880, LP, B/23; Charles Fairfield, *Baron Bramwell* (London 1898), 338; Martin, *Life*, II, 449

8 Lowe to Gladstone, 13 May 1880, GP, Add. MS 44302, ff198-9; Lowe to Gladstone, 11 June 1885, ibid., f211; Martin, *Life*, II, 458

9 Lucy, *Two Parliaments*, II, 468-9

10 *The Times*, 25 Oct. 1877, 8; Lord Sherbrooke, 'Obstruction or "Clôture,"' *19th Century*, VIII, 1880, 515-22; 'Business in the House of Commons,' ibid., IX, 1881, 732-6; 'The Cloture and the Tories,' ibid., XI, 1882, 149-56

11 Ibid.

12 Lord Sherbrooke, 'Parliamentary Oaths,' ibid., XII, 1882, 313-20

13 Henry Bruce, *Letters of ... Austin Bruce, Lord Aberdare of Duffryn* (Oxford 1902), II, 191; Martin, *Life*, II, 452; *Poems of a Life* (London 1885)

14 Augustus Hare, *The Story of My Life* (London 1900), IV, 401-2

15 Martin, *Life*, II, 469-70; Sherbrooke to Henry Sherbrooke, 14 Nov. 1882, LP, B/29 b; M. Ezekiel to Lady Sherbrooke, 27 Feb. 1889, LP, D/11

Bibliography

The Lowe Papers, privately owned and presently kept at the National Register of Archives in London, are, for the most part, remnants left over by A.P. Martin after he finished his commissioned official life in 1892. They do contain a number of interesting letters, written by Lowe's wife during their years in New South Wales. The letters to and from Lowe himself add little to what is already known, although they do provide evidence that Martin did a great deal of heavy editing. Because these papers are scanty, it has been necessary to piece together a coherent account of Lowe's life from letters scattered through a great many manuscript collections. Three collections have been particularly useful: the Delane Papers in *The Times* Archives, the Ellice Papers, and the Gladstone Papers. The correspondence between Lowe and Lady Salisbury, edited by Winifred Burghclere and published under the title *A Great Lady's Friendships*, gives by far the best insights into the workings of Lowe's mind and heart.

Much use has been made of Lowe's editorials in *The Times*. Before 1857 identification of authorship is difficult, although occasionally Delane or his assistant editor, Dasent, will mention in their correspondence specific leading articles and their authors. After 1857, however, positive identification can be made from an office diary. The Delane Papers show that Lowe would not be dictated to about the general line he should follow in his contributions; therefore, the positions he takes can, I believe, be accepted as his own, or at least not opposed to his private judgment.

I have depended heavily on Ruth Knight's recent account of Lowe's career in Australia. My account does not differ in any important respect from her interpretation; what it does do is extend the examination of Lowe's connections with Australia after he returned to England in 1850.

Two excellent accounts of the Reform bills of 1866 and 1867, one by Maurice Cowling and the other by F.B. Smith, appeared while I was preparing the biography. I decided, therefore, to concentrate on Lowe's part in those events and not to attempt yet another full-scale examination of that significant constitutional change.

MANUSCRIPT SOURCES

Barry Papers, Mitchell Library, Sydney
Bodleian Manuscripts, Oxford
Brand Papers, House of Lords Record Office
Bright Papers, British Museum
Broadlands Papers, National Register of Archives, London
Brougham Papers, University College, London
Canning Papers, India Office Library
Cardwell Papers, Public Record Office
Henry Cole Diaries, Victoria and Albert Museum
Colonial Office Records, Public Record Office
Cunningham Papers, Mitchell Library, Sydney
Delane Papers, *The Times* Archives
Dilke Papers, British Museum
Donaldson Papers, Mitchell Library, Sydney
Ellice Papers, National Library of Scotland (references to copy in National Archives, Ottawa)
Gladstone Papers, British Museum
Granville Papers, Public Record Office
Hamilton Papers, British Museum
Harpton Court Papers, National Library of Wales
Howick Papers, Durham
Hudson's Bay Company Archives, National Archives, Ottawa
Hughenden Papers, High Wycombe
Iddesleigh Papers, British Museum
Lang Papers, Mitchell Library, Sydney
Layard Papers, British Museum
Lowe Papers, National Register of Archives, London
Macarthur Papers, Mitchell Library, Sydney
Macleay Papers, Mitchell Library, Sydney
Miscellaneous Manuscripts, Mitchell Library, Sydney
Palmerston Papers, British Museum
Parkes (Henry) Papers, Mitchell Library, Sydney
Parkes (Joseph) Papers, University College, London
Ripon Papers, British Museum
Royal Archives, Windsor
Russell Papers, Public Record Office
Stephen Papers, Mitchell Library, Sydney
Tait Papers, Lambeth Palace Library

OFFICIAL PAPERS

Hansard's Parliamentary Debates, 3rd series
Parliamentary Papers

*Votes and Proceedings of the Legislative Council
    of New South Wales*

NEWSPAPERS AND JOURNALS

Atlas
Baltimore American
Berrow's Worcester Journal
British Medical Journal
British Quarterly Review
Daily News
Economist
Illustrated London News
Lancet
Leeds Mercury
London Review
Manchester Guardian
Medical Mirror
New York Times
Notes and Queries
Pall Mall Gazette
Spectator
Sunday Times, Sydney
Sydney Morning Herald
The Day
The Echo
The Elector: A Magazine of Politics and Literature, Sydney
The Times
The Truth, Sydney
Toronto Globe
Worcestershire Chronicle
Worcester Herald
Zoist

CONTEMPORARY BOOKS, PAMPHLETS, AND ARTICLES

Arnold, Matthew, 'The Code Out of Danger,' in R.H. Super, ed., *Democratic Education*. Ann Arbor 1962
- *Culture and Anarchy*, in R.H. Super, ed., *The Complete Prose Works of Matthew Arnold*. Vol. 5. Ann Arbor 1965
- *A French Eton*, in R.H. Super, ed., *Democratic Education*. Ann Arbor 1962
- 'Mr. Walter and Schoolmasters' Certificates,' in R.H. Super, ed., *Democratic Education*. Ann Arbor 1962
- 'The Twice Revised Code,' *Fraser's Magazine*, March 1862, 347-65

- *The Works of Matthew Arnold.* 15 vols. London 1903-4
Bagehot, Walter, *Biographical Studies.* London 1881
Bagenal, Philip, *Life of Ralph Bernal Osborne.* London 1884
Baines, F.E., *Forty Years at the Post Office.* London 1895
Baxter, Mary, *In Memoriam: R. Dudley Baxter.* London 1878
Baxter, R. Dudley, *The Taxation of the United Kingdom.* London 1869
Brodrick, G.C., *Essays on Reform.* London 1867
- *Memories and Impressions.* London 1900
Bruce, Henry, *Letters of the Rt. Hon. Henry Austin Bruce, Lord Aberdare of Duffryn.* 2 vols. Oxford 1902
Buckle, G.E., ed., *The Letters of Queen Victoria.* 2nd series, 3 vols. London 1926-8
Burghclere, Winifred, ed., *A Great Lady's Friendships: Letters to Mary, Marchioness of Salisbury Countess of Derby 1862-1890.* London 1933
- *A Great Man's Friendship: Letters of the Duke of Wellington and Mary, Marchioness of Salisbury.* London 1927
Burton, John, *A History of Kidderminster.* London 1890
Buxton, Sydney, *Finance and Politics.* 2 vols. London 1888
Church, Richard W., *The Oxford Movement: Twelve Years.* London 1891
Cole, Henry, *The Duty of Government Towards Education, Science and Art.* London 1875
Collier, E.C.F., ed., *A Victorian Diarist: Extracts from the Journals of Mary, Lady Monkswell.* London 1944
Cox, Homersham, *A History of the Reform Bills of 1866 and 1867.* London 1868
Davidson, R.T. and W. Benham, *Life of Archibald Campbell Tait.* 2 vols. London 1891
Denison, John, *Notes from My Journal.* London 1899
Doyle, Francis, *Reminiscences and Opinions.* London 1886
Duff, M.E. Grant, *Notes from a Diary 1889-1891.* 2 vols. London 1901
Duffy, Sir Gavin, *My Life in Two Hemispheres.* 2 vols. London 1898
Fagan, Louis, ed., *Letters of Prosper Merimée to Panizzi.* 2 vols. London 1881
Fairfield, Charles, *Baron Bramwell.* London 1898
Farrer, T.H., ed., *Some Farrer Memorials.* London 1923
Fawcett, Henry, 'The Present Position of the Government,' *Fortnightly Review*, X, 1871, 544-58
Gathorne-Hardy, A.E., ed., *Gathorne Hardy, First Earl of Cranbrook: A Memoir.* 2 vols. London 1910
[Gilbert, W.S.], F. Latour Tomline and Gilbert A'Beckett, *The Happy Land.* London 1873
Gladstone, W.E., 'The County Franchise and Mr. Lowe Thereon,' *Nineteenth Century*, Nov. 1877, 537-60
- 'Last Words on the County Franchise,' *Nineteenth Century*, Jan. 1878, 196-208
Gooch, G.P., *The Later Correspondence of Lord John Russell, 1840-1878.* 2 vols. London 1925

Gregory, William, *An Autobiography*. Ed. Lady Gregory. London 1894

Grey, Henry George, *Parliamentary Government*. 2nd rev. ed. London 1864

Hardinge, A.H., *The Life of Henry Howard Molyneux Herbert, Fourth Earl of Carnarvon, 1831-1890*. 3 vols. London 1925

Hare, Augustus, *The Story of My Life*. 6 vols. London 1896-1900

Hayward, Abraham, *Correspondence of Abraham Hayward*. Ed. H. Carlisle. 2 vols. London 1886

Helps, A.E., ed., *Correspondence of Arthur Helps*. London 1917

Hewitt, Osbert, *And Mr. Fortescue: A Selection from the Diaries from 1851 to 1867 of Chichester Fortescue*. London 1958

Higginson, Thomas, *English Statesmen*. New York 1875

Hodder, Edwin, *The Life and Work of the Seventh Earl of Shaftesbury*. 3 vols. London 1886

Hogan, James, *Robert Lowe: Viscount Sherbrooke*. London 1893

Hogarth, G. and M. Dickens, *The Letters of Charles Dickens*. 2 vols. London 1879-81

Irving, Joseph, *Annals of Our Time, 1837-1871*. London 1871

Jevons, W.S., *The Match Tax: A Problem in Finance*. London 1871

Jones, Evan, *The Life and Speeches of Joseph Cowen*. London 1886

Jowett, Benjamin, 'Lord Sherbrooke, A Personal Memoire,' in A.P. Martin, *Life and Letters of the Right Honourable Robert Lowe, Viscount Sherbrooke*. London 1892, II, 482-500

[Kent, W.C.M.], *The Gladstone Government: Being Cabinet Pictures by a Templar*. London 1869

Kimberley, John, *Journal of Events During the Gladstone Ministry*. Ed. E. Drus. London 1958

Lang, Andrew, *Life, Letters and Diaries of Sir Stafford Northcote*. 2 vols. Edinburgh 1890

Laughton, J.K., ed., *Memoirs of the Life and Correspondence of Henry Reeve*. 2 vols. London 1898

Legge, J. Gordon, ed., *A Selection of Supreme Court Cases in New South Wales from 1825 to 1862*. 2 vols. Sydney 1896

Lowe, Robert, *The Articles Construed By Themselves*. Oxford 1841

– 'The Birmingham Plan for Public-House Reform,' *Fortnightly Review*, XXI, 1877, 1-9

– 'Business in the House of Commons,' *Nineteenth Century*, IX, 1881, 727-36

– 'A Chapter of Autobiography,' 1876, in A.P. Martin, *Life and Letters of the Right Honourable Robert Lowe, Viscount Sherbrooke*. London 1892, I, 3-43

– 'The Docility of an Imperial Parliament,' *Nineteenth Century*, VII, 1880, 557-66

– *General Education Vindicated*. Sydney 1844

– 'Have We Abolished Imprisonment for Debt?' *Fortnightly Review*, XXI, 1877, 307-16

– *The Impending Crisis: An Address to the Colonists of New South Wales, on the Proposed Land Orders*. Sydney 1847

- 'Imperialism,' *Fortnightly Review*, XXIV, 1878, 453-65
- *Middle Class and Primary Education: Two Speeches by the Rt. Hon. Robert Lowe, MP.* Liverpool 1868
- 'Mr. Gladstone on Manhood Suffrage,' *Fortnightly Review*, XXII, 1877, 733-46
- 'A New Reform Bill,' *Fortnightly Review*, XXII, 1877, 437-52
- *Observations Suggested by 'A Few More Words' (by W.G. Ward) in Support of No. 90 (by J.H. Newman).* Oxford 1841
- *Primary and Classical Education: An Address Delivered Before the Philosphical Institution of Edinburgh.* Edinburgh 1867
- 'Recent Attacks on Political Economy,' *Nineteenth Century*, IV, 1878, 858-68
- 'Shall We Create a New University?' *Fortnightly Review*, XXI, 1877, 160-71
- *Speeches and Letters on Reform.* London 1867
- *The Speech of Robert Lowe, Esq. Delivered at the Victoria Theatre on the 19th January, 1848.* Sydney 1848
- *Speech on the Australian Colonies Bill at a Meeting at the Rooms of the Society for the Reform of Colonial Government.* London 1850
- 'The Value to the United Kingdom of the Foreign Dominions of the Crown,' *Fortnightly Review*, XXII, 1877, 618-30
[Lowe, Robert], 'Criminal Law Reform,' *Edinburgh Review*, CXXI, 1865, 109-36
- 'The Hudson's Bay Territory,' *Edinburgh Review*, CIX, 1859, 122-56
- 'Mr. Gladstone's Financial Statements,' *The Home and Foreign Review*, Jan. 1864, 1-18
- 'The Past Session and the New Parliament,' *Edinburgh Review*, CV, 1857, 552-78
- 'What Shall We Do for Ireland?' *Quarterly Review*, CXXIV, 1868, 255-86
Lowe, Robert, Lord Sherbrooke, 'The Cloture and the Tories,' *Nineteenth Century*, XI, 1881, 149-56
- 'Obstruction or "Clôture,"' *Nineteenth Century*, VIII, 1880, 513-25
- 'Parliamentary Oaths,' *Nineteenth Century*, XII, 1882, 313-20
- *Poems of a Life.* London 1885
- 'What Shall We Do With Our Bankrupts?' *Nineteenth Century*, X, 1881, 308-16
Lowry, K., K. Young, and W. Dunn, eds., *The Notebooks of Matthew Arnold.* Oxford 1952
Lucy, H., *A Diary of Two Parliaments.* 2 vols. London 1886
- *Men and Manner in Parliament.* London 1874
Malmsbury, Earl of, *Memoirs of an Ex-Minister.* 2 vols. London 1884
Martin, Arthur P., *Life and Letters of the Right Honourable Robert Lowe, Viscount Sherbrooke.* 2 vols. London 1892
Maxwell, Herbert, *Life and Times of the Rt. Hon. William Henry Smith.* 2 vols. Edinburgh 1893
McCarthy, Justin, *History of Our Own Times.* 4 vols. London 1879, 1880
- *Reminiscences.* 2 vols. London 1871
Morley, John, *The Life of William Ewart Gladstone.* 3 vols. London 1903
Morris, W. O'Connor, *Memories and Thoughts of a Life.* London 1900
Mowbray, John, *Seventy Years at Westminster.* Edinburgh 1900

O'Brien, D.P., ed., *The Correspondence of Lord Overstone.* 3 vols. Cambridge 1971

Palmer, Roundell, *Memorials.* 4 vols. London 1896-8

Parker, Charles, *Life and Letters of Sir James Graham 1792-1861.* 2 vols. London 1907

Parkes, Henry, *An Emigrant's Home Letters.* Sydney 1896

Political Economy Club, Revised Report. London 1876

Pope, Joseph, ed., *The Correspondence of Sir John A. Macdonald.* Toronto 1921

Potter, George, 'The Labourer and the Vote,' *Nineteenth Century*, Jan. 1878, 53-70

Proceedings of the Political Economy Club, vol. VI. London 1921

Pycroft, James, *Oxford Memories.* 2 vols. London 1886

Ramm, Agatha, ed., *The Political Correspondence of Mr. Gladstone and Lord Granville 1868-1876.* Camden Third Series, vols. 81, 82. London 1952

- *The Political Correspondence of Mr. Gladstone and Lord Granville 1876-1886.* 2 vols. Oxford 1962

Redgrave, F.M., ed., *Richard Redgrave: A Memoir Compiled from his Diary.* London 1891

Reid, T. Wemyss, *Memoirs and Correspondence of Lyon Playfair.* London 1900

- *Richard Monckton Milnes.* 2nd ed. 2 vols. London 1890

Rogers, James Thorold, ed., *Speeches by John Bright.* London 1880

Rusden, G.W., *History of Australia.* 2nd ed. 3 vols. Melbourne 1897

Scudamore, Frank, *The Day Dreams of a Sleepless Man.* London 1875

Shuttleworth, Sir James Kay, *Letter to Earl Granville on the Revised Code.* London 1861

Simon, Sir John, *English Sanitary Institutions.* London 1890

Smith, Adam, *The Wealth of Nations.* 2 vols. Camden ed. London 1904

Smith, Goldwyn, *Reminiscences.* Ed. A. Haultain. New York 1910

Sproat, Gilbert, *Physical Politics of Mr. Lowe in 1867.* London 1867

Stephen, Leslie, *Life of Henry Fawcett.* London 1885

- *The 'Times' on the American War.* London 1865

Strachey, Lytton and Roger Fulford, eds., *The Greville Memoirs.* 8 vols. London 1938

Street, Arthur, *Memoirs of George Edmund Street, R.A.* London 1888

The Wasted Session of 1873. London 1874

Ticknor, George, *Life and Journals.* 2 vols. Boston 1876

Torrens, W. McCullagh, *Twenty Years in Parliament.* London 1893

Ward, W.G., *A Few More Words in Support of No. 90 of the Tracts for the Times.* Oxford 1841

Warner, Sir William Lee, *Life of the Marquis of Dalhousie.* 2 vols. London 1904

Weir, A.C., *Primary Education Considered in Relation to the State.* Edinburgh 1868

West, Algernon, *Private Diaries of Sir Algernon West.* New York 1922

White, William, *The Inner Life of the House of Commons.* 2 vols. London 1897

Wilberforce, Reginald, *The Life of Samuel Wilberforce.* 3 vols. London 1882

Wilson, Rivers, *Chapters from My Official Life.* London 1916

Wilson, Robert, *The Life and Times of Queen Victoria.* 2 vols. London 1887-8

SECONDARY AUTHORITIES

Adams, Ephraim, *Great Britain and the American Civil War.* 2 vols. New York 1958
Anderson, Olive, 'The Janus Face of Mid-Nineteenth Century English Radicalism: The Administrative Reform Association of 1855,' *Victorian Studies*, VIII, 1965, 23-42
– *A Liberal State at War.* New York 1967
Annan, Noel, 'The Intellectual Aristocracy,' in J.H. Plumb, ed., *Studies in Social History.* London 1955
Armytage, W.H.G., *A.J. Mundella.* London 1951
Bassett, A. Tilney, *Gladstone to his Wife.* London 1936
Battiscombe, Georgina, *Mr. Gladstone.* London 1956
Bishop, A.S., *The Rise of a Central Authority for English Education.* Cambridge 1971
Blake, Robert, *Disraeli.* London 1966
Boys-Smith, S., 'The Relation Between the British Treasury and the Departments of the Central Government in the Nineteenth Century.' Unpublished MA thesis, University of British Columbia, 1967
Briggs, Asa, *Victorian People.* London 1954
Brooks, Constance, *Antonio Panizzi.* Manchester 1931
Brown, Lucy, *The Board of Trade and the Free Trade Movement.* Oxford 1958
Bryce, James, *Studies in Contemporary Biography.* London 1903
Buckle, G.E. and Monypenny, W.F., *The Life of Benjamin Disraeli, Earl of Beaconsfield.* 6 vols. London 1910-20
Cecil, Lady Gwendolyn, *Life of the Marquis of Salisbury.* 4 vols. London 1921-32
Clapham, John, *An Economic History of Modern Britain: Free Trade and Steel.* Cambridge 1932
Colsen, Percy, ed., *Lord Goschen and His Friends.* London 1946
Conacher, James B., *The Aberdeen Coalition.* Cambridge 1968
Cowling, Maurice, *1867, Disraeli, Gladstone and Revolution.* Cambridge 1967
Dasent, Arthur, *John Thadeus Delane.* 2 vols. London 1908
Davis, John D., *Phrenology, Fad and Science, A 19th Century American Crusade.* New Haven 1955
Duke, Christopher, 'Robert Lowe: A Reappraisal,' *British Journal of Educational Studies*, XIV, 1965, 19-35
Durell, A.J.V., *Parliamentary Grants.* London 1917
Elliot, R.D., *The Life of George Joachim Goschen, First Viscount Goschen, 1831-1907.* 2 vols. London 1911
Erickson, Arvel, 'The Cattle Plague in England, 1865-7,' *Agricultural History*, XXXV, 1961, 94-103
Farr, David, *The Colonial Office and Canada 1867-1887.* Toronto 1955
Fawcett, Millicent, *The Life of Sir William Molesworth.* London 1901
Fitzmaurice, Edmond, *The Life of Granville George Leveson Gower, Second Earl Granville, KG, 1815-1891.* 2 vols. London 1905

Galbraith, John S., *The Hudson's Bay Company as an Imperial Factor.* Berkeley 1957

Gillespie, Francis, *Labor and Politics in England 1850-1867.* Durham, NC 1927

Gooch, G.P., *The Life of Lord Courtenay.* London 1920

Guedalla, Philip, *The Queen and Mr. Gladstone.* 2 vols. London 1933

Hamilton, Lord George, *Parliamentary Reminiscences and Reflections.* 2 vols. London 1917

Hardman, Sir William, *The Hardman Papers.* London 1930

Harrison, J.F.C., *Learning and Living.* Toronto 1961

Harrison, Royden, *Before the Socialists 1861-1881.* London 1965

Hemmeon, J.C., *History of the British Post Office.* Cambridge, Mass. 1912

Historical Records of Australia. Series I. Sydney 1925

Hurt, John, *Education in Evolution.* London 1971

Huxley, Gervas, *Victorian Duke: The Life of Hugh Lupus Grosvenor, First Duke of Westminster.* London 1967

Irving, T.H., 'The Idea of Responsible Government in New South Wales Before 1856,' *Historical Studies Australia and New Zealand*, XI, 1965, 192-205

Jenkins, Roy, *Sir Charles Dilke.* Rev. ed. London 1965

Jones, Gareth S., *Outcast London.* Oxford 1971

Kerr, Donald, 'Edmund Head, Robert Lowe, and Confederation,' *Canadian Historical Review*, XX, 1939, 409-20

– *Sir Edmund Head.* Toronto 1954

Knight, L.A., 'The Royal Titles Act and India,' *Historical Journal*, XI, 1968, 488-507

Knight, Ruth, *Illiberal Liberal: Robert Lowe in New South Wales, 1842-1850.* Melbourne 1966

Lambert, Royston, *Sir John Simon.* London 1963

– 'A Victorian National Health Service: State Vaccination 1855-71,' *Historical Journal*, V, 1962, 1-18

Lawrence, E.P., '"The Happy Land": W.S. Gilbert as Political Satirist,' *Victorian Studies*, XV, 1971

Lloyd, Trevor, *The General Election of 1880.* Oxford 1968

Lyall, Alfred, *Life of the Marquis of Dufferin and Ava.* 2 vols. London 1905

Melbourne, A.C.V., *William Charles Wentworth.* Brisbane 1934

Meyer, H.R., *The British State Telegraphs.* New York 1907

Mitford, Nancy, *The Stanleys of Alderley.* London 1968

Moore, R.J., 'The Abolition of Patronage in the Indian Civil Service and the Closure of Haileybury College,' *Historical Journal*, VII, 1964, 246-57

– *Sir Charles Wood's Indian Policy.* Manchester 1966

[Morison, Stanley], *History of The Times.* 4 vols. London 1935-52

Mulhauser, F.L., *The Correspondence of Arthur Hugh Clough.* 2 vols. Oxford 1957

Oldham, John and Alfred Stirling, *Victorian.* Melbourne 1934

Ponsonby, Arthur, *Henry Ponsonby.* London 1942

Prest, John, *Lord John Russell.* London 1972

Prouty, Roger, *The Transformation of the Board of Trade, 1830-1855.* London 1957

Rich, E.E., *The History of the Hudson's Bay Company, 1670-1870.* 2 vols. London 1959

Roberts, B.C., *The Trades Union Congress.* London 1958

Roberts, Stephen, *History of Australian Land Settlement.* 2nd ed. Melbourne 1968

Roderick, Colin, *John Knatchbull: From Quarterdeck to Gallows.* Sydney 1965

Roseveare, Henry, *The Treasury.* London 1969

Russell, Bertrand and Patricia, *The Amberley Papers.* 2 vols. London 1937

Sabine, B.E.V., *A History of the Income Tax.* London 1966

Schweinitz, Karl de, *England's Road to Social Security.* London 1943

Shannon, H.A., 'The Coming of General Limited Liability,' *Economic History*, II, 1931, 267-91

Smith, F.B., *The Making of the Second Reform Bill.* Cambridge 1966

Smith, Frank, *History of Elementary Education 1760-1902.* London 1931

Smith, Paul, *Disraelian Conservatism and Social Reform.* London 1967

Stacey, C.P., *Canada and the British Army 1846-1871.* Toronto 1963

Stokes, Eric, *The English Utilitarians and India.* Oxford 1959

Sturt, Mary, *The Education of the People.* London 1967

Sylvester, D.W., *Robert Lowe and Education.* Cambridge 1974

Thring, Henry, *The Joint Stock Companies Act, 1856.* London 1956

Trevelyan, George, *The Life of John Bright.* London 1913

Tropp, Asher, *The School Teachers.* London 1957

Victoria History of the Counties of England: Worcestershire. London 1913

Ward, John, *Earl Grey and the Australian Colonies, 1846-1857.* Melbourne 1958

Waterfield, G., *Layard of Nineveh.* London 1963

Webb, Robert K., *Harriet Martineau: A Radical Victorian.* London 1960

West, Algernon, *Contemporary Portraits.* London 1920

Whibley, Charles, *Lord John Manners.* 2 vols. Edinburgh 1925

Whitty, Edward, *St. Stephen's in the Fifties.* London 1906

Winter, James, 'The Cave of Adullam and Parliamentary Reform,' *English Historical Review*, LXXXI, 1966, 38-55

Wolf, Lucien, *Life of the First Marquis of Ripon.* 2 vols. London 1921

Workley, Adelaide, *A History of Bingham.* Oxford 1954

Wright, Maurice, *Treasury Control of the Civil Service 1854-1874.* Oxford 1969

Young, Michael, *The Rise of the Meritocracy, 1870-2033.* London 1958

Index

Lowe, Robert (continued)
British North America and the
United States 113-16; injured in
Kidderminster riot 141-4; becomes
MP for Calne 146-9; serves as vice-
president of the Board of Education
at the Privy Council 150-1; supports
sanitary reforms 152-6; and Revised
Code of Education 173-86; while
defending American Confederates in
The Times 128-31; resigns as vice-
president after censure 189-93;
opposes 1866 Franchise Reform bill
212-26; and 1867 bill 232-7, 239-
41; elected MP for London University
156-7; becomes chancellor of the
exchequer 244-5; contributes to
Forster's Education Act of 1870
188-9; brings in budget of 1869
255-8; of 1870 257-8; of 1871
272-9; of 1872 and 1873 279; puts
through reform of the civil service
262-8; is involved in telegraph and
Zansibar scandals 283-92; is shifted
to the Home Office 293-6; is
attacked for part in royal titles question 310-12; and made Viscount
Sherbrooke (1880) 315-16
general views: contracts 103-4, 304-6;
crime and punishment 25-9; democracy (franchise reform) 7-9, 49-50,
87, 90-3, 115-16, 139-40, 145-6,
159-61, 198-202, 314-15, 317-18,
237-40; education, role of the state
in 181-3, 185-8; federalism 120,
132; finance and taxation 272-3,
276-9; free trade and retrenchment
xii-xiii, 135-6, 162-4, 245-6, 248, 253,
259-60; foreign policy 271, 279-82,
309-10; human nature 28-30, 167-8,
302-4; imperialism 118-19, 126-7,
307-9; meritocracy xiii-xiv, 87, 170-1;
'new' liberalism 300-4; 'practical'
(Palmerstonian) liberalism 105-10,

149-50; religion 31-2; slavery 115,
129-31, 288; university reform 10-
14, 157-8; utilitarianism 5-6, 109-10
personal characteristics xii-xiii, 4-5,
41-2, 54-5, 58-60, 206, 231, 249-55,
292-3, 294-5, 298, 314
Lowell, James Russell 113
Lubbock, John 157
Lucy, Henry 306-7
Lyttleton, Lord 163-4
Lytton, Bulwer 87

McCarthy, Justin 60
Macauley, Thomas 7, 72, 73, 74, 318
McClellan, General George 133
McCullock, John xii
Macdermott, Alderman Henry 34, 35,
39, 311
MacDonald, Alexander 306
Macdonald, John A. 117, 120, 123
Mackay, Charles 128
Macleay, William Sharp 152
Macmillans 62
Malthus, Thomas xii, 6
Manchester Guardian 215
Manchester School radicals 106, 141
Marshall, Alfred xii, 301
Martin, A.P. ii, 152
Martineau, Harriet 29
Mason, J.M. 129, 132
Master and Servant Act of 1867 304
Match tax 273-5, 277
Maurice, F.D. 82
Merchant Shipping bill of 1849 96
Merimée, Prosper 240
Meritocracy xiii-xiv
Merivale, Herman 16
Mill, John Stuart: debates cattle tax
with Lowe 207-8; and Irish land re-
form 259-60; supports Lowe's motion
on endowed schools 165; contributes
to redefinition of liberalism 110; on
parliamentary reform 201, 202, 213,
214, 220-1; on plural voting scheme